MiG Aces
OF THE VIETNAM WAR

ISTVÁN TOPERCZER

Schiffer Publishing Ltd
4880 Lower Valley Road • Atglen, PA 19310

Dedication:

To all the aces and their comrades, who credited air victories and lost their lives in the dogfights over North Vietnam

Library of Congress Control Number: 2015932137

Book Design by Péter Somos and István Toperczer.
Cover Design by Matt Goodman
Type set in Frutiger Regular

ISBN: 978-0-7643-4895-2
Printed in China

Published by Schiffer Publishing, Ltd.
4880 Lower Valley Road
Atglen, PA 19310
Phone: (610) 593-1777; Fax: (610) 593-2002
E-mail: Info@schifferbooks.com

Contents

Foreword

Ambassador Pete Peterson

Until now, only the American side of the story about the war fought in the air over North Vietnam has been told. Numerous books have been published documenting American pilots' narratives of the furious air battles that took place during the Vietnam War, but virtually nothing has been published depicting the Vietnamese side of that story. That comes as no surprise as all information related to the war was classified by the Vietnamese Government for decades. Fortunately, this policy has been relaxed in recent years and researchers now have access to Vietnamese archived records of the air battles. This stimulated the author of this excellent book to begin to tell the "other side" of the air war story.

If you have ever wondered what it is like to sit in the cockpit of a fighter jet during a fierce aerial battle, this book will take you into the cockpits of a North Vietnamese MiG fighter jets as they engage in a dogfights against skilled American fighter pilots. Through careful analysis of available data and extensive personal interviews with Vietnamese fighter pilots, the author skillfully describes the strategy and tactics that were employed by the Vietnamese People's Air Force during the war. He personalizes the story by introducing you (in a literal sense) to the North Vietnamese pilots who actually flew these combat missions. The story of their successes and their failures is seen through these pilots' eyes. This book does indeed give us a discerning look at the air war from the "other side", creating a valuable Vietnamese historical account of what took place in the skies over North Vietnam during the war. However, as we learn more from the Vietnamese side we are discovering significant differences in their accounts of the air war and those from the American side. Hopefully, one day the two sides can tell the story together.

I first met Dr. István Toperczer while serving as America's first post-war ambassador in Hanoi in 1998, shortly after his first book, "Air War over North Vietnam" was published. In my early conversations with him, I assumed he was a former fighter pilot for he was extremely well informed on all aspects of aerial combat and possessed an in-depth knowledge of the military air power capabilities deployed during the Vietnam War on both sides. I was amazed to find that he was instead a highly trained trauma physician turned Hungarian Air Force flight surgeon. I also learned that he was an avid aviation enthusiast who conducted years of extensive research into North Vietnamese air power capabilities. The author is recognized as one of the very few foreign experts on the history, organizational structure, combat operations and capabilities of the MiG aircraft flown by the Vietnamese People's Air Force.

As a former American fighter pilot flying some of those daunting combat missions over North Vietnam, I found it captivating to get a behind the scenes look at the "other side" of the story. The history of the Vietnam War is still being written and analyzed by people of all persuasions and because air combat was such a large part of the war there is still much more of this story to be told. This well documented book gives us a new perspective and historians, war buffs and indeed those involved in the air war over Vietnam – on both sides – will find this book an exciting read and professionally informative.

Ambassador Pete Peterson

Acknowledgments

I would like to thank the following individuals who have helped and supported me in this project: North Vietnamese MiG-17 pilots – Nguyen Van Bay, Luu Huy Chao, Le Hai, Pham Ngoc Lan, Ho Van Quy, Bui Van Suu, Tu De; MiG-19 pilots – Nguyen Manh Tung, Nguyen Hong Son "A"; MiG-21 pilots – Nguyen Van Coc, Vu Ngoc Dinh, Le Thanh Dao, Nguyen Van Nghia, Nguyen Thanh Quy, Ha Quang Hung, Nguyen Sy Hung, Nguyen Hong My, Pham Tuan; other pilots and officers of VPAF – Nguyen Nam Lien, Nguyen Van San, Bui Van Co, Nguyen Huu Dac.

I am especially indebted to my Vietnamese friends – Tran Dinh Kiem, Nguyen Van Dinh, Thuy Huong Duong, Dao Hoang Giang, Truong Van Minh, Nguyen Viet Phuc, Trung H. Huynh, Le Trong Sanh, Nguyen Duc Huy, Le Minh Trung, Nguyen Xuan Thang, Nguyen The Thang, Nguyen Thanh Binh, Dang Thai Son; American friends – Ambassador Pete Peterson, John D. Sherwood, Peter B. Mersky, Frank Olynyk, Peter Chilelli; English friends – Peter E. Davies, Tony Morris and Hungarian friends – Péter Barna (maps), Balázs Kakuk (color MiG-profiles), József Beke, Tibor Hajdú, Zoltán Pintér, Miklós Takács.

I wish to offer a special thanks to the following who have helped me in the translation of Vietnamese written material: Pham Truong Son, Tran Dinh Kiem, Nguyen Van Dinh, and Phan Le Lam Son.

I am also especially grateful to my friends Péter Szöllösi, Ildikó Hortobágyi and Gergely Gróf for their devotion and full commitment in correction of the English manuscript.

I must say a special thanks for their assistance to the Ministry of Foreign Affairs of Vietnam, Embassy of the Socialist Republic of Vietnam – Budapest, Embassy of Hungarian Republic – Hanoi, Hungarian-Vietnamese Friendship Association and Vietnamese Military Museums (Hanoi, Bac Giang, Thai Nguyen, Viet Tri, Hai Phong, Thai Binh, Nam Dinh, Vinh, Dong Hoi, Da Nang, Nha Trang, Bien Hoa, Cu Chi, Ho Chi Minh City).

István Toperczer

MiG-21PFM (Type 94) Fishbed F

Introduction

The placard of the "Aerial Dien Bien Phu" demonstrates the fights of the Air Defenses Forces and Vietnamese People's Air Force against enemy B-52 bombers.
(István Toperczer)

The term *"Ace"* is unofficially bestowed on those military pilots who have shot down five or more enemy aircraft during air combat missions. The label became popular among military pilots during World War I, when French aviator Adolphe Célestin Pégoud was christened as *"l'as"* and he was awarded the Croix de Guerre (Cross of War) after he downed several German airplanes. The British, like the Americans, never officially accepted this term. The French, British, and Germans set ten confirmed air victories as the standard qualification for an Ace. At the beginning of 1918, American air units had still not gone into action, so the likelihood of any American pilot scoring ten kills before Germany's collapse seemed remote. Accordingly, it was decided to reduce the American qualification for an ace to five aerial victories. The same standard of five now applies generally throughout the world.

The United States of America has changed the rules for achieving "Ace" status from one war to the next. In World War I, an airman earned a whole air victory for each of the aircraft he helped to bring down. During World War II and the Korean War, the credit for bringing down a single enemy aircraft was divided into fractions for each of the airmen who contributed to the air victory. Over North Vietnam, if an F-4 Phantom or F-105F Thunderchief crew shot down one enemy aircraft; both the pilot and the weapon systems officer (WSO) each earned a whole air victory credit.

The Vietnamese People's Air Force (VPAF) was armed with a large number of MiG-fighters during Vietnam War, so this allowed many North Vietnamese MiG-pilots to claim "Ace" status. American F-4 Phantom, F-8 Crusader, and F-105 Thunderchief aircraft crews usually had to contend with both surface-to-air missiles (SAM) and anti-aircraft artillery (AAA) units before opposing North Vietnamese MiG-fighters attacked them.

The longest war conflict produced 24 *"flying aces":* 19 North Vietnamese MiG-17 and MiG-21 pilots; two American pilots, and three American weapons systems officers from the US Air Force and US Navy.

In the decades that have passed since the end of the air war over North Vietnam, a great number of books have been published all over the world, which focused mainly on the American side of the conflict. As such, the careers of the North Vietnamese pilots and MiG-aircraft did not receive authentic publicity outside Vietnam. In 1994 I had decided to travel there and collect written and photo archives, and meanwhile meet MiG-pilots from "the other side."

My first book was published a few years after the trip, and was followed by new visits in Vietnam and new books.

The turn of the century has brought significant changes in the historical accounts of the Vietnamese People's Air Force, as more publications appeared about the history of air force units, air victories, and losses in the air war. The North Vietnamese MiG-pilots had retired and talked about the events of the air war without constraints. There will always be differences in describing the air combats between the Americans and the Vietnamese pilots, but close knowledge of these events from both perspectives definitely takes us closer to reality.

The current book presents the North Vietnamese Flying Aces careers and the service of their MiG-fighters during the air war, the results of my twenty years old research work in the "theatre of air war."

István Toperczer

The famous North Vietnamese Ace-pilots: Le Hai (MiG-17 – 6 kills), Vu Ngoc Dinh (MiG-21 – 6 kills) and Nguyen Van Nghia (MiG-21 – 5 kills) are seen currently in Ho Chi Minh City (Saigon). (István Toperczer)

The Beginnings and Years of Training

Ho Chi Minh's Flying Pioneers

The last Emperor of the Nguyen Dynasty, Bao Dai owned two private planes. The British biplane Tiger Moth was used for training; the second was the French Morane-Saulnier MS.343 sport monoplane, which could perform aerobatic.

After the revolt against the French colonial regime and his abdication, Bao Dai arrived in Hanoi as an advisor to the Democratic Republic of Vietnam in August 1945. President Ho Chi Minh requested him to bring the two planes from Hue to Hanoi. The government accepted and intended to establish an aviation club to train pilots, and set the basics for the air force's development in the future.

Ta Quang Buu, Deputy Minister of Defense, ordered Phan Phac, Director of the Military Training Bureau, to transport the planes to the North. The wings were disassembled, the planes were put on a train and secretly transported to Hanoi. In January 1946, Bach Mai and Gia Lam airports were occupied by Chinese troops with the task of disarming the Japanese, so the planes were transferred by road to the Kim Dai, Tong airfield in Son Tay.

In January 1947, the planes were transported to Binh Ca airstrip (Tuyen Quang Province). After two months, the Tiger Moth was shot by an enemy aircraft and received several holes. The maintenance team repaired and repainted it with the red flag and gold star insignia. Then they moved again. After a protected journey by land and water, the planes were moved again by boats, to be finally stationed in Chiem Hoa. The soldiers prepared an airstrip from the corn field, 400 meters long and 25m wide. The planes were kept on waiting.

At the beginning of 1949, General Vo Nguyen Giap the Chief Commander of the Ministry of Defense, Brigadier General Hoang Van Thai, Chief of Staff, and Phan Phac, Chief of Military Training, personally approached Ho Chi Minh for guidance concerning the establishment of the Vietnamese Air Force and Navy. The Ministry of Defense created the Air Force Research Committee (Ban Nghien Cuu Khong Quan) on 9 March 1949, under the codename "Experimental Farm," stationed in Ngoi Liem hamlet, Huu Loc commune (Tuyen Quang Province) headed by Ha Dong. The aim of the committee was to create the foundations of a future Air Force and to research the French Air Force.

The Research Section's mission was to set up basic research for the air force, investigate the French air force's operations and the means to fight them back, prepare documents, material facilities, training men step-by-step and take the chance to put them into action. Other units, as such as administrative, political, airport research, air defense and meteorology

The Emperor Bao Dai's Morane-Saulnier MS.343 became a trainer plane for pilots and mechanics of the Air Force Research Committee, which was established on 9 March 1949.
(István Toperczer Collection)

departments, mechanical workshop, maintenance teams, and training team were also organized. The Research Section retrieved "gifts" from the French air force: a downed Junkers Ju-52 transport aircraft and a downed Bell P-63 King Cobra fighter. The lecturers were section officers and some airmen who voluntarily surrendered (Japanese, German, Austrian and etc.). The curriculum was collected from French-controlled territories.

Nguyen Duc Viet, a German ex-liaison aircraft pilot was among the first officers assigned to the committee. He was a soldier of German nationality (his mother was German), who had served in the French Légion Étrangére (French Foreign Legion). Viet had switched his allegiance to the revolutionary fighters in the early days of the conflict in Trung Bo (Central Vietnam).

On 15 August 1949, at 17:00 hours, Nguyen Duc Viet had made the first flight in the Tiger Moth from Soi Dung sand bar on the side of the Gam River, with Nguyen Van Dong as his passenger. The plane ran taxi on the strip about 250 meters, then took off to 100 meters altitude, turned to the south, and at 800 meters the pilot began to perform aerobatics. After the second turn, Viet intended to fly along the Gam River to return and land. But, they were too low in altitude; the left wing touched the water surface and the plane crashed into the river. The pilots were safe thanks to the water. After the accidents, the two planes, Tiger Moth and Morane-Saulnier MS.343, were unable to take off again and became valuable trainers for pilots and mechanics.

The Airforce Research Committee trained in two courses. The first course began in autumn-winter 1949 and finished in early 1950. The second course began in May 1950 with 87 students in 3 classes: navigators, meteorologists, and mechanics. After finishing the theoretical class, the students moved to Chiem Hoa to practice opening, operating and taxiing the planes.

The Airforce Research Committee also studied about airfield and airport construction, methods of shooting enemy aircraft by infantry machine guns and rifles, and placed two-light machine guns on a combined stand with an iron sight for aircraft down shooting.

In the late phase of resistance war against French colonialists, the development of the Airforce Research Committee was stopped and focused to build other branches: artillery and air defense. All facilities of the Airforce Research Committee, including two planes, were sealed and transferred. The others items and components were sent to local people for safe-keeping. After a long time they were forgotten, all documents and items were lost or damaged.

Cadets and Schools

The selection and training of personnel for the new air force was given priority, and so in March 1956, the first group of 110 students was sent abroad. From the 80 persons sent to China, two groups were formed with the first 50 commanded by Pham Dung, receiving fighter pilot training. The second group (training on Tu-2 aircraft) of 30 students was led by Dao Dinh Luyen. During the course, because of changing priorities, Dao Dinh Luyen took over the fighter pilot group while Pham Dung headed the Li-2/Mi-4 group.

In mid-1956, under the organization of the Vietnam Air Club (Cau Lac Bo Hang Khong Viet Nam – established in January 1956), a delegation of twelve was sent to Czechoslovakia to study the operation and flying of the two-seater Zlin-226 Trener 6 sport aircraft.

The North Vietnamese flying cadets were sent to China for their basic training on Yak-18. In April 1959, thirteen pilots returning to North Vietnam became the tutors at the No.1 Training School located at Cat Bi airfield. (István Toperczer Collection)

All 8 of the Czech-built Zlin-226 Trener 6s were the primary two seat trainers and were operated from May 1959 by the VPAF 910th Training Regiment at Cat Bi airfield. (István Toperczer)

In the last months of 1956, at Cat Bi airfield, the Ministry of Defense created the Flying Club of Civil Aviation Department, and by doing so also formed the first training unit for the air force. In this No.1 Training School (Truong Hang Khong So 1) with the help of Chinese advisers, technical personnel (meteorologist, signal officers, generator operators) was trained. After Cat Bi, the No.2 Training School (Truong Hang Khong So 2) was established at Gia Lam where radio operators and mechanical engineers were trained. The No.1 Training School received eight Zlin-226 Trener 6s from Czechoslovakia and eight Yak-18s from China on April 1959. The first 25 pilots trained on Zlin-226 Trener 6s in Czechoslovakia (12 pilots) and on Yak-18s in China (13 pilots) became the teachers in the No.1 Training School as well as five Czech instructors who arrived to North Vietnam. The first local training started with 30 applicants at Cat Bi on 31 May 1959.

Under order 429/ND dated 30 September 1959, the Ministry of Defense established the 919th Air Transport Regiment and the 910th Training Regiment (Trung Doan Khong Quan 910), and the Air Force Training School (Truong Khong Quan Viet Nam). The primary trainer

All 8 of the Chinese-built Yak-18 trainers (Nanchang CJ-6) were supplied by the People's Republic of China and operated by the VPAF 910th Training Regiment. (István Toperczer)

aircraft type at the 910th Training Regiment was the Yak-18. By 6 October 1959, the first 12 students reached 20 flight hours on the Yak-18 and were transferred to 919th Air Transport Regiment for further training on the Il-14, Li-2, and An-2 types. The next year the course started with 87 students at Cat Bi.

A group of 52 pilots, who had already received training on the Yak-18 were sent to China in 1960 for conversion training to the MiG-17. The first group of North Vietnamese pilots, who trained on MiG-15 in China, had returned by 1960. The 31 trained pilots were taken to the Chinese base at Tianjin for conversion training to MiG-17 fighters. The pilots and some 200 technical service personnel were moved, at the end of 1963, to the Chinese base at Mong Tu (Mengzi) near the North Vietnamese border so that they could return home, if the need should arise at short notice. By the end of 1962, the first groups of fighter pilot training in the Soviet Union and China had successfully finished the courses and returned to North Vietnam.

The majority of the North Vietnamese pilots were trained in the Soviet Union for MiG-17 and MiG-21 types. The Krasnodar Flight Officers School, in the eastern region of the Black Sea and Sea of Azov, had four airfields attached to it. On the air bases of Bataysk, Primorsko-Ahtarsk, Kushchovskaya and Krasnodar, different types of aircraft were used for training in the sixties and seventies.

The North Vietnamese cadets looked forward to several grueling tests. The Russians allowed them to participate in the final stages of training only when found fit both in health and mental ground and with skills shown during their evaluation flights. The drop-out ratio was very high, sometimes only 20 out of 100 students made it to flight status with the rest becoming ground technicians. On the other hand, the training program for the Vietnamese was shorter and at a faster pace, which became even more intense from the mid-sixties.

Later a Russian language pre-school training program was started in the autumn with close to twenty theoretical subjects: aircraft and propulsion system structure, flight theory, radio-electronics and on board equipment, meteorology, map reading, tactics, and so on. The autumn and winter months were taken up with theory and static training, while the spring and summer months were ideal for flight training. The student groups, with the progress of time, received different practical training.

In April 1961, training started on Yak-18s at Bataysk grass airfield near Rostov-on-Don, to be continued from September at Kushchovskaya on MiG-15UTI and MiG-17As, until the end of 1962. They flew 100 hours on the Yak-18 and 150 hours on the MiGs. Only daytime flying was conducted and the North Vietnamese had an advantage over all other nations when allocating training time from Monday to Saturday. Still, the North Vietnamese in comparison to others, needed about twice as much flight time before the first solo take-off.

The Russian instructor shows the take-off characteristics with the help of a MiG-model to two Vietnamese flying cadets next to a MiG-15UTI at Kushchovskaya airfield, in the Soviet Union.
(István Toperczer Collection)

The North Vietnamese and Hungarian flying cadets were training together in Primorsko-Ahtarsk, Soviet Union. Vu Ngoc Dinh, who later became a famous Ace-pilot, stands in the middle between Hungarians Dezsö Miklós and Károly Janka, in September of 1963. (István Toperczer Collection)

The flight training was made up of simple aerobatics, route flight, simple dogfight, air-to-air against non-maneuvering targets and attack on ground targets, but of course only in good weather. Live gun firing was conducted once or twice a year with the MiG-15UTI or the MiG-17, both in solo and in a flight of two, with 30 rounds for each cannon, while for dogfight and intercept practice only the gun-camera was fired.

Ejection seat training and parachute jumps were also part of the curriculum. Once a year, an explosive charge operating a ground ejection seat simulator was used, and twice a year parachute jumps were conducted from An-2 aircraft. Each year, a day-long medical was conducted at Krasnodar for the students.

The students of the 1962 class received the theoretical lessons in Bataysk, but the primary training on the Yak-18s was conducted from Primorsko-Ahtarsk. The next year they also had the MiG-15UTI and MiG-17 flights from Kushchovskaya.

In the first half of the year, before delivering to Vietnam in 1965 new Russian MiG-21s, a group of Vietnamese pilots arrived at Krasnodar for type conversion and were joined by some of the best graduates from Kushchovskaya. With the introduction of the MiG-21, the tactical tasks

The Vietnamese pilot is on his first solo-flight with a MiG-17A in August 1964, over the Kushchovskaya airfield.
(István Toperczer Collection)

were further expanded. Against ground targets, both bombing runs and unguided missile firing from the UB-16-57 launcher were practiced.

The year 1966 had brought about several changes in the training syllabus. The Yak-18s were changed over for the Czech made L-29 Delfin jets at Primorsko-Ahtarsk. The students had to complete 80 hours on the Delfins before moving on to Kushchovskaya for the MiG-15 UTI and MiG-17 with 40 hours on each of them. Before completing the course in the first half of 1968, they were back in Krasnodar to complete 40 hours on MiG-21PFM Fishbed F and MiG-21US trainers. This was the first group to complete night training too, with 8-10 hours on L-29, 10-12 hours on MiG-17, and 8-10 hours on MiG-21. During this course some Vietnamese pilots arrived who had already completed flight training on the MiG-17 in China.

This Aero L-29 Delfin was operated as a trainer jet in Vietnam from 1971. Nowadays it is displayed in VPAF Museum of Hanoi.
(István Toperczer)

The North Vietnamese MiG-pilots, who were trained in the Soviet Union, in a group photograph, in 1966. The famous Ace pilots Nguyen Duc Soat, Le Thanh Dao and Nguyen Tien Sam are seen on the picture.
(ISTVÁN TOPERCZER COLLECTION)

For them, after the L-29, it was straight into the cockpit of the MiG-21. All war experiences gained, both successes and failures by North Vietnamese pilots graduated in the Soviet Union, were used by Russian instructors in teaching the new students. In the early seventies, the trend of using a L-29 – MiG-17 – MiG-21 combination continued, but with fewer pilots due to the air war over Vietnam in 1972.

In the summer of 1965, another 30 fighter pilots returned from Krasnodar in the Soviet Union and from China, doubling the number of available pilots. The North Vietnamese were ordered to be trained as fighter pilots instead of training transport pilots in the flight school near Tuong Van airfield (Kunming, Yunnan) in China. So, after the re-opening of Kep airbase, the Ministry of Defense (MOD) decided to establish a second, the 923rd "Yen The" Fighter Regiment (Trung Doan Khong Quan Tiem Kich 923), on 7 September 1965, under the command of Major Nguyen Phuc Trach. The 923rd Fighter Regiment was to equip with MiG-17s at Kep airbase and the 921st Fighter Regiment with MiG-17 and MiG-21 fighters at Noi Bai airbase. Since the MiG-21U and L-29's necessary for the local training were not available, MiG-15UTI two seaters were used.

By June 1966, MiG-17 pilots finished their studies in the Soviet Union. In November 1966, another 18 pilots on MiG-17 conversion had graduated. Sixty percent of them had already seen combat by the end of the year.

In 1967, apart from MiG-21 pilots, two thirds of the pilots trained on MiG-17 were also assigned on MiG-21s. The freshly trained MiG-17 pilots were sent to battle immediately.

In January of 1968, in all, 29 new MiG-21 pilots returned from the Soviet Union and 14 MiG-17 pilots graduated from courses with the 910th Training Regiment. They were all posted to the 921st and 923rd Fighter Regiments.

In February 1969, after 36 Chinese-built MiG-19S (Shenyang J-6) aircraft arrived in Vietnam, the MOD decided that the creation of the 925th Fighter Regiment (Trung Doan Khong Quan Tiem Kich 925) was to be equipped with MiG-17F and Shenyang J-6 (Chinese version of the MiG-19 Farmer) fighters. Nguyen Quang Trung was appointed as the Regiment Commander and he was to be based at Yen Bai airbase. The pilots of the regiment came from those MiG-21 pilots who had studied in the Soviet Union and MiG-17 pilots trained in North Vietnam by the 910th Training Regiment. The pilots were training in flights of 4-8-12 aircraft from already repaired airfields, both in bad weather as well as during the night. In April 1969, the 925th Fighter Regiment already had 9 MiG-19 and 4 MiG-17 pilots who had enough qualification for combat duties. The number of trained pilots had increased, but the level of combat experience varied considerably.

In 1971, on order from VPAF High Command and Chiefs of Staff, ten MiG-17 pilots were selected from the 923rd Fighter Regiment for future ground attack missions. In March 1972, the 923rd Fighter Regiment already had six pilots qualified for attacking targets at sea.

By the beginning of 1972, the number of pilots who were combat ready, under adverse weather conditions and for night missions, steadily increased. In each regiment, new training courses were started where the MiG-17 pilots received conversion to the MiG-21. All pilots

The trainer MiG-21UM Mongol B (5903) of the 927th Fighter Regiment in the foreground is followed by a row of MiG-21 PFM and MiG-21MF Fishbeds on the ramp of Noi Bai airbase in 1972.
(István Toperczer Collection)

The unnumbered grey MiG-21PFM (Type 94) and the MiG-21MF, No.5137, are prepared for night sorties at Noi Bai airbase, in 1972. (István Toperczer Collection)

of the 921st Fighter Regiment had now converted to the MiG-21MF (Type 96). In July 1972, the command of the VPAF approved an order for further training programs, showing that the air force was not only fighting the war but also training new pilots. The new pilots were receiving training primarily for MiG-21MF, and conversion training from MiG-17 to MiG-21 also continued. The Chiefs of Staff approved an attack plan against the B-52s and made it possible for 12 pilots, including 8 trained for night missions to practice according to the plan. MiG-21MF training flights were carried out in adverse weather, both day and night and from short landing strips. After the course, at the end of 1972, most MiG-21 pilots were ready for engagement with B-52s at an altitude of 10,000 meters.

After the Linebacker II campaign and the beginning of 1973, the training units did not have enough aircraft and they had to move to China. The Air Force Training Schools and Aircraft Repair Facility were put under direct supervision of the VPAF High Command, and at the end of 1973 training began of future personal for the Chiefs of Staff.

The First Air Victories of North Vietnamese MiGs

In June 1963, at the meeting of the Political Comity of the Military, a decision was made to join the Air Force and the Air Defense Forces. The new force, the Air Defense Forces – Vietnamese People's Air Force (ADF-VPAF) (Phong Khong – Khong Quan Nhan Dan Viet Nam) was formed on the 22 October 1963, by Chief Commander Colonel General Phung The Tai and Colonel General Dang Tinh as the second in command.

The Soviet government decided that it would give 32 MiG-17s and 4 MiG-15UTIs as a gift to North Vietnam, so on 3 February 1964 Lieutenant General Hoang Van Thai, the Deputy Defense Minister signed order 18/QD on the establishment of the 921st "Sao Do" Fighter Regiment (Trung Doan Khong Quan Tiem Kich 921) with Lieutenant Colonel Dao Dinh Luyen as the Commanding Officer.

The First Air Victory of the VPAF

On 16 February 1964, Nguyen Van Ba shot down a SVNAF C-123 Provider over the Laotian – Vietnamese border using a T-28 Trojan. This was the first aerial victory of the Vietnamese People's Air Force.
(István Toperczer Collection)

In September 1963, a Thai national Lt Chert Saibory, went to North Vietnam from an air show of the Royal Lao Air Force. Landing his T-28, he offered his services to the communist government in Hanoi, but they placed him in prison. The aircraft remained in storage at the A-33 Aircraft Repair Facility for half a year, after which it was refurbished and commissioned as the first fighter aircraft in the Vietnamese People's Air Force. The T-28 Trojan was incorporated into the VPAF structure and received aircraft number "963" (9 standing for September and 63 for 1963 – the month and year of the defection).

The training program was assigned to instructors Nguyen Van Ba and Le Tien Phuoc. Nguyen Van Ba made joint flights together with the defecting Laotian pilot, Lt Chert Saibory, after which later Nguyen Van Ba, Le Tien Phuoc, and Hoang Ngoc Trung took control of the aircraft. After several flights, No. 963 was combat ready in little more than three months, in January 1964.

At 23:30 hours on 15 February 1964, the radar units reported that an American aircraft was approaching Con Cuong in Nghe An Province. Later, they reported it was flying over Truong Son (the Ho Chi Minh Trail) in a northern direction towards Hoi Xuan in Thanh Hoa Province. The the crew, Nguyen Van Ba and Le Tien Phuoc, of the No. 963 received an order to take off at 01.07 hours on 16 February. After getting to altitude 1,200 meters, crew was informed that the enemy was ahead 15 degrees right, distance 15 kilometers. Nguyen Van Ba asked for attack permission, turned on the sights equipment's light, and armed his guns. When the target was at distance of 3 kilometers, Le Tien Phuoc had found the

The ex-Laotian Trojan was "incorporated" into the VPAF and received aircraft number "963" (which means September and 1963, of the defection date). Nguyen Van Ba and Le Tien Phuoc took off with this T-28 Trojan from Gia Lam airfield to attack a C-123 Provider, on 16 February 1964.
(István Toperczer Collection)

enemy above the right side of the No. 963 over a white cloud. When the South Vietnamese Air Force (SVNAF) C-123 Provider was within a distance of 500 meters, Nguyen Van Ba fired two rounds, with bullets pouring constantly into the right engine and cockpit. Following this, he flew up, into a cloud, and was guided by command post to land safety at Gia Lam airfield. The hit C-123 crashed into a forest near the North Vietnam – Laos border. The T-28 was not equipped with a ombat camera, there was no film to record the action and no evidence to check damages of the C-123. Only after 3 months, from extract intelligence information of a captured South Vietnamese soldier, could they confirm all paratroopers and crew on board of that SVNAF transport C-123 were dead after its crash.

This was the first aerial victory of the Vietnamese People's Air Force.

The MiGs over North Vietnam

From 1 May 1960, the construction of the Noi Bai airbase had begun. By mid-1964, the main structures of the airfield were standing and this was especially important for making possible the return of the first MiG-17 fighters from China.

At the beginning of August 1964, with the Tonkin-incident, the Americans extended the war to the North Vietnam. Both the Ministry and the Command of Air Defense Forces – Vietnamese People's Air Force – decided to call home the 921st Fighter Regiment from China.

Chief of the General Staff Van Tien Dung commanded the secret "X-1" project. Lieutenant Colonel Nguyen Van Tien, Deputy Commander of the VPAF, revealed the project to the pilots in China. On the morning of 6 August 1964, a valedictory ceremony was held at Mong Tu (Mengzi) airfield. Ground crews conducted final checks on the flight line while the fully equipped pilots were awaiting take off. Noi Bai reported sunshine, but the sky over southern China was overcast until noon.

The first group of MiG-pilots in the Vietnamese People's Air Force, who were trained in China, between 1956 and 1964.
(István Toperczer Collection)

When the weather cleared, flights of four MiG-17As began to take off heading southeast. Wing Commander Dao Dinh Luyen, Pham Ngoc Lan, Tao Song Minh (Chinese pilot) and Lam Van Lich took off first, to be followed by three more four-ship formations (in all 16 MiG-17s). At Noi Bai airbase, Van Tien Dung, the Chief of the General Staff, Phung The Tai, the VPAF Commander, and Dang Tinh, Deputy Commander, were present when Pham Ngoc Lan came in first to land. After all aircraft of the 921st Fighter Regiment landed at Noi Bai airbase, the Chief of Staff personally congratulated each pilot. The date, 6 August 1964, became a highlight in North Vietnam's history.

On the same date, the VPAF already had the very first, two pair, of alert aircraft (MiG-17A) ready for scrambling with Pham Ngoc Lan and wingman Lam Van Lich in the first flight and Tran Hanh with wingman Nguyen Nhat Chieu in the second flight.

Following the arrival of the MiG-17 fighters, the military Party Committee and ADF-VPAF Headquarters (HQ) held conferences to discuss ideas and draw up the details of preparations to succeed in the first engagement. A handful of young, inexperienced pilots flying obsolete aircraft would fight against a numerically and technically superior enemy. However, the North Vietnamese had the advantages of flying over friendly territory and of collaboration with radar and anti-aircraft units.

Pilots regularly talked over their ideas about air combat tactics. They preferred tactics that ensured victory at the expense of the smallest possible loss. In order to get to know the adversaries better, the command of VPAF organized meetings between captured US air crews and its own pilots. They studied photographs of US aircraft for more precise visual recognition. It was after some time that the military plans and tactics of VPAF started to materialize. In this, they stated that the Achilles heel of the intruders is that they come in with predetermined objectives and heavily loaded with bombs which take away their agility.

On 3 February 1964, the 921st "Sao Do" (Red Star) Fighter Regiment was established under the command of Lieutenant Colonel Dao Dinh Luyen.
(István Toperczer Collection)

The North Vietnamese MiG-bases and the Air Operations Area during the Vietnam Air War.

Pham Giay, Nguyen Phi Hung, Le Minh Huan, Ho Van Quy, Tran Hanh and Nguyen Nhat Chieu stand in front of their new MiG-17s at Noi Bai airbase in September 1964.
(István Toperczer Collection)

On each strike, large numbers of aircraft were used which flew on routes which were rarely changed, so they were very vulnerable. The MiG-17 was considered to be able to fight at the same altitude as the intruding fighters, to be able to use their guns effectively when within range, and so a close dogfight should be provoked with the Americans. To achieve a kill on the first pass, they practiced opening fire from 300 meters or even 150 meters.

Before the first VPAF counter attack, a conference was called at which everyone agreed that from the first air battle the North Vietnamese side must come out victoriously, and that they will attack only if the Americans crossed the 20th parallel at Thanh Hoa.

The First Air Victories of MiG-17

Following the start of the American Operation Flaming Dart I-II and Rolling Thunder, the supreme command of VPAF decided, on 2 April 1965, that in the first counter offensive 2 flights would take part.

My flight – says Pham Ngoc Lan – consisted of Phan Van Tuc (my wingman), Ho Van Quy and Tran Minh Phuong, while the second flight was made up of Tran Hanh and Pham Giay. In the morning of 3 April 1965, the weather was foggy over Noi Bai airbase, with visibility of 4-5

AIR COMBAT MAP – 3 APRIL 1965

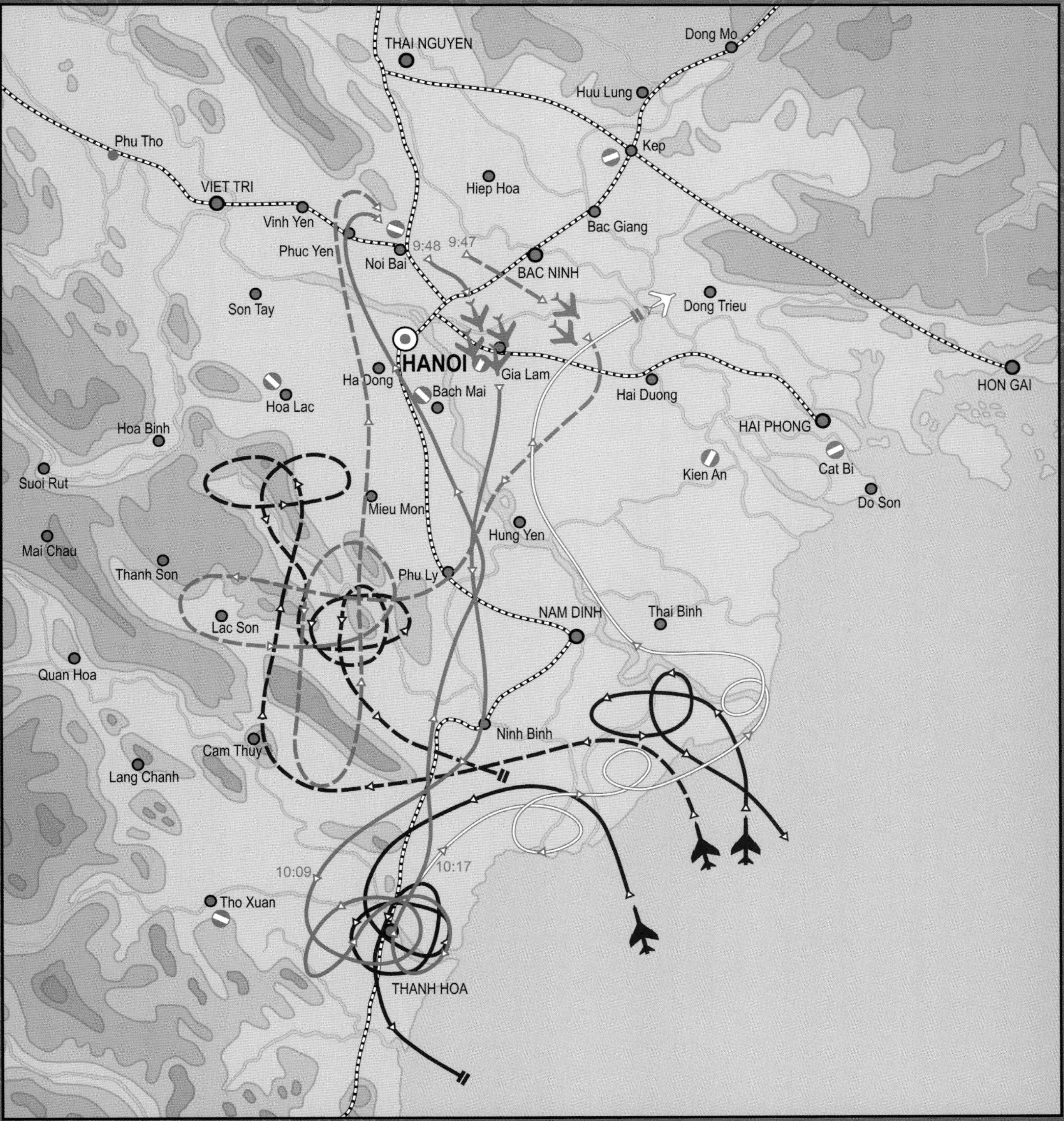

The first air victory of North Vietnamese MiG-17s was on 3 April 1965 over Thanh Hoa Province. Pham Ngoc Lan and Phan Van Tuc shot down two F-8 Crusaders by Vietnamese records. (CARTOGRAPH: PÉTER BARNA)

Pham Ngoc Lan (LEFT) and Pham Van Tuc (RIGHT) participated in the first Vietnamese-American dogfight on 3 April 1965. They shot down two F-8s, but US Navy sources say that only Lt Cdr Thomas had managed to land his damaged F-8 Crusader at Da Nang.
(ISTVÁN TOPERCZER COLLECTION)

kilometers, volume of cloud 6/10, and cloud base at 300 meters. Over the anticipated battle area, the volume of cloud was 5-6/10 with cloud base at 700 meters and a visibility of 10 kilometers. At 07:00 hours, the radar operators reported a group of intruding fighters in North Vietnamese airspace, which left after carrying out reconnaissance duties. The North Vietnamese command felt that a large formation will attack the bridge at Ham Rong. Colonel General Phung, The Tai the Commander of VPAF, once again briefed the pilots on the objectives and ordered a Class One Alert. As anticipated, at 09:40 hours, American aircraft attacked the bridges at Tao, Do Len, and Ham Rong.

With a deceptive maneuver in mind at 09:47 hours the second flight was launched from Noi Bai. The leader of the first attack flight I took off at 09:48 hours and took a heading of 210 towards the province of Thanh Hoa. Our flight closed up to 45 kilometers on the intruders at 10:08 hours while the second flight was still flying over Ninh Binh Province. I have informed the air control at 10:09 hours that we had a visual contact with the intruders, in response to which an order was given to drop the tanks and we went into an attack.

The bridge at Ham Rong was attacked in pairs by the American fighter bombers that were at this time still unaware of our fighters. In very short time, together with my wingman, we were following a pair of American fighters. When in range, I opened fire with my guns and the F-8 Crusader in front of me exploded in a ball of fire and crashed. I was later credited with the first downed American fighter bomber to be shot down by a North Vietnamese fighter pilot. At the same time, the aircraft of Ho Van Quy and Tran Minh Phuong were also pursuing another pair of intruders, where Tran Minh Phuong was the wingman to Ho Van Quy. Ho Van Quy opened fire, but the Americans were out of range and managed to escape, but the battle between the MiG-17s and the F-8 Crusaders was still far from over in the area of Ham Rong. At 10:15 hours my wingman, Phan Van Tuc, reported on the radio an American fighter to his right, and immediately received an order from me to attack, while I was acting as his wingman. When he managed to close in on the American, the cannons of my wingman opened up and the F-8 crashed.

At 10:17 hours, Phan Van Tuc, Ho Van Quy and Tran Minh Phuong received an order to land and they returned to the home base. In the meantime, I was running out of fuel in the vicinity of the home airfield and the Ground Controlled Interception (GCI) gave me the order to eject. I thought that there is still a chance to save the aircraft, which represented a considerable value to the VPAF and still had the possibility of many more battles in it. I looked for a suitable landing place and found a long sandy strip on the bank of Duong River where I made a successful landing.

On the gun camera film, the blazing F-8 was perfectly visible. US sources

Pham Ngoc Lan

Date of Birth: 19 February 1934
Enlisted: July 1952
Pilot training:
1956 – 1964 (MiG-17 – China)
1967 (MiG-21 – Vietnam)
War Service and Unit:
1964 – 1971 (921st Fighter Regiment)
1971 – 1975 (371st Air Division)
Aircraft: MiG-17, MiG-21
Hero of the Vietnamese People's Armed Forces:
28 May 2010
Rank: Major General

Each MiG-17 pilot, Tran Hanh (LEFT) and Pham Ngoc Lan (RIGHT), shot down an American aircraft during the first air battles in April 1965.

Tran Hanh

Date of Birth: 28 November 1932
Enlisted: 1 September 1949
Pilot training: 1956 – 1964 (MiG-17 – China)
War Service and Unit: 1964 – 1972 (921st Fighter Regiment), 1972 – 1975 (371st Air Division)
Aircraft: MiG-17, MiG-21
Hero of the Vietnamese People's Armed Forces: 1 January 1967
Rank: Lieutenant General

Shenyang J-5 (MiG-17F Fresco C) of the 921st Fighter Regiment, 1965
These MiG-17s were used by Pham Ngoc Lan (No. 2310) and Tran Hanh (No. 2316) during air battles of 3 and 4 April 1965, over Thanh Hoa Province. (ARTWORK: BALÁZS KAKUK)

claimed only one F-8E of VF-211 damaged by MiGs, with two other aircraft lost to air defense forces. According to US official sources, all F-8 Crusaders from USS *Hancock* (CVA-19) recovered from the encounter, only Spence Thomas' Crusader so was badly damaged that he had to land at Da Nang.

Due to this first victory in 1965, the 3 April is the "Day of the Vietnamese People's Air Force."

On the evening of the 3 April, the commanders of the 921st Fighter Regiment gathered for a meeting to evaluate the success and make plans for future encounters. They felt that both the pilots and the wing, as a whole, were correctly prepared for the encounter and this was the main reason for the success. Everything was kept in secret so they were able to use the element of surprise, in the heat of the battle the pilots stuck to the basic tactics: shoot down as many enemies as possible, protect your own aircraft, engage only in close dogfight, and concentrate the attacking force against a single group. Other lessons were also learned from mistakes of the battle. There were some pilots who fired even when out of range and they used a lot of ammunition without success. On this date, altogether 686 rounds of ammunition were fired out of which 160 were of 37mm and 526 of 23mm caliber. The commanders felt that since the Americans were not successful in destroying the bridge at Ham Rong, they would surely be back the next day with a new flight and attack plan.

The command, on the other hand, felt that the enemy will not have enough time in one day to change its tactics, so with a correct choice of time for the North Vietnamese attack, the Americans can be surprised again. If the Americans continue with the bombing runs and attack the Ham Rong Bridge on the 4 April, then it will be left in the first place for the air defenses and only after this will the fighters attack. The plan was, for the deception flight, to take off first and to fly at an altitude of 7,000-8,000 meters to the West. The attack flight would follow at low altitude, heading to the south-east and climbing to a higher altitude only when

The MiG-17 pilots, Tran Hanh, Pham Giay, Tran Nguyen Nam and Le Minh Huan are seen before take-off. On 4 April 1965, Tran Hanh and Le Minh Huan shot down two USAF F-105D Thunderchiefs over Ham Rong Bridge. This was the first confirmed aerial victories of the Vietnamese People's Air Force. (István Toperczer Collection)

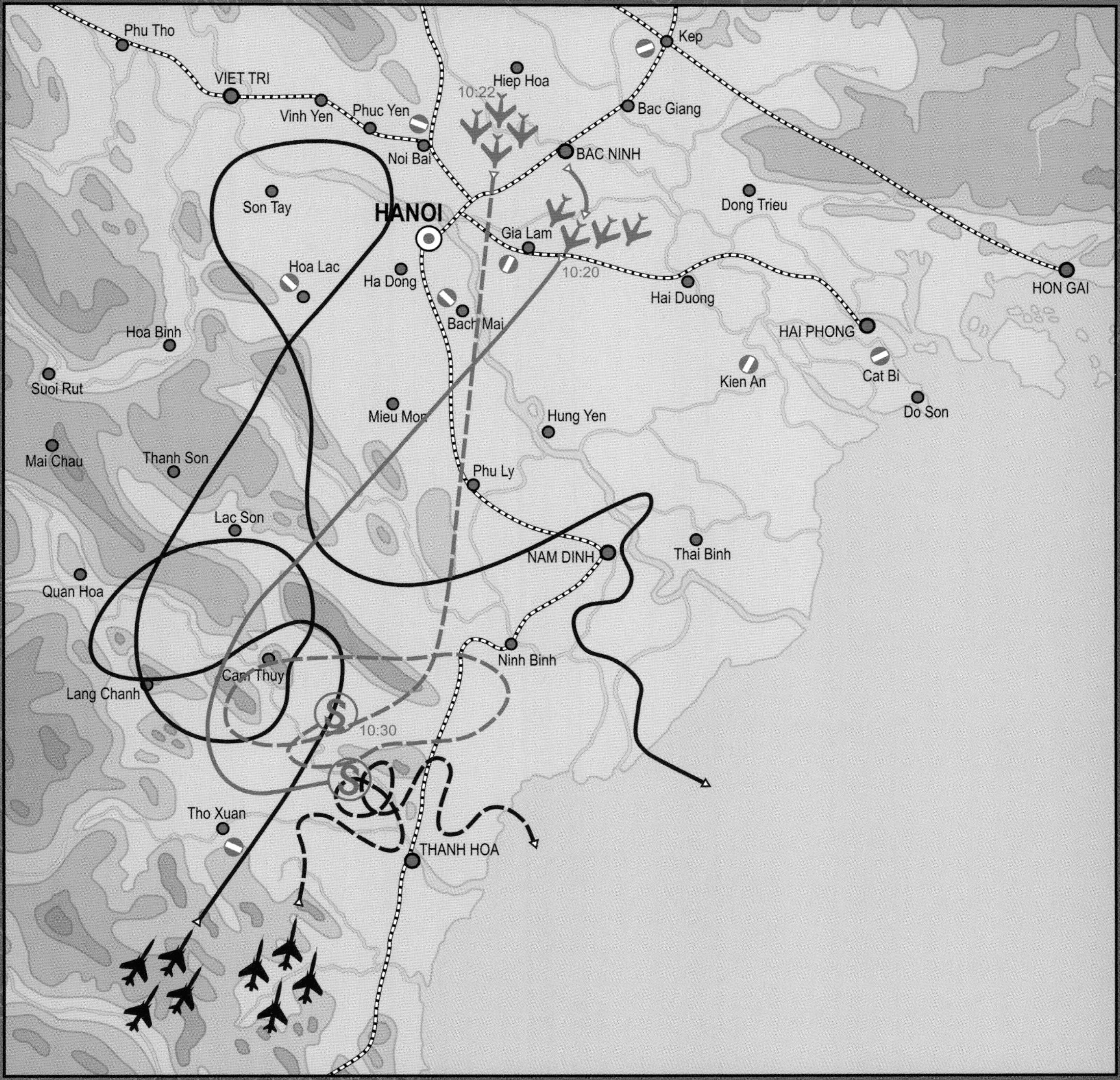

On 4 April 1965, the MiG-17 flight of Tran Hanh and Le Minh Huan shot down two F-105D Thunderchiefs in a dogfight over Ham Rong Bridge. (CARTOGRAPH: PÉTER BARNA)

approaching the enemy to gain altitude advantage. The battle will be led by Nguyen Van Tien, the second in command, while the GCI will be the task of Dao Ngoc Ngu.

On the morning of 4 April 1965, the Americans made several reconnaissance flights over Thanh Hoa which was to precede an attack on Ham Rong Bridge and the power plant at Thanh Hoa. At 10:20 hours ,the second flight took off with the following pilots: Le Trong Long, Phan Van Tuc, Ho Van Quy, and Tran Minh Phuong. They climbed to 8,000 meters and flew over Vu Ban and Phu Ly in Nam Ha Province to attract the attention of the attackers.

Ho Van Quy, as a member of second flight tells: The attack flight, Tran Hanh, Pham Giay, Le Minh Huan and Tran Nguyen Nam, took off at 10:22 hours. The weather was very cloudy with considerable areas covered by fog. They received orders from the GCI to descend to low altitude and head east, then again on order sharply changed heading to southeast. As Tran Hanh's flight approached the area of the anticipated intercept, they quickly gathered altitude to gain advantage. Tran Hanh reported at 10:30 hours that they had visual contact of the Americans. He had spotted a group of four F-105Ds which had just started dropping their bomb-load and ordered his wingman, Pham Giay, to cover him in the attack. At a distance of 400 meters, Tran Hanh opened up with all three guns downing one of the Thunderchiefs, which fell in flames into the sea. The Americans turned to attack, while they split into two groups. Together with his wingman, Tran Hanh's flight staying on the southern side of Ham Rong Bridge with Le Minh Huan and Tran Nguyen Nam going to the northern side. Supported by Tran Nguyen Nam, Le Minh Huan shot down another F-105D. In the ensuing combat, the numerical superiority of the Americans claimed the loss of Pham Giay, Le Minh Huan, and Tran Nguyen Nam. Tran Hanh was only able to escape by hard maneuvering, but he lost contact with the GCI. Short on fuel, he had to land at the first possible opportunity. With his MiG-17, he successfully landed in Ke Tam valley (Nghe An Province) but was arrested immediately by the locals. Tran Hanh was able to clear himself only after showing the VPAF badge. He was taken to the provincial capital where the commander turned out to be his friend with whom he had fought against the French in the 320th Army Division. After bidding the host farewell, Tran Hanh returned to his unit.

In this second engagement the VPAF pilots did not have the element of surprise as on the day before, but still these two encounters had shown that even though the VPAF was very young and not so well equipped, it was able to conduct successful air combats. The USAF did confirm the destruction two F-105Ds (59-1754 and 59-1764) from 355th TFW on this day, although their records indicate that no kill claims were made by any of the returning pilots. Maybe the Vietnamese pilots fell victim to

DATE OF BIRTH: 22 December 1936
ENLISTED: 25 May 1952
PILOT TRAINING:
March 1961 (910th Air Training Regiment – Vietnam)
1961 – 1964 (MiG-21 – Soviet Union)
WAR SERVICE AND UNIT:
1964 – 1972 (921st Fighter Regiment)
1972 – 1973 (927th Fighter Regiment)
AIRCRAFT: MiG-21
HERO OF THE VIETNAMESE PEOPLE'S ARMED FORCES: 18 June 1969
RANK: Major General

AIR VICTORIES: 8 kills
(2 F-4s, 3 F-105s, 1 RF-101, 1 F-8, 1 Firebee – VPAF official credit)

DATE	AIRCRAFT	UNIT	KILL – US PILOT (VPAF – US DATABASES)
04 Mar 66	MiG-21	921.	Firebee
31 Aug 67	MiG-21	921.	RF-4C – US not confirmed
10 Sep 67	MiG-21	921.	RF-101C – US not confirmed
26 Sep 67	MiG-21	921.	F-4D – US not confirmed
09 Oct 67	MiG-21	921.	F-105D – Clements (POW)
07 Nov 67	MiG-21	921.	F-105D – Diehl (KIA)
17 Dec 67	MiG-21	921.	F-105 – US not confirmed
01 Aug 68	MiG-21	921.	F-8 – US not confirmed

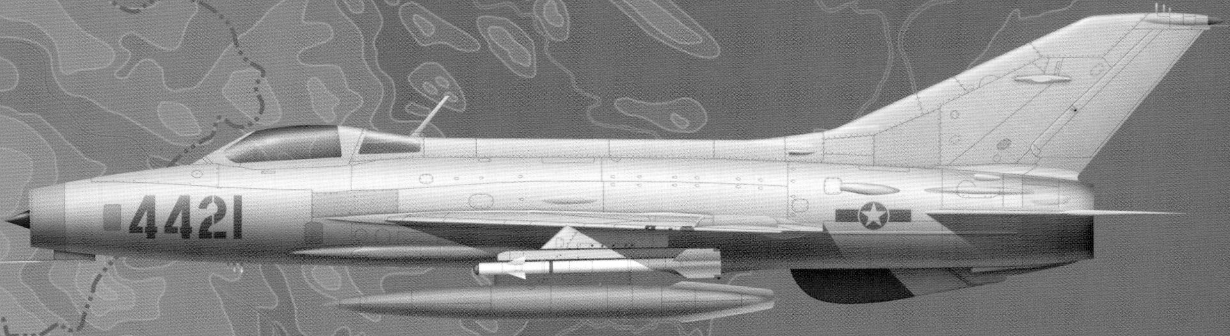

MiG-21F-13 Fishbed C, No. 4421 of the 921st Fighter Regiment, 1967
Nguyen Hong Nhi, who claimed the first victory of MiG-21 during the Vietnam War, used this MiG-21F-13 to destroy Maj Clements' F-105D Thunderchief (60-0434) over northwest of Thai Nguyen, on 9 October 1967. (ARTWORK: BALÁZS KAKUK)

friendly fire and Donald W. Kilgus's F-100D Super Sabre.

On 5 April, Vo Nguyen Giap, the Defense Minister, and Van Tien Dung, Chief of Staff, received a briefing on air combat of the previous two days when they visited 921st Fighter Regiment. To complement the victory Uncle Ho sent a wire to the VPAF:

> *You have fought bravely and shot down the American planes and you are worthy the traditions of our people and army. I am congratulating you but at the same time asking you to further improve your fighting spirit against the American aggressors. Don't be conceited with your victories and do not let yourself be stopped by difficulties on the way.*

The First Air Victory of MiG-21

From the end of 1965, USAF and Vietnamese People's Air Force changed their tactics and strategy basically. At the same time, MiG-21PFL Fishbed-D aircraft arrived from the Soviet Union and, in April 1966, the Vietnamese already introduced their first MiG-21 interceptors. One of the squadrons of the 921st Fighter Regiment was involved in night-fighting training. Together with all those who had their training on MiG-21 in the Soviet Union, also MiG-17 pilots were chosen for conversion training to MiG-21 in the 921st Fighter Regiment.

In January 1966, the command of the 921st Fighter Regiment officially asked for the introduction into service of the MiG-21 fighters. As a result, MiG-21s were taking part in the fighting besides the MiG-17s, from February 1966. They were first used to intercept unmanned reconnaissance drones.

The North Vietnamese MiG-21 type claimed its first air victory on 4 March 1966, when Nguyen Hong Nhi shot down a Firebee reconnaissance drone north of Hanoi. (István Toperczer Collection)

At noon, on 4 March 1966, receiving information that an enemy drone appeared, command ordered to watch it and Tran Hanh, who was second in command, ordered a MiG-21 of the 921st Fighter Regiment ready to take off. At 13:53 hours, a flight appeared at the Vietnamese – Laotian border, west of Quan Hoa, which flew through Suoi Rut then to Viet Tri, Bac Can, at an altitude of 9,000 meters, then ascended to 18,000 meters, with a speed of 800 km/h. At 13:56 hours, another flight appeared at Vu Ban, at an altitude of 5,000 meters, and flew east of Hanoi to Thai Nguyen. At a 921st Fighter Regiment command, ground control officer Pham Cong Thanh informed ground control officer Trinh Van Tuat at the C-45 station. At that time, guidance radar had not caught the target yet, but after consideration Pham Cong Thanh requested to launch the MiG-21. Commander Dao Dinh Luyen accepted it.

At 14:05 hours, Nguyen Hong Nhi took off from Noi Bai, bearing 285 degrees and two minutes later, he was informed of a target at bearing 110 degrees, at an altitude of 19,500 meters. At Viet Tri, command ordered a bearing 320 degrees, ascending to 6,000 meters then later 7,000

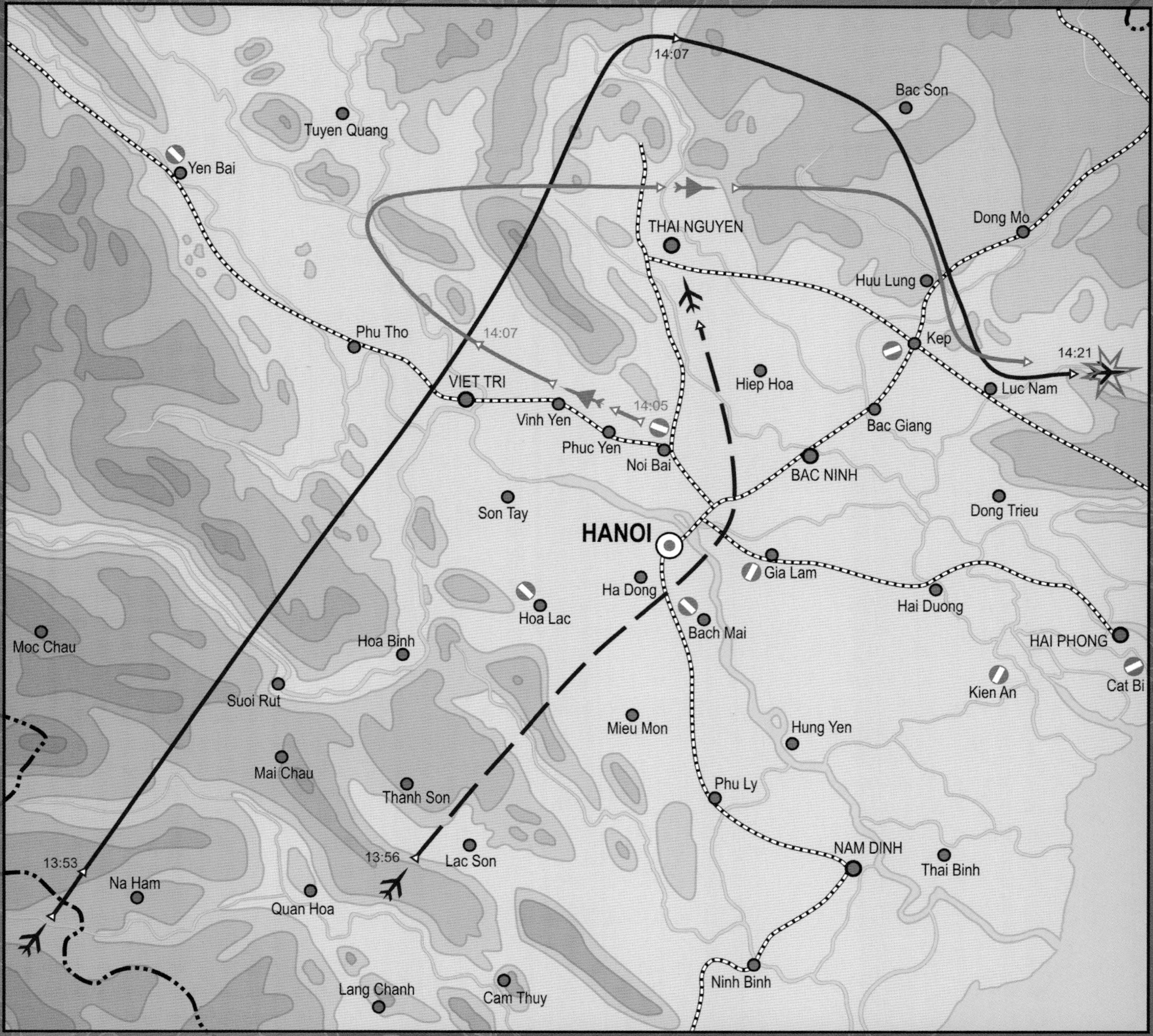

The first air victory of North Vietnamese MiG-21s was on 4 March 1966 at a high altitude north of Hanoi. Nguyen Hong Nhi shot down an AQM-34 Firebee unmanned aerial vehicle. (CARTOGRAPH: PÉTER BARNA)

meters. At Doan Hung, seeing the ability to be lost behind and below the enemy, a ground control officer ordered the pilot to turn right and start the afterburner to reach Mach 1.3 (1,400 km/h), ascending to 13,000 meters, bearing 90 degrees, then Mach 1.6 (1.700 km/h), at an altitude of 14,000 meters, but still behind and below. Dao Dinh Luyen was ordered to check and guide the MiG-pilot based on the actual data of a drone. After reaching southeast 15 kilometers of Bac Son, the target turned right and at Luc Nam it turned left to the east at an altitude of 19,500 meters. Nguyen Hong Nhi turned right bearing 150 degrees and accelerated to Mach 1.7 (1,800 km/h) at an altitude of 17,000 meters. After the MiG-21 turned left to bearing 90 degrees, the target was ahead 30 kilometers and 2,500 meters above. The control centre ordered Nguyen Hong Nhi to attack the drone, which he did after closing on it. Approximately at 70 kilometers northeast of Hanoi, a Firebee was destroyed at an altitude of 18,000 meters. It was downed with an R-3S (K-13 Atoll) air-to-air missile (AAM) from 2 kilometers respectively.

This was the first victory with a MiG-21, Nguyen Hong Nhi's first aerial victory, and the first kill of an unmanned reconnaissance drone over North Vietnam.

The First Air Victories of MiG-19

In September 1965, a group of 80 people (pilot cadets, technicians) travelled to China for training on MiG-19. In 1966, new pilot cadets joined the training. Following the flying time on Yak-18 (Nanchang CJ-6) and MiG-15UTI (Shenyang JJ-2) trainers, the cadets continued training on MiG-19 (Shenyang J-6). Training in China ended in January 1969 and the crews started deployment back to Vietnam. At the end of 1968, USAF focused on an area south of the 20th Parallel. In February 1969 North Vietnam was enjoying a four-month break from American air raids, and the MiG-19 group moved from China to Kep airbase. The MOD decided on the creation of the 925th Fighter Regiment (Trung Doan Khong Quan Tiem Kich 925) to be equipped with Chinese-built MiG-19 Farmers, called Shenyang J-6 fighters. Le Quang Trung was appointed Regiment Commander and Mai Duc Toai as Vice Commander. Air Force engineers, with help from other units and people of Lang Giang (Ha Bac Province), quickly repaired the Kep airbase.

After its creation, the 925th Fighter Regiment had only the core officers from the 923rd Fighter Regiment, while others still trained in China. In a short period before MiG-19s moved to Kep, the ground control section of the regiment quickly organized the training and helped the pilots in terrain research. After MiG-19s arrived at Kep in February, they had to build up basic combat plans and improve flight training data. At the beginning, there were 37 pilots, using 36 MiG-19s (J-6) and 4 MiG-15UTIs. The intense tactical and advanced flying training resulted

Nguyen Ngoc Tiep

Date of Birth: 1942
Enlisted: February 1965
Pilot training:
1965 – 1969 (MiG-19 – China)
War Service and Unit:
1969 – 1975 (925th Fighter Regiment)
Aircraft: MiG-19
Died: 15 August 1975 – during training flight over Vinh Phuc
Rank: First Lieutenant

Nguyen Hong Son "A", Phung Van Quang and Nguyen Ngoc Tiep are seen after the air battle of 8 May 1972.

Nguyen Hung Son "B"

Date of Birth: 22 June 1947
Enlisted: 1965
Pilot training: 1965 – 1969 (MiG-19 – China)
War Service and Unit: 1969 – 1975 (925th Fighter Regiment)
Aircraft: MiG-19
Rank: Senior Colonel

Shenyang J-6 (MiG-19S) Farmer Cs, No. 6005 and 6029 of the 925th Fighter Regiment, 1972
Each MiG-19 pilot, Nguyen Ngoc Tiep (No. 6005) and Nguyen Hung Son "B" (No. 6029), shot down an F-4 Phantom during the air battle of 8 May 1972. (Artwork: Balázs Kakuk)

in nine combat-capable MiG-19 pilots by April 1969. Other pilots of the 925th Fighter Regiment came from Gia Lam to MiG-17s and Soviet flying schools, where they had undergone MiG-21 training.

In September 1969, the 925th Fighter Regiment, with MiG-19s and MiG-17s, moved to Yen Bai airbase to protect the northwest airspace of Vietnam. From late 1969 to early 1970, with experiences in Kep, the ground control section quickly organized operations in the new base, they supported combat training flight for MiG-19, switched training to MiG-17 for several MiG-19 pilots, and supported for 10 MiG-19s and 12 MiG-21s moved from Tuong Van airfield (Kunming, Yunnan) to Yen Bai, then MiG-21s to Noi Bai airbase.

The previously gained MiG-19 experience was taken into account in the expected combat. The pilots returned from China after nearly 200 hours of flight time and entered wartime conditions right away. Their combat experience was limited, but they tried to exploit the characteristics of the aircraft. For the Vietnamese People's Air Force (VPAF) this had been the first, two-engine, supersonic fighter. Because of the two engines, the MiG-19 needed a lot of fuel, so this remained in shorter range. These aircraft were unable to attack the American bombers from Combat Air Patrol (CAP) ties, but could only be deployed from ground alert. The horizontal maneuverability of the aircraft was good, even at an altitude of 2,000-4,000 meters. It had only three 30 mm cannons, and had been equipped with air- to-air missiles only later, because the Chinese could fit the missile rails onto the aircraft only in 1974. However, if they could get into close range to the Americans, there was an increased risk that the enemy would shoot first and down them. When they approached the enemy at high speed, to prevent the Americans from counter attack, they usually missed the hit. So the firing power of the MiG-19s firepower could not be fully exploited.

By the spring of 1972, the MiG-19 force had matured into an effective element of North Vietnam's air defense system. The 925th Fighter Regiment was ordered to defend the western and the northwestern airspace of North Vietnam. Under "Operation Pocket Money", President Nixon announced the mining of the most important ports in the North, at the beginning of May.

On 8 May, when "Operation Linebacker" started, the VPAF headquarters had ordered the 925th Fighter Regiment to put up a constant CAP over Yen Bai airbase, to protect the Thac Ba hydroelectric power station. The 921st Fighter Regiment was to help the 925th Fighter Regiment by distracting the attention of the Americans. According to the plan, the 925th Fighter Regiment had in air two flights of MiGs at opposite ends of the Yen Bai. Number I flight in the north operated four MiG-19 fighters flown by: Nguyen Ngoc Tiep, Nguyen Duc Tiem, Nguyen Hong Son "A," and Nguyen Hung Son "B." Number II flight patrolled in the South with: Pham Ngoc Tam, Pham Hung Son "C", Phung Van Quang, and Nguyen Manh Tung (instead of Vu Chinh Nghi).

The famous MiG-19 pilot, Nguyen Hong Son "A" demonstrates his dogfight-maneuvers, nowadays in Da Nang.
(István Toperczer)

Nguyen Hong Son "A," as a member of first flight recalls: Radar units reported on 8 May 1972 that at an altitude of 5,000 meters, 35 kilometers southwest from Moc Chau, a group of four aircraft was approaching towards Yen Bai. Two MiG-21s from the 921st Fighter Regiment took off at 08.40 hours and headed towards Tuyen Quang. Our flight also took off, with four MiG-19s, at 08.47 hours. We broke through the clouds overhead between 1,000-1,200 meters and turned left. When they reached 4,000 meters at 08:52 hours, I spotted the American aircraft to my right, at 30 degrees, at a distance of 6 kilometers and at an altitude of 4,000 meters. I reported the position also to the MiG-21s. Nguyen Ngoc Tiep reported that he could see four F-4 Phantoms. The American aircraft also discovered our MiG-19 aircraft and launched AAMs which missed its targets. My flight leader, Nguyen Ngoc Tiep had ordered everyone to attack as they approached the targets quickly. In response, the Phantoms split into pairs, with flight leader Nguyen Ngoc Tiep and Nguyen Duc Tiem following the left pair while Nguyen Hung Son "B" and I went after the right pair. As Nguyen Duc Tiem followed the F-4, he noticed that from another Phantom flight two missiles were fired at him, from which he was able to escape with hard maneuvering after which he turned around. Nguyen Ngoc Tiep continued his chase after the F-4, which descended to 1,500 meters and tried to escape with a left turn, but Nguyen Ngoc Tiep increased his speed and opened up with his cannons only to miss his target, which flew into a cloud. Tiep turned to the right and noticed two F-4s, at an altitude of 2,000 meters, which became his new centre of attention. One of the Phantoms tried to escape into the clouds, but Tiep fired his cannons again to score a hit this time. The F-4 Phantom crashed. Nguyen Duc Tiem, after turning around, returned to cover his flight leader, only to find that he was once again under attack from an F-4. Nguyen Duc Tiem again turned around and counterattacked the American. Nguyen Duc Tiem did not drop his auxiliary fuel tanks and so the plane had a considerable yaw and he could not aim precisely. Soon Nguyen Duc Tiem received an order to land. The F-4 Phantom, which was chased by Nguyen Hung Son "B" and me, descended rapidly to 1,500 meters when I fired my cannon with no success. The American climbed to 2,000 meters, where it was followed by me and I fired again with no hits scored before the Phantom disappeared into the clouds. Nguyen Hung Son "B" did not receive an order to drop his auxiliary fuel tanks but when he saw what I did in confusion, he pulled the "Release Brake Chute" lever, and it was opened up and was ripped away instantly. Nguyen Ngoc Tiep thought that he saw an American pilot ejecting. Eventually, Nguyen Hung Son "B" managed to get rid of the auxiliary fuel tank only to notice that he was fired on with an AAM from which he escaped with a sudden diving evasive maneuver. The attacking F-4 followed him, but because of his greater speed over ran Nguyen Hung Son "B", who became the attacker opened up on the Phantom at an altitude of 1.200 meters with no success. The Phantom flew into a cloud but Nguyen Hung Son "B" pressed on with the attack, and when they reached 500 meters he fired again. He noticed big flames at the back of the Phantom but Nguyen

Tran Trong Vuong teaches his comrades in May of 1972, at Yen Bai airbase.
(István Toperczer Collection)

Hung Son "B" broke off the engagement since they were approaching fast a high mountain. He landed safely at Yen Bai. Although having only 1,100 liters of fuel left, Nguyen Ngoc Tiep remained airborne until two MiG-19s took off to assume his task. Nguyen Ngoc Tiep fired 24 30 mm rounds and Nguyen Hung Son "B" fired 105 rounds against Phantoms, but US records did not confirm any losses. The command ordered the flight of Pham Ngoc Tam, Pham Hung Son "C" took off to cover while Phung Van Quang and Nguyen Manh Tung stayed on ready. At 09.06 hours, Tam-Son "C" took off, went through clouds, bearing 314 degrees then turned back to our flight landed safely. The second MiG-19 pair apparently did not meet American aircraft. At 09:16 hours all MiG-19s were safely back at the base. The US records did not confirm MiG-19s kills.

This was the first dogfight with a MiG-19 (Shenyang J-6) and the first victories of the 925th Fighter Regiment at its home, over Yen Bai, by VPAF records.

The North Vietnamese continuously analyzed enemy tactics, using data from observations or acquired during interrogations of captured American pilots. US fighters avoided turning with the agile MiG-17s and MiG-19s and stressed vertical flight. Their formations ingressed the combat area with the pairs well spaced, because it required less concentration to maintain the position and the pilots could pay more attention to the MiGs sneaking up on them. When facing a lone MiG, they attacked it by working together. Meeting a pair of MiGs, the US went after the wingman until they succeeded or the lead could force them to break off. Encountering a larger formation, they separated and engaged the MiGs in pairs.

The Aces were born in the Sixties

Operation "Rolling Thunder" in 1965

Operation "Rolling Thunder" was the title of the US Seventh Air Force, US Navy, and South Vietnamese Air Force (SVNAF) aerial bombardment campaign conducted against the North Vietnam from 2 March 1965 until 2 November 1968, during the Vietnam War.

The targets, timing of the attack, and other details of the operation were all decided in Washington D.C., United States. The North Vietnamese's real strength around Hanoi and Haiphong was not touched, nor even threatened.

In "Rolling Thunder," the US attacked North Vietnam with all sorts of aircraft, but the worst of the fighting was borne by the F-105 Thunderchiefs and the F-4 Phantoms. The F-105 Thunderchief flew 75 percent of the strikes and took more losses over North Vietnam than any other kind of aircraft. The F-4 Phantom, better able to attack North Vietnamese MiGs, flew both strike missions and close support for the F-105s. Later the F-4 became the dominant USAF fighter-bomber. The F-105s and F-4s flew mostly from bases in Thailand and worked the northern and western "Route Packs" in North Vietnam. US pilots were credited with a full combat tour after 100 missions over North Vietnam. That was not an easy mark to reach. US Navy F-4 Phantom, F-8 Crusader, A-4 Skyhawk, A-6 Intruder and A-7 Corsair pilots from carriers at Yankee Station in the Tonkin Gulf flew mainly against targets at the coastline.

The other aircraft flying north or supporting the operation were tankers, jammers, search-and-rescue, and reconnaissance aircraft, as well as command and control airplanes. The everyday refueling of combat aircraft was one of the big operational changes in the Vietnam War. Fighters on their way into North Vietnam topped up their tanks from KC-135 tankers, which flew orbits above Thailand, Laos, and the Gulf of Tonkin, then met the tankers again on the way out to get enough fuel to make it home.

The successful North Vietnamese fighters that operated over North Vietnam were MiG-17 Frescos and MiG-21 Fishbeds. The MiG-17 Fresco performed well as an interceptor, especially effective at lower altitudes where it used its heavy machine guns to good advantage. Six of North Vietnamese 19 aces flew on MiG-17s. The MiG-21 Fishbed was the best North Vietnamese fighter and a close match in capability with the F-4 Phantom. The MiG-21F-13 and MiG-21MF were equipped with a gun, but together MiG-21PFL and PFM, they relied primarily on their R-3S (K-13 Atoll) air-to-air missiles. Thirteen MiG-21 pilots became "flying aces" during Vietnam Air War.

On 17 June 1965, there was a dogfight between MiG-17s and US Navy Skyraiders and Phantoms, over Nho Quan in Ninh Binh Province. Nguyen Nhat Chieu (SECOND FROM LEFT) was shot down by an F-4B Phantom, but he ejected and landed safely.
(ISTVÁN TOPERCZER COLLECTION)

The North Vietnamese were able to expand and develop their airbases and airfields (Noi Bai, Kep, Hoa Lac, Gia Lam, etc). The main fighter base was Noi Bai north of Hanoi. Gia Lam remained free from attack throughout the war because US officials decided to permit transport aircraft from China, the Soviet Union, and the International Control Commission to have safe access to North Vietnam. However, the VPAF used Gia Lam as an active MiG-base, also.

The summer of 1965 brought decimation to the still-maturing fighter force. Combat losses were due to lack of combat experience, inferior hardware, and the over-efficient air defense units. Heavy casualties were also a consequence of the high accident rate.

Early on the morning of June 4, 1965, American aircraft attacked on Road No. 15 over Quan Hoa. At 05:55 hours MiG-17 pilots Lam Van Lich, Nguyen Nhat Chieu, Ho Van Quy, and Tran Minh Phuong took off from Noi Bai to Nho Quan. At 06:11 hours, Lam Van Lich detected the enemy in front of him at 8 kilometers. Two minutes later, Ho Van Quy immediately shot down an F-4 Phantom at 15 kilometers east of Tho Xuan. The US sources did not confirm this loss.

On the 17 June 1965, an aerial combat developed over Nho Quan in Ninh Binh Province between 4 MiG-17s from the 921st Fighter Regiment and 20 A-1H Skyraiders and F-4s from the USS *Midway* (CVA-41). As a result of the battle, two Phantoms were lost, but the US side did not confirm these losses. Two MiG-17s were shot down by the Americans F-4Bs, Cao Thanh Tinh and Nguyen Nhat Chieu ejected and landed, while one MiG-17 crashed into a mountain side killing Le Trong Long.

The VPAF managed to shoot down American aircraft, but in each case they also had losses. On an order from the VPAF Headquarters in the third quarter of 1965, the fighters participated in fewer air combats. The Headquarters analyzed the situation and found many deficiencies in air combat tactics. For example, instead of attacking the heavily laden strike aircraft, Vietnamese pilots regularly tangled with escort fighters. Some flight leaders had acted in confusion or, because of the first successes, had contempt for the Americans.

According to the plans, the airfield at Kep had to be ready by September 1965 for the arrival of the newly formed 923rd Fighter Regiment. On 7 September the base was ready and the 923rd Fighter Regiment (Trung Doan Khong Quan Tiem Kich 923), under the command of Major Nguyen Phuc Trach, was formed.

In late 1965, MiG-21PFL (Type 76) Fishbeds and MiG-17PF Fresco Ds arrived from the Soviet Union, so both fighter wings were reorganized with two squadrons in each of them. The 921st Fighter Regiment was located at Noi Bai, while the 923rd Fighter Regiment at Kep. Based on a MOD decision, the 921st Fighter Regiment was to be equipped with MiG-17 and MiG-21 fighters and the 923rd Fighter Regiment with MiG-17s.

Beginning from the summer of 1965, the American forces concentrated on the destruction of roads and railroads in Lang Son, Lao Cai, Hai Phong Provinces, near Hanoi and in the 4th Military District. After a two-month lull, from September 1965, VPAF aircraft were once again fighting in the sky over North Vietnam based on a decision by the Chief of Staff and the General Command.

The Route No.1 was attacked on 20 September 1965, between Lang Son and Hanoi. American A-4s flew from Hong Gai through Yen Tu ridge to Bac Le railway station and Song Hoa Bridge, F-4 fighters also flew close support at Nha Nam. A flight of four MiG-17Fs of the 921st Fighter Regiment departed from Noi Bai. The Air Force ground control team was Nguyen Van Chuyen at command post and Vu Duc Binh at C-29A at Bach Mai.

On 7 September 1965, the Kep airbase was combat ready and the 923rd "Yen The" Fighter Regiment was formed under the command of Major Nguyen Phuc Trach.
(István Toperczer Collection)

Pham Ngoc Lan was the flight leader of MiG-17s from Noi Bai airbase, which attacked US Navy Phantoms on 20 September 1965. Nguyen Nhat Chieu shot down one F-4 Phantom via VPAF records. (István Toperczer Collection)

I was the leader of the flight with Nguyen Nhat Chieu, Tran Van Tri and Nguyen Ngoc Do on that day – says Pham Ngoc Lan. Our flight was guided to Phuc Yen then headed north. When we arrived over Cho Moi and American F-4s left Nha Nam, command ordered us to turn right to an eastern direction. We immediately turned right, dropped our wing tanks and attacked a flight of four US Navy F-4s. The Phantom pilots apparently had not noticed our MiGs coming until it was too late. Two Phantoms pulled hard up while the other pair broke to the starboard. Not intending to get into a vertical fight, we stayed with the turning Phantoms. One of them was attempting to disappear into a cloud, while his wingman made a dive towards the earth. My wingman, Nguyen Nhat Chieu, was in ideal position to follow the former, which started to turn left into the clouds. The Phantom's predictable flight path allowed my wingman to take a short cut and close in on him. Popping out of the cloud, the Phantom headed for the sea, with Nguyen Nhat Chieu on his tail, opening fire when he was within 400 meters. Trailing black smoke, the F-4 began a slow descent and tried to escape, the Phantom received another burst from the triple cannon pack of the MiG. The Phantom crashed into a mountain near Nha Ham in Ha Bac Province. Our flight returned home safely. It was Nguyen Nhat Chieu's first aerial victory by VPAF official credit. Opposite to the Vietnamese sources, the US side did not confirm this F-4 Phantom kill.

During the dogfight, two close support pairs, Bui Dinh Kinh-Dao Cong Xuong and Ho Van Quy-Nguyen Van Bien, with MiG-17s of the 921st Fighter Regiment, also were in the air to protect Pham Ngoc Lan's fight. According to a cooperated plan, after all MiGs broke off, SAM and

Capt Tran Hanh gets in a MiG-17PF at the Noi Bai AB. The first MiG-17PFs arrived to North Vietnam from the Soviet Union at the end of 1965.
(István Toperczer Collection)

Earth revetments were constructed to protect the MiG aircraft on the ground at Noi Bai, Kep, Kien An, Gia Lam and other airfields. The guards stand at the end of a MiG-21-shelter, at Tho Xuan during 1966.
(István Toperczer Collection)

AAA, at Bac Le railway station and Song Hoa bridge, fired at the enemy, and shot down an A-4E Skyhawk of VA-72, from the USS *Independence*.

On 6 October 1965, US Navy F-4 Phantoms from the USS *Coral Sea* (CVA-43) flew to attack Kep airbase, when the MiG-17 flight of Tran Huyen, Le Trong Huyen, Nguyen Van Bay and Luu Huy Chao from the 923rd Fighter Regiment was ordered to take off against enemy. The Americans detected the MiGs from distance of 25 kilometers and they flew above the MiG-17s at high speed. They supposed that the Vietnamese pilots were frightened and will land at the closest airfield. However, Tran Huyen attacked Lt Cdr MacIntyre's F-4B Phantom, but did not hit. The US Phantom made a barrel roll attack and fired at Tran Huyen's MiG-17, without success. At the same time Nguyen Van Bay's MiG-17 was damaged by shrapnel from a Sparrow missile. His canopy received a big hole, so he was ordered to land at Noi Bai airbase. On the ground, he counted 84 holes on his MiG-17 fuselage. Opposite to the US sources, the Vietnamese side confirmed this kill for next day, 7 October 1965.

The last aerial victory of 1965 was on 6 November when the MiG-17 flight from the 921st Fighter Regiment, with Tran Hanh, Ngo Doan Nhung, Pham Ngoc Lan and Tran Minh Phuong, shot down a US helicopter (CH-3C) over Hoa Binh.

From 3 April 1965 to December of that year, VPAF aircraft took off in 156 cases with 12 victories. The aerial combats in 1965 had proven that the subsonic MiG-17s could fight effectively against the superior F-105 and F-4 fighters. At low altitude, the F-105 was not as maneuverable while the MiG-17 had a considerable advantage. The MiG-17s were successful against the F-105's when they were on a bombing run, with the pilot concentrating on aiming, with a decreasing awareness of fighter attack. The F-4s had only guided missiles, which required an optimal launch range, while the maneuvering MiG-17 had an advantage with its cannons in a dogfight.

One has to admit that the Vietnamese pilots had numerous unsuccessful aerial combats which were due, primarily, to poor training standards. Pilots also had difficulties during fights requiring precision formation flying and in keeping the required battle formation. North Vietnamese MiG-17s were sent into combat almost exclusively in flights of four. Initially, they kept rather tight formations with 50-100 meters separation between lead and wingman, and 100-200 meters between the two pairs. This may have been good for formation display flight, but not for air combat, as it required too much attention to maintaining position. Other tactical disadvantages were the lack of possibility for energetic maneuvering and individual initiative. Digesting the lessons of air battles, the Vietnamese spread the formation out to 600-800 meters between aircraft and 800-1,200 meters between pairs. Later, the flights became even more spaced, with 2,000 meters horizontal and 400-500 meters vertical separation between the pairs. Altogether, the MiG-17s

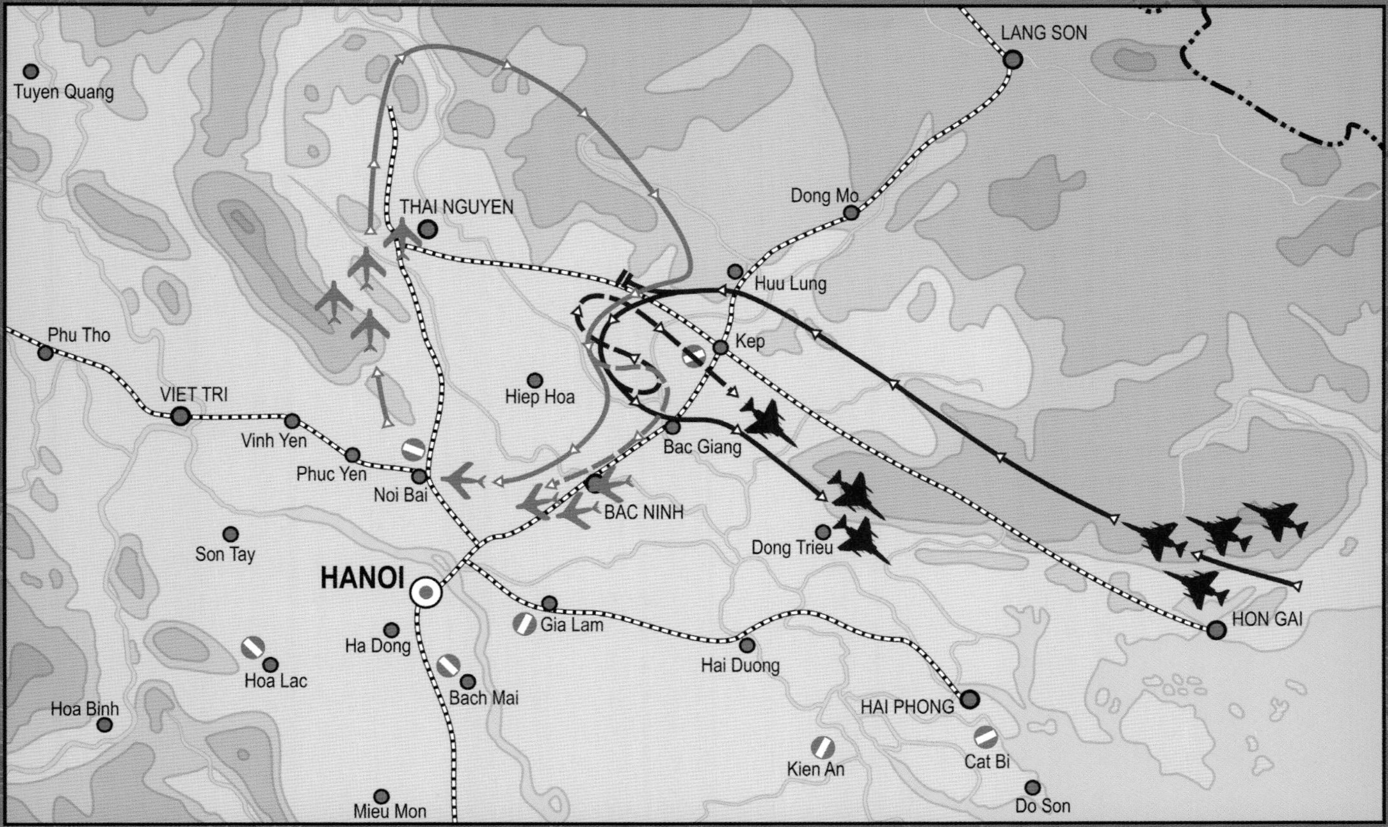

On 20 September 1965, the flight of MiG-17s attacked a US Navy strike formation and shot down one F-4 Phantom over Nha Ham in Ha Bac Province by Vietnamese records.
(Cartograph: Péter Barna)

had shown good flight characteristics and tactical fighting capabilities against the supersonic American fighter aircraft at low altitude, in dogfight and fights in the horizontal plane.

Air Battles during 1966

In February 1966, after 37 days of lull (24 December 1965 to 31 January 1966), the Johnson cabinet had ordered the resumption of the aerial bombing of North Vietnam. At the same time, the role given to the VPAF was the protection of important transport infrastructure, attacking the land and water installations of the enemy, and transportation.

Opening in 1966, an unforgettable battle was on 4 March, when Nguyen Hong Nhi shot down a Firebee over North Vietnam, as his first aerial victory. After shooting down the first reconnaissance drones, the new fighters of the 921st Fighter Regiment participated in several aerial engagements, but were unable to achieve a kill. The first combat took place on the 23 April 1966 when two MiG-21s, Nguyen Dang Kinh and Dong Van Song, targeted a flight of F-4s, but were unable to fire the R-3S AAMs since they could not achieve launch parameters. There were instances when, in three engagements, all 14 AAMs were launched with

Tran Hanh briefs for his comrades, Nguyen Cat A, Nguyen Van Coc, Nguyen Van Minh, Nguyen Van Ly, Mai Van Cuong and Pham Thanh Ngan, who later became famous Ace-pilots of the VPAF.
(István Toperczer Collection)

none achieving a hit, while in other cases the Nguyen Dang Kinh flew until they completely ran out of fuel and had to eject. Although US records mention the two F-4C, crew (555th TFS/8th TFW) claimed two MiG-17 kills on that day. After three days, on 26 April, Nguyen Hong Nhi and Dong Van Song took off from Noi Bai and attacked an F-4 Phantom over Bac Can – Thai Nguyen. Maj Gilmore fired a Sidewinder missile from his Phantom and he downed the first North Vietnamese MiG-21 of the war. Nguyen Hong Nhi ejected and injured his spine; he received treatment an extended period of time.

On 17 April 1966, four MiG-17 pilots, Ho Van Quy, Luu Huy Chao, Nguyen Van Bien, and Tran Van Triem, from the 923rd Fighter Regiment, were ordered to take off against a C-47 Skytrain, which flew at an altitude of 3,000 meters over Hoi Xuan (Thanh Hoa Province). At 13:01 hours the MiG-17 flight took a heading of 230 degrees, at an altitude of 3,000 meters, but they did not discover the enemy. After 21 minutes Ho Van Quy discovered a C-47 and he turned left and fired without success. At 13:39 hours Luu Huy Chao also attacked a Skytrain and his shots hit the right engine of the enemy aircraft. After attacking, Quy and Chao turned back and Nguyen Van Bien also fired the enemy aircraft. The right wing of the C-47 broke off and the aircraft crashed down. The US records did not confirm this kill for the North Vietnamese MiG-17s.

The heads of the 923rd Fighter Regiment guided three MiG-17 flights, on 23 April 1966. Ho Van Quy, Luu Huy Chao, Nguyen Van Bien, and Tran Van Triem took off from Noi Bai airbase at 11:20 hours, to beat the enemy in the region Vu Ban – Cam Thuy, with no results. The second flight, Mai Duc Toai, Vo Van Man, Nguyen Khac Loc, Do Huy Hoang from Kep airbase hit attack aircraft in the western region of Binh Gia – Bac

Son. With a 30 degree angle, after detecting F–105s with F-4s, Nguyen Khac Loc shot down one F-4 Phantom. The US sources did not confirm this loss. The third MiG-flight, Le Quang Trung, Nguyen The Hon, Ngo Duc Mai, and Duong Trung Tan, took off from the airfield of Kien An, at 17:13 hours, but they did not fight with the enemy and returned to base.

In the afternoon of 26 April 1966, enemy strikers attacked Route No.10 at Bac Son-Binh Gia, and their fighters covered them, at 30 kilometers east of Cho Moi. MiG-17 flight of Ho Van Quy, Luu Huy Chao, Nguyen Van Bay, and Tran Van Triem took off from Kep. The GCI ordered them to fly at an altitude of 2,500 meters, and 15 kilometers south of Bac Son-Binh Gia. American aircraft continuously changed their direction so MiG-17s went in head-on. Informed by GCI, Ho Van Quy detected an F-4 Phantom at 6 kilometers. In 5 minutes, Luu Huy Chao and Nguyen Van Bay, each shot down F-4C Phantoms and damaged another Phantom over Lang Son Province. After breaking off, the regiment command guided three MiG-17s to land at Kep. US records note no losses to fighters on this day. There was no confirmed US victory over MiG-17s on that day, so Tran Van Triem's MiG-17 might have been the victim of friendly fire.

At the end of April, two air battles were over North Vietnam. On 29 April 1966, Bui Dinh Kinh (MiG-17 – 923rd F.R.) shot down Capt. Boston's A-4E over mountainous terrain 16 kilometers east of Na San. That afternoon, another MiG-17 unit fought with USAF F-4C Phantoms, when Nguyen Van Bay shot down an F-105D Thunderchief, but US records did not confirm it. His comrade, Nguyen Khac Loc, ejected because of F-4C Phantom's AIM-9 missile, and he landed safely. Next day, on 30 April 1966, MiG-17s from the 923rd Fighter Regiment were involved in a dogfight with F-4s and F-105s over Nghia Lo. Pham Ngoc Lan ejected and landed safely, but Tran Tan Duc was killed in action by an F-4C Phantom.

By the summer of 1966, the American forces were attacking Hanoi, Hai Phong, and other military and industrial centers. Air battles began in June and in ten engagements, 15 US aircraft were shot down by VPAF fighters until the autumn of 1966.

On 12 June 1966, at 14:41 hours, the enemy was detected over Cai Bau Island at an altitude of 1,900 meters. After they passed Yen Thu, at 14:43 hours, Le Quang Trung and Vo Van Man took off from Kep. At 14:45 hours the pair of MiG-17s rounded to the west and to the top of Kep, held an altitude of 1,000 meters, and then took a heading of 90 degrees. Le Quang Trung immediately discovered two F-8s about 10 kilometers east of Luc Nam. He had rounded, closed down spacing to keep the confrontation to his advantage, and then turned right to left. After two rounds, Le Quang Trung shot down an F-8 Crusader. At 14:53 hours, the second flight, Pham Thanh Chung and Duong Trung Tan took off to protect their comrades. At 15:00 hours Trung – Man landed and three minutes later Chung. Tan also landed safely at Kep airbase. The US sources did not confirm this loss.

On 12 June 1966, Le Quang Trung shot down an F-8 Crusader east of Luc Nam, in Ha Bac Province, by VPAF records. It was Trung's first air victory during the war.
(István Toperczer Collection)

In the afternoon of June 21, 1966, the heads of the 923rd F.R. ordered Pham Thanh Chung, Duong Trung Tan, Nguyen Van Bay and Phan Van Tuc to take off from Kep and to fly on low-level altitude to the Kep – Chu area. The radar captured the enemy (4 F-8s and 6 A-4s) but was not in good position to attack; the flight changed their angle to 60 degrees. In two minutes and twenty seconds of combat, Pham Thanh Chung and Phan Van Tuc shot down an RF-8A and F-8E, but Duong Trung Tan ejected, because he was hit by Lt. Chancy's AIM-9 missile. The RF-8A loss records state that it fell to North Vietnamese AAA fire.

At noon of 29 June 1966, bombing efforts were made against petrol facilities in Duc Giang (Hanoi), Thuong Ly (Hai Phong) and the capital. Attempting to oppose the raids, the 923rd Fighter Regiment sent four MiG-17s into combat. Tran Huyen, Vo Van Man, Nguyen Van Bay and Phan Van Tuc flew at an altitude of 500 meters, turned to the Da Phuc Bridge and alongside the south of Tam Dao ridge, then pulled up and intercepted enemy between Hill 1591 and 1263. With a 60 degree inbound angle, Nguyen Van Bay detected the enemy from 15 kilometers away. It gave a chance for Nguyen Van Bay and Phan Van Tuc to shoot down two F-105Ds over Tam Dao (Thai Nguyen Province). When returning to Noi Bai, they received information of the enemy from command assist post at Am Lon Mountain, 10 kilometers north of Noi Bai and a command post at Noi Bai, instead they turned and landed at Gia Lam. The solitary F-105 officially listed as missing was credited to AAA by the USAF.

Twelve F-105s with no bombs, just rockets and the machine gun, flying over Tam Dao between 600 and 1,500 meters, were heading north of Hanoi to Noi Bai on 19 July 1966. The lack of bombs and the missile armament implied that the American aircraft were on a MiG-hunting

The MiG-17 pilots (Le Hai, Tran Van Triem, Luu Huy Chao, Ngo Duc Mai, Nguyen Van Bien, Le Quang Trung and Pham Thanh Chung) from the 923rd Fighter Regiment pose for a group photo at Kep airbase, in July 1966. (István Toperczer Collection)

Phan Van Tuc

Date of Birth: 1934
Enlisted: June 1953
Pilot training:
1956 – 1964 (MiG-17 – China)
War Service and Unit:
1964 – 1965 (921st Fighter Regiment)
1965 – 1967 (923rd Fighter Regiment)
Aircraft: MiG-17
Died: 31 December 1967 – during training flight over Vinh Phuc
Hero of the Vietnamese People's Armed Forces: 28 April 2000
Rank: Captain

Air Victories: 4 kills
(2 F-8s, 1 F-4, 1 F-105 – VPAF official credit)

Date	Aircraft	Unit	Kill – US Pilot (VPAF – US databases)
03 Apr 65	MiG-17	921.	F-8E – US not confirmed
21 Jun 66	MiG-17	921.	F-8E – Black (POW)
29 Jun 66	MiG-17	921.	F-105D – US not confirmed
19 Apr 67	MiG-17	923.	F-105F – Madison, Sterling (POWs) (Shared)

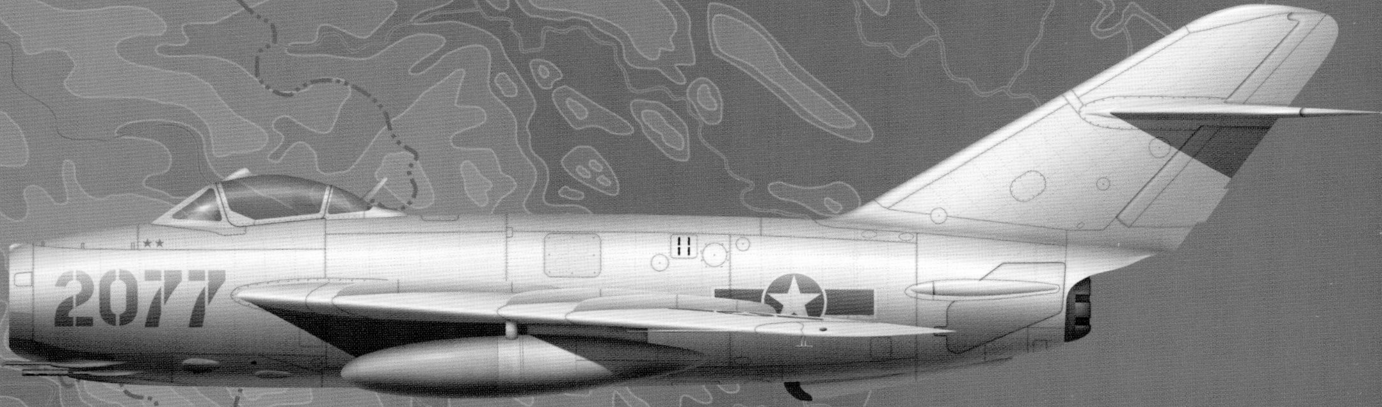

MiG-17F Fresco C, No. 2077 (2 kills) of the 923rd Fighter Regiment, 1966
This MiG-17 was used by Phan Van Tuc, who shot down Lt Cdr Black's F-8E Crusader (149152) of the VF-211 from USS Hancock, on 21 June 1966. (Artwork: Balázs Kakuk)

mission. Nguyen Van Bien and Vo Van Man were ordered to attack and were instructed not to open fire unless closing to at least 400-600 meters. At 14:50 hours two MiG-17s of the 923rd Fighter Regiment took off and soon ran into two pairs of F-105s, separated by 1,500 meters. The MiGs flew diagonally through the airbase. First, the enemy flight appeared ahead with 4 F-105s in a ladder formation, the first two ahead of the others about 1,500 meters with an altitude not much higher than the MiGs. Nguyen Bien informed Vo Van Man, who then pulled up to surprise the enemy. The Vietnamese pilots increased speed and a steep climb brought them behind an F-105. Nguyen Van Bien opened fire from 600 meters, but the Thunderchief had noticed him and evaded. Getting behind the MiG, the American pilot tried to shoot it down with numerous bursts, but missed. A furious dogfight developed upon the arrival of the remaining eight F-105s. Attempting to bait their chasers into the fire of the AAA, the MiGs rushed for Noi Bai. East of the base, Vo Van Man abruptly reversed and got behind the F-105. After two bursts, one of the American aircraft crashed and its pilot (1Lt Diamond) was killed. Despite the determination of the American pilots to shoot down the MiGs, their efforts were defeated by fierce AAA fire. Two minutes later, another F-105 fell victim to Nguyen Bien, while the third F-105 was hit by flak and exploded over Tuyen Quang. Vo Van Man's aircraft was shot with several holes in his wings. The two MiGs landed at Gia Lam airfield (Hanoi).

On 29 July 1966, an RC-47D set off for a surveillance mission over Sam Neua. The Skytrain flew close to the Vietnamese – Laotian border, and later it was between Yen Chau and Son La. At 14:37 hours, the GCI ordered the Class One Alert for a pair of MiG-17 in Noi Bai. At 14:55 hours, Tran Huyen and Vo Van Man took off, bearing 240 degrees at an altitude of 3,000 meters and two minutes later they discovered the enemy at a

Two grey-colored MiG-17s (2044, 2037) are seen on the runway of Kep airbase during the summer of 1966.
(István Toperczer Collection)

Date of Birth: 2 August 1940
Enlisted: 1961
Pilot training:
1962 – 1965 (MiG-21 – Soviet Union)
War Service and Unit:
1965 – 1968 (921st Fighter Regiment)
Aircraft: MiG-21
Rank: Senior Colonel

Air Victories: 4 kills
(3 F-105s, 1 EB-66 – VPAF official credit)

Date	Aircraft	Unit	Kill – US Pilot (VPAF – US databases)
12 May 67	MiG-21	921.	F-105D – Grenzebach (KIA) (AAA)
14 Jan 68	MiG-21	921.	EB-66C – Mercer + 6 crews (Rescued – POWs)

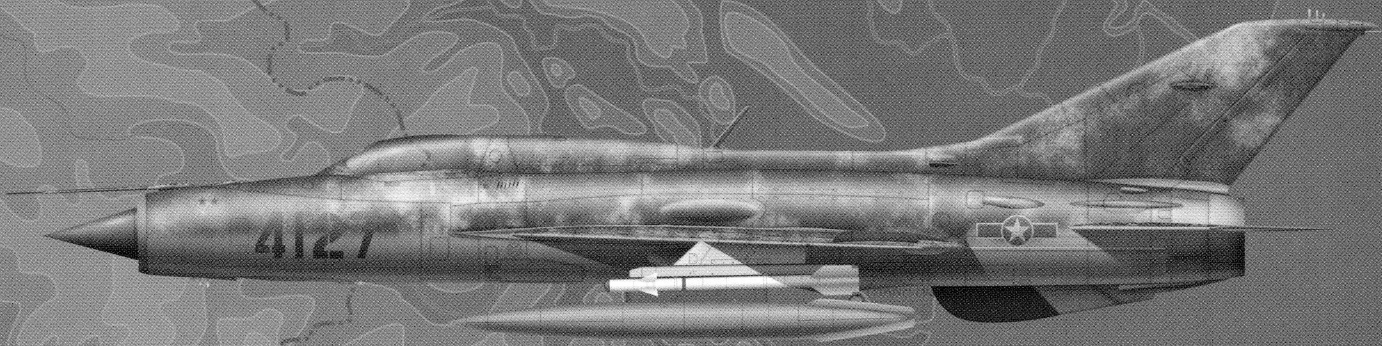

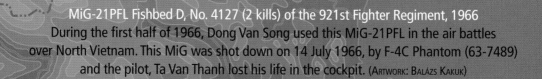

MiG-21PFL Fishbed D, No. 4127 (2 kills) of the 921st Fighter Regiment, 1966
During the first half of 1966, Dong Van Song used this MiG-21PFL in the air battles over North Vietnam. This MiG was shot down on 14 July 1966, by F-4C Phantom (63-7489) and the pilot, Ta Van Thanh lost his life in the cockpit. (Artwork: Balázs Kakuk)

distance of 20 kilometers. When they arrived closer to the RC-47, they dropped their auxiliary fuel tanks and attacked the enemy aircraft. They fired two bursts of cannons and hit the left wing of Skytrain. Because of the higher speed, the MiG-17s overran their damaged enemy and they turned back to attack once more. They fired and shot down the RC-47 enemy aircraft over Mai Chau – Hoa Binh airspace. They detected two parachutes, but the crew of the aircraft did not survive this accident. At 15:15 hours two MiG-17s landed safely at Noi Bai AB.

In the last month of the summer, the 923rd Fighter Regiment was also active. In the afternoon of 12 August 1966, receiving the information that the enemy would attack targets around Hanoi and Hai Phong, Commander Nguyen Van Tien ordered MiG-17s and MiG-21s ready to take off. The plan of the 923rd Fighter Regiment was to intercept the enemy coming from Yen Chau to Yen Bai – Tuyen Quang was granted and MiG-21s were allowed to use to cover. At 16:39 hours, an enemy flight was detected at 25 kilometers east of Phu Yen; they maneuvered and moved position to Nghia Lo. Ten minutes later, the MiG-17 flight of Phan Van Tuc and Luu Huy Chao took off from Gia Lam, flew alongside the Red River, through Son Tay and Thanh Son. At 25 kilometers east of Van Yen, they turned right and headed to an area 25 kilometers southeast of Nghia Lo. At 16:57 hours, a MiG-21 pair took off from Noi Bai, flew along the west side of the Tam Dao ridge to Son Duong. The GCI guided MiG-17s approached from behind, the enemy at 30 degrees. Phan Van Tuc detected F-105s at 15 kilometers at the front. MiG-17s gained the initiative and attacked 4 F-105s at an altitude of 500 to 1,000 meters. Luu Huy Chao shot down an F-105D, then broke off, went low

Le Quang Trung (LEFT) and Ngo Duc Mai (RIGHT) prepare to take off from Noi Bai on 17 August 1966. Le Quang Trung shot down an F-105F Thunderchief over Duong River on that day. (ISTVÁN TOPERCZER COLLECTION)

Date of Birth: 1939
Enlisted: February 1959
Pilot training:
1960 – 1964 (MiG-17 – China)
War Service and Unit:
1964 – 1965 (921st Fighter Regiment)
1965 – 1967 (923rd Fighter Regiment)
Aircraft: MiG-17
Died: 14 May 1967 – shot down by USAF F-4C Phantom (63-7699 / Bakke – Lambert)
Hero of the Vietnamese People's Armed Forces: 28 April 2000
Rank: First Lieutenant

Air Victories: 5 kills
(3 F-4s, 1 F-8, 1 F-105 – VPAF official credit)

Date	Aircraft	Unit	Kill – US Pilot (VPAF – US databases)
19 Jul 66	MiG-17	923.	F-105D – Diamond (KIA)
29 Jul 66	MiG-17	923.	RC-47 – Hoskinson + 7 crew (KIA) (Shared)
05 Sep 66	MiG-17	923.	F-8E – US not confirmed (F-8 damaged)
21 Sep 66	MiG-17	923.	F-4C – Kellems, Thomas (Rescued)
24 Apr 67	MiG-17	923.	F-4C – Knapp, Austin (KIAs) (AAA)
14 May 67	MiG-17	923.	F-4 – US not confirmed

MiG-17F Fresco C, No. 2047 (7 kills) of the 923rd Fighter Regiment, 1966
This MiG-17F had flown by Vo Van Man, who shot down an USAF RC-47 enemy aircraft (43-48388) over airspace Mai Chau – Hoa Binh, on 29 July 1966. (Artwork: Balázs Kakuk)

and flew southeast. At the same time, two MiG-21s were guided from Son Duong to 15 kilometers south of Yen Bai and covered the MiG-17 retreat. After the MiG-17s crossed the Red River, they went down to the north of Gia Lam and landed safely. The MiG-21s turned left to Thanh Son and turned back, at 15 kilometers of Doan Hung; finally they turned right to land at Noi Bai.

On 17 August, two MiG-17 pairs, Le Quang Trung – Ngo Duc Mai and Nguyen Van Bien – Phan Van Tuc, took off from Noi Bai and Gia Lam, and had to fight F-105s for their Hanoi. They broke enemy's intention to use low-flying groups to attack the Bridge of Duong River. Le Quang Trung shot down an F-105F and the two MiG-pairs landed safely. According to US sources, Maj Brand and Maj Singer were shot down when their Thunderchief was hit by AAA over a target 20 kilometers north of Van Yen and at 100 kilometers west of Hanoi.

The standard pair of MiG-21s was more successful in combat when they had a mix of weapons fitted. The lead aircraft had two infra-red guided R-3S AAMs, while his wingman was carrying two UB-16-57 rocket pods with unguided S-5M air-to-air missiles.

With a dissimilar load like this, on 7 July 1966, a pair of MiG-21PFL Fishbed-Ds attacked two F-105s. The air defense radar grid indicated that a number of US aircraft were approaching from Thailand. Two MiG-21s scrambled from the 921st Fighter Regiment and remained on Combat Air Patrol (CAP) over Noi Bai. When the F-105Ds appeared from behind the Tam Dao Mountain at an altitude of 500 meters, the wingman, Tran Ngoc Siu, opened fire from 1,500 meters, but the Thunderchief made an evasive left turn. Two more salvos of rockets from 500 and 200 meters destroyed Capt Tomes' F-105D northwest of Hanoi. This was basically the first aerial victory by a MiG-21 over piloted American aircraft. The leader, Nguyen Nhat Chieu, in the meantime, was unable to achieve a lock with the R-3S AAM on another F-105 making energetic maneuvers, and so did not launch his AAMs. The official USAF loss records confirmed this claim to the AAA unit.

Soon, two similar dogfights followed, which showed that the fighters could have been more effective if, besides the missiles, they had an onboard cannon. At this time, the MiG-21PFL Fishbed-Ds delivered to Vietnam did not yet have the option of the centerline GP-9 cannon pod. On 11 July, F-105s and F-4s were heading to Yen Bai – Bac Can, when Vu Ngoc Dinh and Dong Van Song attacked the American flights. Vu Ngoc Dinh launched a missile against an F-105D over Son Duong, in Tuyen Quang Province, and damaged a Thunderchief. Trying to make it back to Thailand, but running out of fuel, Maj McClelland ejected over Laos. On 14 July, two MiG-21s attacked 12 F-4s and F-105s. But Hoang Bieu and Ta Van Thanh were shot down by Sidewinders of F-4C Phantoms. Bieu ejected, but Ta Van Thanh's ejection seat did not work, he lost his life in the cockpit.

LE QUANG TRUNG

DATE OF BIRTH: 1934
ENLISTED: May 1949
PILOT TRAINING:
1956 – 1964 (MiG-17 – China)
1969 – 1970 (MiG-19 – Vietnam)
WAR SERVICE AND UNIT:
1964 – 1968 (921st and 923rd Fighter Regiments)
1969 – 1970 (925th Fighter Regiment)
AIRCRAFT: MiG-17, MiG-19
DIED: 6 April 1970 – during training flight over Yen Bai
HERO OF THE VIETNAMESE PEOPLE'S ARMED FORCES: 20 December 1994
RANK: Major

AIR VICTORIES: 5 kills
(2 F-105s, 1 F-8, 1 A-4, 1 AD-6 – VPAF official credit)

DATE	AIRCRAFT	UNIT	KILL – US PILOT (VPAF – US DATABASES)
12 Jun 66	MiG-17	923.	F-8 – US not confirmed
17 Aug 66	MiG-17	923.	F-105F – Brand, Singer (KIA) (AAA)
20 Sep 66	MiG-17	923.	F-105 – US not confirmed
04 Dec 66	MiG-17	923.	F-105 – US not confirmed (Shared)
25 Apr 67	MiG-17	923.	F-105 – US not confirmed

MiG-17F Fresco C, No. 2072 (5 kills) of the 923rd Fighter Regiment, 1966
On 17 August 1966, two MiG-17 pairs had to fight F-105s for Hanoi. Le Quang Trung shot down Maj Brand and Maj Singer's F-105F Thunderchief (63-8308) with this MiG-17. (ARTWORK: BALÁZS KAKUK)

Scrambling the MiG-21s was on direct orders from the central command post, while the commander of the fighter regiment could order the take-off for the alert aircraft only when in imminent danger. They adhered to the principle: scrambling from the central command post, vectoring in from the regimental control post or from forward air control positions. The order of battle for the MiG-21s was as follows: in pairs a separation of 50-200 meters, for flights of four a separations between the two pairs 300-700 meters. Later these numbers were modified to 500-800 and 800 meters respectively. A change to open formations became possible only after the MiG-21s started to operate above the 2,500 meters level. In order to provide better maneuvering capabilities, a choice was made in favor of the R-3S AAMs instead of the unguided S-5M rockets from the UB-16-57 pod.

The North Vietnamese discovered that the launch of similar American missiles (AIM-9 Sidewinder) was more difficult than in a MiG-17. In a pair of MiG-21s it was the task of the wingman to watch the rear hemisphere, and when he saw a launch they made an energetic turn towards and below the missile at maximum G limits. The maneuver carried out in time provided a protection against a Sidewinder hit.

The combat effectiveness of the VPAF improved considerably, especially that of the MiG-17 fighters, but the same could not be said for the MiG-21s. The fighters of the 921st Fighter Regiment took part in several dogfights but with no results. After several meetings and discussions, the conclusion was that the MiG-21 was less successful because the pilots were not yet fully familiar with the aircraft and most of the pilots used tactics learned and practiced with the MiG-17s. In this situation, the "intercept from combat air patrol" principle was used. The MiG-21s together with MiG-17s were on Combat Air Patrol missions in regions most often used by incoming American fighter bombers. The MiG-17s had their job at low altitude (to 1,500 meters), while the MiG-21s were patrolling at high altitude (over 2,500 meters). The altitude segment between 1,500 and 2,500 meters was considered to be an intermediate zone where both aircraft types could operate in case of a dogfight. The North Vietnamese pilots were at an advantage since they were more familiar with the local geography, the mountains, and also had a good support by the ground control units on their side. The North Vietnamese side studied the patterns of US attacks and decided to put up MiG-21s from Noi Bai on Combat Air Patrol on the known American routes.

The American reconnaissance drones were active during 1966. Nguyen Dang Kinh claimed the second Firebee kill for MiG-21, after his comrade, Nguyen Hong Nhi's drone kill. On 21 July 1966, at 10:13 hours, an enemy flight was coming from Thanh Son to Noi Bai at an altitude of 8,000 meters with high speed. Likely, they were recons before the attack or decoys. At 10:36 hours, another flight crossed the Vietnamese – Laotian border 50 kilometers west of Lang Chanh, at an altitude of 17,000 meters. Commander Nguyen Van Tien and Hoang Ngoc Dieu judged they were Firebees but they lost signals three minutes later. Based on their flight path, command ordered to follow the Firebees, opened other ground control radars, and put MiG-21 on ready. At 10:47 hours, the enemy appeared 10 kilometers west of Thanh Son, heading to Phu Tho. Nguyen Dang Kinh was ordered to take off with a MiG-21 of the 921st Fighter Regiment. The Firebee arrived over Phu Tho and turned left, followed Route No.2 through Thac Ba, at a stable speed of 800 km/h, then flew alongside the Yen Bai – Lao Cai railway, at an altitude of 16,000 meters. After take-off at bearing of 300 degrees, theMiG-21 was ordered to altitude of 8.000 meters. But at 10:54 hours, over Viet Tri, Nguyen Dang Kinh only climbed to 6,000 meters and began to turn right to bearing 350-360 degrees to create an approach angle. After two minutes, the GCI ordered the MiG-21 to ascend to 13,000 meters, but he only got to 8,000 meters, and then 10,000 meters, as his speed rose from 900 km/h to 1,200 km/h. At 15 kilometers north of Tuyen Quang, the MiG-21 turned right to a bearing 270 degrees, at an altitude of 12,000 meters and 1,500 km/h speed. Over Luc Yen, the MiG-21 turned left and began to approach, at an altitude of 14,000 meters and followed the Firebee. At 11:02 hours, Nguyen Dang Kinh reached Bao Ha and the target was 30 kilometers ahead. After a few seconds, he detected the target and ascended. One minute later, the MiG-21 arrived to Bao Thang at an altitude of 16,000 meters, where the target was 15 kilometers ahead, at an altitude of 17,000 meters. Ground control allowed opening radar. Nguyen Dang Kinh followed target by radar and fired his R-3S missiles, shot down the AQM-34 Firebee. He broke off right, turned back 180 degrees to land at Noi Bai.

One month later, Dang Ngoc Ngu was also successful in shooting down a Firebee drone with his MiG-21. At noon of 13 August 1966, an AQM-34 drone was detected east at Bach Long Vi Island, flying to the north. It might have came to scout Route No.4. At 12:47 hours, MiG-21 pilot Ha Van Chuc took off from Noi Bai to Cam Pha. After twelve minutes, he arrived over Hong Gai, at an altitude of 14,000 meters, with a 1,500 km/h speed and at a distance of 90 kilometers from the target. But the target continued to fly straight, so he was ordered to come back. At Mong Cai, a Firebee turned left and flew alongside north of the Vietnam – China border. At 13:11 hours, the target signal was lost, reappeared after two minutes, and then lost again. Commanders Phung The Tai and Nguyen Van Tien judged the enemy might fly to the Cao Bang – Bac Can area and ordered a MiG-21 to take off again. At 13:14 hours, Dang Ngoc Ngu took off. At that moment the radar still had yet not located exact enemy position. The MiG-21 was guided through Vinh Yen to Son Duong, accelerated and ascended. At 13:18 hours, when the MiG was near Dai Tu, the target signal was located at 13 kilometers east of Dong Khe, but the radar lost the MiG-21 signal two minutes later, at the moment the target turned left. The GCI asked a pilot and "blindly" guided him to Chiem Hoa, then turned right, bearing 90 degrees and ascended his MiG. At 13:24 hours, the radar caught a MiG-21 signal at Ba Be Lake, which headed to the east while the target had crossed Na Ri at 15 kilometers northwest of Binh Gia, at an altitude of 18,000 meters. The MiG-21 was 80 kilometers behind the drone. Dang Ngoc Ngu was ordered to turn left, bearing 125 degrees, accelerated to 1,800 km/h, but ascended slowly. After four minutes, at 13:28 hours, the MiG-21 arrived over Binh Gia, 30 kilometers behind and below 1,000 meters from target. During the next one and half minutes, the battle turned out like the battle on 21 July1966, Dang Ngoc Ngu shot down that AQM-34 Firebee reconnaissance drone.

In the second half of 1966, there were many aerial engagements. At this time, the Americans were already using air-to-air missiles (AAM), but the Vietnamese, with MiG-17s, employed successful evasive maneuvers against the air-to-air missiles. In September of 1966 a MiG-17 was returning to his home base when two F-4s started to chase it and launched missiles from a distance of 1,500-2,000 meters. The MiG pilot used evasive maneuvers and none of the AAMs found their target. In the MiG to observe the rear hemisphere and to discover a Sidewinder missile was possible only by flying in a snaking pattern. The missile's flame was clearly visible at launch. The basic maneuver involved the Vietnamese pilots turning with their MiG-17s at a 70-degree banking angle and pulling 3-4 Gs towards the incoming missile, at a speed of 700-900 km/h. In most cases, this maneuver was enough to break the lock of the missile. If the MiG was flying higher than 800 meters and the "basic turn" was not successful in shaking off the Sidewinder, he started a more elaborate maneuver. By increasing the bank angle, he slowly started a dive. The pilot did not push forward the control stick, and so carried on with a constantly changing movement of the aircraft in different planes. The maneuver, in its early stage, was similar to a spiral, while the pilot performed a slow descending roll. The simultaneous movement of the aircraft, both in vertical and horizontal plane, was enough to break the lock of the missiles guidance head.

In the afternoon of 5 September 1966, Nguyen Van Bay shot down the USAF exchange pilot Capt Abbott's F-8E Crusader, from the USS Oriskany, in the area of Nam Dinh.
(István Toperczer Collection)

At 16:30 hours on 5 September 1966, Nguyen Van Bay – Vo Van Man and Tran Huyen – Luu Huy Chao, from the 923rd Fighter Regiment, were ordered to take off, according to the enemy-attacked area of Phu Ly, Nam Dinh. Nguyen Van Bay quickly discovered two American aircraft right in front, about 30 km in an altitude from 1,800 to 2,000 meters. He dropped the auxiliary fuel tanks and jumped to 1,500 meters. Detecting the MiGs, the F-8 escaped through the clouds, but Nguyen Van Bay accurately predicted the enemy routes. As he was at about 400 – 500 meters from enemy, he had a series of shots, but the bullets missed the target. He corrected the line of sight and the second shot series hit the cockpit of the F-8E Crusader. By the third bullet series, the F-8E caught fire and crashed into the ground. While Nguyen Van Bay attacked, Vo Van Man was the close support for his leader, so he had seen the American

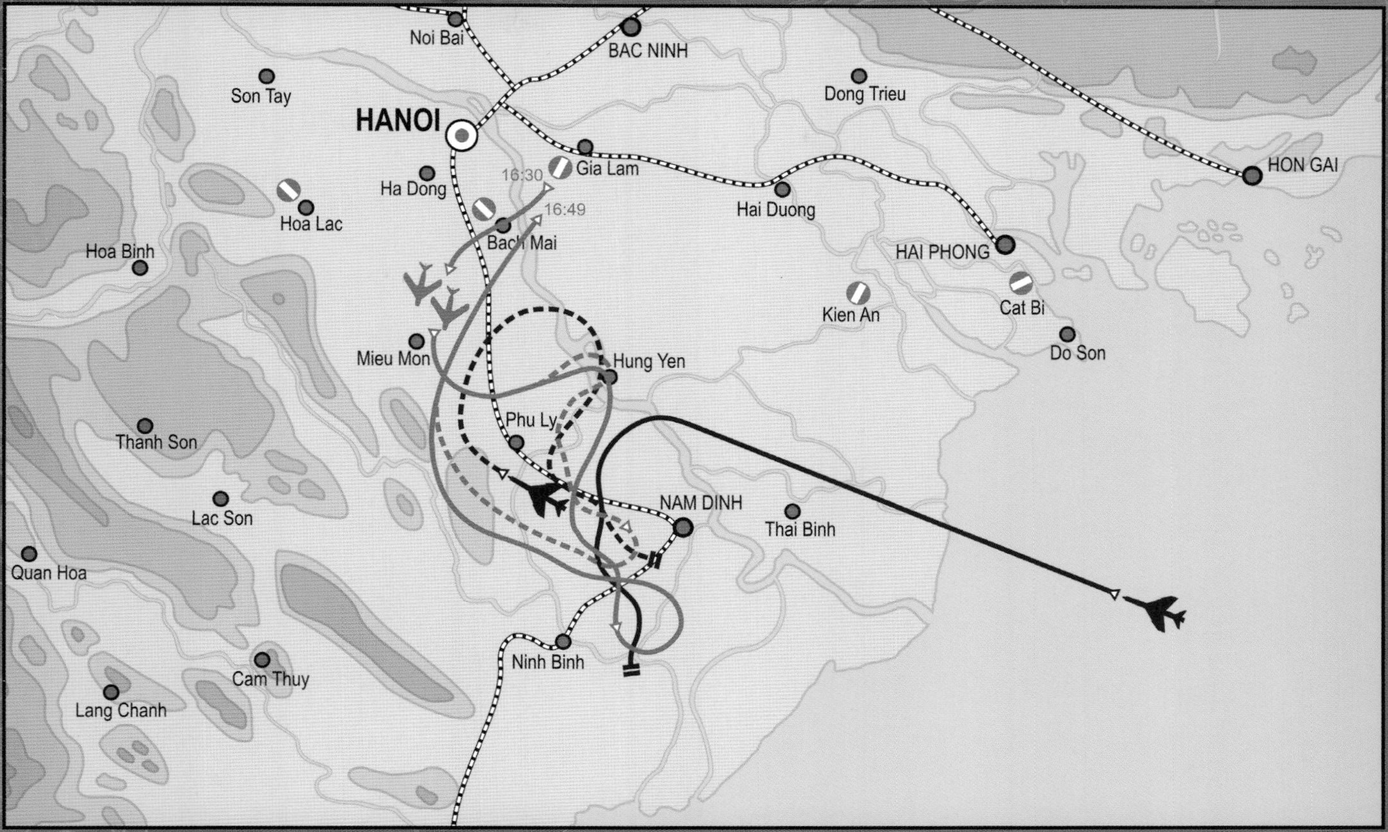

On 5 September 1966, Nguyen Van Bay and Vo Van Manshot down two US Navy F-8E Crusaders at area of Ninh Binh - Nam Dinh.
(CARTOGRAPH: PÉTER BARNA)

aircraft catch fire. Vo Van Man reached 500 meters to the other F-8 and he began shooting the first series but did not win. He immediately shot three more series at close range and the American aircraft caught fire and crashed. Nguyen Van Bay and Vo Van Man landed safely at Gia Lam airfield. The USAF exchange pilot Capt Abbott from USS *Oriskany* was downed by Nguyen Van Bay, but the other F-8 was only damaged.

After ten days, on 16 September, a MiG-17 flight, including Ho Van Quy, Do Huy Hoang, Nguyen Van Bay and Vo Van Man, was ordered to take the enemy in the northeast sky. Taking off from Gia Lam, they flew toward Pha Lai – Dong Trieu (Quang Ninh). They detected the attack formation, six F-105 Thunderchiefs and eight F-4C Phantoms aircraft were at an altitude of 700 meters. The MiG-17 flight got into a dogfight with four F-4Cs over Nam Mau Mountain. The Phantoms fired 8 missiles, but the MiGs were able to avoid them. Nguyen Van Bay claimed Maj Robertson's F-4C Phantom loss at southeast of Kep airbase. They wounded another Phantom too, and returned safely.

In the afternoon of 20 September, a MiG-17 flight of Le Quang Trung, Hoang Van Ky, Tran Minh Phuong and Luu Duc Sy was ordered to take off from Noi Bai, because at 15:30 hours the enemy across Yen Bai – Tuyen Quang had flown up north. The MiG-17 flight was guided alongside the west of Route No.3, near AAA fire perimeter of Thai Nguyen, with a speed 750 km/h, at an altitude of 1,000 meters then turned left, bearing

The famous Ace-pilot Nguyen Van Bay used this MiG-17 during the war. The No.2505 can be seen in the city museum of Cao Lanh, Dong Thap Province, South Vietnam. (Le Minh Trung)

100 degrees to intercept at Vo Nhai. After two minutes of straight flight, they turned left to intercept. Le Quang Trung detected F-105s and F-4s at a distance of 8 kilometers. Covered by Tran Minh Phuong and Luu Duc Sy, he shot down one F-105 and damaged the other one. Hoang Van Ky shot down one more F-105. Command ordered them to break off to Dai Tu, over Tam Dao ridge then to west Noi Bai. As a close support team to MiG-17 landing, at 15:40 hours, MiG-21 flight of Le Trong Huyen and Tran Thien Luong also took off from Noi Bai, and flew over Vinh Yen , on the west side of the Tam Dao ridge, then turned right over Hill 1591 to Dai Tu, Thai Nguyen and made several circles from Da Phuc to Phuc Yen to cover the MiG-17s landing. While the MiG-21s prepared to land, there were still enemies at north Dinh Hoa, Cho Moi, so the 923rd Fighter Regiment requested a pair of MiG-17s with Tran Huyen – Nguyen Van Bien to take off from Gia Lam, operate over the airbase, and be ready to respond if necessary. The USAF sources did not confirm the losses on this day.

Next day, on 21 September 1966, an attacking group of F-4 Phantoms came to the attention of a flight of MiG-17s. The enemies were coming from the sea, over the Yen Tu ridge to attack targets in Bac Giang. At 08.58 hours, four MiG–17s, Nguyen Van Bay, Do Huy Hoang, Luu Huy Chao and Vo Van Man, took off from Kien An airfield, flew low level through Kinh Mon to Dong Trieu, turned left and ascended. At 09:05 hours, the pilots detected F-105s, at a distance of 10 kilometers and at higher altitudes were also F-4s. The F-4s had flown as close support team behind the F-105s, at an altitude of 1.000 meters. After 8 minutes, Vo Van Man had an altitude advantage and opened up with his cannons

Le Trong Huyen

Date of Birth: 1934
Enlisted: December 1953
Pilot training:
1960 – 1964 (MiG-17 – China)
1966 (MiG-21 – Vietnam)
War Service and Unit:
1964 – 1972 (921st Fighter Regiment)
Aircraft: MiG-17, MiG-21
Died: 3 March 1972 – during task flight by friendly SAM fire, over Vinh
Hero of the Vietnamese People's Armed Forces: 28 April 2000
Rank: Major

Air Victories: 4 kills
(3 F-105s, 1 A-4 – VPAF official credit)

Date	Aircraft	Unit	Kill – US Pilot (VPAF – US databases)
21 Sep 66	MiG-21	921.	F-105D – Ammon (KIA) (AAA)
02 Dec 66	MiG-21	921.	F-105D – Moorberg (KIA) (AAA)
30 Apr 67	MiG-21	921.	F-105D – J. Abbott (POW)
11 Jul 67	MiG-21	921.	A-4 – US not confirmed

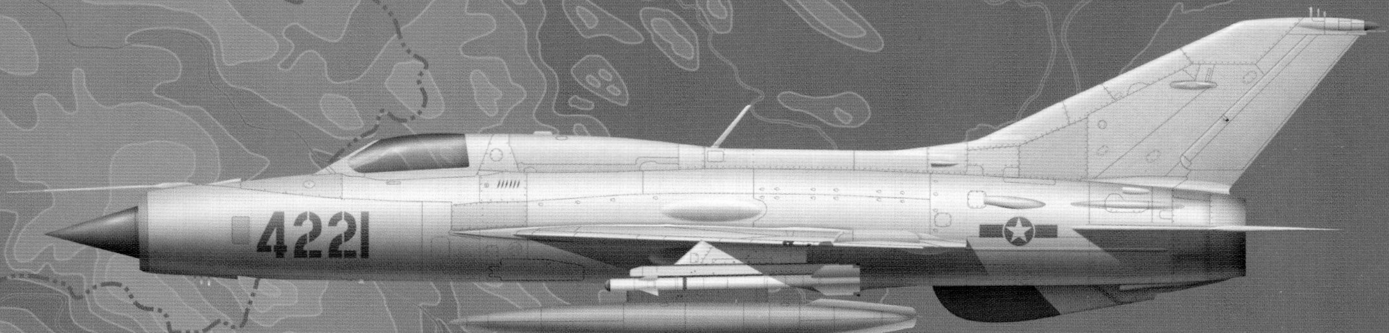

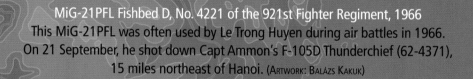

MiG-21PFL Fishbed D, No. 4221 of the 921st Fighter Regiment, 1966
This MiG-21PFL was often used by Le Trong Huyen during air battles in 1966.
On 21 September, he shot down Capt Ammon's F-105D Thunderchief (62-4371),
15 miles northeast of Hanoi. (Artwork: Balázs Kakuk)

from 500 meters, and then from 200 meters, downing Capt. Kellems's F-4C Phantom. After coming out of a dive at 3,000 meters the other MiG-17 attacked another Phantom, opening up on him from 1,000-1,200 meters, when it lit its afterburners and ran away. Do Huy Hoang's MiG was hit by enemy cannon; he ejected and landed to ground safely. The other MiG-17 returned to Gia Lam airfield.

At 09:09 hours, a MiG-21 flight of Le Trong Huyen and Tran Thien Luong took off from Noi Bai, made one turn on the top and were guided east 30 kilometers to Luc Nam. After eleven minutes, MiG-21s detected F-105s and F-4s head on, at a distance of 10 kilometers. The MiG-21s caught another F-105 flight at an altitude of 2,000 meters. The leader, Le Trong Huyen attacked a Thunderchief and shot it down with an R-3S missile launched from a 1,500 meters distance. The missile was launched on the edge of the operational envelop WEZ (weapon engagement zone) for the targeting system, at a altitude of 1,200 meters and at a speed of 700 km/h – the USAF admitted the loss of F-105D, but credited its destruction to AAA over the northeast area of Hanoi.

On 23 September 1966, an enemy drone was coming from the sea. MiG-21s were ready to take off but radar could not catch an enemy signal. At 15:01 hours, the target was detected 8 kilometers east of My Duc, at an altitude of 500 meters, and then turned right to Hanoi at Mieu Mon. Three minutes later, when the target was 5 kilometers east of Ha Dong, a MiG-17 flight of Ho Van Quy and Nguyen Hong Thanh took off from Gia Lam to Noi Bai. At 15:06 hours, the target flew over Hanoi and went alongside Route No.1 to the North, when Nguyen Hong Nhi took off from Noi Bai. After it left Hanoi, the Firebee ascended. Command guessed a drone would fly to an eastern direction and ordered a MiG-21 to a bearing of 80 degrees. At 15:13 hours, a Firebee was 10 kilometers southwest of Dong Mo. It began to turn right, with a speed of 900 km/h, at an altitude of 4,500 meters then bearing 180 degrees and continued to ascend. Two minutes later, a MiG-21 was 5 kilometers west of Luc Nam and was ordered to turn right and ascended to altitude of 6,000 meters. The next moment the target was 8 kilometers north of Chu, 15 kilometers ahead and 1,500 meters above, with an approach angle of about 90 degrees. Then it turned left to Son Dong and ascended to 10,000 meters, Nguyen Hong Nhi turned right, bearing 120 degrees with his MiG-21. He detected a Firebee on his left, 10 kilometers ahead and much higher. He fired a missile, but because of long range, he did not make a hit.

At the beginning of October 1966, two pairs of MiG-21s claimed two kills. On 5 October, a flight of four Phantoms was assigned to provide an escort to two EB-66s southwest of Yen Bai. 1Lt Garland's Phantom had been hit by Bui Dinh Kinh's R-3S missile from a MiG-21. On 8 October, Tran Ngoc Siu and Mai Van Cuong took off at 14:38 hours to attack four F-105s. The wingman, Mai Van Cuong, claimed an F-105 kill over Vinh Yen, but US sources did not mention a Thunderchief loss on this date.

On 5 November 1966, a pair of MiG-21s, Bui Dinh Kinh and Dong Van Song, took off at 14:30 hours from Noi Bai. The second pair of MiG-21s, Le Trong Huyen and Tran Thien Luong, took off 4 minutes later. The first flight was on approach to Ham Yen – Van Yen, where they discovered EB-66, under support team of F-4s at a distance of 10 kilometers. Bui Dinh Kinh and Dong Van Song did not see all of them when they were on the offensive. They could not shoot the enemy and were fired upon in the rear from two USAF F-4C Phantoms, so the first pair had to eject.

Between 2 and 24 December 1966, Americans attacked North Vietnam with 280 bombing missions. The main targets were around Hanoi, at Gia Lam, Yen Vien, Van Dien and Noi Bai airbase. The North Vietnamese air defense units claimed 26 American aircraft kills during this period.

The airbase at Noi Bai was attacked by USAF F-4s and F-105s from an altitude of 2,000-2,500 meters on the 2nd of December. For the defense of the base, MiG-21s and MiG-17s were alerted, with the former operating above 2,000 meters and the later below this level. The principle for the MiG-21s was to engage the enemy when they started the dive for the bombing run, while the MiG-17s were to attack when the American aircraft were pulling out of the dive. A pair of MiG-17s discovered two F-105s to their right and attacked them. The wingman of the MiG pair opened up first on the F-105 wingman, but he was too far to achieve success. The pilot of the Thunderchief used his afterburner and disappeared from the scene.

At noon, the Americans attacked Noi Bai. For the defense of the base two pairs of MiG-21s were scrambled. Le Trong Huyen, and Tran Thien Luong took off from Noi Bai, approached their targets with a 160 degrees angle. The leader of the first flight, Le Trong Huyen detected F-105s at a distance of 6 kilometers and launched an R-3S AAM from 1,200-1,500 meters against a Thunderchief scoring a kill, while his wingman, Tran Thien Luong, was not able to fire his UB missile containers, since his target was too far. With the remaining missile, the leader attacked another formation of Phantoms, but the R-3S AAM launched from 4 kilometers missed and finally exploded on impact with the ground. The leader of the second flight, Nghiem Dinh Hieu, also added a Phantom to his list of victories. The USAF recorded the victory of first flight, but once again attributed its destruction to 37 mm AAA unit.

Two days later, on the afternoon of the 4th of December, two MiG-17 flights, by Tran Huyen, Truong Van Cung, Ngo Duc Mai, Hoang Van Ky and Le Quang Trung, Le Xuan Di, Nguyen Xuan Dung, Luu Duc Sy, were rated to take off on enemy airspace at Bac Ninh, Vinh Phu. Tran Huyen and Le Quang Trung shot down an F-105 aircraft, and Luu Duc Sy was shot down by USAF Maj Dickey's F-105 cannon. He lost his life and the other MiG-17s landed safely at Noi Bai.

The tactics of moving the intercept area away from the zone of the intended target was first used at the end of 1966. Until then the fighters

This MiG-21PFL, No. 4128, waits in the earth revetment for the next sortie, at the 921st Fighter Regiment, in December 1966. (István Toperczer Collection)

were active in the vicinity of their own airfield and attacked only American aircraft intruding into this airspace. Based on recommendations from Soviet advisors, the intercept area was moved further away, where the strike package was still flying in a closed formation.

On 5 December 1966, in the morning, an American EB-66 Destroyer was covered by fighters from Sam Neua, which operated at Cho Don – Nghia Lo area. As per their normal strategy, the fighters would come from Moc Chau – Yen Bai – Tuyen Quang route, then along west side of the Tam Dao ridge to attack targets north of Hanoi. Three pairs of MiG-21s were scrambled from Noi Bai to an area 35 kilometers from the airbase. The 24 American aircraft, a mix of F-4s and F-105s, were flying in a long formation with 1-2 minutes separation between the flights. Nguyen Dang Kinh and Bui Duc Nhu took off from Noi Bai at 08:55 hours, bearing 130 degrees and at an altitude of 3,000 meters, highly coordinated, and synergetic with MiG-17s in the area of Lap Thach. At 08:58 hours, the enemy suddenly turned left and came back. MiG-21s turned right 180 degrees twice at Lap Thach. At the same time, a MiG-17 flight of Ho Van Quy, Nguyen The Hon, Nguyen Van Bay and Vo Van Man, took off from Noi Bai to Vinh Yen – Phuc Yen, at an altitude of 1,000 meters ready to fight low, but all enemies were turned back. At 09:02 hours, the first pair of MiGs attacked the lead flight and Nguyen Dang Kinh scored a hit on Maj Begley's Thunderchief, the American pilot killed in action. The US records noted that the F-105 had been downed by a MiG-17. The second pair attacked the next flight, without results, and then the strike package jettisoned their bombs, turned around and left the area. In the afternoon, another pair of MiG-21s continued the attack against another package of American enemy. Vu Ngoc Dinh and Nghiem Dinh Hieu took off from Noi Bai to fly to the area of Vinh Yen – Dai Tu

– Doan Hung. Vu Ngoc Dinh fired two R-3S missiles and shot down one F-105 with a 100 degrees angle and the speed difference was 100 km/h. The US records did not confirm his kill.

On 14 December, a group of twenty F-105s was attacked by 4 MiG-21s, which shot down two US aircraft. The flight of the 921st Fighter Regiment, Nguyen Nhat Chieu, Dang Ngoc Ngu, Dong Van De and Nguyen Van Coc, was led into Tam Dao region, with a 60 degree angle to the next enemy, where they found F-105s, at a distance of 10 kilometers. Dang Ngoc Ngu shot down one F-105, and later he shot down his second F-105. The old North Vietnamese records mention his name as the first MiG-21 pilot who had shot down two enemy aircraft using missiles in an air battle. The new records claimed a second victory for Dong Van De. The USAF only credits the destruction of an F-105D, flown by Capt Cooley, who was rescued, to AAM fired by MiG-21.

On this day the radar detected a Firebee coming at an altitude of 4,000 meters. The MiG-21 flight of Pham Thanh Ngan – Hoang Bieu took off from Noi Bai. After GCI informed them of the target position, Hoang Bieu reported a detection of it at a distance of 4 kilometers, below at an altitude of 100 meters and Pham Thanh Ngan quickly detected it, too. Pham Thanh Ngan followed and hit the drone with a R-3S missile when it arrived over Noi Bai. In the mean time, a MiG-21 flight of Tran Ngoc Siu and Mai Van Cuong took off to cover Chieu – Ngu – De – Coc and Ngan – Bieu to land.

The last MiG-21 action was on 19 December, when Nguyen Hong Nhi – Nguyen Dang Kinh – Vu Ngoc Dinh – Nghiem Dinh Hieu were led on to the enemy at a 50 degree angle, to detect 32 F-105 Thunderchiefs and F-4 Phantoms, at a distance of 10 kilometers over Vinh Yen. Vu Ngoc Dinh shot down an F-105 in the Noi Bai area, but the US did not confirm it.

In the course of aerial engagements during December 1966, the Vietnamese pilots were convinced of the R-3S AAMs capabilities, but only when the attack was unexpected. To achieve this they could use only visual search for the Americans, and if they were in the blind spot of the intruding aircraft's radar. Most of the missiles were launched from an average distance of 1,200-2,500 meters. The Soviet instructors recommended launching the missiles at the distance 1,500 meters. After launching missiles, the Vietnamese pilot made a roll and arrived back to base immediately in low level flight.

But the hunter would often become the hunted and due to the MiG-21 heavily framed canopy, detecting a launched Sidewinder was much more difficult for MiG-21 pilots than for those flying MiG-17s. It was the task of the Fishbed wingman to watch his back, and that of his leader, and if he spotted an AIM-9 closing on either of them he would yell out a warning so they could perform a high-G turn into and below the round. This maneuver would usually break the lock of the Sidewinder infrared seeker head on the tailpipe of a MiG-21.

During 1966, the Commander of the 921st Fighter Regiment was Tran Manh, who also took part in the conversion program from MiG-17 to MiG-21 fighter.
(István Toperczer Collection)

During 1966, 55 percent of enemy aircraft were destroyed by fighter aircraft, and by doing so they had managed to stop 1991 missions to the Hanoi region. There were 196 aerial combats with a loss of 54 US aircraft (30 kills by MiG-17s). With growing combat experience, the average usage of ammunition was improved on the MiG-17. In 1965, to achieve a kill the pilot had to use 65 rounds of 37 millimeters and 247 rounds of 23 millimeters ammunition, while in 1966 they only needed in average 43 rounds of the former and 150 of the later.

Year of a Hundred Dogfights – 1967

In the dry season of 1967 the Americans continued to attack power plants, industrial locations, major routes and military locations in the area of Hanoi and Hai Phong, and also the air defense locations in Viet Tri, Thai Nguyen and Quang Ninh Provinces. The Americans were attempting to isolate Hanoi from Hai Phong and the two cities from other regions.

The attacks against airbases also continued to limit the operational capabilities of the VPAF. Trying to make good use of the small fighter force, activity was concentrated on the defense of Hanoi. Although MiG-21s had already been initiated into the war, the major share of fighting was still falling to the proven MiG-17s. Combined use of the two types, utilizing their capabilities to the fullest, was regarded to have paramount importance.

The military leadership of the North Vietnamese and North Korean forces agreed to set up the "Doan Z" in February 1967. North Korea had agreed to provide "volunteering" pilots to the MiG-17 and MiG-21 units. The North Korean pilots were performing training and combat tasks primarily at the 923rd Fighter Regiment at Kep airbase. Noi Bai airbase had since been declared a reserve-airfield. The "volunteering" North Korean pilots had been in Vietnam until the beginning of 1969.

BELOW LEFT: two MiG-17s and two MiG-15UTIs are seen in separated L-shaped earth revetments close to the runway of a MiG airbase in 1966.
(USAF, COURTESY OF JOHN D. SHERWOOD)

BELOW RIGHT: After a half-century, the earth revetments are in unserviceable status close to Noi Bai airbase, so the villagers used them as volleyball courts.
(ISTVÁN TOPERCZER)

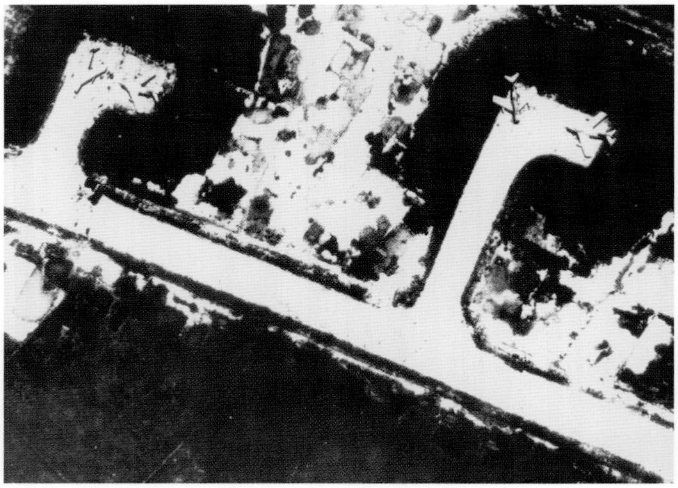

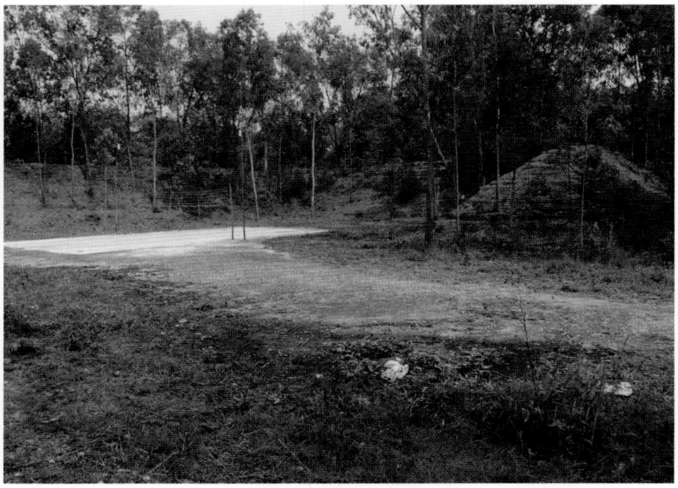

Ho Chi Minh had sent a "Flower Basket" for pilots of the 923rd Fighter regiment as a sign of his respect to their air victories in 1966. The famous MiG-17 pilots, Le Quang Trung (LEFT) and Nguyen Van Bay (RIGHT) are holding a gift. Vo Van Man, Luu Huy Chao, Tran Huyen, Nguyen Ngoc Phieu (COM), Nguyen Khac Loc, Tieu and Vu The Xuan are standing in front of a MiG-17.
(ISTVÁN TOPERCZER COLLECTION)

On 24 March 1967 Vo Nguyen Giap the Minister of Defense, with the order 04/QD-GP, had established the missile and radar units of the ADF-VPAF. The structure of the VPAF was also changed, officially named the 371st "Thang Long" Air Division (Su Doan Khong Quan 371) with the 921st, 923rd Fighter Regiments and the 919th Air Transport Regiment subordinated to it, as well as the airfields at Gia Lam, Noi Bai, Kep, Hoa Lac, Kien An, Tho Xuan and Vinh. The new Chief Command was made up of Lt Col Nguyen Van Tien as commander, and Lt Col Hoang Ngoc Dieu and Lt Col Dao Dinh Luyen as vice commanders. Lt Col Tran Manh and Lt Col Nguyen Phuc Trach became second in command. The main aim of the VPAF was still to defend Hanoi and the dike system around the Red River. Primarily due to the few pilots available, the air force did not respond to all intrusions, and only when important targets were attacked. At this time the VPAF had 64 fighter pilots, 1,685 technicians and 1,024 ground controllers.

The new year started badly for the VPAF. On 2 January 1967, five MiG-21s were shot down over Noi Bai with each of the pilots ejecting successfully.

At noon of that day, the enemy activities increased in the Sam Neua area with several flights heading to Phu Tho. The MiGs at Noi Bai and Kep were placed on Class One Alert. In the area of the bases, the cloud density was 10/10, with a bottom at 1,500 meters and a top at 3,000 meters. The central command post forbade the launch of the MiGs until the incoming attacking formation was just 40 kilometers from Noi Bai, which by this time two flights of American fighters were holding above the clouds. At 13:56 hours, the first flight of Vu Ngoc Dinh, Nguyen Duc Thuan, Nguyen Dang Kinh and Bui Duc Nhu took off from Noi Bai. They encountered four F-4 Phantoms coming from Phu Tho at Phu Ninh.

Le Trong Huyen briefs for his comrades, Nguyen Ngoc Do, Bui Duc Nhu, Nguyen Duc Thuan and Nguyen Dang Kinh, who were shot down by USAF F-4s in the afternoon of 2 January 1967. All the MiG-pilots ejected and landed safely.
(István Toperczer Collection)

The MiG-21s chased their enemies to west of Noi Bai and encountered another four F-4 Phantoms. All Vietnamese MiGs were shot down and pilots ejected. The same fate was waiting for the leader of the second MiG-21 formation. The second flight of Nguyen Ngoc Do, Dang Ngoc Ngu, Dong Van De and Nguyen Van Coc took off also from Noi Bai at the same time. After breaking through the clouds, they were guided to intercept with an approach angle of 120 degrees. The flight leader detected F-4s and F-105s at a distance of 8 kilometers. During the fight, Nguyen Ngoc Do's MiG-21 was shot down and he ejected, while the other MiG-21s broke off and landed at Noi Bai.

This serious loss was due to the late take-off of the alert aircraft, indecisiveness in the central command post, and a faulty concept. The Fishbeds should have broken through the cloud layer only at a distance from the base and then would have had to attack the ambushing F-4s with a joint force.

Four days later, on 6 January, the VPAF lost two more MiG-21s. From the 921st Fighter Regiment, one MiG-21 flight took off from Noi Bai at 09:24 hours. Tran Hanh, Mai Van Cuong, Dong Van De and Nguyen Van Coc were led to the enemy with a 20 degree angle to the Viet Tri – Phu Tho area. Tran Hanh discovered two F-4 Phantoms, at a distance of 9 kilometers, but he was followed by several other enemies. Mai Van Cuong and Dong Van De were under fire by enemy AIM-7 Sparrow missiles, so Cuong ejected safely, but De did not eject and was killed.

According to the VPAF records on 2 January 1967, five MiG-21PFLs were shot down by USAF F-4C Phantoms. Vu Ngoc Dinh had to eject from his MiG-21PFL, although he landed safely.
(István Toperczer Collection)

Based on experiences of the 921st Fighter Regiment on 8 January, the High Command of the VPAF discussed the aerial combat between 2 and 6 January 1967. The new tactic was to attack partisan style, with quick attack and quick retreat, with small aircraft groups of 2 or 4 and

DATE OF BIRTH: 2 February 1941
ENLISTED: 28 March 1959
PILOT TRAINING:
1961 – 1964 (MiG-17 – Soviet Union)
1965 – 1966 (MiG-21 – Soviet Union)
WAR SERVICE AND UNIT:
1964 – 1965 (921st Fighter Regiment)
1966 – 1975 (921st Fighter Regiment)
AIRCRAFT: MiG-21
HERO OF THE VIETNAMESE PEOPLE'S ARMED FORCES: 22 December 1969
RANK: Major General

AIR VICTORIES: 8 kills
(2 F-4s, 3 F-105s, 3 Firebees – VPAF official credit)

DATE	AIRCRAFT	UNIT	KILL – US PILOT (VPAF – US DATABASES)
08 Oct 66	MiG-21	921.	F-105 – US not confirmed
28 Apr 67	MiG-21	921.	F-105D – Caras (KIA)
16 May 67	MiG-21	921.	Firebee
30 Sep 67	MiG-21	921.	F-105 – US not confirmed
07 Oct 67	MiG-21	921.	F-4 damaged
19 Jun 68	MiG-21	921.	Firebee
03 Sep 68	MiG-21	921.	Firebee
20 Sep 68	MiG-21	921.	Firebee
09 Feb 69	MiG-21	921.	Firebee
24 Jun 69	MiG-21	921.	Firebee

MiG-21PFL Fishbed D, No. 4023 of the 921st Fighter Regiment, 1967
Ace-pilot Mai Van Cuong's MiG-21PFL, No.4023 was under fire by Maj Hirsch's AIM-7 Sparrow missile from F-4C Phantom (64-0849), so Mai Van Cuong had to eject and landed safely, on 6 January 1967. (ARTWORK: BALÁZS KAKUK)

Nguyen Phi Hung and Phan Van Tuc are waiting for the next sortie in front of their MiG-17Fs, in February of 1967. The identification patch on pilots' leather helmet was standard in the VPAF during the war. (István Toperczer Collection)

using the maximum of 8-10 aircraft in each combat. The altitude and the speed of the attacking group should be constantly changed. After studying the American tactics, it was decided to attack with MiG-21s by diving onto the enemy from overhead, while with the MiG-17s from the sides, forcing the intruders into a dogfight, but the MiG-21s were withdrawn from combat for a time.

The MiG-17s proved to be successful once again on 21 January 1967. On this day the radars detected intruders, which arrived from Thailand and Da Nang to attack Thai Nguyen and Kep airbase. At 14:45 hours, a MiG-17flight of the 923rd Fighter Regiment, Ho Van Quy, Phan Thanh Tai, Nguyen Van Bay and Vo Van Man, took off with a 220 degree angle. After three and half minutes, the MiGs turned left, when the leader and Nguyen Van Bay detected 20 F-105s and 4 F-4 Phantoms at a distance of 10 kilometers, over Dinh Lap. The enemy also detected the North Vietnamese MiG-17s, so the F-105 Thunderchiefs dropped their bombs and the F-4 Phantoms attacked the MiGs without success. Ho Van Quy was ordered to fly low level towards Chu, for his flight. When Quy was at a distance of 500-600 meters from F-105, he shot, but did not get a hit. Nguyen Van Bay also fired 5-6 bursts from his cannon and shot down Capt Wyatt's F-105D in the area of Kep. This Thunderchief officially listed as missing was credited to AAA by the US sources.

The next month, on 5 February 1967, four enemy groups arrived from the direction of Laos over Luong Son – Hoa Binh area. At 14:12 hours the flight of MiG-17s, Le Quang Trung, Hoang Van Ky, Ngo Duc Mai and Truong Van Cung, were scrambled at Kep airbase. They took off with a 220 degree angle and after twelve minutes the flight leader detected F-4 Phantoms on their right side at a distance 3 kilometers. After the flight made a hard right turn, Le Quang Trung fired three bursts and he observed no hits. Hoang Van Ky also attacked them and he shoot down an F-4 Phantom, over Luong Son in Hoa Binh Province, although US sources did not confirm this loss.

The MiG-17s of the 923rd Fighter Regiment took part in the air battles on 19 April 1967, over Suoi Rut in Hoa Binh Province. The F-105 flight supported a raid on army barracks at Xuan Mai, 60 kilometers southwest of Hanoi. At 15:52 hours, Vo Van Man, Ha Dinh Bon, Phan Van Tuc and Nguyen Ba Dich took off from Gia Lam airfield and Dich shot down Maj Madison's F-105 in the Hoa Binh airspace and landed safely at Gia Lam. At 17:01 hours Luu Huy Chao, Le Hai, Nguyen Van Bay and Hoang Van Ky took off from Gia Lam airfield. After two minutes the radar stations discovered the enemy at 40 kilometers west-northwest of Quan Hoa at 3,500 meters. The US rescue forces moved into high gear as soon as the F-105F crew went down. Within less than an hour a pair of A-1E Skyraiders was approaching the location of the downed crew. The MiG-17s flew in an east – southeast direction, and descended to 2,500 meters. At 17:10 hours, radar stations suddenly found the enemy at 20 kilometers southeast of Hoa Binh, as they flew to the west of Vu Ban. At 17:11 hours, Le Quang Trung, Nguyen Van Tho, Nguyen Xuan Dung and Duong Trung Tan were on duty at the airfield of Hoa Lac, and they were ordered to take off. At 17:18 hours, the flight of Chao – Hai – Bay – Ky went a heading of 250 degrees to Hoa Binh, while the other flight of Trung – Tho – Dung – Tan went a heading of 210 degrees. The F-105s were east of the Cam Thuy flying to Road No. 12., so the flight of Chao – Hai – Bay – Ky were forced to escape to Gia Lam. At 17:24 hours, the flight of Trung – Tho – Dung – Tan was flying towards 140 degrees, west of Vu Ban, but found no enemy. The command discovered that the enemy flew west to 5 kilometers north of Vu Ban. The MiG-17s changed their direction to 250 degrees and Le Quang Trung discovered F-105s and A-1s at a distance of 7 kilometers. He immediately ordered the close

In March of 1967, Nguyen Phi Hung, Ho Van Quy, Luu Huy Chao and Hoang Van Ky walk to their fighters at Kep airbase. The black SRD-1M radar range finder antenna is seen on the nose panel of the Red 2431 MiG-17 Fresco.
(István Toperczer Collection)

The MiG-17 pilots from the 923rd Fighter Regiment, Luu Huy Chao, Le Hai, Mai Duc Toai and Hoang Van Ky downed three F-105 Thunderchiefs on 24, 25 and 28 April 1967, by VPAF records.
(István Toperczer Collection)

support to the second pair of MiG-17s, and Nguyen Van Tho shot down Maj Hamilton's Skyraider. Duong Trung Tan claimed one F-105 and one A-1 loss, although USAF sources did not confirm his victories.

The North Vietnamese pilots, at about this time, started to use the "ambush on ground" method with the help of ambush airfields. Early in the morning, using all camouflage methods, the MiG-17 flight transferred from the home-base to the ambush airfield. The news of the approaching American aircraft was relayed by radio or telephone from the visual observation post. The MiGs were soon in the air and took up position in a predetermined location at low altitude to remain hidden from US airborne command posts. The approach and attack was made on the same heading by increasing their speed. The attack was carried out from above and from behind to be followed by a quick escape back to the home-base at low altitude, using the masking of the surrounding countryside.

On 23 April, Kien An airfield, near Hai Phong, was struck from the air. The raid inflicted heavy damage both to the runway and buildings. On the 23 and 24 April, it was repaired by civilians and the military from Truong Son and Thai Son. Hanoi, Kep airbase and Hoa Lac airfield were attacked by 24 F-105s and 6 F-4s enemy aircraft on the 24 April 1967, to which two MiG-17 flights of the 923rd Fighter Regiment responded.

At 09:15 hours, Mai Duc Toai, Le Hai, Luu Huy Chao and Hoang Van Ky took off from Gia Lam airfield. The flight of MiG-17s was divided into two pairs at a distance of 1,500 meters from each other and they flew towards Xuan Mai – Hoa Binh. There were heavy clouds up to the altitude of 2,000 meters, so MiG-17s flew at a speed of 700 km/h over the clouds. Hoang Van Ky discovered enemies on their left side at a distance of 6 kilometers over the Dang River. Mai Duc Toai ordered to drop auxiliary fuel tanks and he attacked a group of F-105s with his wingman, Le Hai. Mai Duc Toai destroyed an F-105, but the US did not confirm it. It was

DATE OF BIRTH: 2 February 1936
ENLISTED: 3 April 1954
PILOT TRAINING:
1959 (910th Air Training Regiment – Vietnam)
1960 – 1964 (MiG-17 – China)
WAR SERVICE AND UNIT:
1964 – 1965 (921st Fighter Regiment)
1965 – 1973 (923rd Fighter Regiment)
AIRCRAFT: MiG-17
HERO OF THE VIETNAMESE PEOPLE'S ARMED FORCES: 1 January 1967
RANK: Senior Colonel

AIR VICTORIES: 7 kills
(4 F-4s, 2 F-105s, 1 F-8 – VPAF official credit)

DATE	AIRCRAFT	UNIT	KILL – US PILOT (VPAF – US DATABASES)
26 Apr 66	MiG-17	923.	F-4C damaged – US not confirmed
29 Apr 66	MiG-17	923.	F-105D – Bruch (KIA) (AAA)
29 Jun 66	MiG-17	923.	F-105D damaged – Jones (POW) (AAA)
05 Sep 66	MiG-17	923.	F-8E – Abbott (POW)
16 Sep 66	MiG-17	923.	F-4C – Robertson (KIA) Buchanan (POW)
21 Jan 67	MiG-17	923.	F-105D – Wyatt (AAA)
24 Apr 67	MiG-17	923.	F-4B – Southwick, Laing (AAA)
29 Apr 67	MiG-17	923.	F-4C – Torkleson (POW) Pollin (KIA) (AAA)

MiG-17F Fresco C, No. 2537 of the 923rd Fighter Regiment, 1967
On 24 April 1967, the most successful MiG-17 pilot, Nguyen Van Bay used this MiG-17 to shoot down an F-4B Phantom (153000) of VF-114, from USS Kitty Hawk. (ARTWORK: BALÁZS KAKUK)

The flight line at the 923rd Fighter Regiment, at Kep airbase. Some grey and green colored MiG-17Fs are ready to take-off in front of the earth revetments, in April 1967.
(István Toperczer Collection)

Le Hai's first air combat, so he was very excited and pushed the trigger about five seconds to run out of ammunition. Meanwhile, the other pair of MiG-17s attacked the F-4 Phantoms, but without any hits.

One day earlier, on 23 April, Vo Van Man, Nguyen Ba Dich, Nguyen Van Bay and Nguyen The Hon were transferred from Gia Lam to Kien An. On 24 April, at 16:30 hours, F-4 Phantoms arrived from the Gulf of Tonkin, and they flew from Quang Yen – Dong Trieu towards Kep and Hoa Lac airfields. Vo Van Man's flight took off from Kien An, and Nguyen Ba Dich discovered the enemy at a distance of 10 kilometers. Vo Van Man ordered two pair of MiG-17s to divide and he shot down a F-4 Phantom over Pha Lai (Hai Hung Province). Vo Van Man and Nguyen Ba Dich turned back and they saw that Nguyen Van Bay and Nguyen The Hon were in a dogfight with other Phantoms. Nguyen Van Bay managed to shoot down another F-4 Phantom over Son Dong (Ha Bac Province). The MiG-17s landed safely at Gia Lam. Nevertheless, US records state that they fell to AAA. Later the same day, based on an order from the Chief Command, four MiG-17s from the 923rd Fighter Regiment, with Nguyen Van Bay, Nguyen The Hon, Ha Dinh Bon and Nguyen Ba Dich, took off from Gia Lam and, to avoid detection flew low with no ground control to Kien An.

Hanoi came under attack again on 25 April 1967. The MiG-17 flight of Mai Duc Toai, Le Hai, Luu Huy Chao and Hoang Van Ky shot down 1Lt Weskamp's F-105D over Gia Lam. On the same morning, another raid struck the port of Hai Phong. While MiG-17s deployed to Kien An on the previous day stayed away, AAA fire brought down 10 American aircraft. At 10:04 hours, the four MiG-17s (Bay – Bon – Hon – Dich) at Kien An were ordered up. On their way to the rendezvous they flew over Voi Mountain, and climbed to 1,500 meters, heading for the Van Uc River. The enemy was completely unaware of the MiG-17s because Kien An was thought to be incapacitated. The four MiG-17s shot down three navy aircraft. The MiGs returned to Gia Lam undamaged. Ha Dinh Bon claimed an A-4C, Nguyen The Hon killed an F-8 Crusader, and Nguyen Ba Dich shot down another A-4E. By the US Navy sources, Lt Stackhouse's A-4C Skyhawk was hit in the engine by 37mm cannon shells, Lt Cdr Almberg's Skyhawk was damaged by an SA-2 missile and the F-8 was not a loss.

At 11:00 hours, the Americans were coming from southwest of Suoi Rut, towards Hoa Binh. At 11:25 hours, Le Quang Trung, Nguyen Huu Diet, Phan Thanh Tai and Nguyen Van Tho took off from the Hoa Lac airfield. They flew at a heading of 120 degrees to Hoa Binh, when Le Quang Trung detected F-105s at a distance of 7 kilometers over Hoa Binh. He flew closer and immediately shot down one F-105, and the flight returned to Hoa Lac airfield. The USAF sources only mentioned Weskamp's Thunderchief as a loss on that day.

On 28 April, the enemy attacked the area to the west and south of Hanoi. At 14:25 hours, four MiG-17s took off from Gia Lam airfield and headed to Chuong My. At the same time, another flight of MiG-17s took off from Hoa Lac airfield and they flew to the western region of Ba Vi. The enemy F-105s arrived from a heading of 120 degrees, at a distance of 8 kilometers, when the MiG-17s detected them. Le Hai and Phan Thanh Tai both claimed F-105 losses, although USAF records did not confirm them. The enemy continued the attacks for one hour and the MiG-17 pair, Ho Van Quy and Phan Trong Van, with a simultaneous flight of MiG-17s, Nguyen Van Bay, Nguyen Hong Diep, Vo Van Man and Nguyen Ba Dich, were scrambled from Gia Lam. The MiG-17 pair flew to over Hoa Binh, while the flight headed to Xuan Mai. The pair detected enemy aircraft, they shot no results and all MiG-17s returned to their airfields.

In the last two days of April 1967, MiG-17s took off every day, but they claimed only one kill. In the afternoon of April 29, a flight of MiG-17 took off from Hoa Lac and flew a heading of 120 degrees, over to Hoa Binh. Nguyen Van Bay detected F-4 Phantoms, at a distance of 8 kilometers. After 3 minutes he shot down one USAF F-4C Phantom, and the flights returned safely to Hoa Lac airfield. The flight of four Phantoms from Da Nang was tasked to fly CAPs around Hanoi as F-105 strike force went in. By the US records, 1Lt Torkleson's Phantom was about 25 kilometers west of the capital, and flying at 1,400 meters, when the aircraft was hit by AAA. The following day, Ho Van Quy, Nguyen Van Phi, Nguyen Xuan Dung and Nguyen Van Tho from Hoa Lac flew over an area of 15 kilometers southwest of Hoa Binh. Because the radar station had technical problems, the flight of MiG-17s circled and all efforts of the crew were not successful to navigate.

During 12 days of April 1967, the GCIs of the ADF – VPAF HQ and the 923rd Fighter Regiment organized 18 battles, and in 9 battles they approached at an angle from 80 to 140 degrees, and detected targets at a distance from 3-10 kilometers. In four battles they used a lower speed than the enemy (-50 km/h) and in two with the same speed. The pilots maneuvered so well, all of them shot down a target. Two battles also used lower speeds (-50 km/h and -100 km/h), where pilots followed the targets, but with no success.

After a long pause, the first pair of MiG-21s appeared over North Vietnam, in April 1967.

On 23 April, two MiG-21 pairs were scrambled and they attacked an F-105 strike package at Thai Nguyen. Nguyen Dang Kinh and Tran Thien Luong turned into the "Thuds" when Maj Anderson's F-4C Phantom attacked the MiG-21 and crew, shot Nguyen Dang Kinh's Fishbed, ejected safely.

On 28 April 1967, the Americans attacked Hanoi. Commander Phung The Tai decided to use MiG-21s to intercept enemy flights that came from Tuyen Quang along the Tam Dao ridge to Hanoi. At 15:17 hours, the MiG-21 flight of Le Trong Huyen and Dong Van Song took off from Noi Bai towards Tuyen Quang. The MiG-21s were guided along east side of the Tam Dao ridge to Ham Yen, Doan Hung then Tuyen Quang – Chiem Hoa, but did not meet an enemy. At 15:41 hours, an enemy flight appeared at 10 kilometers south of Son Duong, flew to Tuyen Quang and then made a left turn. Ground control guided the MiGs to turn back, since pilots detected enemies but were unable to attack. Command ordered them to come back home.

Meanwhile, at 15:34 hours, Dang Ngoc Ngu and Mai Van Cuong were ordered to take off and flew along the west side of the Tam Dao ridge to 15 kilometers north of Son Duong, where they turned left to Van Yen and then to the north of Nghia Lo to intercept the enemy in their return. The enemy was surprised when the MiG-21s intercepted them at 30 kilometers northeast of Bac Yen. Approaching at a 30 degree heading, Dang Ngoc Ngu detected targets to the left 4 kilometers, closed in and fired a missile but missed. Mai Van Cuong launched an R-3S missile from 1,500-2,000 meters away, at an altitude of 2,500 meters, and Capt Caras's aircraft crashed 50 kilometers east of Na San and he died in the crash.

On the last day of April 1967, the radar units were alerted to incoming American aircraft from Lao airspace towards Vinh Phu. The 921st Fighter Regiment received an order to send two flights with a pair of MiGs in each. The MiG-21 flight of Nguyen Ngoc Do and Nguyen Van Coc took off to Moc Chau and they flew about 40 kilometers west of Son Tay, where they turned left to west Suoi Rut and Mai Chau. A few minutes later, the GCI followed an enemy flight, which went through Co Noi – Ta Khoa. The MiG-21s turned right to Yen Chau to intercept in the Bac Yen – Phu Yen – Yen Lap area.

On 30 April 1967, Nguyen Ngoc Do shot down Maj Thorsness' F-105F Thunderchief. It was Do's first air victory during the war. (István Toperczer Collection)

As the wingman of Nguyen Ngoc Do, I took off for the mission – tells Nguyen Van Coc. At an altitude of 2,500 meters I noticed F-105s flying under us at 30 degrees to our course. My leader also saw the Thunderchiefs. We both increased our speed and made a dive towards

Hoang Van Ky

Date of Birth: 1939
Enlisted: March 1959
Pilot training:
1962 – 1965 (MiG-17 – Soviet Union)
War Service and Unit:
1965 – 1966 (921st Fighter Regiment)
1967 (923rd Fighter Regiment)
Aircraft: MiG-17
Died: 5 June 1967 – shot down by USAF F-4C Phantom
(64-0660 / Priester – Pankhurst)
Hero of the Vietnamese People's Armed Forces: 28 April 2000
Rank: First Lieutenant

Air Victories: 4 kills
(2 F-4s, 2 F-105s – VPAF official credit)

Date	Aircraft	Unit	Kill – US Pilot (VPAF – US databases)
20 Sep 66	MiG-17	923.	F-105 – US not confirmed
05 Feb 67	MiG-17	923.	F-4 – US not confirmed
25 Apr 67	MiG-17	923.	F-105D – Weskamp (KIA) (AAA) (Shared)
04 May 67	MiG-17	923.	F-4C – US not confirmed
12 May 67	MiG-17	923.	F-4C – US not confirmed

MiG-17F Fresco C, No. 2076 (3 kills) of the 923rd Fighter Regiment, 1967
The Kep-based MiG-17 pilots claimed three air victories with this MiG-17 from 1966 to the end of March 1967. Hoang Van Ky also used No. 2076 during air battles of 1967. (Artwork: Balázs Kakuk)

the American fighter bombers unaware of our presence. The leader shot down the second aircraft in a group of four F-105s. Until now I was protecting my leader, but when in position I also opened fire downing another Thunderchief. We received an order to return to base and made a successful landing, while the eight F-105s dropped their bombs and started a search for the ejected pilots.

A few minutes later, Le Trong Huyen and Vu Ngoc Dinh, in MiG-21s of the same regiment, added two more F-105s to the tally of the day over Thanh Son. The USAF recorded the loss of two F-105Ds, and a single F-105F, all four Americans became POWs. Maj Lenski's "Thud" was badly damaged, but he landed safely at Udorn RTAFB.

In the spring of 1967, seven pilots, including four flying MiG-17s (Nguyen Van Bay, Luu Huy Chao, Le Hai and Nguyen Dinh Phuc), were awarded by Ho Chi Minh for their distinguished service since the outbreak of the air war.

In May 1967, the battles over Hanoi continued with the same intensity. VPAF aircraft flew 30-40 or even 78 sorties daily, with increasing effectiveness.

At the beginning of the month, the VPAF lost one MiG-21 on 4 May, when Nguyen Van Coc ejected safely from his MiG-21PFL Fishbed D.

On 4 May 1967, I took off with my leader, Pham Thanh Ngan, from Noi Bai – remembers Nguyen Van Coc. The enemy strike package arrived from Nghia Lo towards Tam Dao ridge, when we flew at 350 degrees and at an altitude of 2.000 meters. We discovered 12 F-105s and 8 F-4s

Nguyen Ngoc Do just returned from an air battle on 5 May 1967, where he shot down an F-105D Thunderchief, by VPAF records. (István Toperczer Collection)

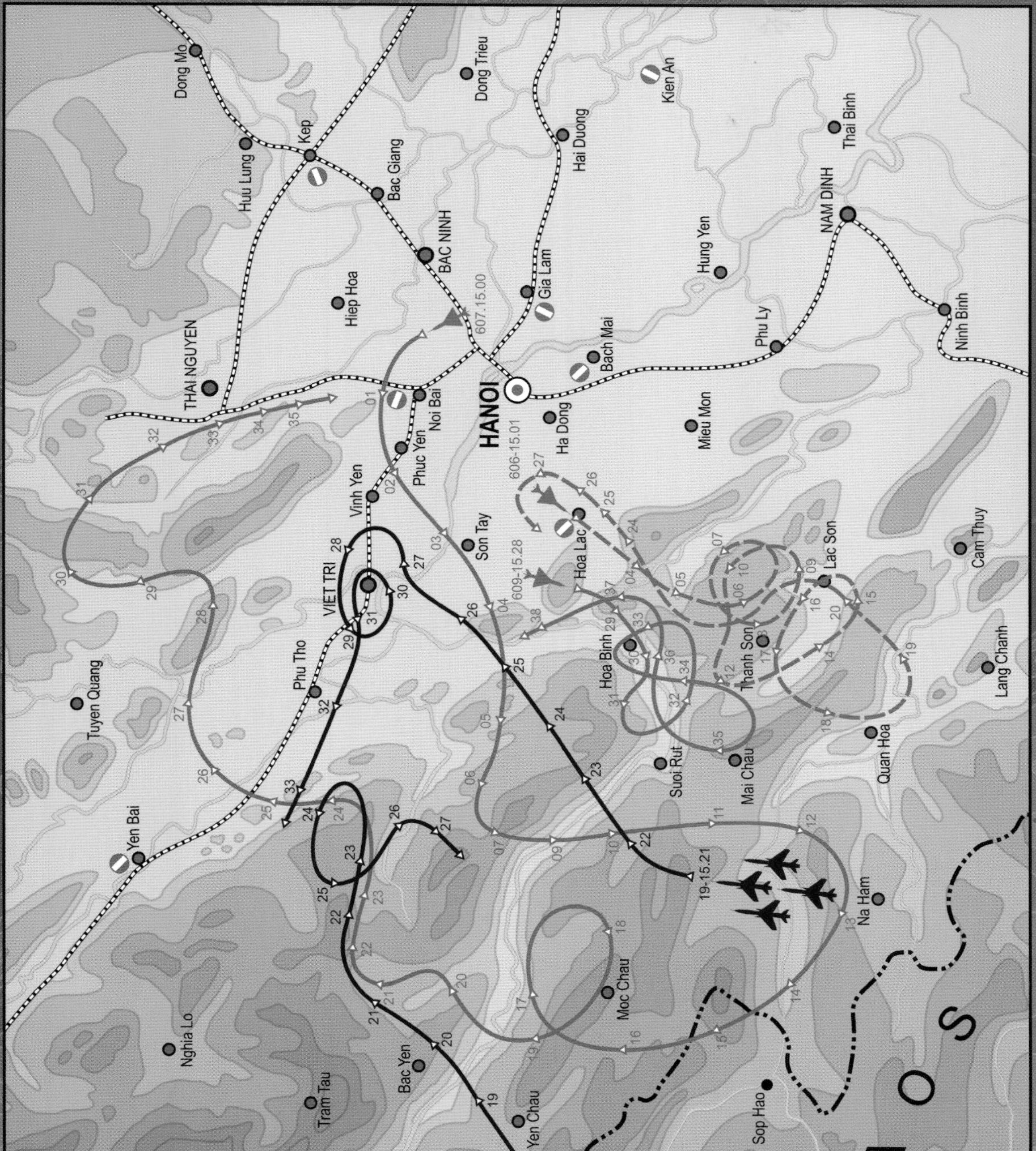

On 30 April 1967, two MiG-21 pairs, Le Trong Huyen – Vu Ngoc Dinh and Nguyen Ngoc Do – Nguyen Van Coc from 921st Fighter Regiment shot down four F-105 Thunderchiefs over Vinh Phu Province. (CARTOGRAPH: PETER BARNA)

On 5 May 1967, Nguyen Nhat Chieu intercepted and shot down Maj Van Loan's F-4C Phantom. This was Nguyen Nhat Chieu's first air victory flying with a MiG-21 Fishbed.
(István Toperczer Collection)

at a distance of 7 kilometers, where the F-105s flew in three flights over Tam Dao. My leader, Ngan, increased his speed and attacked with his R-3S missile an F-105 left side. He discovered three other Thunderchiefs and fired another missile at a distance of 1,200-1,500 meters. I did not see any hits, while Pham Thanh Ngan broke off to land. I discovered four F-4 Phantoms on my left side and attacked them, but I heard a big detonation behind my MiG's tailpipe... I got hit from an American F-4 Phantom and I had to decide to land at Noi Bai. When my speed was 360 km/h, I turned the gear control lever into "out" position. At an altitude of 100 meters I only flew with speed of 260 km/h, so I ejected safely from my MiG and that crashed at a distance of 500 meters from the runway of Noi Bai.

On this day, another strike formation, 16 F-105s and 8 F-4s, attacked Hoa Lac airfield. From the 923rd Fighter Regiment, a pair of MiG-17s, Cao Thanh Tinh and Hoang Van Ky, were scrambled and the wingman, Ky, claimed a F-4 Phantom kill over Hoa Lac. The USAF records did not confirm his kill.

The next day, on 5 May, Nguyen Ngoc Do claimed an F-105D kill, although the USAF listed Shively's F-105 as having been downed by an AAA unit. After one week, on 12 May, a pair of MiG-21s, Le Trong Huyen and Dong Van Song, from the 921st Fighter Regiment were also successful in shooting down an F-105 over Van Yen, at 16:45 hours. The USAF again listed this aircraft as having been downed by ground fire.

The MiG-17s from the 923rd Fighter Regiment were successful also in May. On 12 May, three MiG-17 flights of the 923rd Fighter Regiment scored 5 kills in all. The flight of Cao Thanh Tinh, Le Hai, Ngo Duc Mai and Hoang Van Ky took credit together with Air Defense Forces for

The pilots of a MiG-17 flight, Cao Thanh Tinh, Le Hai, Ngo Duc Mai, Hoang Van Ky and their unknown comrades, are seen after the air battle on 12 May 1967. In this battle, Ngo Duc Mai shot down Col Norman C. Gaddis' F-4C Phantom.
(István Toperczer Collection)

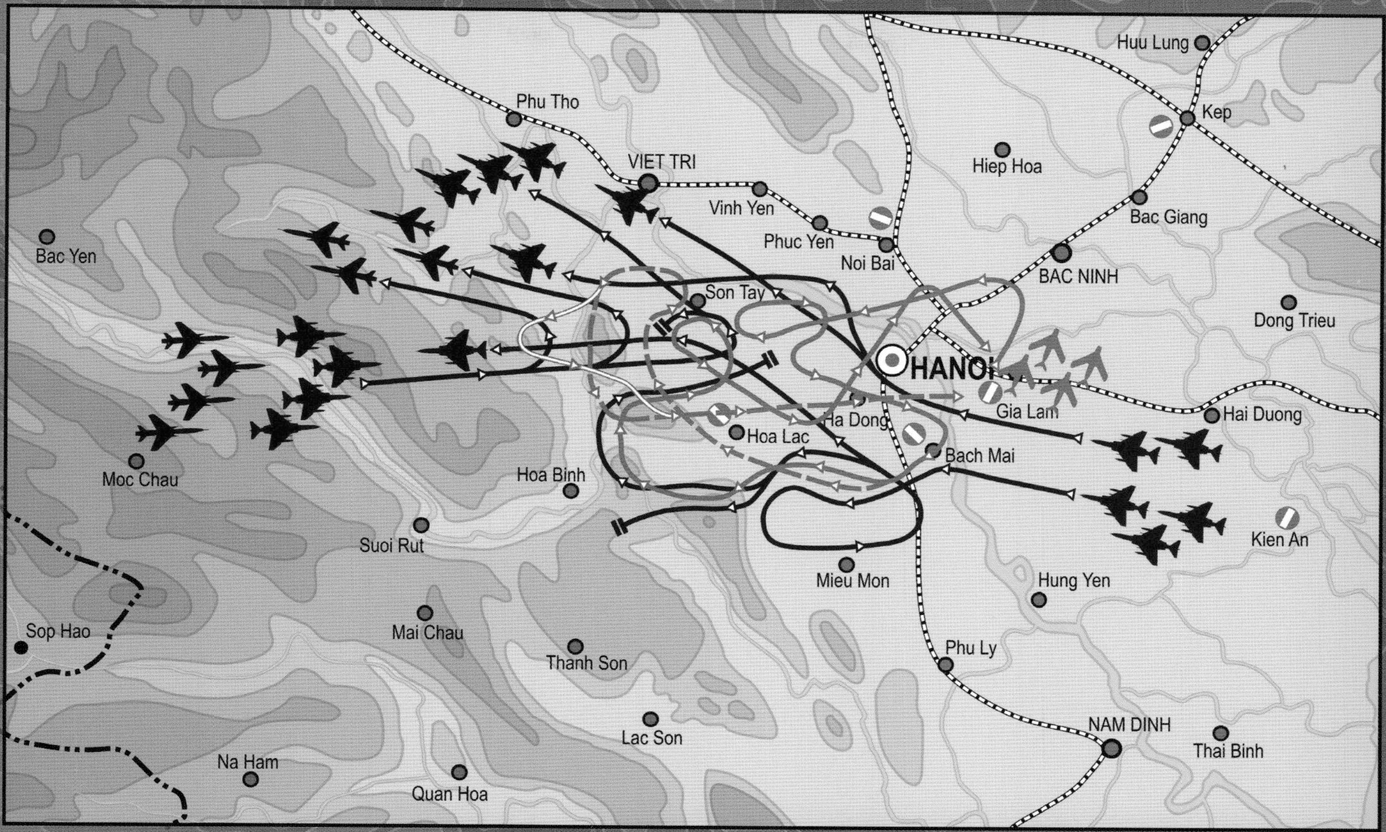

On 12 May 1967, the MiG-17 flight of Cao Thanh Tinh, Le Hai, Ngo Duc Mai and Hoang Van Ky shot down three F-4C Phantoms over Hoa Lac in Ha Tay Province. In this battle, Ngo Duc Mai shot down Col Norman C. Gaddis, who arrived from the US-based Fighter Weapons School to the Vietnam Air War. (CARTOGRAPH: PÉTER BARNA)

three F-4Cs over Hoa Lac, in Ha Tay Province. The low flying enemies came from the southwest, most of their forces attacked Hanoi while the rest turned to Son Duong alongside Tam Dao ridge. At 15:31 hours, a MiG-17 flight took off from Gia Lam and they were guided over Hoa Lac. The enemy F-4 flights arrived in a heading of 120 degrees to the battle zone. Cao Thanh Tinh detected F-4s and F-105s at a distance of 6 kilometers and attacked them, shooting down the first Phantom. Ngo Duc Mai, and Hoang Van Ky each shot down an F-4C Phantom. In this battle, Ngo Duc Mai shot down Col Norman C. Gaddis, who arrived from the Fighter Weapons School, Nellis AFB, to find a way of defeating North Vietnamese MiGs. At 15:50 hours, the MiG–17 pair of Phan Thanh Tai and Nguyen Huu Diet also took off from Gia Lam airfield and flew south of Hanoi towards Son Tay – Hoa Lac to cover Tinh – Hai – Mai – Ky. One more flight of MiG-17s took off from Noi Bai airbase and headed to the west side of Tam Dao Hill over Phuc Yen – Vinh Yen. Duong Trung Tan and Nguyen Van Tho each shot down an F-105 over Vinh Yen, but Phan Trong Van's MiG-17 was hit by cannon shells of Capt Suzanne's F-105D. He ejected and landed safely.

Two days later, on 14 May, the 923rd Fighter Regiment lost his two well-experienced pilots, Vo Van Man (4 air victories) and Nguyen The Hon (3 air victories) in a battle with 24 F-4s and F-105s over Hoa Binh. Two F-4C Phantoms from the 480th TFS/366th TFW, Da Nang AB, claimed MiG kills.

Lt Ngo Duc Mai's unusually camouflaged Shenyang J-5 (MiG-17F Fresco C), No. 2011, is on display at the VPAF Museum in Hanoi. (István Toperczer)

On Uncle Ho's 77th Birthday, 19 May, Phan Thanh Tai and Nguyen Huu Diet destroyed two F-4 over Xuan Mai (Hoa Binh Province). With these kills the scoreboard of the 923rd Fighter Regiment totaled 62 enemy aircraft. The fighter unit received a challenge pennant from that day on. Unfortunately, three MiG-17 pilots (Tran Minh Phuong, Nguyen Van Phi and Phan Thanh Tai) of the 923rd Fighter Regiment lost their lives in the battles of 19 May over Ha Tay province, and Nguyen Huu Diet had to eject from his MiG-17 Fresco.

On 20 May 1967, USAF F-4C Phantoms from the 433rd TFS, 8th TFW, Ubon AFB, Thailand, were flying MiG Combat Air Patrol (MiGCAP) mission for an F-105 strike force from Takhli AFB. The Thuds were heading for the Bac Le railroad yard. During the mission, the MiGCAP flights engaged between 12-14 MiG-17s, downing four of them. The MiG-17 flights came from "Doan Z," Kep airbase. While 22 F-4s and F-105s were flying to their target, two pairs of the MiG-21 attempted to attack the strike force. At 15:16 hours, Nguyen Nhat Chieu and Pham Thanh Ngan, and four minutes later, Vu Ngoc Dinh and Nghiem Dinh Hieu from the 921st Fighter Regiment, took off and bearing 320 degrees, flew over Tam Dao. They discovered enemies at a heading of 45 degrees on their left, at a distance of 18 kilometers. Nguyen Nhat Chieu increased his speed and fired an R-3S missile at a distance of 2,000 meters without a hit. Pham Thanh Ngan warned him that enemies came behind them. Chieu made some maneuvers, turned right and left, descended, and then discovered four Phantoms above his MiG-21. He ascended to 3,500 meters, then fired another R-3S missile and shot down an F-4C Phantom from the 433rd TFS / 8th TFW Ubon RTAFB. At the same time, another pair of MiG-21s, Vu Ngoc Dinh and Nghiem Dinh Hieu, flew behind the

Date of Birth: 12 February 1941
Enlisted: 28 March 1959
Pilot training:
1962 – 1964 (MiG-17 – Soviet Union)
1965 – 1966 (MiG-21 – Soviet Union)
War Service and Unit:
1964 – 1965 (921st Fighter Regiment)
1966 – 1970 (921st Fighter Regiment)
Aircraft: MiG-21
Hero of the Vietnamese People's Armed Forces: 25 August 1970
Rank: Senior Colonel

Air Victories: 6 kills
(5 F-105s, 1 HH-53 – VPAF official credit)

Date	Aircraft	Unit	Kill – US Pilot (VPAF – US databases)
11 Jul 66	MiG-21	921.	F-105D – McClelland (Run out fuel)
05 Dec 66	MiG-21	921.	F-105 – US not confirmed
19 Dec 66	MiG-21	921.	F-105 – US not confirmed
30 Apr 67	MiG-21	921.	F-105 – Lenski (Badly damaged)
17 Dec 67	MiG-21	921.	F-105D – Ellis (POW)
28 Jan 70	MiG-21	921.	HH-53B – Bell + 5 crews (KIAs)

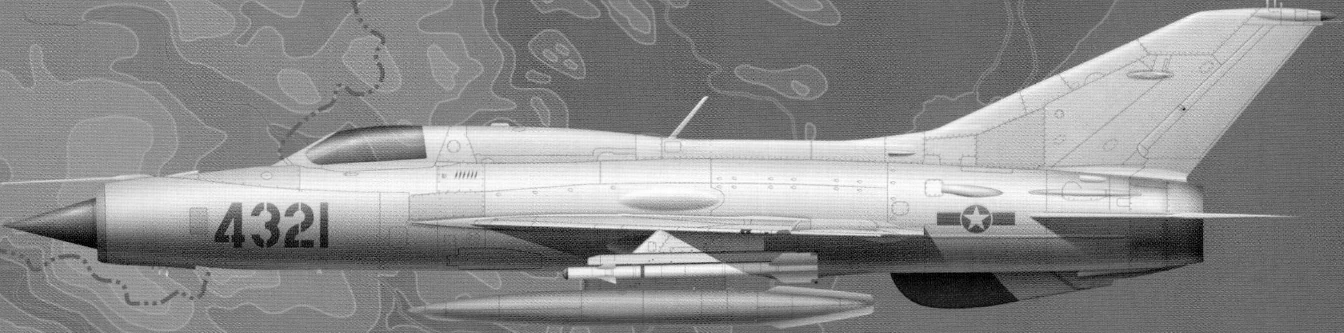

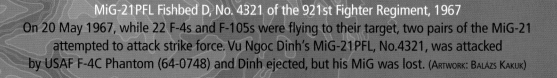

MiG-21PFL Fishbed D, No. 4321 of the 921st Fighter Regiment, 1967
On 20 May 1967, while 22 F-4s and F-105s were flying to their target, two pairs of the MiG-21 attempted to attack strike force. Vu Ngoc Dinh's MiG-21PFL, No.4321, was attacked by USAF F-4C Phantom (64-0748) and Dinh ejected, but his MiG was lost. (Artwork: Balázs Kakuk)

This North Vietnamese ground crew refuels and performs routine maintenance on an overall dark green painted MiG-17F before the next take-off.
(István Toperczer Collection)

first MiG-21 pair, at a distance of 15–20 kilometers over Tam Dao. Dinh asked the order to attack the four F-4s, but it was rejected because of the Air Defense Forces fire. Dinh discovered four other F-4 Phantoms at a distance of 4 kilometers behind their MiGs, and he made a hard left turn, but two Sidewinder missiles exploded on their right side. The hydraulic system was seriously damaged, so Dinh ejected but his MiG began diving in a flat spiral until impacting the ground at Thanh Van (Bac Thai Province). Unfortunately, Dinh's wingman Nghiem Dinh Hieu also was shot down by Sparrow missiles from Lt Col Titus's Phantom; he ejected and died on the way to the hospital.

After two days, on 22 May, four MiG-21s of the 921st Fighter Regiment were scrambled against enemies over Tuyen Quang – Phu Tho. At 14:52 hours, Tran Ngoc Siu and Dang Ngoc Ngu took off and flew over Ba Vi, and four minutes later Vu Ngoc Dinh and Nguyen Dang Kinh were ordered over Tam Dao. Vu Ngoc Dinh was on duty two days after his incident, although he was unconscious after ejecting. Over Hoa Binh, the Siu – Ngu pair discovered four F-105s on their left side at a distance of 8-10 kilometers, so they dropped auxiliary fuel tanks and attacked the Thunderchiefs. They fired R-3S missiles, but did not claim any kills. Siu – Ngu further pursued F-105s on their left side at a distance of 4 kilometers, when Siu discovered four F-4 Phantoms behind their MiGs at a distance of 6 kilometers. He knew that was an unfavorable situation, so broke off to the left and returned to Noi Bai. Meanwhile, Dang Ngoc Ngu detected four F-105s and ascended to 7,000 meters. During this maneuver his MiG-21 ran into 12 F-4 Phantoms, which covered the Thunderchiefs, but the enemies did not discover him. He fired an R-3S missile at a distance of 1,000-1,500 meters and shot down an F-4 Phantom over Hanoi, although US records list the hit as an AAA shoot-down.

Nghiem Dinh Hieu (LEFT) discusses the details of the next sortie with Vu Ngoc Dinh (RIGHT), on 20 May 1967. Both pilots were shot down by USAF F-4C Phantoms on that day. After ejecting the injured Hieu died on the way to the hospital, while Vu Ngoc Dinh landed safely.
(ISTVÁN TOPERCZER COLLECTION)

In May 1967 the United States had lost 85 aircraft from which 34 were claimed by SAMs, 32 by AAA and 19 by the VPAF. In the month from 24 April to 25 May, VPAF aircraft had 469 sorties, took part in 34 dogfights and prevented 222 American attacks.

In the first air battles of June, the 923rd F.R was unsuccessful. On 3 June, Ngo Duc Mai, Phan Tan Duan and North Korean pilot, Kim The Dun, were sacrificed, over Bac Giang. After two days, on 5 June, Hoang Van Ky an experienced (4 air victories) MiG pilot was killed in a dogfight over Vinh Phuc, and his two comrades, Tran Huyen and Truong Van Cung, became victims of USAF F-4C Phantoms.

The Ace-pilot Dang Ngoc Ngu claimed Capt Perrine's F-4C Phantom kill on 22 May 1967. It was his third air victory during the war.
(ISTVÁN TOPERCZER COLLECTION)

The pilots of this flight run to the overall dark green MiG-17s at Kep airbase, in June 1967. The pilots nicknamed these Frescos "Snake" because of their green colors.
(István Toperczer Collection)

Owing to these achievements, some pilots became conceited, scornful and careless – for which they paid a heavy price. At the end of May and at the beginning of June, ten MiG-17 pilots perished in seven air battles. The loss of experienced airmen in rapid succession was detrimental to the morale of the novices.

By the summer of 1967, the number of pilots in the two fighter regiments did not reach the required size for one single regiment. When the airbase at Kep came under attack on 19 May, the ground crew did not have time to withdraw the aircraft from the vicinity of the runway and many MiG-17s were damaged. The six airfields that were suitable for operating fighter aircraft – Noi Bai, Gia Lam, Kep, Hoa Lac, Kien An and Tho Xuan – were repeatedly attacked, and except for Noi Bai and Gia Lam, were not always quickly repaired. General Van Tien Dung, Commander in Chief and Chief of Staff, ordered the VPAF to conserve its resources in order to be able to provide defense in the long run. For a time the aircraft did not participate in action; only in a few cases and even then only against EB-66 electronic warfare (EW) aircraft.

In July, August and September of 1967, the American reconnaissance aircraft using repeatedly the same routes were very active over the North Vietnamese air bases. It was no surprise that the Vietnamese managed to bring down several reconnaissance aircraft.

According to North Vietnamese records, USAF RF-4 Phantom became the victim of two MiG-21PFL Fishbed-Ds, with Nguyen Ngoc Do and Pham Thanh Ngan at the controls, over Nho Quan in Ninh Binh Province, on 20 July 1967. In the afternoon of this day, radar detected groups of F-105s and F-4s over Nho Quan – Ninh Binh. At 15:28 hours, a MiG-21 pair of the

921st Fighter Regiment took off from Noi Bai, and bearing 200 degrees ascended to altitude of 2,000 meters. The GCI reported enemies at a distance of 12-15 kilometers on right side of MiG-21s. Nguyen Ngoc Do reported that he had a visual of the intruder some 8-10 kilometers ahead of him. Going into afterburner, he started to chase the Phantom which also increased its speed to 1,200 km/h and started to descend. At a speed of 1,400 km/h and an altitude of 3,000 meters, the MiG-21 launched an R-3S AAM from a distance of 1,500 meters destroying the Phantom. The other two Phantoms made a hard turn and tried to attack Do's MiG-21, but he ascended to an altitude of 10,000 meters and returned to Noi Bai. Simultaneously, Pham Thanh Ngan broke off and ascended to an altitude of 7,000 meters and landed on Noi Bai also. The USAF records did not confirm any RF-4 losses on that day, but they recognized an RF-4C Phantom loss (Maj Corbitt and 1Lt Bare) on 26 July 1967 to North Vietnamese MiG-21s. The American crew was killed in action.

In the morning of 31 August 1967, Nguyen Hong Nhi and Nguyen Dang Kinh took off from Noi Bai, and flying toward Thanh Son at an altitude of 8,000 meters, they discovered enemies at 60 degrees at a distance of 14 kilometers. They dropped their auxiliary fuel tanks and Nguyen Hong Nhi attacked from the right side, while Nguyen Dang Kinh was on the left side of the enemy. Nguyen Hong Nhi launched an R-3S missile from a distance of 1,200 meters and hit an RF-4C. The attack took only 21 minutes. The USAF did not list any RF-4Cs as having been downed by a MiG on that day.

The same "routine" was repeated with an RF-101C Voodoo, on the morning of 10 September 1967. At 10:12 hours, Nguyen Hong Nhi and Nguyen Dang Kinh were scrambled at Noi Bai to fly to the eastern

The MiGs were delivered by Mi-6 helicopters to the caverns and they were pushed inside by trucks. This MiG-17 strike camera can be seen in this preflight check by technicians, in a mountainside concrete shelter.
(ISTVÁN TOPERCZER COLLECTION)

Nguyen Hong Nhi shot down an USAF RF-101 Voodoo on 9 September 1967, east of Moc Chau, by VPAF records.
(István Toperczer Collection)

region of Vinh Yen, at a heading of 240 degrees and an altitude of 9,000 meters. From the distance of 15 kilometers east of Moc Chau, at a 30 degree angle, they detected the enemies at an altitude of 6,000 meters. Navigation oscilloscope helped pilots to detect the next targets left, at a distance of 10 kilometers. When Nguyen Hong Nhi was close enough, he launched an R-3S missile from distance of 2,000 meters and an RF-101C had fallen. After his kill, Nhi ascended to an altitude of 9,000 meters and returned to Noi Bai with 100 liters fuel in his MiG. Once again, no such loss is included in US official records.

On 16 September 1967, radars detected the enemy coming from Sam Neua (Laos), and later two RF-101C Voodoos flew a bearing of 360 degrees between Nghia Lo and Thanh Son. At 10:55 hours, a flight of two MiG-21F-13 Fishbed-Cs (ex-Cuban) was scrambled against a pair of recce aircraft at Noi Bai airbase. At 11:14 hours, the Voodoos were at an altitude of 5,500 meters, a speed of 950 km/h, and at a distance of 8 kilometers from Nguyen Ngoc Do and Pham Thanh Ngan. The MiGs, with afterburners increased their speed to Mach 1.4 and ascended to an altitude of 6,000 meters. The Voodoos responded by increasing their speed and using active jamming. According to the experience of a dogfight on 10 September, it was planned that the MiG-leader will attack the American wingman, and then the MiG-wingman attacks the American leader. If the MiG leader attacks the US leader from behind, then it will be recognized by the US wingman and the surprise of attack would be lost. Nguyen Ngoc Do, from an altitude of 6,000 meters and a distance of 1,500 meters, using an R-3S missile, claimed Capt Patterson's reconnaissance aircraft kill. Pham Thanh Ngan also fired an R-3S missile destroying Maj Bagley's RF-101C Voodoo over Son La. Nevertheless, the first kill was credited to AAA by the USAF.

On 16 September 1967, Pham Thanh Ngan and Nguyen Ngoc Do shot down two USAF RF-101C Voodoos with their MiG-21F-13s over Son La. US records credited Nguyen Ngoc Do's kill to an AAA unit.
(István Toperczer Collection)

From the middle of June 1967, meetings were held to discuss the causes that had led to the defeats the VPAF suffered in the previous weeks. While the enemy had been developing air combat tactics and had switched to two-level formations, the Vietnamese had continued to employ intercept-procedures and maneuvers that had once been successful, but which by then were outdated. Some pilots still thought that impromptu shots would certainly be followed by quick victories. With many airmen, mainly experienced ones dying in combat the survivors were overburdened by being on duty and fighting around the clock.

Two MiG-21s, Le Trong Huyen and Dong Van Song from the 921st Fighter Regiment in co-ordination with a flight of MiG-17s, attacked a group of US Navy 12 A-4s and 4 F-8s over Hai Duong on the morning of 11 July 1967. Le Trong Huyen shot down an A-4 Skyhawk, so the two bridges at Lai Vu and Phu Luong were defended. The US Navy did not confirm this loss on that day.

It was the first MiG-17s ambush with cooperation from MiG-21s. Despite that it was unsuccessful, GCI had handled it well in some cases: guiding the first MiG-21 pair from a cover changed to main fighting flight at the right moment to intercept the enemies that attacked Hai Duong, and contributed in the defense of the two important bridges on the Route No.5 (Lai Vu and Phu Luong); guiding the second MiG-21 pair into the diversion area at the right altitude, then changed to cover for the first MiG-21 pair and MiG-17 flight during their landing.

On 10 August 1967, the US Navy attacked the Phu Ly area. MiG-21s from the 921st Fighter Regiment were guided by the regimental headquarters and pilot Dang Ngoc Ngu. Bui Dinh Kinh and Dong Van Song, in their MiG-21s, flew toward Hoa Binh – Cam Thuy. They suddenly stormed the Lac Thuy area when they met the enemy fighters. Bui Dinh Kinh detected F-4 flights at a distance of 10 kilometers and 5 kilometers. After 2 minutes 30 seconds, at an altitude of 4,000 meters, the enemy shot down the MiGs in the area. They ejected safely but Bui Dinh Kinh was killed by a mistake of the militia, during his descent with his parachute.

In the afternoon of 23 August 1967, the radar stations reported a large package of 60 American aircraft bound for Hanoi approaching from Sam Neua (Laos), Yen Bai, and north of Tuyen Quang, along the west side of the Tam Dao ridge, Pho Yen and Da Phuc to Hanoi. Two MiG-21s and two flights (4 North Vietnamese and 4 aircraft of "Doan Z") of MiG-17s were scrambled to intercept them. The MiG-21s took off at 14:51 hours from Noi Bai, to the west, through Thanh Son, and then turned right to the north. The MiG-21s flew with an approach angle of 60 degrees, accelerated and ascended. At Tuyen Quang, Nguyen Nhat Chieu detected four aircraft at a distance of 15 kilometers, and then all the flights detected 8, then 12 F-4s and F- 105s. Nguyen Van Coc takes up the story:

Nguyen Van Coc and Nguyen Nhat Chieu are walking from their MiG-21s after they shot down two USAF F-4D Phantoms northwest of Hanoi.
(István Toperczer Collection)

The leader Nguyen Nhat Chieu and I went the long way around to get into a better attack position from the back. Nguyen Nhat Chieu fired an AAM bringing down an F-4D, while I attacked successfully the other Phantom, also with an R-3S AAM. In the meantime, Nguyen Nhat Chieu commenced another attack with his second missile, but it missed and he went into a cloud overhead only to reappear moments later with an attack from his cannon. Following the leader, I also attacked the Phantom with a missile, but I was too close and came into the line of Nguyen Nhat Chieu's fire diving from above. My MiG-21 was damaged by the friendly-fire, but all controls operated normally and I requested to carry on the engagement. The command post ordered me to return to base since due to the damage, my aircraft was only able to do a maximum speed of 600 km/h.

The Maj Tyler and Capt Sittner's F-4D, claimed by Nguyen Nhat Chieu, was listed in USAF records. Nguyen Van Coc's F-4D Phantom (Carrigan/Lane) was confirmed by American sources as a MiG-21 kill.

In air battles from late May to early June 1967, MiG-17s were not successful in being guided to intercept enemy strikers. Command decided to ease combat missions for MiG-17s. From late August to early September 1967, MiG-17s could fight effectively again. In the second half of 1967, MiG-17s first used the "ambush in the air" method. On the anticipated route of the attacking aircraft, a waiting area, or the ambush area, was selected. The MiGs arrived in the waiting area just a few minutes before the Americans were due and maintained, until then, an altitude of 50-100 meters.

On 23 August 1967, while MiG-21s were launched, the MiG-17 flight, Cao Thanh Tinh, Le Van Phong, Nguyen Van Tho and Nguyen Hong Diep, joined in by initiating a head-on attack. MiG-17s took off from Gia Lam at 15:00 hours to Da Phuc – Phuc Yen. Cao Thanh Tinh and Le Van Phong contacted the control center through radio, and continued with the air patrol. On discovering the F-105 strike package flying high above them, they first had fallen behind before commencing a climb in full afterburner. When in firing position behind the last F-105 pair, Cao Thanh Tinh opened up with cannon fire from a distance of 200-250 meters, downing the leader and then from 50-100 meters his wingman, too. The second pair of MiG-17s, Nguyen Van Tho and Nguyen Hong Diep, was each credited an F-4 kill. Le Van Phong was killed in the dogfight by 1Lt Waldrop's F-105D cannon shells. During this time, GCI also guided MiG-17s from "Doan Z" (North Korean group). At 14:58 hours, they took off from Kep airbase to fight over Bac Ninh, where they shot down one F-4 Phantom and landed at Noi Bai.

In comparison to the second quarter of 1967, the number of missions was only one third during the summer. From September, the enemy was apparently concentrating again on the utter destruction of the North Vietnamese airfields – Noi Bai, Kep, Hoa Lac Kien An and Cat Bi.

Air combat map – 23 August 1967

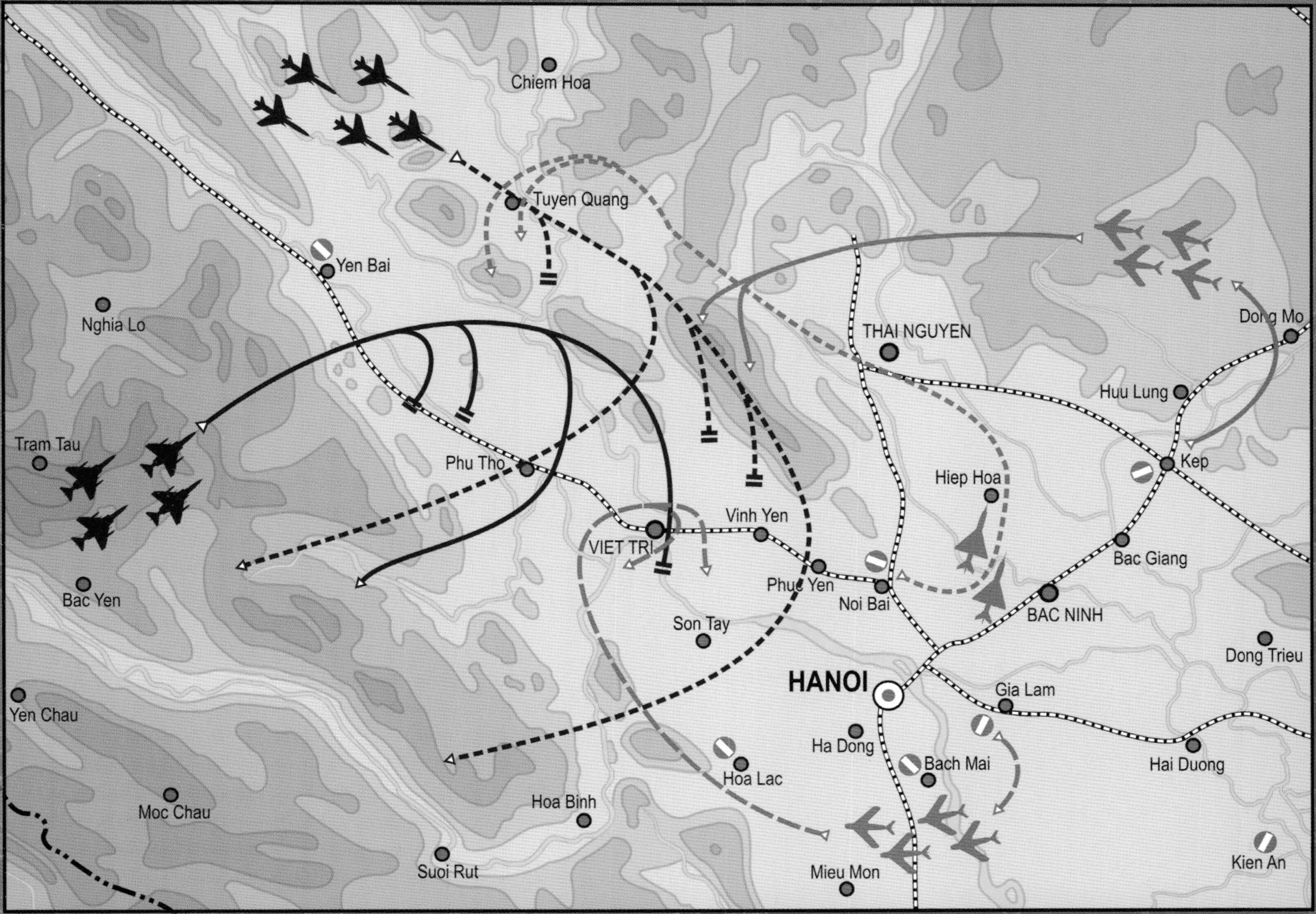

On 23 August 1967, North Vietnamese MiG-17 flight of the 923rd Fighter Regiment, North Korean MiG-17 flight of "Doan Z" and a MiG-21 pair of the 921st Fighter Regiment shot down six USAF aircraft over Phu Tho and Viet Tri area.
(Cartograph: Péter Barna)

On 21 September 1967, a flight of MiG-17s, Ho Van Quy, Nguyen Dinh Phuc, Bui Van Suu and Le Si Diep, took off in the morning, but did not meet an enemy. Commander Hoang Ngoc Dieu decided to move some MiG-17s to Kien An airbase to organize an ambush, and then these MiGs would return to Gia Lam and requested cover from MiG-17s at Gia Lam and MiG-21s at Noi Bai.

At 15:15 hours, the flight of Quy – Phuc – Suu – Diep secretly landed at Kien An, and they were in Class Two Alert. At 16:37 hours, radars detected three low flying enemy flights, coming from north of Cat Ba Island, and the north of Do Son and the Diem Dien mouth. The MiG-17s prepared to take off from Kien An, but after forming their formation, command ordered Le Si Diep to replace Nguyen Dinh Phuc, because he could not start his engine. Three MiG-17s Quy – Diep – Suu were guided to intercept the enemy on the top of the airbase, approaching at an angle of 50 degrees. Ho Van Quy detected F-4s and A-4s, at a distance of 6 kilometers. After four minutes of fighting, Ho Van Quy and Bui Van Suu, each shot down an F-4B Phantom. The US Navy records did not confirm their kills. The MiGs landed at Gia Lam as planned. Another

On 21 September 1967, Ho Van Quy (in picture) and his comrades Bui Van Suu shot down two US Navy F-4B Phantoms, but US sources did not confirm these losses.
(István Toperczer Collection)

MiG-17 flight of Cao Thanh Tinh, Nguyen Phu Ninh, Nguyen Van Tho, and Nguyen Phi Hung, took off from Gia Lam over Gia Loc – My Hao, and a MiG-21 flight of Vu Ngoc Dinh and Dong Van Song from Noi Bai to Tien Lu – Phu Cu to cover at the time MiG-17s return to Ke Sat – My Hao.

At the end of September and the beginning of October, North Vietnamese MiG-21s were successful against F-4 Phantoms and F-105 Thunderchiefs.

In the morning of 26 September 1967, enemies flew towards Tuyen Quang – Yen Bai – Phu Tho to attack Hanoi. Two MiG-21s from the 921st Fighter Regiment, Nguyen Hong Nhi and Dong Van Song, were

The North Vietnamese pilot is seen in a MiG-17 of the 923rd Fighter Regiment, at Kep airbase, in September of 1967.
(István Toperczer Collection)

Dong Van Song used this MiG-21PFL during the air battle on 26 September 1967. His flight leader, Nguyen Hong Nhi, shot down an F-4 Phantom on that day, by VPAF records. This famous No.4324 was operated by nine pilots of the 921st Fighter Regiment, who shot down 14 US aircraft, from November 1967 to May 1968.
(ISTVÁN TOPERCZER)

scrambled at Noi Bai airbase. At 07:34 hours, a pair of MiG-21s took off bearing 250 degrees, and increased their speed and ascended. They discovered four F-4 Phantoms to their right, about a distance of 10 kilometers. There was a good position to fire the missile on their right side, so Nhi accelerated and attacked them. He fired the first R-3S missile against the second F-4 Phantom in formation, but missed. Continuing the attack, he fired his second missile at a distance of 1,200 meters and shot down a flight-leader Phantom. The MiG-21s broke off, ascended to an altitude of 9,000 meters, and returned Noi Bai. The USAF records did not confirm this kill for Nguyen Hong Nhi.

In the afternoon of 27 September, Nguyen Ngoc Do and Nguyen Van Ly were on duty at Noi Bai. At 14:53 hours, MiG-21s took off and ascended with a bearing of 90 degrees. At 15:03 hours, radar detected enemies over Route No.1 towards Thai Nguyen. After six minutes, Nguyen Van Ly discovered an F-105 formation on the right side, from a heading of 120 degrees. The MiGs dropped their auxiliary fuel tanks and attacked the Thunderchiefs. Nguyen Ngoc Do fired an R-3S missile from a distance of 1,500-2,000 meters and damaged an F-105 Thunderchief. The MiG-21 pair broke off and returned safely to Noi Bai airbase.

The enemy formation of F-105s and F-4s attacked Kep airbase from the northeast on 30 September 1967. The Command of the VPAF decided to order an attack for MiG-17s from "Doan Z" and a MiG-21 pair from the 921st Fighter Regiment. At 15.08 hours, Tran Ngoc Siu and Mai Van Cuong took off from Noi Bai and ascended to an altitude of 6,000 meters towards Kep airbase. The GCI guided them to a heading of 210 degrees, when Cuong discovered some F-105 Thunderchiefs on his left side at a distance of 15 kilometers. The MiGs attacked the enemy formation, but

Pham Thanh Ngan shot down Maj Moore's F-4D Phantom over North Vietnam, on 3 October 1967. The F-4 crew was able to fly to the border of Laos, where they ejected and were picked up by rescue teams over there. (István Toperczer Collection)

Mai Van Cuong chose the last US aircraft, and immediately launched an R-3S missile to shoot down an F-105 bomber. At 15:23 hours, Cuong did not see his leader and called him on the radio, but no answer. Unfortunately, Tran Ngoc Siu lost his life on that day by friendly fire from a missile from the ADF. The USAF did not lose a Thunderchief and the North Korean Lim Dang An lost his life in the air battle. However, the US sources did not confirm their own air victory on that day.

In October 1967, the Soviet Union agreed to provide Vietnam with the new MiG-21 PFM Fishbed F (F94). The first MiG-21 PFMs arrived at Hai Phong Harbor in late 1967. During 1967 and to mid-1968, the MiG-21F-13 and MiG-21PFL Fishbeds were involved in the air battles. From the second half of 1968, the MiG-21PFM became the primary fighter aircraft of the Vietnamese People's Air Force.

On 3 October, the Americans were on a raid against Hoa Lac, Noi Bai airfields and the bridge at Cao Bang, when a pair of MiG-21s from the 921st Fighter Regiment, Pham Thanh Ngan and Nguyen Van Ly, took off from Noi Bai. The MiGs ascended to an altitude of 800 meters and later 9,000 meters, to a heading of 270 degrees. At 13:52 hours, Ngan – Ly detected enemies and dropped their auxiliary fuel tanks. They attacked the formation of two F-4D and two RF-4C Phantoms, when Maj Moore's aircraft was damaged by the MiG leader's R-3S missile. The F-4D Phantom was on fire and its port engine had to be shut down, but it flew to the border of Laos. The crew ejected and was rescued.

In the morning of 7 October 1967, the Americans attacked Hanoi from the west and south. Meanwhile, several other flights flew patrols at Son Duong – Dai Tu – Lap Thach and My Duc – Thanh Oai. At 07:32 hours, the MiG-21 pair of Pham Thanh Ngan and Mai Van Cuong took off from Noi

The military museum stores Ace-pilot Pham Thanh Ngan's ex-No.4520 MiG-21F-13 Fishbed C at Thai Nguyen city. (Nguyen Duc Huy)

Technicians load R-3S missiles to Noi Bai-based MiG-21F-13 Fishbed C fighters. On 9 October 1967, Nguyen Hong Nhi shot down an USAF F-105D Thunderchief, and he became an "Ace" with this air victory.
(István Toperczer Collection)

Bai flying toward Son Tay and Thanh Son. At 07:34 hours, radar detected an enemy group of 12 aircraft 15 kilometers south of Na San, at an altitude of 4,000 meters that flew to Bac Yen- Phu Yen. After Thanh Son, MiG-21s turned right, bearing 360 degrees, and flew for one more minute to choose the time to attack. They then turned hard left and ascended to an altitude of 3,000 meters. They intercepted the group of enemy aircraft coming from Phu Yen to Hoa Lac. The MiGs were guided with an approach angle of 70 degrees, and they detected F-4 Phantoms to the right, at a distance of 15 kilometers. The MiGs accelerated and attacked, each pilot shot down an F-4 Phantom with R-3S missiles and broke off before crossing the Da River. The total fight time was 22 minutes.

The duty navigation crew made the twin lead and also coordinated the MiG-21 pair of Nguyen Nhat Chieu and Nguyen Van Coc in the afternoon. They took off from Noi Bai to fight in the area of Yen Tu Hill (1068). At a heading of 130 degrees and at a distance of 10 kilometers, the enemy targets were detected. Chieu and Coc each shot down an F-105 Thunderchief by using missiles. The USAF records confirmed only three kills (F-4D, F-105D and F-105F) for two MiG-21 pairs.

On that day, eight minutes after Ngan – Cuong's MiG-21s take off, the MiG-17 flight of Nguyen Huu Tao, Nguyen Phu Ninh, Nguyen Hong Diep and Nguyen Phi Hung took off from Gia Lam to Noi Bai, and fought at Son Tay – Ba Vi – Hoa Lac at an altitude of 1,000 meters. With an approach angle of 110 degrees, MiG pilots detected F-4s and F-105s at a distance of 7 kilometers, and Nguyen Phi Hung shot down an F-4 Phantom. An American flight came from the west to Hanoi, jettisoned their bombs and retreated. USAF records did not confirm any MiG-17's kill.

On 9 October, between 15:00 and 16:00 hours, the enemy groups of F-4s and F-105s arrived from Sam Neua towards Yen Chau – Nghia Lo as always. At 15:28 hours, two MiG-21F-13s, Nguyen Hong Nhi and Dong Van Song, took off at Noi Bai, ascended to an altitude of 5,000 meters and flew west of Thanh Son over Route No.2. The MiGs reaching Thanh Son detected enemy at a distance of 20 kilometers. The American bomber group did not discover the MiGs and the F-105s were en route to bomb the railway at Quang Hien. Nguyen Hong Nhi attacked the last flight of F-105s in the formation and fired two R-3S missiles. Maj Clement's F-105D was hit in the tailpipe by missiles and he ejected safely. Meanwhile, Dong Van Song also shot down another F-105 Thunderchief, but US records confirmed only one loss in this incident.

In the afternoon of 24 October 1967, the enemy came from Na San and Yen Chau, formed formations 15 kilometers northwest of Phu Yen, and flew to Doan Hung, along the east side of the Tam Dao ridge to Hanoi. At 14:54 hours, a MiG-21 flight of Nguyen Dang Kinh and Dong Van Song took off from Noi Bai. At 15 kilometers northwest of Hoa Binh, the MiGs turned right, bearing 280 degrees; at 15 kilometers northeast of Moc Chau, they turned right again, bearing 350 degrees. At Phu Yen, they turned right to intercept with an approach angle of 15 degrees. After detecting F-105s and F-4s at a distance of 6 kilometers, the pilots requested to drop their auxiliary fuel tanks, but right after that they reported there were F-4s coming in head-on without detection by radar. At the same time, radar detected enemies from the east. Seeing the MiG-21s were at a disadvantage, command ordered them to break off, bearing 160 degrees. After breaking off, Nguyen Dang Kinh did not check Dong Van Song's position and radar did not either, when Kinh returned to Suoi Rut Song was still fighting. When radar caught Dong Van Song's signal and ordered him to break off, it was too late. He was hit by missile of a USAF F-4 Phantom and ejected safely.

The ex-Chinese MiG-17Fs are seen before take-off in October 1967. The original Chinese markings are painted over with North Vietnamese insignias. (István Toperczer Collection)

From October 1967, three versions of the MiG-21 fighter (F-13, PFL and PFM) were in service together at the 921st Fighter Regiment. The famous No.4326 wears 13 red stars as a sign of MiG-21 pilots' aerial victories.
(ISTVÁN TOPERCZER COLLECTION)

After two days, on 26 October, 32 F-105s and F-4s flown from Laos on route Nghia Lo – Tuyen Quang – Dai Tu – Thai Nguyen to Hanoi. Two MiG-17 flights were ordered to take off from Noi Bai, and they were guided in a heading of 330 degrees, at an altitude of 4,700-5,000 meters. In the battle zone, the USAF F-4D Phantoms fired 12 missiles (AIM-4, AIM-7) toward MiGs. Nguyen Hong Thai, Le Sy Diep and Duong Trung Tan had to eject, and all landed safely. The 921st Fighter Regiment lost a MiG-21 also in the air battle over Nho Quan. Mai Van Cuong's MiG-21 was shot down by a Sparrow missile of an F-4B Phantom of the VF-143, from the USS *Constellation* (CVA-64). He ejected safely and his wingman, Nguyen Van Coc landed on their base.

At the end of month, on 29 October, American aircraft, F-4s and F-105s flew in the direction of Hanoi. A pair of MiG-21F-13s, Nguyen Nhat Chieu and Dang Ngoc Ngu, were scrambled from Noi Bai to intercept the enemy in the Nam Dinh – Ninh Binh area. At 15:28 hours, MiGs took off, bearing 160 degrees over Phu Ly, and after 16 minutes they turned left to 120 degrees towards USAF F-4 Phantoms. The enemy discovered the MiG-21s and fired missiles, but Chieu – Ngu were able to evade hits. At an altitude of 7,500 meters, Chieu made a hard turn and fired an R-3S missile from distance of 1,800 meters. An F-4 Phantom smoked after a hit. The MiG-21s broke off and ascended to an altitude of 8.000 meters, flying to a heading of 330 degrees to Kep airbase. It was Nguyen Nhat Chieu's sixth air victory during Vietnam War. The USAF records did not confirm this loss.

In the morning of 6 November 1967, American aircraft flew from Hong Gai, along the south side of the Yen Tu ridge over Uong Bi, and headed to Pha Lai, while others went from the southwest over Suoi Rut – Hoa

Binh towards Hoa Lac. The Vietnamese MiGs were tasked to intercept any enemy group east of Hanoi. Commander Dao Dinh Luyen ordered to use aircraft from Gia Lam and Kep airfields for protecting the east part of Hanoi. At 07:38 hours, a pair of MiG-21s, Dang Ngoc Ngu and Nguyen Van Ly, took off from Gia Lam and over Thanh Mien they turned right to Hung Yen – Kim Bang, then turned back to intercept an enemy group of 16 aircraft, at an altitude of 2,000 meters at Dong Trieu. MiG-21s approached at an angle of 120 degrees, but pilots were unable to detect the targets. When the MiGs crossed over the enemy flight path, GCI ordered them to turn back, and the MiGs had to break off. At that time, American aircraft were operating in the Noi Bai area, so command ordered Ngu – Ly to land at Ninh Minh airfield. At 07:48 hours, a MiG-17 flight of Bui Van Suu, Nguyen Duy Tuan, Le Xuan Di and Nguyen Dinh Phuc took off from Kep to Bac Giang. At an approach angle of 70 degrees, MiG pilots detected several F-105 Thunderchiefs at a distance of 5 kilometers. Pilot Nguyen Dinh Phuc shot down one F-105 Thunderchief and the MiGs landed at Kep airbase. At 07:50 hours, another MiG-17 flight, with Nguyen Huu Tao, Phan Trong Van, Nguyen Van Tho and Nguyen Phi Hung, took off from Gia Lam and fought over Pha Lai. Only Phan Trong Van had an opportunity to fire, but with no results.

In the afternoon of this day, a large USAF Thunderchiefs and Phantoms strike formation came from Cam Pha – Tien Yen, flew along the north of the Yen Tu ridge to Son Dong – Luc Nam towards Hanoi. At 15:35 hours, a pair of MiG-21s, Dang Ngoc Ngu and Nguyen Van Ly, took off from Gia Lam (after landing at Ninh Minh in the morning, they moved back to Gia Lam and were on ready right away), to Ninh Giang, turned left to Kien An – Hai Phong – Quang Yen. When MiG-21s turned left, they approached at an angle of 60 degrees, 10 kilometers north of Uong Bi, but enemy aircraft had an advantage to maneuver. The MiGs had to break off to the north and landed at Ninh Minh again. At 15:38 hours, a MiG-17 flight from the 923rd Fighter Regiment, Nguyen Huu Tao, Phan Trong Van, Nguyen Van Tho and Nguyen Phi Hung, took off from Gia Lam and they were guided to fly along the south of Route No.5 to Cam Giang, and then turned left to Chi Linh to meet the F-4s and F-105s. The MiGs fought with disadvantage and flew to Luc Ngan. Nguyen Van Tho and Nguyen Phi Hung, each shot down an F-105, but Nguyen Huu Tao and Phan Trong Van had to eject. Unfortunately, a flight leader, Tao, lost his life in this incident. At 15:44 hours, a second MiG-17 flight, Bui Van Suu, Nguyen Duy Tuan, Le Xuan Di and Nguyen Dinh Phuc, took off from Kep and flew to Luc Ngan to support and cover Tho – Hung, the first flight to break off. With an approach angle of 60 degrees, Nguyen Dinh Phuc detected F-105s, at a distance of 6 kilometers. Bui Van Suu shot down an F-105 Thunderchief, and after the dogfights the MiG-17s landed on Gia Lam. The USAF records did not confirm three F-105 losses and the fourth F-105, Maj Hagerman's Thunderchief, was damaged after an SA-2 missile exploded close to the aircraft.

DATE OF BIRTH: 1934
ENLISTED: 12 December 1953
PILOT TRAINING:
1956 – 1964 (MiG-17 – China)
1966 (MiG-21 – Vietnam)
WAR SERVICE AND UNIT:
1964 – 1971 (921st Fighter Regiment)
1972 – 1975 (927th Fighter Regiment)
AIRCRAFT: MiG-17, MiG-21
HERO OF THE VIETNAMESE PEOPLE'S ARMED FORCES: 31 December 1973
RANK: Senior Colonel

AIR VICTORIES: 6 kills
(5 F-4s, 1 F-105 – VPAF official credit)

DATE	AIRCRAFT	UNIT	KILL – US PILOT (VPAF – US DATABASES)
20 Sep 65	MiG-17	921.	F-4 – US not confirmed
20 May 67	MiG-21	921.	F-4C – Van Loan, Milligan (POWs)
23 Aug 67	MiG-21	921.	F-4D – Tyler (POW) Sittner (KIA)
07 Oct 67	MiG-21	921.	F-105F – Howard, Shamblee (Rescued)
29 Oct 67	MiG-21	921.	F-4 – US not confirmed

MiG-21F-13 Fishbed C, No. 4426 of the 921st Fighter Regiment, 1967
This MiG-21F-13 was used by Nguyen Nhat Chieu, who claimed an F-4 Phantom kill on 29 October 1967. (ARTWORK: BALÁZS KAKUK)

The Ace-pilots Nguyen Van Coc, Nguyen Hong Nhi, Nguyen Dang Kinh and Pham Thanh Ngan used this MiG-21PFL Fishbed in November 1967. The veteran MiG-21PFL Fishbed D, No. 4326 (13 kills), is seen in the courtyard of the VPAF Museum, Hanoi. (István Toperczer)

After the air battles of late October and early November 1967, the MiG-17s were unsuccessful, shooting down three American aircraft but losing six MiG-17s. The VPAF Headquarters decided to use MiG-21s more responsibly. The Noi Bai airbase had been so heavily damaged that the 921st Fighter Regiment moved its combat alert duty aircraft to Gia Lam airfield. Because of Gia Lam did not have sufficient support facilities for its operations, their command group decided to move back to Noi Bai. At the end of 1967, to achieve success, the central command decided that at all times a North Vietnamese fighter should be in the air, for which it should use the 16 meters wide taxiway at Noi Bai as its runway. Nguyen Hong Nhi and Nguyen Dang Kinh were the first two pilots to be given this task.

In the early morning of 7 November 1967, a Mi-4 helicopter picked up pilots Nguyen Hong Nhi and Nguyen Danh Kinh at Gia Lam and flew to Noi Bai. In the afternoon information was received from radar stations that F-105 Thunderchiefs and F-4 Phantoms were heading for Hanoi. At 15:09 hours, the two MiG-21s were ordered to take off and fly in a holding pattern directly above the airfield. Later, the MiGs climbed to an altitude of 6,000 meters and flew on a heading of 360 degrees. Pilots were informed that the target was 45 degrees to their right front at a range of 15 kilometers. They dropped their auxiliary fuel tanks and switched on their afterburners. Nguyen Hong Nhi attacked the left side of the F-105 formation. He fired an R-3S missile at a distance of 1,500 meters, which impacted in the tail of an F-105. The F-105 pilots turned hard and flew right under the belly of Nhi's MiG. Nguyen Hong Nhi turned left to get the next flight of F-105 Thunderchiefs. He fired his second missile, and Major Diehl's F-105D began to burn and crashed

Nguyen Dang Kinh

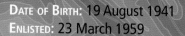

Date of Birth: 19 August 1941
Enlisted: 23 March 1959
Pilot training:
1961 – 1964 (MiG-17 – Soviet Union)
1964 – 1965 (MiG-21 – Soviet Union)
War Service and Unit:
1965 – 1972 (921st Fighter Regiment)
1972 – 1975 (927th Fighter Regiment)
Aircraft: MiG-21
Hero of the Vietnamese People's Armed Forces: 28 May 2010
Rank: Major General

Air Victories: 6 kills
(2 F-4s, 1 F-105, 1 EB-66, 2 Firebees – VPAF official credit)

Date	Aircraft	Unit	Kill – US Pilot (VPAF – US databases)
21 Jul 66	MiG-21	921.	Firebee
05 Dec 66	MiG-21	921.	F-105D – Begley (KIA)
07 Nov 67	MiG-21	921.	F-4 – US not confirmed
19 Nov 67	MiG-21	921.	EB-66 – US not confirmed
19 Dec 67	MiG-21	921.	F-4 damaged
03 Jan 68	MiG-21	921.	F-105 – US not confirmed
21 Sep 68	MiG-21	921.	Firebee
26 Oct 68	MiG-21	921.	F-4 – US not confirmed

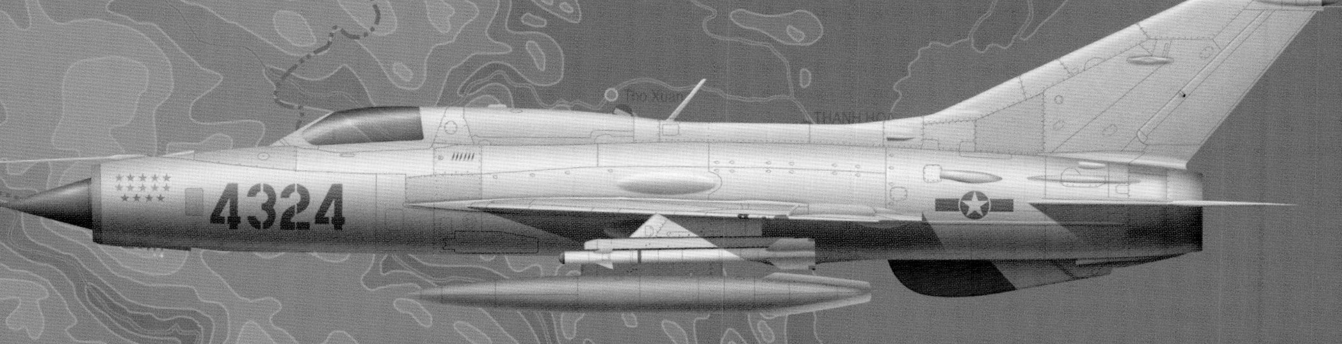

MiG-21PFL Fishbed D, No. 4324 (14 kills) of the 921st Fighter Regiment, 1967
Nguyen Dang Kinh fired R-3S missile from this MiG-21PFL during the dogfight on 7 November 1967, when he claimed an F-4 Phantom kill. (Artwork: Balázs Kakuk)

On 7 November 1967, Nguyen Hong Nhi used the No. 4326 to shoot down Major Diehl's F-105D southwest of Kep airbase. The MiG-21PFM, No.5034, is seen in the background, which was shot down by USAF F-4s on 29 July 1972.
(István Toperczer Collection)

40 kilometers southwest of Kep airbase. The other F-105 bombers of the group dropped their load and turned back. Nguyen Dang Kinh discovered eight enemy aircraft that were chasing his flight leader. He fired a missile to protect Nhi's MiG, but the two flights of F-4 Phantoms made a sharp turn to the right and abandoned their pursuit of his flight leader. Nguyen Dang Kinh pulled his aircraft up into a climb to an altitude of 10,000 meters, flew to Kien An airfield. The control tower of Kien An gave a landing heading and warned them to take special care. Nguyen Hong Nhi made a perfect landing on the taxiway to be followed by Nguyen Dang Kinh. The USAF records did not confirm their losses.

The next day, on 8 November, Dang Ngoc Ngu and Nguyen Van Ly also took off from the runway at Noi Bai airbase, to check in the area 15 kilometers south of Phu Yen to Yen Bai. After take-off, they were directed to intercept a MiGCAP flight of F-4 Phantoms flying at an altitude of 5,500 meters, 40 kilometers northeast of Yen Bai. The Phantoms discovered that the MiGs were chasing them and the F-4 pilots split into two sections. Dang Ngoc Ngu attacked the F-4 flight-leader and ordered Ly to attack another Phantom. The F-4 flight-leader made evasive maneuvers to try to escape. Dang Ngoc Ngu kept on his tail and fired a missile that hit Maj Gordon's F-4D Phantom. Meanwhile, Ly also fired a missile and he saw the F-4 begin to burn and dive toward the ground. A MiG-21 broke off and landed safely at Gia Lam airfield. The US records confirmed Dang Ngoc Ngu's kill, which official was his fourth kill.

At the end of November, Pham Thanh Ngan and Nguyen Van Coc from the 921st Fighter Regiment took part in two air battles over Ha Hoa. They downed F-105 Thunderchiefs and landed at Kep airbase.

On 18 November the weather conditions were bad, but sixteen F-105s along with F-4 fighter escorts, flew in to attack SAM-sites and AAA positions in advance of the next bombers formation that would attack targets at Hanoi and the Noi Bai airbase. During this period USAF aircraft flying in to bomb targets in North Vietnam were provided with navigational support by TSQ-81 position-finding radar, located at Pa Thi in Laos. The USAF would use EB-66s to provide jamming and EC-121s to provide information to their pilots about North Vietnamese MiGs.

The North Vietnamese used radar signals to detect incoming enemy aircraft, guide their MiG fighters, and aim surface-to-air missiles and antiaircraft guns. The USAF EB-66s conducted "electronic warfare" against these radars to render them useless. The first USAF electronic warfare Douglas EB-66 Destroyers went to Southeast Asia in the spring of 1965. EB-66 crews detected and gathered information about enemy radar locations and frequencies. They also used jamming equipment to interrupt enemy radar signals.

The Lockheed EC-121 Constellation played a key role by monitoring airborne North Vietnamese MiGs and guiding USAF fighters to intercept them. Orbiting securely outside the border, EC-121 crews used the aircraft's radar and enemy radio communications to detect and locate MiGs within North Vietnamese airspace. These operations began in the spring of 1965 under the code name "Big Eye", later named "College Eye" and "Disco", and continued beyond the end of the war.

At the 921st Fighter Regiment, Pham Thanh Ngan and Nguyen Van Coc were on combat alert duty that day. They were the most outstanding pilots, who were prepared to use the tactic of "fast attack – deep penetration." At 07:48 hours, pilots Pham Thanh Ngan and Nguyen Van Coc took off and flew out on a heading of 265 degrees over Thanh Son. At 07:53 hours, radar detected a flight of four American aircraft flying from Yen Chau to Ha Hoa. Four minutes later Coc discovered a target at 15 degrees to the right front, at a distance of 8 kilometers.

Two MiG-21PFLs are preparing to take-off on 18 November 1967. Pham Thanh Ngan sits in the No.4324, who shot down an F-105F Thunderchief over Yen Bai Province on that day.
(István Toperczer Collection)

In the afternoon of 18 November, Nguyen Van Coc demonstrates that morning's dogfight for his comrades at Noi Bai airbase. He shot down Lt Col Reed's F-105D Thunderchief on that day.
(István Toperczer Collection)

Pham Thanh Ngan, immediately turned to the left and spotted two more enemy aircraft. Ngan – Coc had clearly identified all four F-105s' formation. The two MiG-21s increased their speed and climbed to gain an altitude advantage of 1,500-2,000 meters over the enemy. They dropped auxiliary fuel tanks and attacked the enemy. When the distance to enemy was 1,800 meters, Pham Thanh Ngan fired an R-3S missile; an F-105F Thunderchief burst into flames and crashed in Van Du hamlet, along the banks of the Lo River. After launching his first missile, Ngan spotted another F-105 flying right in front of him and launched his second missile towards the Thunderchief. He did not observe the results of his second attack. However, Nguyen Van Coc saw the F-105 being hit by Ngan's missile and the F-105 was damaged. Pham Thanh Ngan climbed to an altitude of 7,000 meters, but American aircraft was at a heading of 70 degrees to his rear, at a distance of 40 kilometers. Having seen the American aircraft behind him, he increased his speed and descended to an altitude of 5,000 meters to return to land. Meanwhile, Nguyen Van Coc pursued Lt Col Reed's F-105D, who was leading the F-105 formation. Nguyen Van Coc fired an R-3S missile at a distance of 1,200 meters, and the enemy aircraft burst into flames. The two MiG-21s pilots broke off and flew toward the Nanning airfield (China) to land, but because the weather was bad at that airfield, the pilots returned and landed at Kep airbase.

In the morning of 20 November 1967, the radars detected a group of enemy aircraft southwest of Moc Chau and later another group approaching from Sam Neua. After the reports about the American combat formation changed, the command post ordered a pair of MiG-21s to be prepared to attack against an EB-66 Destroyer. At 07:33 hours, a pair of MiG-21s, Pham Thanh Ngan and Nguyen Van Coc, took off and they were directed to head toward Thanh Son. The command

Date of Birth: 15 December 1942
Enlisted: June 1961
Pilot training:
1962 – 1964 (MiG-17 – Soviet Union)
1965 – 1966 (MiG-21 – Soviet Union)
War Service and Unit:
1966 – 1972 (921st Fighter Regiment)
Aircraft: MiG-21
Hero of the Vietnamese People's Armed Forces: 18 June 1969
Rank: Lieutenant General

Air Victories: 9 kills
(2 F-4s, 5 F-105s, 2 Firebees – VPAF official credit)

Date	Aircraft	Unit	Kill – US Pilot (VPAF – US databases)
30 Apr 67	MiG-21	921.	F-105D – R. Abbott (POW)
23 Aug 67	MiG-21	921.	F-4D – Carrigan (POW) Lane (KIA)
07 Oct 67	MiG-21	921.	F-105D damaged – Fullam (KIA) (AAA)
18 Nov 67	MiG-21	921.	F-105D – Reed (Rescued)
20 Nov 67	MiG-21	921.	F-105 – US not confirmed
12 Dec 67	MiG-21	921.	F-105 damaged
07 May 68	MiG-21	921.	F-4B – Christensen, Kramer (Rescued)
04 Jun 68	MiG-21	921.	Firebee
08 Nov 68	MiG-21	921.	Firebee
03 Aug 69	MiG-21	921.	Firebee (Shared)

MiG-21PFL Fishbed D, No. 4326 (13 kills) of the 921st Fighter Regiment, 1967
The most famous and Top Ace-pilot, Nguyen Van Coc used this Fishbed to shoot down LtCol Reed's F-105D Thunderchief (60-0497) on 18 November 1967. (Artwork: Balázs Kakuk)

post then concluded that the leading enemy group were not bombers and decided to direct the flight up north of Moc Chau to wait for the bombers. The target approached Nghia Lo – Yen Bai at a speed of 900 km/h and an altitude of 9,000 meters, the command post concluded that the target was an EB-66 Destroyer electronic warfare (EW) aircraft. At 07:45 hours, Pham Thanh Ngan and Nguyen Van Coc dropped their auxiliary fuel tanks and increased their speed to attack the EB-66. At 07:53 hours, the MiG-21s were flying on a heading of 250 degrees when the pilots spotted the target, which was not an EB-66. Instead of EW aircraft, two F-4 Phantoms flew at a heading of 15 degrees to their left front, at a distance of 7-10 kilometers. When Pham Thanh Ngan decided to attack, the Phantoms discovered the MiGs. Pham Thanh Ngan turned away and returned to land on Kep airbase. Meanwhile, Nguyen Van Coc had spotted another F-4 Phantom and fired an R-3S missile, but the F-4 had made a sharp turn so the missile missed its target. Coc turned away and returned to Noi Bai airbase.

That afternoon, after an EB-66 began transmitting jamming signals from the southeast of Sam Neua, a large American strike formation of twelve F-105s and four F-4s flew in to attack a target southeast of Yen Bai. At 15:50 hours, Pham Thanh Ngan and Nguyen Van Coc took off from Noi Bai and flew toward Thanh Son – Phu Tho. At 16:01 hours, they discovered the target at a heading of 45 degrees to the left, at a distance of 10 kilometers. The American formation included both F-105 Thunderchiefs and F-4 Phantoms. The MiG-21s dropped their auxiliary fuel tanks and Ngan decided to attack a flight of F-105s on the left side of the formation. At distance of 1,500 meters, Ngan launched his missile and hit Capt Butler's F-105D Thunderchief, which burst into flames. After he launched the first missile, Ngan turned away and spotted another F-105 right in front of him. He fired his second missile and pulled up to break away, so he did not see the missile explosion. He returned and landed on Noi Bai airbase. Meanwhile, Nguyen Van Coc spotted two F-105s climbing in front of him. He quickly fired a missile at a distance of 1,800 meters and an F-105 burst into flames. Nguyen Van Coc broke off and flew north of Thai Nguyen, and then landed at Noi Bai airbase. The USAF records only confirmed Pham Thanh Ngan's victory over a F-105D Thunderchief.

The airfield at Kien An was under attack by US Navy aircraft on 17 November and the runways were destroyed, only to be restored in two days by the 28th Technical Brigade and civilians from Kien An.

The MiG-21s of the 921st Fighter Regiment participated in many air battles but they were not successful due to the electronic jamming aircraft, Douglas EB-66 Destroyer. They had not much experience fighting against the EB-66 Destroyer. In the morning of 19 November, an EB-66 was detected in the region of Thanh Hoa and command ordered MiG-21s to take off. At 07:13 hours, Vu Ngoc Dinh and Nguyen Dang Kinh left Noi Bai airbase at a heading of 180 degrees, at an altitude of

1,200 meters from the clouds, and up to 5,000 meters and later to 7,000 meters. The MiG-21 pair was led toward the enemy, at a heading of 280 degrees, increased their speed as high as 1,100 km/h and an altitude of 10,000 meters. After three minutes, Vu Ngoc Dinh discovered the first close support flight, but the Phantoms were not on the offensive. At that time, Nguyen Dang Kinh spotted one EB-66 Destroyer at a heading of 15 degrees to the left front, and at a distance of 12-15 kilometers. Vu Ngoc Dinh also spotted the target. When the distance was approximately 2,500 meters, and Kinh launched the first R-3S missile, which hit the left engine of EB-66 EW-aircraft, but the range was longer than 1,000 meters and the explosion was behind the tail. He flew closer, and when the target was at a distance of 1,200 meters he fired his second R-3S missile. This missile flew straight into the EB-66 Destroyer and Kinh broke away to climb to an altitude of 13,000 meters, then turned to a heading of 30 degrees to fly over Hoa Binh – Thai Nguyen. The EB-66 was damaged and crashed in flames into the jungles of Lang Chanh (Thanh Hoa Province). The F-4 Phantoms realized that a MiG-21 had shot down the EB-66 and they turned back to attack the MiG-21s. Nguyen Dang Kinh had already fired both of his missiles, so Vu Ngoc Dinh turned back to cover his MiG-21. The Phantoms realized they had no chance to get on the tails of the MiG-21s so they broke off the attack. The two MiG-21s returned and landed at Kep airbase. It was the first time when a MiG-21 attacked the electronic jamming aircraft EB-66 and shot it down. The US records did not confirm the loss of EB-66 on that day.

In early morning on the 19 November, four MiG-17s of the 923rd Fighter Regiment with Ho Van Quy took off from Gia Lam, Le Hai, Nguyen Dinh Phuc and Nguyen Phi Hung took off from Kep in secret, landing shortly after at Kien An airfield. Simultaneously, two MiG-21s by Vu Ngoc Dinh and Nguyen Dang Kinh flew from Kep to Noi Bai to cover MiG-17s. At 10:00 hours, a 20-ship enemy formation, comprising of A-4 Skyhawks and F-4 Phantoms, was observed approaching Hai Phong. At 10:40 hours, the flight of MiG-17s took off from Kien An airfield. After take-off, the communication equipment of flight leader Ho Van Quy was damaged, so command decided to let Le Hai became flight-leader. Le Hai was a young pilot and never was in charge of a flight but he expressed his skills and tactics. He led the flight to Do Son. After accelerating to altitude of 2,500 meters, they dropped their auxiliary fuel tanks. Le Hai assigned Phuc and Hung to intercept the trailing flight, while he and Quy attacked the leading F-4 Phantoms. The enemy detected the MiG-17s, accelerated to ascend and turned to the sea to pull the MiGs from strikers. The A-4 Skyhawks jettisoned their bombs and retreated. The fight took place at an altitude over Hai Phong. After a few minutes, Le Hai followed an F-4B Phantom and shot down it with two bursts. Then he lured another F-4B to let Nguyen Phi Hung shot it down. Meanwhile, Nguyen Dinh Phuc shot down one more F-4B Phantom. After the encounter all MiGs returned safely to Kien An.

Nguyen Dinh Phuc and Le Hai shot down two US Navy F-4B Phantoms, from the USS Coral Sea, on 19 November 1967. US records confirmed only Le Hai's air victory, which was his second air victory during the war. (István Toperczer Collection)

The American sources tell this story as follows. On this day Lt(jg) James E. Teague pilot, and Lt(jg) Theodore G. Stier RIO, were flying the number two F-4B Phantoms, in a flight of two, providing fighter protection for a strike group. As the strike group approached the target area, the two fighters were detached to proceed north-east of the target where American aircraft were reported. The two F-4 aircraft were observed (on radar) to proceed to the assigned area, and then to turn to a south-westerly heading as the strike group attacked. Shortly thereafter, at about 10:49 hours, while they were flying around the southern edge of Hai Phong from Cat Bi toward Kien An airfield, the flight leader reported the enemy MiG-17 aircraft off his right wing. No one saw the actual engagement between the two F-4s and the MiGs. Radio transmissions were heard and recorded which stated they were engaging MiGs, "to light engine afterburners" and to "break." Shortly thereafter, a "Mayday" transmission was heard. Other aircraft on the strike reported seeing a large fireball between 3,000 and 4,500 meters southeast of Cat Bi airfield. Lt(jg) Teague was killed in captivity and Lt(jg) Stier was a POW until March 1973.

At Noi Bai airbase, the MiG-21 pair, Vu Ngoc Dinh and Nguyen Dang Kinh, was in a Class One Alert. The 45th Radar Company detected enemy aircraft from the sea and MiG-21s had to wait for the take-off order at 10:32 hours. After take-off, the MiG-21s flew along the west of Route No.1 to Phu Ly, Nam Dinh and Thai Binh. While MiG-17s were attacking, the MiG-21s turned at Phu Duc, flew over the area of MiG-17s to cover them. The MiG-21s saw American aircraft fires missiles against the MiG-17s, but Dinh – Kinh did not have a chance to attack, and later they landed at Noi Bai.

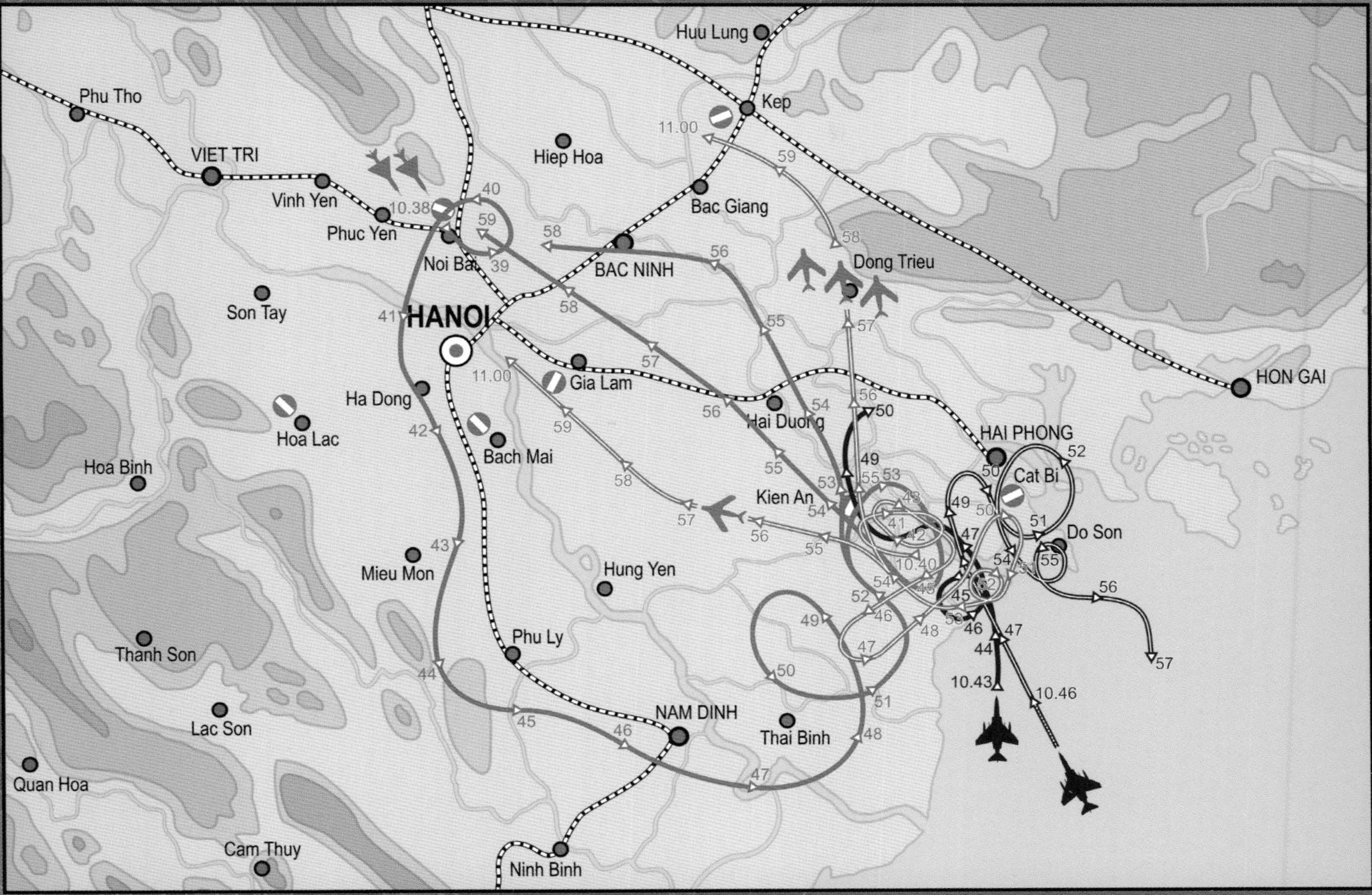

On 19 November 1967, a flight of MiG-17s and a pair of MiG-21s were over Kien An airfield. The MiG-17 pilots, Le Hai, Nguyen Phi Hung and Nguyen Dinh Phuc shot down three US Navy F-4B Phantoms from USS Coral Sea.
(CARTOGRAPH: PÉTER BARNA)

At the beginning of December of 1967, the weather was bad in North Vietnam. The winds of the northeast monsoon arrived early and the visibility was limited because the sky was dark from clouds hiding the sun. From mid-December, the weather improved and the enemy started large air strikes against the Hanoi area.

In the morning of 12 December, the USAF strike formation, consisting of twelve F-105s and four F-4s, flew in to attack targets in the Hanoi area. Nguyen Van Coc and Nguyen Van Ly were on combat alert duty at Noi Bai. At 07:40 hours, the MiG-21 pair was ordered to take off and was directed to fly over Son Dong – Luc Ngan. After five minutes, the command ordered the pilots to change direction and head to Hai Duong and Haiphong. Coc – Ly climbed to an altitude of 6,000 meters, when the enemy was at a distance of 35 kilometers in front of them. Coc discovered the enemy at a heading of 40 degrees to his right. MiGs dropped the auxiliary fuel tanks, increased their speed and began the attack.

Nguyen Van Coc ordered Nguyen Van Ly to attack the tail-end flight of an enemy aircraft while he attacked the aircraft in the flight, in front of the trailing flight. Coc fired his R-3S missile at a distance of 1,500-

The VPAF Mi-6 Hook heavy lift helicopters transported MiG fighters to protect against US bombing runs and to remote those underground hangars in the hills, on no less than 400 occasions. (István Toperczer Collection)

1,700 meters and broke away. He rolled his aircraft back to observe the results of his attack to see that the F-105 was burning. Nguyen Van Ly covered and supported Coc, but there were many F-4 Phantoms behind them, so he pulled up to an altitude of 7,000 meters, and then climbed to an altitude of 11,000 meters. He left the air battle zone and landed at 08:05 hours. The USAF records did not confirm Nguyen Van Coc's victory, because the Thunderchief was only damaged.

On 14 December 1967, a USAF strike package arrived from the Vietnamese – Laotian border and headed for Hanoi, where thirty F-105s and F-4s attacked the Long Bien Bridge and the Yen Phu electrical power plant. At 13:11 hours, the flight of MiG-17s; Luu Huy Chao, Le Hai, Bui Van Suu, and Nguyen Dinh Phuc, took off from Kien An and flew toward Nha Nam to attack a formation of enemy bombers approaching to bomb Kep airbase. Unexpectedly, the enemy bombers turned down over Hai Duong and then turned back to attack Hanoi. The MiG-17 flight was ordered to turn back and land.

During the afternoon, a large US Navy strike force attacked targets in the Red River Delta. At 16:14 hours, the VPAF HQ ordered a MiG-17 flight from the 923rd Fighter Regiment, Luu Huy Chao, Le Hai, Bui Van Suu, and Nguyen Dinh Phuc took off and flew on a heading of 180 degrees while climbing to an altitude of 2,000 meters. The MiG-17s made a turn to the right and climbed to an altitude of 4,000 meters. At 16:26 hours, Nguyen Dinh Phuc spotted four F-4s at a distance of 20 kilometers. The MiG-17s split into two sections and pursued the enemy, with one section, Luu Huy Chao and Le Hai, fighting at an altitude of 3,500-4,000 meters and the other section, Bui Van Suu and Nguyen Dinh Phuc, fighting at an altitude of 1,500-2,000 meters. US Navy F-8s fought the four MiG-17s. An F-8E Crusader got on the tail of Le Hai's MiG-17 and fired a missile,

DATE OF BIRTH: 22 December 1936
ENLISTED: 12 February 1954
PILOT TRAINING:
1960 – 1962 (MiG-17 – China)
1962 – 1963 (Vietnam)
1963 – 1965 (China)
WAR SERVICE AND UNIT:
1965 – 1975 (923rd Fighter Regiment)
AIRCRAFT: MiG-17
HERO OF THE VIETNAMESE PEOPLE'S ARMED FORCES: 22 December 1969
RANK: Senior Colonel

AIR VICTORIES: 6 kills
(2 F-4s, 2 F-8s, 1 F-105, 1 C-47 – VPAF official credit)

DATE	AIRCRAFT	UNIT	KILL – US PILOT (VPAF – US DATABASES)
17 Apr 66	MiG-17	923.	C-47 – US not confirmed
26 Apr 66	MiG-17	923.	F-4C – US not confirmed
12 Aug 66	MiG-17	923.	F-105D – Allison (KIA) (AAA)
21 Sep 66	MiG-17	923.	F-4C – Kellems, Thomas (Rescued) (Shared)
14 Dec 67	MiG-17	923.	F-8 – US not confirmed (Shared)
17 Dec 67	MiG-17	923.	F-4D – Fleenor, Boyer (POWs)
03 Jan 68	MiG-17	923.	F-4 – US not confirmed (Shared)
14 Jun 68	MiG-17	923.	F-4 – US not confirmed
29 Jul 68	MiG-17	923.	F-8 – US not confirmed (Shared)

Shenyang J-5 (MiG-17F Fresco C), No. 2011 (9 kills) of the 923rd Fighter Regiment, 1967
This unusual camouflaged Shenyang J-5 was used by Luu Huy Chao to shot down an F-8 Crusader of US Navy, on 14 December 1967. (ARTWORK: BALÁZS KAKUK)

but it missed. The air battle happened from an altitude of 5,000 meters to a low altitude. The F-8s were constantly making sharp turns and the MiG-17s were not able to cut inside the turns to get into position to fire their guns. The Crusaders repeatedly firing missiles, but the MiGs took evasive maneuvers. The F-8s tried to force the MiG-17s to fly toward the ocean, but the MiG-17s kept circling and did not move far from their original position. Le Hai, flew his aircraft in three tight circles but was still unable to shake the F-8 behind him. Luu Huy Chao saw Le Hai's hopeless situation, and he dove down from above, firing a burst from his cannons. The F-8 finally turned away to avoid the hit. The second MiG-17 pair, Bui Van Suu and Nguyen Dinh Phuc, was engaged in a separate dogfight against three F-8E Crusaders. During seven minutes of air battle, all four MiG-17s fired their guns and Luu Huy Chao shot down one F-8E over Ninh Giang (not confirmed by US Navy records). At 16:30 hours, the command post ordered the pilots to break off the engagement. Luu Huy Chao led his flight up along the Red River, at extremely low altitude over the river to return to Kien An airfield. After the pilots broke off, Luu Huy Chao, Le Hai and Nguyen Dinh Phuc turned back to counterattack when they discovered F-8s pursuing them. The Crusaders dispersed and headed back out to the Gulf of Tonkin. Luu Huy Chao called his comrades to check on them, when Nguyen Dinh Phuc was trailing about 6-7 kilometers behind the rest of the flight. At that moment, six F-8s swept in from the direction of Hai Duong and Phuc turned back toward them. Lt Wyman launched a Sidewinder missile from his F-8E and hit the left side of the fuselage of Phuc's MiG-17. The MiG crashed and Nguyen Dinh Phuc was killed in Dang Quan, Hai Duong Province.

In this air battle the US Navy had changed its tactics. Rather that striving to dogfight with the MiG-17s, they strove to fly away quickly to lure the MiGs to follow them. When the MiGs refused to chase them, the American aircraft waited for the flight of MiGs to form up together to return to the airfield. They then split up into small sections and snuck up, taking advantage of times when MiG pilots dropped their guard, to make surprise attacks when the MiGs were low on fuel and pilots were tired. This experience taught North Vietnamese MiG pilots lessons in timing, formation, and support tactics when breaking off engagements to return to base when the MiGs were heavily outnumbered.

Three days later, in the afternoon of 17 December, a MiG-17 flight assisted three MiG-21s in attacking a formation of 32 F-105s and F-4s heading toward Hanoi. After receiving information that the Americans would attack Hanoi, the VPAF HQ guessed that they would come from two directions: Sam Neua – Yen Chau – Yen Bai – Tuyen Quang, along the Tam Dao ridge and Sam Neua – Suoi Rut – Hoa Binh, along Route No.6. The VPAF Commanders Nguyen Van Tien and Dao Dinh Luyen decided: if they came from the first direction, MiG-21s would fly over Nghia Lo to intercept them before Tuyen Quang and MiG-17s would fly over Doan

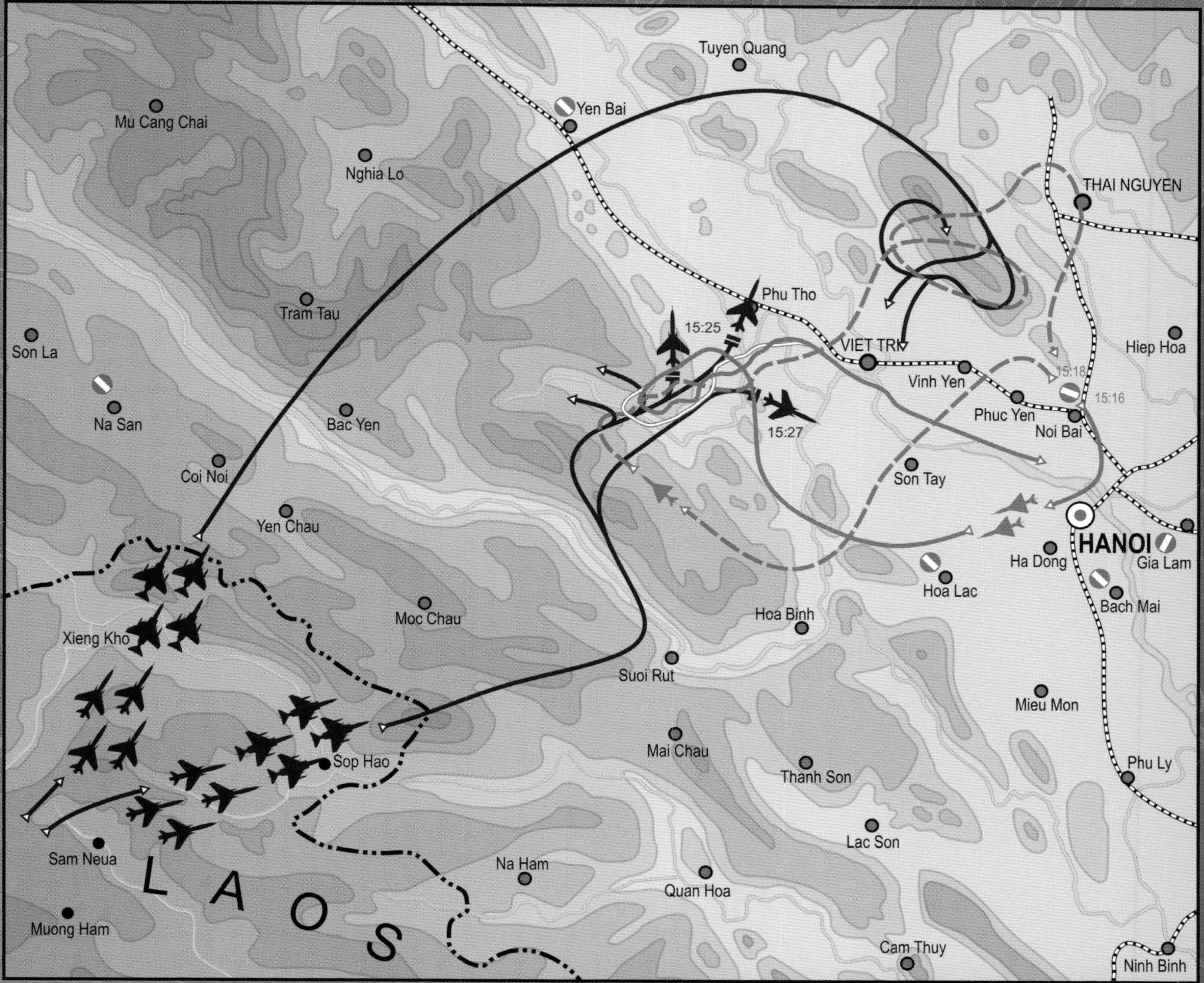

On 17 December 1967, Vu Ngoc Dinh, Nguyen Dang Kinh and Nguyen Hong Nhi used MiG-21s of the 921st Fighter Regiment to shoot downthree F-105 Thunderchiefs over Thanh Son area by Vietnamese records.
(CARTOGRAPH: PÉTER BARNA)

Hung to intercept them before Son Duong. If they came from a second direction, a MiG-21 pair would fly to Van Yen, one MiG-21 to Quan Hoa to intercept them before Suoi Rut and cover MiG-17s. The Kep-based two MiG -21s and four MiG-17s from the "Doan Z" also joined to the air battles to the west, but they had no results.

At 15:10 hours, an enemy appeared, but they did not fly to Yen Bai, but over Phu Tho. Six minutes later, a pair of MiG-21s, Vu Ngoc Dinh and Nguyen Dang Kinh, took off from Noi Bai. The MiG-21s were guided to Hoa Lac, over Vien Nam Mountain, turned right to Thanh Son, turned left and made an "S" maneuver to 7 kilometers west of Yen Lap. The enemy group of 16 aircraft approached from Thanh Ba to Phu Ninh at a heading of 70 degrees. At 15:25 hours, Vu Ngoc Dinh detected F-105s and F-4s, at a distance of 10 to 15 kilometers. Covered by Kinh, Vu Ngoc

Dinh fired two missiles and shot down two F-105 Thunderchiefs, but US records confirmed only 1Lt Ellis' F-105D as a loss. The MiG-21s continued to fight, but then landed at Noi Bai airbase. Two minutes later, after the flight of Dinh – Kinh took off, Nguyen Hong Nhi left Noi Bai with his MiG-21. He turned to Son Tay – Hoa Binh, and then turned right at Suoi Rut, bearing 360 degrees to Yen Lap to intercept the enemy group of 12 aircraft. At 15:27 hours, approaching a heading of 45 degrees, Nguyen Hong Nhi detected F-105s and F-4s, at a distance of 10 to 15 kilometers. He fired an R-3S missile and shot down an F-105 over the Thanh Son area, and broke off by an "S" maneuver to Phu Tho – Viet Tri – Vinh Yen to land at Noi Bai airbase.

While the MiG-21s scattered the bombers and brought down three F-105s, the Gia Lam-based MiG-17s ventured to attack the Phantoms. At 15:18 hours, a flight of MiG-17s, Luu Huy Chao, Nguyen Hong Thai, Bui Van Suu and Le Hai, took off from Gia Lam to intercept enemy flights at the west of Hanoi and fought at Viet Tri – Phu Tho. The MiG-17s turned north toward Hanoi and at the next moment to Hoa Lac. At 15:27 hours, Luu Huy Chao detected 4 F-105s and 4 F-4s at a distance of 10 kilometers. He shot down an F-4D Phantom, and seven minute later, Bui Van Suu also shot down an F-4C Phantom. At 15:39 hours, Luu Huy Chao reported not seeing Nguyen Hong Thai. He was killed in action by Capt Baker's F-4D Phantom, who was an exchange pilot from the USMC to the USAF. The other three MiG-17s landed at Gia Lam airfield.

In the morning of 19 December 1967, the Americans used large forces to attack Hanoi from the northwest and southeast, and they used separated groups of 8 aircraft from the east and northeast. The VPAF continued to fight in a northwest direction, as on 17 December, and they were ready to respond if an enemy came from Sam Neua, to Suoi Rut – Hoa Binh to attack targets west of Hanoi. The MiG- 17s and MiG-21s of "Doan Z" fought east and northeast of Hanoi, while SAM and AAA units covered the southeast region. At 07:04 hours, the radar station determined 8 American aircraft at an altitude of 4,000 meters en route Yen Chau – Yen Bai. At 07:06 hours, a pair of MiG-21s, Nguyen Dang Kinh and Bui Duc Nhu, was ordered to take off from Noi Bai. The GCI suggested not attacking the enemy group of 8 aircraft, because they had changed their route to Doan Hung – Son Duong. If the MiG-21s attacked, they had to intercept the enemy at Phu Luong, making it difficult to cooperate with MiG-17s. So the MiG-21s flew to Son Tay – Hoa Binh. When the MiG-21s arrived over Hoa Binh, enemy strikers approached not as the North Vietnamese supposed, so the command ordered the MiG-21s to turn to Vu Ban, and then turn back left. At 07:19 hours, the radar station reported the second group of 8 aircraft at an altitude of 4,000 meters, which was from Yen Chau to Tuyen Quang. The MiG-21s were guided from Hoa Binh to Yen Lap. At Thanh Son, they turned left to close the distance and then turned right to take a bearing of 360 degrees. At 07:25 hours, enemy aircraft were over the Doan Thuong railway station. The enemy formation suddenly turned to Phu Tho, so the MiG-21s changed their flying direction to 80 degrees, diagonally to the front of the enemy's left, then in a ring to fold back. Nguyen Dang Kinh detected F-4s and F-105s, at a distance of 12 kilometers, and fired an R-3S missile. He shot down an F- 4 Phantom at 3,000 meters altitude to the northeast of Phu Tho. Command ordered the MiG-21 pair to break off and they landed safely at Noi Bai. The US did not list an F-4 Phantom loss on that day.

Meanwhile, the MiG-17 flight was on Class One Alert at Gia Lam airfield. At 07:03 hours, Vu The Xuan, Nguyen Quang Sinh, Nguyen Hong Diep and Nguyen Phi Hung started their MiG-17 engines. Four minutes later, the MiG flight took off and turned north of Hanoi, toward Son Tay – Hoa Lac, at an altitude of 2,000 meters.

At 07:13 hours, Vu The Xuan reported at an altitude of 2,000 meters, where visual was bad. The GCI control followed both MiG-21s, which were guided to attack the second group of 8 aircraft, and changed the MiG-17s' route. When the MiG-21s began to close in on the enemy, GCI control requested to let the MiG-17s to leave Hoa Lac and intercept the enemy at Phu Tho. Commander Dao Dinh Luyen ordered MiG-21s to attack first and the MiG-17s later. The MiG-17s were guided to Son Tay – Thanh Son, where they turned right to Phu Tho at an altitude of 2,000 meters and were informed about the targets' positions. The MiG-17s attacked them with an approach angle of 90 degrees. Nguyen Quang Sinh detected F-4 Phantoms, at a distance of 10 kilometers, and several F-105 Thunderchiefs, and reported there were four F-4 Phantoms behind. The flight leader of the MiG-17s assigned tasks and commanded to attack. Vu The Xuan turned in and dove on the lead enemy aircraft, which was flying at a lower altitude. At a distance of 500 meters he fired a burst of cannon shells. The F-105D was hit, rolled over, and then dove toward the ground. Nguyen Hong Diep and Nguyen Phi Hung

At the end of 1967, Nguyen Hong Nhi, Pham Thanh Ngan and Nguyen Van Coc discuss their experiences about air tactics against US aircraft, in front of an unusually camouflaged MiG-21PFM.
(István Toperczer Collection)

On 19 December 1967, Vu The Xuan (in the cockpit of No.2077) and his wingman, Nguyen Phi Hung, shot down two F-105s over Tam Dao Hill, close to Hanoi. One of kills was credited as the fourth air victory for Nguyen Phi Hung by VPAF records. (István Toperczer Collection)

chased another flight of F-105Ds and both fired their guns. Nguyen Phi Hung fired a long burst at an F-105 Thunderchief, and he saw his shells hitting the fuselage of the enemy aircraft. Vu The Xuan and Nguyen Phi Hung each shot down an F-105 Thunderchief, although no losses were recorded by the Americans on this day. At 07:44 hours, all MiGs landed safely at Noi Bai airbase.

At the west of Hanoi, four MiG-17s and 2 MiG-21s from "Doan Z" also participated to hit the enemy, but they had no results.

In the afternoon the air battles continued. After receiving information that between 15:00 and 15:30 hours there would be 60 enemy sorties, the VPAF Commanders, Nguyen Van Tien and Dao Dinh Luyen, decided to use MiG-17s and MiG-21s of the "Doan Z" to fight west and northwest Hanoi. The GCI guessed that at 15:30 hours, enemies would arrive to targets and requested to take off not later than 15:09 hours. The 921st Fighter Regiment Commander, Tran Hanh, and the 923rd Fighter Regiment Commander, Nguyen Phuc Trach, ordered take-offs from 14:59 to 15:05 hours, but commander Nguyen Van Tien thought it was too soon and he agreed only at 15:07 hours.

Two minutes later, the MiG-21 flight of Dang Ngoc Ngu and Nguyen Van Coc took off from Noi Bai. The MiG-21s flew to Luong Son – Vu Ban, but the enemy had not come yet, so they turned left at Vu Ban, took a bearing of 270 degrees to Mai Chau. At 15:20 hours, two American flights were 50 kilometers east of Sam Neua, heading to Suoi Rut. The MiG-21s kept their bearing at 270 degrees. One minute later, radars also detected the targets, but the MiGs were already head-on with them and lost the signal after a minute. At 15:22 hours, the 921st Fighter Regiment command requested assistance, but it was too late, so the MiGs had to break off and landed at Kep airbase.

Also at 15:09 hours, the MiG-17 flight of Vu The Xuan, Nguyen Quang Sinh, Nguyen Hong Diep and Nguyen Phi Hung took off from Gia Lam (after the morning battle they landed at Noi Bai and then returned to

Gia Lam), and they flew to Kim Boi. The same situation happened with the MiG-21s. The MiG-17s were ordered to turn right to Hoa Binh, then turned left to Vu Ban. At 15:21 hours, the 923rd Fighter Regiment radar detected a target. The MiG-17s turned left to Suoi Rut, approached at an angle of 90 degrees, flew straight and leveled for a minute. The pilots detected four F-4 Phantoms at a distance of 25 kilometers and, during their left turn to Hoa Binh, they saw 8 and then 12 F-4 Phantoms. The enemy, seeing the MiGs, jettisoned their bombs and turned left to the northwest. The fight took place from Hoa Binh to Suoi Rut. At 15:28 hours, the 923rd Fighter Regiment command ordered the MiGs to break off to avoid a disadvantage. Until 15:34 hours, all the MiG-17s were able to break off and landed at Hoa Lac airfield.

Based on the air battles against the USAF aircraft on 19 December 1967, the VPAF Headquarters command post and MiG pilots concluded that the American pilots had learned lessons from the air battles of early December. The enemy had changed their tactics by having their individual flights split into two-aircraft sections in order to counter both MiG-17s and MiG-21s. However, the lead enemy flight had a hard time fighting off the MiG-17s, which had caused all the bombers to be forced to jettison their bombs in order to be able to deal with the VPAF MiGs.

In assessing the aerial encounters of 1967, the VPAF felt that the effectiveness of the force increased in fights defending Hanoi and Hai Phong. The co-operation between different types was good, just as with the units of the Air Defense Forces. A major contributing factor to the success was the quick repair of the damaged airfields. Unfortunately amongst pilots, the victory-defeat-reinforcement-victory line of action was more prevailing than the required victory-improvement-victory combination. During 1967 there were 129 aerial combats with the loss of 124 US aircraft (MiG-17 – 74 kills).

Close to Kep airbase, the North Korean pilots' cemetery is in the forest on Hoang Hill at Tan Dinh village, Lang Giang District, Bac Giang Province. The 14 tombstones are carved with Vietnamese – Korean languages names of the martyrs.
(ISTVÁN TOPERCZER)

Fourth year and Fourth Military District – 1968

Early in the morning of 3 January 1968, the radar stations reported an EB-66C coming from the northwest. At 07:33 hours, American aircraft appeared over Mai Chau Province. Four MiG-17s of the 923rd Fighter Regiment took off from Gia Lam at 07:39 hours. Luu Huy Chao, Le Hong Diep, Bui Van Suu and Le Hai were directed over Thai Nguyen, but the haze prevented visual contact and therefore they missed the rendezvous with the enemy. Following the order to turn back and land, they suddenly spotted eight F-4s flying at a heading of 45 degrees to port at a distance of 8 kilometers. Luu Huy Chao increased his speed and began to chase an F-4 Phantom, just as his wingman Le Hong Diep got a hit and ejected safely from his MiG-17. Luu Huy Chao also took a pounding, but managed to keep his tattered aircraft in the air and continued fighting. Veering away and down on the numerous F-4s that appeared low on his left, he accelerated and soon found himself behind the tail of a Phantom. After firing three bursts from 700 meters he observed no hits. Luu Huy Chao's MiG was hit and he disengaged, set a course for Bac Ninh, and landed at Noi Bai. Bui Van Suu pursued another F-4 Phantom flight, opened fire, but missed too. Turning back, he caught sight of more F-4s and, closing to 500 meters of one, he opened fire and apparently damaged an F-4 Phantom. The other enemy aircraft escaped into the clouds and disappeared. Bui Van Suu descended to low altitude and returned to Noi Bai airbase at 08:15 hours. Le Hai also attacked an F-4, squeezing the trigger from 800 meters, but the F-4 escaped unharmed. The North Vietnamese pilot spent the next moments of his life avoiding AAMs being shot at him. In doing so, he became disorientated and ran into friendly AAA fire over Viet Tri. Le Hai reassured himself and flew along the Red River to land at Gia Lam airfield at 08:16 hours.

In the morning of 3 January 1968, Le Hong Diep is preparing to take-off with his MiG-17F at Gia Lam airfield. His wingman, Bui Van Suu, shot down an F-4 Phantom according to VPAF sources, and Luu Huy Chao's MiG was damaged during this dogfight.
(István Toperczer Collection)

Date of Birth: 11 December 1943
Enlisted: 1961
Pilot training:
1961 – 1965 (MiG-17 – Soviet Union)
1969 (MiG-19 – Vietnam)
War Service and Unit:
1965 – 1969 (921st Fighter Regiment)
1969 – 1975 (925th Fighter Regiment)
Aircraft: MiG-17, MiG-19
Rank: Senior Colonel

Air Victories: 4 kills
(3 F-4s, 1 F-105 – VPAF official credit)

Date	Aircraft	Unit	Kill – US Pilot (VPAF – US databases)
21 Sep 67	MiG-17	923.	F-4B – US not confirmed
06 Nov 67	MiG-17	923.	F-105 – US not confirmed
17 Dec 67	MiG-17	923.	F-4C – US not confirmed
03 Jan 68	MiG-17	923.	F-4 – US not confirmed

Shenyang J-5 (MiG-17F Fresco C), No. 2037 of the 923rd Fighter Regiment, 1968
By VPAF records, Bui Van Suu used this MiG-17 on 3 January 1968,
when he claimed an F-4 Phantom kill over Thai Nguyen. (Artwork: Balázs Kakuk)

In the first month of 1968, all together there were 29 new MiG-21 pilots that returned from the Soviet Union and they were all posted to the 921st Fighter Regiment. These freshly trained MiG-pilots were sent to air battles immediately.

Early the same morning, on 3 January 1968, another radar detected an EB-66 aircraft operating at northwest region. At 07:33 hours, American aircraft popped up over Moc Chau. A pair of MiG-21s scrambled from Noi Bai, piloted by Nguyen Dang Kinh and Bui Duc Nhu. They were heading towards Thanh Son in Vinh Phu Province. Taking advantage of the fact that the 48 American aircraft were flying against the sun, they attacked the formation. There was no contact between Nguyen Dang Kinh and Bui Duc Nhu and they lost each other during the engagement, but still managed to shoot down an F-105 each. On returning to Kep airbase, Nguyen Dang Kinh overran the runway and broke the nose landing gear and damaged the cockpit. Nguyen Dang Kinh could only be extracted from the cockpit after the canopy was broken.

After the morning engagements, due to Nguyen Dang Kinh's aircraft crashing at the end of the runway, only one MiG-21 was left able to fly a combat mission. Ha Van Chuc and Bui Duc Nhu were taking turns on duty. In the afternoon, at 15:00 hours, a group of 36 American aircraft was reported to be on their way to Yen Chau, heading for Hanoi. At 15:16 hours, Ha Van Chuc took off and found a formation of F-105s at an altitude of 5,500 meters over Yen Chau, but he was overshot by four F-4s before he could open an attack. Turning back, he climbed to 10,000 meters only to notice that the Thunderchiefs were flying under him. Diving to 5,000 meters he prepared for an attack, but the F-105s turned around to make a counter-attack and he ran away by climbing to 9,000 meters. Four more F-105s were to his left, which he tried unsuccessfully to approach by diving, but soon he was back at 9,000 meters looking for a new target. By this time he only had 700 liters of fuel left in his aircraft. Looking towards Tam Dao, he saw a group of eight F-105s and after descending to 3,500 meters, he attacked them, bringing down Col Bean's F-105D Thunderchief with an R-3S missile. The other F-105s were forced to jettison their bomb loads and this time they gave up their plans to bomb Hanoi. Only Ha Van Chuc's claim was confirmed by USAF records.

Ha Van Chuc participated in air battles against F-105s on 14 January, when the intelligence reported that the USAF might send between 30 and 40 aircraft, F-105s and F-4s, from the west to attack targets along Route No.2. At 07:37 hours, EB-66 Destroyers EW aircraft and ten minutes later other flights of American aircraft were detected, at a heading from 230 to 265 degrees. Ha Van Chuc and Nguyen Duc Thuan took off from Noi Bai with their MiG-21s and flew out on a heading of 270 degrees at 07:45 hours. After take-off, they turned to a heading of 290 degrees. The MiGs increased their speed and turned right to a heading of 90 degrees. Ha Van Chuc spotted four aircraft headed in the opposite direction

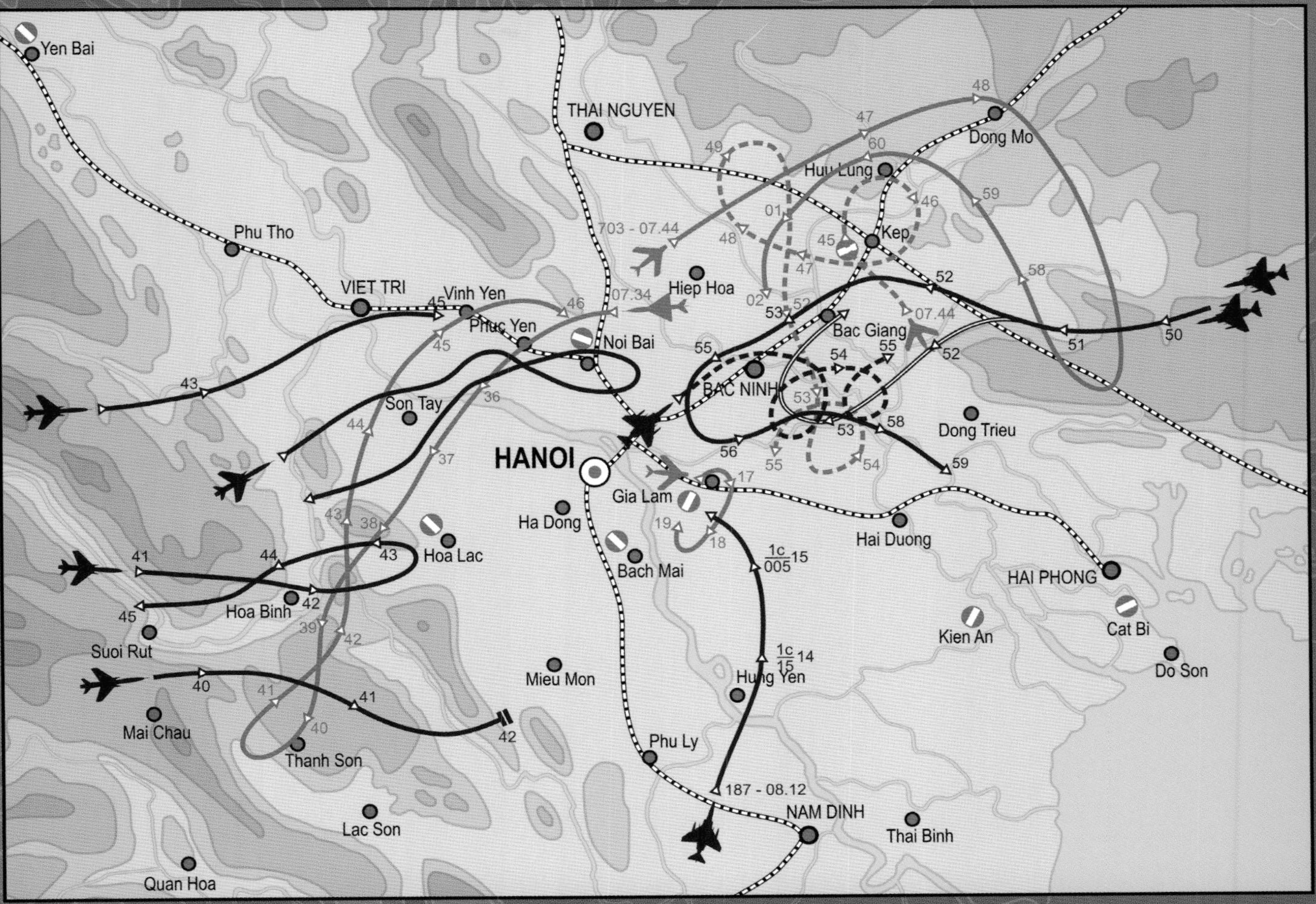

On 3 January 1968, a MiG-21 pair of Nguyen Dang Kinh and Bui Duc Nhu shot down two F-105 Thunderchiefs, while MiG-17 pilots Bui Van Suu and Luu Huy Chao also claimed one F-4 Phantom kill over Bac Ninh – Bac Giangby Vietnamese records. (CARTOGRAPH: PÉTER BARNA)

from their MiG-21s and at a lower altitude. At the same time, MiG-pilots discovered four more aircraft to the left front of MiGs. Chuc and Thuan switched on MiG-21 afterburners and attacked the flight of F-105 Thunderchiefs. The flight of F-105s was 3-4 kilometers ahead of MiG-21s and Chuc wanted to fire his R-3S Atoll missile, but it did not leave the pylon. Chuc immediately dropped a wing and pressed the firing button again. The Atoll missile left the pylon and headed straight for the F-105. Maj Horne's F-105D Thunderchief got hit in its wing, setting the aircraft on fire and it went down east of Yen Bai. The pilot was listed as killed in action and the other F-105s jettisoned their bombs. Chuc broke off to the right, and climbed to an altitude of 9,000 meters to fly back to the airbase. Meanwhile, as Chuc attacked the F-105D, Nguyen Duc Thuan checked on all sides and noticed a flight of four enemy aircraft making a right turn below his MiG. He started to chase an F-4 Phantom. However, after the two sides engaged in a turning dogfight for a short time and being unable to get an enemy aircraft into his sights, Thuan joined Ha Van Chuc in returning to Noi Bai airbase. Unfortunately, Ha Van Chuc's MiG-21 was damaged and he was wounded in the dogfight. Five days later Ha Van Chuc died in Hospital No.108.

The North Vietnamese MiG-21s had accelerated away and escaped, in accordance with their tactic of "fast attack – fast withdrawal," during this air battle.

In the afternoon of the same day, two MiG-21s of the 921st Fighter Regiment, with Nguyen Dang Kinh and Dong Van Song, scored the second EB-66 kill on the afternoon 14 January. The radar station detected EB-66 activity at Road No.15 and a pair of MiG-21s took off from Noi Bai. The MiG-21s flew from Phuc Yen, headed south and took advantage of the altitude. At 15:33 hours, the target was turning right at 30 kilometers south of Moc Chau to Thuong Xuan. Accordingly, the MiGs were at Phu Ly and made a turn to adjust their position and then flew to the south. At 15:40 hours, enemy aircraft arrived 10 kilometers northwest of Thuong Xuan and began to turn left to Moc Chau. The MiGs turned right back to a northern direction and accelerated at Dong Son. At 15:44 hours, the Americans were stable, flying from Ngoc Lac to Lang Chanh. The MiG-21s turned left, to follow, but lost them, behind by 35km. After 3 minutes, one EB-66 was discovered at a distance of 12km. Nguyen Dang Kinh shot twice without any results, while Dong Van Song flew closest to the EB-66. He fired an R-3S missile and hit the starboard engine of EB-66 Destroyer. The American electronic jamming aircraft came down about 65 kilometers east of Sam Neua.

On 3 February, in the afternoon, the enemy was detected about 30 kilometers south of Moc Chau. They were at an altitude of 10,000 meters with a speed of 950 km/h, about 170 kilometers from Noi Bai. At 15:50 hours, a pair of Pham Thanh Ngan and Nguyen Van Coc took off and turned south, keeping a speed of 850 km/h, then ascended slowly to an altitude of 6,000 meters toward Quy Chau. At 15:54 hours, Mai Van

On 3 February 1968, Nguyen Van Coc and Pham Thanh Ngan attacked an enemy formation close to the Laotian border. Pham Thanh Ngan shot down the first USAF F-102 Delta Dagger in the air battle, over North Vietnam.
(István Toperczer Collection)

Cuong took off to close air support and flew toward Thanh Son, at an altitude of 10,000 meters to Suoi Rut. The pair kept the flight heading of 280 degrees over Road No.12A, at an altitude of 10,000 meters. Pham Thanh Ngan reported about the EB-66 at a distance of 5 kilometers, over Que Phong. He had turned left and, when arrived behind the target, he did not see the EB-66 but two fighters instead. He discovered a close air support team and launched the first missile, but it did not leave its rail. He launched a second missile and the enemy Wiggins' F-102 Delta Dagger aircraft was on fire. Nguyen Van Coc also fired a missile from a shorter distance, but with no result. The command ordered to break off. When this MiG-21 pair began to attack, Mai Van Cuong turned south to assist, but considered that his fuel was not enough and he was ordered to turn back. When the main flight was back to Noi Bai, Mai Van Cuong left Thanh Son. All MiGs landed safely at Noi Bai from the east. This was the first F-102A which was shot down by a MiG-21 over North Vietnam.

In the early morning of 5 February 1968, the USAF sent a large formation of F-105s, escorted by flights of F-4 Phantoms to attack targets in the Son Duong, Tuyen Quang and Thai Nguyen areas. At 07:39 hours, Nguyen Ngoc Do and Hoang Bieu, from the 921st Fighter Regiment, took off and climbed to an altitude of 4,000 meters, heading in a direction of 310 degrees over Son Duong and Hoa Binh. Five minutes later, they were ordered to turn left to a heading of 220 degrees. When the enemy was about 15 kilometers from the MiG-21s, Hoang Bieu spotted them. At the same time Nguyen Ngoc Do saw a group of F-105s flying across their front from left to right. The F-105s were followed by an escort-flight of four F-4 Phantoms flying in an extended step-ladder formation.

The MiG pilots made a hard turn to pursue the enemy formation, which was approaching to attack targets in the Thai Nguyen area. The F-4 Phantoms were assigned to MiG suppression duty, but they failed to spot the MiG-21s. The American F-4s were looked for by North Vietnamese aircraft. Meanwhile, Do and Bieu following the tactic of "fast attack – deep penetration" appeared, flew over the top of the escort flight, and closed with the F-105 Thunderchiefs.

After scanning the American formation, Nguyen Ngoc Do decided to fire one missile at the F-4 Phantoms in order to force them to break their formation. When the enemy aircraft saw the MiG-21 firing a missile, the F-4 pilots immediately split up and broke formation. Nguyen Ngoc Do flew right past the F-4s and closed on the flight of F-105s flying out in front. He fired an R-3S missile from a distance of 1,500 meters, which then headed straight at the enemy aircraft, that turned into a ball of fire. After this hit, Nguyen Ngoc Do rolled his aircraft back and he saw Capt Lasiter's F-105D Thunderchief was shot down by his missile. He quickly broke off and headed back to land at Noi Bai airbase. The other F-4s turned back to attack the MiGs and fired one AIM-7 Sparrow missile after another at the MiG, but both missiles missed. Nguyen Ngoc Do took maximum advantage of the MiG-21s ability to make sharp turns at high speed and he pulled into a climb up to 10,000 meters. The enemy aircraft were quite some distance behind him, Nguyen Ngoc Do climbed to an altitude of 10,000 meters, turned back toward his base, and landed at the airfield. It was Nguyen Ngoc Do's sixth air victory and his 10th air battle during the Vietnam War.

Presumably, because of the difference in time zones, the date that the North Vietnamese records claimed for Nguyen Ngoc Do's air victory was next day (5 February 1968), while USAF records mentioned 4 February 1968.

Between April and October 1968, the Americans carried out 79,000 missions against the 4th Military District (4th MD) of North Vietnam from the Lam River (Nghe An Province) to the Gianh River (Quang Binh Province). The VPAF, apart from the defense of Hanoi, took active part in protecting the transport routes of the 4th MD as well as fights on front "B" (South Vietnam) and front "C" (Laos). Apart from aerial warfare, there were considerable preparations for ground and sea battles. The Americans felt that in the 4th MD, the North Vietnamese MiGs were not able to fight effectively and so they did not attach special importance to their operations. It is true that the VPAF had problems, since the American carrier groups were very close. The country is narrow and long in this region, with mountains on one side and the sea on the other. The weather is also usually bad and very unpredictable.

Commander in Chief Nguyen Van Tien, Chief of the General Staff Tran Manh, his deputy Nguyen Phuc Trach, and other high ranking VPAF officers visited the 4th Military District to assess the state of airfields study weather conditions and enemy tactics. The construction of new airfields in the 4th MD was ordered along with the reconstruction of existing ones, and Tho Xuan in Thanh Hoa Province was soon to be opened. The few serviceable aircraft were regularly subjected to temporary deployments to Noi Bai, Gia Lam, Kep, Hoa Lac, Kien An, Tho Xuan, and Vinh airfields, according to operational requirements.

The ground crewmen make a post-flight check on a MiG-21PFM of the 921st Fighter Regiment at Noi Bai airbase. The MiG lacks a centerline auxiliary fuel tank, so perhaps the fighter was on an unsuccessful combat mission, during March of 1968.
(István Toperczer Collection)

DATE OF BIRTH: 1 November 1934
ENLISTED: 16 June 1953
PILOT TRAINING:
1956 – 1964 (MiG-17 – China)
1966 (MiG-21 – Vietnam)
WAR SERVICE AND UNIT:
1964 – 1973 (921st Fighter Regiment)
AIRCRAFT: MiG-21
HERO OF THE VIETNAMESE PEOPLE'S ARMED FORCES: 25 August 1970
RANK: Major General

AIR VICTORIES: 6 kills
(2 F-105s, 3 F-4s, 1 RF-101 – VPAF official credit)

DATE	AIRCRAFT	UNIT	KILL – US PILOT (VPAF – US DATABASES)
30 Apr 67	MiG-21	921.	F-105F – Thorness, Johnson (POWs)
05 May 67	MiG-21	921.	F-105D – Shively (POW) (AAA)
20 Jul 67	MiG-21	921.	RF-4C – Corbitt, Bare (KIA) (26-Jul-67 by USAF)
02 Aug 67	MiG-21	921.	F-105 – US not confirmed
16 Sep 67	MiG-21	921.	RF-101C – Patterson (AAA)
27 Sep 67	MiG-21	921.	F-105 damaged
05 Feb 68	MiG-21	921.	F-105D – Lasiter (POW) (04-Feb-68 by USAF)

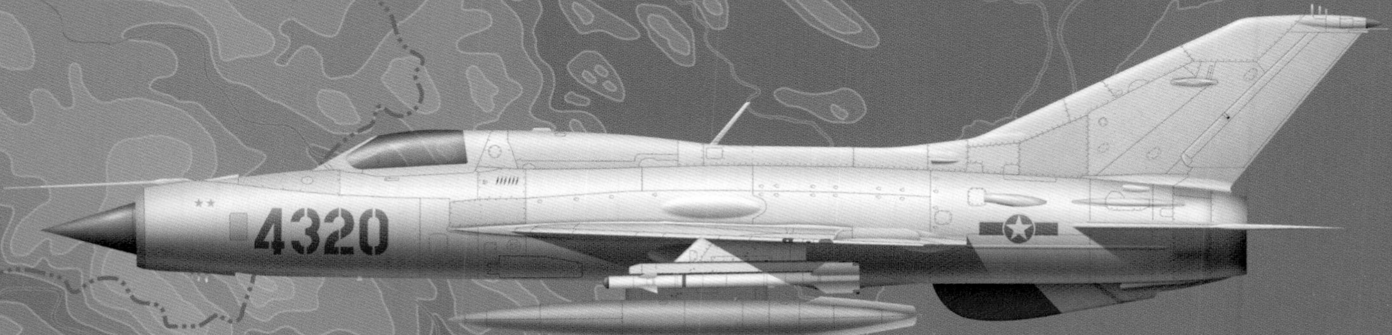

MiG-21PFL Fishbed D, No. 4320 (2 kills) of the 921st Fighter Regiment, 1968
On 5 February 1968, Nguyen Ngoc Do used this MiG-21PFL to launch a R-3S missile against Capt Lasiter's F-105D Thunderchief (60-5384) over Tuyen Quang. By USAF records this F-105D was lost one day earlier, on 4 February at Thai Nguyen. (ARTWORK: BALÁZS KAKUK)

From April of 1968, the MiG-17 flights were active over the 4th Military District of North Vietnam. Tran Hanh's MiG-17 F Fresco C, Red 2010 is seen in the military museum of Vinh city.
(István Toperczer)

There were communication and control centers all the way from Tho Xuan to Quang Binh. Headquarters designated them as X1, X2, X3... (at Tho Xuan, Do Luong, Anh Son...), which were arranged on duty shifts in two levels of navigation.

In May, three flights of MiG-21s, under the command of Dang Ngoc Ngu, Nguyen Van Coc, and Nguyen Van Minh, were sent to Tho Xuan.

Early morning on 7 May 1968, the VPAF HQ guessed the enemy might attacked the Route No.7 area. The MiG-21 pair of Nguyen Dang Kinh and Nguyen Van Lung, after take-off from Noi Bai, flew to Con Cuong – Anh Son, and then west to Do Luong as a diversion and to cover at high altitude. At 08:23 hours, another MiG-21 pair, Dang Ngoc Ngu and Nguyen Van Coc took off from Tho Xuan airfield, and kept low altitude, alongside Route No.15 to Do Luong. During the flight route, the MiGs had to navigate by themselves to avoid low clouds and rain, but kept landmarks and planned altitudes.

As a member of the 921st Fighter Regiment, Nguyen Van Coc describes this air battle:

Together with my leader Dang Ngoc Nhu, we took off from Tho Xuan on the 7 May 1968. A second pair of MiGs with Nguyen Dang Kinh and Nguyen Van Lung took off as an escort of our flight. Because of poor co-ordination with the air defense forces, the MiGs were mistaken for American fighters and the AAA opened fire on us. This was not the only mistake as Dang Ngoc Nhu first mistook the escort MiGs for Americans and preparing for an attack dropped his fuel tanks, but soon he recognized them as North Vietnamese. We made three circles of Combat Air Patrol over Do Luong before being informed of approaching fighters from the direction of the sea, this time real Americans. Dang Ngoc Nhu noticed two F-4 Phantoms 5 kilometers to the starboard and, due to the very cloudy weather had to make a tight turn for the attack but was unable to get into firing position. I could not follow my leader and was fell behind by some 7 kilometers. I was looking for my leader but at the same time noticed that I was running low on fuel and wanted to land at Tho Xuan. At this moment I noticed a Phantom ahead of me at an altitude of 2,500 meters. I went after it and launched two missiles when at a distance of 1,500 meters. The US Navy F-4B Phantom (Christensen/Kramer) of VF-92 from the USS Enterprise crashed in flames into the sea, after which both of us made a safe landing back at Tho Xuan.

This was the first aerial victory that the VPAF achieved over the 4th Military District. From then on, the Americans regularly attacked the airfields at Vinh and Dong Hoi and, using the radars on the carrier, controlled the airspace from Vinh Linh to Ninh Binh. When threatened, US aircraft regularly escaped towards the sea and lured the MiGs towards the carrier group, where they were met with anti-aircraft fire.

Following endeavors with MiG-21s in May 1968, a pair of MiG-17s of the 923rd Fighter Regiment was dispatched south again in morning of 14 June 1968.

The MiG-17 pair of Luu Huy Chao and Le Hai moved from Gia Lam to Tho Xuan at 08:30 hours. At 09:30 hours, they were in Class Two Alert. In the afternoon, radar detected several enemy groups operating 60 kilometers east of Sot Mouth (Nghen River) and then fly to Dien Chau.

The camouflaged MiG-17F Fresco is armed with an ORO-57K rocket pod on an underwing pylon. The MiG-21US and MiG-21F-13s also wait for the next mission in the background, at Noi Bai airbase.
(István Toperczer Collection)

During three months of 1968, Dinh Ton shot down three AQM-34 Firebees and one F-4 Phantom with a MiG-21PFM of the 921st Fighter Regiment.
(István Toperczer Collection)

Luu Huy Chao and Le Hai started the engines of their MiG-17s, took off from Tho Xuan at 14:34 hours and climbed to 500 meters. Following Route No.15 at 650 km/h, they soon reached Nghia Dan where they climbed up to 1,000 meters. Over Thanh Chuong they were flying at 1,500 meters when GCI warned them of six F-4s on a heading of 100 degrees to port, flying at 3,000 meters. The MiG-17s increased their speed to 730 km/h and upon reaching 2,000 meters, Le Hai saw the American aircraft coasting in at right angles to their direction. A missile launch indicated that the enemy had spotted them, too. Le Hai jettisoned the auxiliary fuel tanks, accelerated to 800 km/h, evaded the oncoming missile, and climbed to 2,700 meters. Luu Huy Chao followed his wingman and gave cover while Le Hai was turning left and tried to hit an F-4 Phantom, but with no success. The enemy lead made a steep turn. Le Hai chose the wingman to follow, turned left, and dropped the nose of his MiG to lose some altitude and close up. From 300 meters he opened fire. After the second burst, the F-4 Phantom caught fire and crashed into the sea. Le Hai made a left climbing turn to regain his original wingman position. Suddenly, an F-4 Phantom popped up 1,000 meters in front of him. He closed in before opening fire, but not enough to hit the F-4, which escaped. Luu Huy Chao recognized the enemy's attempt to leave south-easterly, so he turned right and found an F-4 dead ahead. He fired a burst but was out of range and missed. Turning right he saw another Phantom making for the coast. Accompanied by Le Hai on his wing, Luu Huy Chao positioned himself behind his quarry and gave him three bursts. The F-4 Phantom blew up and crashed. As the rest of the US Navy Phantoms cleared to the coast, the MiG-17 pair set course for Tho Xuan. After crossing Route No.7, they flew along Route No.15 and landed at 15:00 hours. Meanwhile, an enemy group appeared 60 kilometers east of Lach Quen, so another pair of MiG-21s took off at 14:57 hours, flew to a holding area north of Nghia Dan, but the enemy flights did not come in. The US sources did not confirm two Phantom losses on that day.

Two days later, on 16 June, a MiG-21 pair, with Dinh Ton and Nguyen Tien Sam was sent from Noi Bai, at 14:30 hours, to Tho Xuan. The MiG-21s landed at 14:50 hours at Tho Xuan airfield. One hour later, they were ordered to a Class One Alert. At 16:00 hours, they took off and flew along Route No.15, at an altitude of 250-300 meters and a speed of 800 km/h. At 16:10 hours, an enemy came from Hon Mat to Dien Chau and to Route No.7. The MiG-21s turned right, and then changed their direction to Yen Thanh. After two minutes, the enemy suddenly made an "S" maneuver south of Route No.7, so the MiG-21s turned right hard to Anh Son, accelerated and ascended. A few minutes later, Nguyen Tien Sam reported fire from an AAA unit at Do Luong. When the MiG-21s crossed Route No.7, they had to turn left to Thanh Chuong to intercept head on. Dinh Ton noticed four F-4 Phantoms, 10 kilometers on his left were turning left to Do Luong and so started an attack by dropping his external fuel tanks as well as applying power. When the MiGs and the Phantoms were closing in head-on, the latter went into a dive and tried to make a run for it. The lead MiG-21 followed them and when they realized this, the Phantoms made a left turn and went into a climb. Sticking to their prey, the MiG pair followed and when the Phantoms were only 300 meters from the leader, they were already flying towards the sea. Dinh Ton continued the pursuit, increased his speed and opened fire. Cdr Wilber's F-4J of VF-102, from the USS *America* (CVA-66), exploded and the crew ejected. The wingman, Nguyen Tien Sam was providing cover for his leader. One of the American aircraft was set on fire with the first round and Dinh Ton broke away from the engagement. Back at the home base of Tho Xuan, the control tower noticed that the MiG-21s were followed by the Americans and so they made a quick landing. The Americans, afraid of an AAA ambush around the base, returned home. For Nguyen Tien Sam, this was his very first live engagement.

In the 4th Military District, the North Vietnamese MiGs continued to stand on combat alert duty, ready to intercept USAF and US Navy strike formations. During May and June of 1968, the North Vietnamese tried to attack US ships five times, with no success and losing two MiG-21s in the process. On 23 May, Ha Quang Hung's MiG was shot down by a RIM-8 Talos naval, surface-to-air missile. The pilot ejected successfully.

On 26 June, the 921st Fighter Regiment placed a flight consisting of Vu Ngoc Dinh and Bui Duc Nhu on combat alert duty. After take-off, they spotted four F-8 Crusaders from the USS *Bon Homme Richard* heading toward their MiG-21s. The F-8s were directed-in to intercept a

This MiG-17F Fresco C, of the 923rd Fighter Regiment, is undergoing maintenance in a makeshift bamboo hangar. It was a good camouflage against American bombers, because the huts were usually located in villages or agricultural co-operatives in the 4th Military District.
(István Toperczer Collection)

flight of MiG-21s near Vinh airfield. In spite of support from American electronic warfare aircraft that jammed Vietnamese radars and radio communications, Vu Ngoc Dinh and Bui Duc Nhu still were able to spot the F-8 fighters in time. The two MiG-21s made a hard turn inside, but the F-8s were also trying to get on the tails of the MiGs. The MiG-21s got into position above and behind the enemy aircraft and fired a missile at the formation of F-8 Crusaders. However, the MiG's missile failed to hit its target. The North Vietnamese records mention that one MiG-21 crashed. On that day, another Talos hit Vu Ngoc Dinh's MiG-21 and he was able to eject safely.

The pilots of the 921st and 923rd Fighter Regiments had won four air battles since the VPAF first deployed forces to the 4th Military District. The USAF and US Navy forces, which were initially surprised by the appearance of MiG fighters in the 4th Military District, so far from MiG-bases in the North, sought new methods and tactics to deal with this new threat. The US Navy decided to assign a large number of F-8 Crusaders to carry out fighter missions and deception operations designed to lure MiGs into taking off to intercept. The F-8s usually flew in a stair-step formation with extended separation between aircraft in order to be able to split up to combat North Vietnamese MiGs. The Americans also tried to draw MiG-17s into flying out over the sea, where the surface-to-air missiles of warships could fire at MiGs. The U.S. Navy usually preferred locations where there were two parallel mountain ranges in order to fly into Vietnamese airspace at low altitude to avoid the radar detection.

On 9 and 29 July, the 923rd Fighter Regiment lost its two well-experienced MiG-17 pilots; Nguyen Phi Hung (5 air victories) and Le Sy Diep were shot down by US Navy F-8 Crusaders.

Nguyen Phi Hung claimed his fifth air victory with an F-8 Crusader kill on 9 July 1968, but unfortunately he was killed by another F-8E Crusader on the same day.
(István Toperczer Collection)

In order to support MiG-17 formations, the regiment established a number of visual observation posts in the area of Cam Bridge and the Vinh airfield. The regiment also formed a forward combat element headed by GCI officer Le Viet Dien. The pilots assigned to this forward combat element were Nguyen Phi Hung and Nguyen Phu Ninh, who were ready to fly from Kep airbase to carry out the mission. According to the plan, they would secretly take off and wait to fight in the air over Thung Nua Mountain. In the afternoon of 6 July 1968, the pair of MiG-17s was ordered to take off and move to Tho Xuan airfield.

At 06:30 hours, on the morning of 9 July 1968, intelligence reported US Navy aircraft operating off the coast of the Dien Chau – Cua Hoi area of Nghe An Province. At 07:34 hours, two MiG-17s were ordered to take off and the pair was directed to fly on a heading of 170 degrees, flying east in parallel to Route No.15, at an altitude of 150 meters. The MiG-17 pilots maintained total radio silence and upon reaching Nghia Dan climbed to an altitude of 700 meters. After the MiGs passed Nghia Dan, the auxiliary ground control station informed the pilots that there were two F-4s flying over the area of Cau Cam. One moment later, Nguyen Phu Ninh spotted two F-8s, at a heading of 45 degrees to the right front, which were flying as an escort to an RF-8 reconnaissance aircraft. Nguyen Phi Hung and Nguyen Phu Ninh climbed to an altitude of 1,500 meters to make the attack. The two F-8s switched on their afterburners and made a shallow turn toward the mountains. The second MiG continued to chase them while the MiG-leader shifted position to cover him. At that time the two F-8s split up, with one Crusader continuing to fly straight and level, while the other Crusader turned to the left. Nguyen Phu Ninh pursued the F-8 turning left and increased his speed to close in on his target. He fired three bursts from his guns and saw the hits on the top of the F-8's fuselage. Ninh made a hard turn to the left to break away. Nguyen Phi Hung was pursuing another F-8 out toward the Gulf of Tonkin. The F-8 increased its speed and pulled into a sharp climb. Hung stuck right with the F-8 and he fired a burst that hit the Crusader fuselage. The command post ordered the MiGs to turn back to the coast, but no response from Hung. At that time, Hung was diving to continue chasing the F-8, but another F-8 fired a Sidewinder missile at Hung's MiG. Ninh then turned to close in with the attackers, but all three F-8s dove to a low altitude and fled out to sea. Ninh flew one complete circle looking for Hung's MiG, but did not see him. Nguyen Phu Ninh descended to a lower altitude and then returned to land at Tho Xuan airfield.

Nguyen Phi Hung managed to avoid two enemy missiles, but just as he leveled out from a turn to look around, a third missile by Lt Cdr Nichols' F-8E, of VF-191 from the USS *Ticonderoga*, hit his aircraft. When he realized that his aircraft had been hit, Hung turned back toward the coast in order to be able to eject. However, he was too low, so his ejection was unsuccessful.

Nguyen Phi Hung shot down a total of five American aircraft. During this air battle, he shot down an F-8 over Ha Tinh, which was his last and fifth victory during Vietnam War. The US Navy records did not confirm this loss.

During the early morning hours of 29 July, groups of US Navy attack bombers, supported by fighters, began attacking transportation traffic targets at Thanh Chuong – Vinh in Nghe An Province. According to the plan, MiG-17s would fight at low altitude while two MiG-21s would engage the enemy at high altitude. At the auxiliary GCI on Troc Mountain, the command duty officer was Lam Van Lich and the ground control officer was Le Viet Dien. From 09:00 hours, the commanders Dao Dinh Luyen, Tran Manh, Nguyen Phuc Trach, and Nguyen Ngoc Phieu focused on enemy operations east of Vinh, and were ordered to watch out for enemy groups that might attack Route No.7.

At 10:16 hours, a MiG-17 flight of Luu Huy Chao, Hoang Ich, Le Hai and Le Si Diep took off and formed their formation; the flight was then directed to fly on a heading of 180 degrees toward Nghia Dan. At 10:20 hours, MiG-21 pair of Pham Thanh Ngan and Nguyen Ngoc Thien took off to cover the MiG-17s without using radio. At 10:26 hours, the MiG-17s arrived at the planned orbit, but the enemy still turned at the sea. The MiGs had to wait 15 kilometers east of Tan Ky.

At 10:35 hours, the auxiliary ground control station directed the four MiG-17s to climb to an altitude of 2,000 meters. One minutes later, at an intercept angle of 140 degrees, Luu Huy Chao detected F-8s at a distance of 4km. The MiG-17s dropped their auxiliary fuel tanks and started to fight against eight F- 8 Crusaders. While the flight leader was chasing one F-8, he spotted another aircraft flying across his nose from left to right. Chao immediately turned in and fired from a distance of 400 meters and a speed of 600 km/h. His cannon shells hit the nose of F-8 Crusader, but Chao had fired all of his ammunition. When he saw the smoke from the F-8, he broke off and made a hard turn. As he rolled his MiG back, he saw a missile streaking toward Hoang Ich's MiG. He then ordered Ich to turn hard to evade the missile. Meanwhile, Le Hai spotted an F-8 on his left side and he turned inside the F-8's turn. From an appropriate distance, he fired a first burst, but his shells missed behind the enemy Crusader's tail. He fired a second burst and hit the enemy aircraft, which rolled upside-down. Le Hai made a break-off maneuver, pulling over into a climbing turn to gain altitude. After seeing another F-8 Crusader flying parallel and below him, he rolled upside-down and dove to pursue this target. He attacked the enemy, but after a short burst his guns ran out of ammunition and the F-8 flew out over the Gulf of Tonkin. The F-8 that Le Hai shot down was his fifth victory during the war.

While Le Si Diep flew as a wingman to cover Le Hai's MiG, his aircraft was hit by an AIM-9 missile fired by Cdr Cane's F-8E Crusader of VF-53 from the USS *Bon Homme Richard*. As a result of the missile impact,

NGUYEN PHI HUNG

DATE OF BIRTH: 1942
ENLISTED: May 1961
PILOT TRAINING:
1961 (MiG-17 – 910th Air Training Regiment – Vietnam)
1961 – 1964 (MiG-17 – Soviet Union)
1964 – 1965 (919th Air Transport Regiment – Vietnam)
1965 – 1966 (910th Air Training Regiment – Vietnam)
WAR SERVICE AND UNIT:
1966 – 1968 (923rd Fighter Regiment)
AIRCRAFT: MiG-17
DIED: 9 July 1968 – shot down by US NAVY F-8E Crusader (150926 / Nichols III)
HERO OF THE VIETNAMESE PEOPLE'S ARMED FORCES: 10 December 1994
RANK: First Lieutenant

AIR VICTORIES: 5 kills
(2 F-4s, 2 F-105s, 1 F-8 – VPAF official credit)

DATE	AIRCRAFT	UNIT	KILL – US PILOT (VPAF – US DATABASES)
07 Oct 67	MiG-17	923.	F-4 – US not confirmed
06 Nov 67	MiG-17	923.	F-105 – US not confirmed
19 Nov 67	MiG-17	923.	F-4B – Clower (POW) Estes (KIA)
19 Dec 67	MiG-17	923.	F-105 – US not confirmed
09 Jul 68	MiG-17	923.	F-8E – US not confirmed

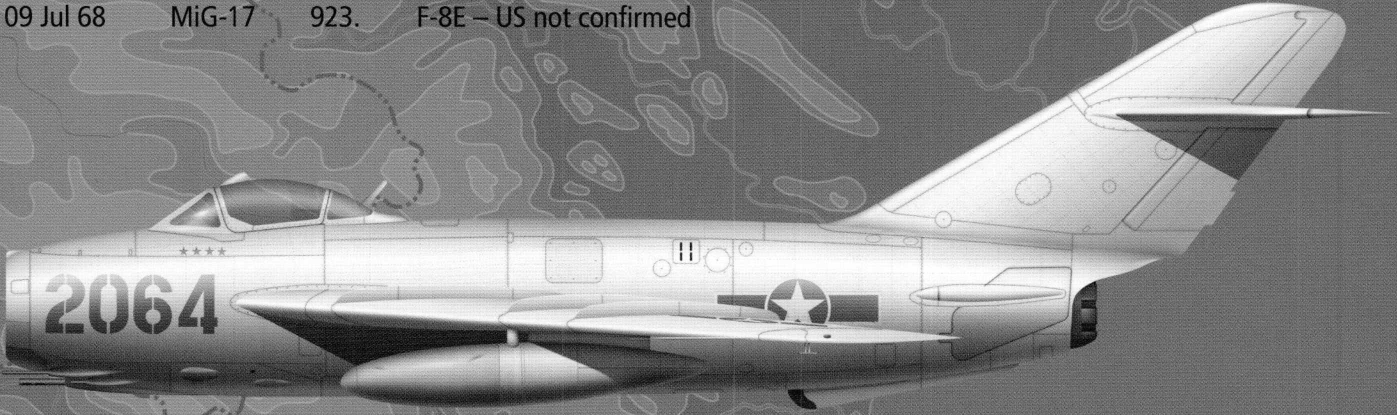

MiG-17F Fresco C, No. 2064 (4 kills) of the 923rd Fighter Regiment, 1968
The four red stars symbolize the MiG-pilots' air victories, which were credited on board of this MiG-17F at the 923rd Fighter Regiment. Nguyen Phi Hung used frequently this Fresco during air battles, but unfortunately he was shot down by Lt Cdr Nichols' F-8E Crusader on 9 July 1968 and lost his life. (ARTWORK: BALÁZS KAKUK)

a large section of the MiG-17's right wing was seen to separate from the aircraft. Diep tried to level his MiG, but he could not and his aircraft crashed northwest of Tan Ky. He had just returned to service from the hospital after being injured, so he had not yet recovered his strength. Because of it, his ejection was unsuccessful and he was killed in action (KIA).

At 10:41 hours, command ordered the three MiG-17s to break off and one minute later a MiG-21 pair arrived to cover their return back to Tho Xuan.

The three-aircraft formation would help the MiG-pilots by giving them better early warning capability in the air. During attacks this formation also would increase their capabilities and effectiveness when attacking the large US Navy strike formations.

On 10 July 1968, USAF and US Navy aircraft again flew in to attack targets along the transportation routes in the 4th Military District. The VPAF Headquarters ordered the 921st Fighter Regiment to have a flight of three MiG-21s to take off and intercept the American strike formation.

The three pilots, Pham Thanh Ngan, Pham Phu Thai and Dang Ngoc Ngu, went on combat alert duty at Noi Bai airbase. In the afternoon of 10 July, the MiG-21 flight was ordered to secretly fly down to the Tho Xuan airfield. The pilots were ordered to take off in the late afternoon. Intelligence information revealed that F-4J Phantoms of VF-33 from the USS *America*, would carry out the MiGCAP mission to support a formation of attack bombers flying in to attack traffic and transportation targets in the 4th Military District. The US Navy strike formation and the MiGCAP fighters were supported by electronic warfare aircraft (EKA-3B Skywarrior, EA-6A Intruder, EB-66 Destroyer), which jammed signals to disrupt radar and radio communication at Vietnamese units.

When the MiGs appeared and intercepted, the American bombers quickly turned away and withdrew to allow the F-4J Phantom fighters to

The pilots of MiG-21PFM are preparing to take-off in July of 1968 in earth revetments at Noi Bai airbase. After redeployment, the MiG-21s started from Tho Xuan airfield to intercept enemy formations over the 4th Military District.
(István Toperczer Collection)

On 1 August 1968, Nguyen Hong Nhi and Nguyen Dang Kinh attacked US Navy formation. Nguyen Hong Nhi claimed his 8th air victory with an F-8 kill, but his MiG-21 was shot down also in this engagement by another F-8 Crusader.
(István Toperczer Collection)

fire missiles at long range to threaten MiGs and frighten them away. As the MiG-21 flight was looking for their target, Dang Ngoc Ngu suddenly warned his comrades: "The enemy is firing missiles!" Pham Thanh Ngan and Pham Phu Thai did not know that the enemy was firing missiles from the forward hemisphere, and they immediately made a sharp turn. Pham Phu Thai, who was flying in the rear, ended up in the sights of the F-4J Phantoms. Due to the inexperience of both the GCI and of the pilots, they failed to achieve a kill. Pham Phu Thai's MiG-21 was shot down by a Sidewinder missile from Lt Cash's F-4J of VF-33, USS *America*, and he ejected safely.

On 1 August 1968, the VPAF used the trio-formation of MiG-21s again. Their tasks were the same as on the 10 July 1968 battle. The flight-leader and his wingman were the main fighters, while the third MiG-21 covered them both. In the afternoon of 31 July, preparations were conducted at Noi Bai and the MiG-21s moved to Tho Xuan. Three MiG-21s, with Nguyen Dang Kinh, Pham Van Mao and Nguyen Hong Nhi, of the 921st Fighter Regiment took part in an air battle over Do Luong, Thanh Chuong and Nam Dan in Nghe An Province.

At 12:37 hours, a trio of MiG-21s took off from Tho Xuan and flew below the clouds as planned. After five minutes, they were 10 kilometers north of Nghia Dan, when X1 command post ordered them to go above the clouds. After good signals on both enemies, X3 ordered the MiG-21s to keep a heading of 210 degrees, at an altitude of 4,000 meters. At 12:43 hours, X3 informed the flight that the enemy was on their left, at a heading of 50 degrees, 15 kilometers east of Do Luong, at an altitude from 3,000 to 3,500 meters. One minute later, the MiG-21s were ordered to turn a direction of 160 degrees. At 12:46 hours, MiG-21s were close to Do Luong, turned left to avoid an enemy group from the east, flew along south of Route No.7 to Do Luong. Thirty seconds later, Nguyen Dang Kinh and Pham Van Mao detected two F-4 Phantoms, ahead at a distance of 13km and were turning right to go north on Route No.7 and below the clouds. From a distance of 15 kilometers, the opposing aircraft were clearly visible. Nguyen Dang Kinh turned right hard, followed the enemy and launched an R-3S missile, but missed his target and it went into the clouds. Pham Van Mao could not follow the enemy and lost them. Kinh ordered Mao to break off to X1, bearing 330 degrees and turned right and above the clouds.

Nguyen Hong Nhi was going after two F-8s, and when, at a distance of 1,000 meters and at a heading of 60 degrees, he launched the first R-3S missile at the American aircraft, turning at a heading of 45 degrees. His first AAM missed, but the second was a direct hit. The other Crusader, who noticed the MiG, made a turn and started to chase it. The distance was 2,500 meters between them. Nguyen Hong Nhi increased his speed and with a right turn started a climb, but the control of the aircraft was too strong. He made a 30 degree turn and noticed that the Americans were firing at him. One F-8 also made a left turn and was just 300 meters behind him, when the MiG tried to make a tighter turn to avoid being hit. Nguyen Hong Nhi was successful for the third time and by turning around was able to attack the F-8 Crusader. However, due to a malfunction of the electrical system he could only fire at random. At this moment, two F-8s arriving on the scene from the direction of Sot Mouth (Nghen River) opened fire on them. Nguyen Hong Nhi tried to climb, but was hit by a Sidewinder missile from Lt McCoy's F-8H Crusader of VF-51 from USS *Bon Homme Richard*. He had to eject and returned to his unit three days later. Before take-off, Nguyen Hong Nhi had noticed that the throttle was not working properly, but did not report this to anyone. The US Navy records did not confirm Nhi's kill.

In September 1968, the VPAF Headquarters for the 4th Military District was moved to Do Luong. At Tho Xuan, the Commanding officer was Tran Hanh and the Regimental Vice Commanding officers post was given to Pham Ngoc Lan from the 921st Fighter Regiment.

On 17 September, over Yen Thanh, Thanh Chuong and Do Luong, with a mixture of MiG-21s and MiG-17s, took part in an air battle, when the US Navy sent in attack bombers escorted by F-8s to bomb targets in the 4th Military District.

Nguyen Van Coc and Pham Phu Thai from the 921st Fighter Regiment were ready to take off. At 11:17 hours, the MiG-21 pair started from Tho Xuan and flew out on a heading of 200 degrees, at an altitude of 800 meters. One minute after passing over Anh Son, the command post ordered them to turn to a heading of 120 degrees. After the MiG-21s increased their speed and made a climbing left turn, they spotted two F-8 Crusaders at a heading of 90 degrees to their left side, at a distance

The flight of MiG-21PFMs prepares to take-off at the 921st Fighter Regiment on Noi Bai airbase, in 1968. The fifth MiG-21 (No. 4520) in the line is F-13 Fishbed C version.
(ISTVÁN TOPERCZER COLLECTION)

of 6 kilometers and an altitude of 5,000 meters. The F-8 Crusaders were on a BARCAP (Barrier Combat Air Patrol) mission to support the bomber attack group. The MiG-21s dropped their auxiliary fuel tanks and Coc turned left to head toward the two F-8 Crusaders. He made five or six complete circles in this dogfight with an F-8, but was not able to get into attack position. The two F-8s were still behind Coc's MiG-21 at an angle of 70 to 80 degrees. The Crusaders of VF-24, from USS *Hancock*, launched four missiles at the MiG-21 with no results. Nguyen Van Coc decided to continue the dogfight, his MiG-21 had only 700 or 800 liters of fuel. After a break-off maneuver, he made a spiraling combat climb from his altitude of 2,000 meters up to 5,000 meters. When Coc rolled his aircraft upside-down to look around, he saw he was not being pursued by enemy aircraft. He switched off the afterburner and returned to land. After the landing, the mechanics checked his aircraft and found 24 separate pieces of missile shrapnel imbedded in the tail and flaps of Coc's MiG-21 fighter.

Meanwhile, Pham Phu Thai spotted two other F-8s at a heading of 60 degrees. He reported this to Coc and turned in to attack the other F-8s. The F-8 Crusaders took turns firing missiles at Pham Phu Thai, but he was able to evade them and turned back hard to counterattack. The F-8s increased their speed and decided to withdraw from the air battle, since their fuel was also running low. Both aircraft flew out to the coast of Gulf of Tonkin and a few minutes later the engine of Lt(jg) Swigart's F-8H Crusader (148648) shut down. He had to eject and was picked up by a SAR (Search and Rescue) helicopter. Pham Phu Thai broke off and turned to climb to an altitude of 7,000 meters, and then descended to land safely at Tho Xuan.

During this air battle, the 923rd Fighter Regiment launched a flight of four MiG-17s, which flew over Yen Thanh to fight in coordination with the MiG-21s. After a dogfight with F-8s in which neither side was able to get into position to fire their weapons, the MiG-17s returned to base and landed.

On 19 September, there was an encounter with two MiG-21s, but due to an electrical fault the flight leader, Dinh Ton, could not launch his missiles while his wingman, Vu Dinh Rang, was shot down by Lt Nargi's F-8C of VF-111 from USS *Intrepid* (CV-11). Vu Dinh Rang ejected safely.

After three days, on 22 September, a trio of MiG-21s was in the airspace of 4th Military District. The US Navy fired RIM-8 Talos SAMs and hit the North Vietnamese MiG-21 Fishbeds. Pham Thanh Ngan's MiG was damaged, Nguyen Van Ly and Vu Dinh Rang ejected safely. It was the second ejecting of Vu Dinh Rang in three days!

By October, the enemy had increased its air activity along Routes No.1 and No.15 and enhanced radar surveillance of this region in the 4th Military District.

On 26 October, a MiG-17 pair of Nguyen Quang Sinh and Bui Dinh Doan took off from Tho Xuan to fly Combat Air Patrol over Tan Ky, at 08:17 hours. A minute later, a pair of MiG-21s was also launched from the airfield. Both flights flew alongside Route No.15 at low altitude to Tan Ky, then turned to a holding area north of Route No.7.

At 08:27 hours, the MiG-17s turned hard to a heading of 180 degrees, then bearing 150 degrees at an altitude of 2,000 meters to attack the enemy south of Yen Thanh. After crossing Route No.7, they were informed that the enemy aircraft flew to Vinh, so the Americans did not come as they supposed. Due to heavy overcast, they could not make visual contact with the enemy flying at the same altitude, so the X3 command post ordered MiG- 17s to return to Tho Xuan.

The MiG-17 Fresco is covered with canvas in the greenwood of a village somewhere in the 4th Military District during October of 1968. (István Toperczer Collection)

Pham Thanh Ngan

Date of Birth: 18 April 1939
Enlisted: 21 March 1959
Pilot training:
1961 – 1964 (MiG-17 – Soviet Union)
1965 – 1966 (MiG-21 – Soviet Union)
War Service and Unit:
1966 – 1969 (921st Fighter Regiment)
Aircraft: MiG-21
Hero of the Vietnamese People's Armed Forces: 18 June 1969
Rank: Colonel General

Air Victories: 8 kills
(3 F-4s, 2 F-105s, 1 RF-101, 1 F-102, 1 Firebee – VPAF official credit)

Date	Aircraft	Unit	Kill – US Pilot (VPAF – US databases)
14 Dec 66	MiG-21	921.	Firebee
16 Sep 67	MiG-21	921.	RF-101C – Bagley (POW)
03 Oct 67	MiG-21	921.	F-4D – Moore, Gulbrandson (Rescued)
07 Oct 67	MiG-21	921.	F-4D – Appleby (POW) Austin (KIA) (SA2)
18 Nov 67	MiG-21	921.	F-105F – Dardeau, Lehnhoff (KIAs)
20 Nov 67	MiG-21	921.	F-105D – Butler (POW)
03 Feb 68	MiG-21	921.	F-102A – Wiggins (KIA)

MiG-21F-13 Fishbed C, No. 4520 (8 kills) of the 921st Fighter Regiment, 1968
The Ace-pilot Pham Thanh Ngan credited eight air victories during Vietnam Air War.
He and his comrades shot down eight American aircraft with this MiG-21F-13
that is symbolized by eight red stars on its nose. (Artwork: Balázs Kakuk)

The MiG-21 pair Nguyen Dang Kinh and Vu Xuan Thieu was flying at 500 meters over Route No.15, when they noticed American aircraft on their left. Based on information from the Dai Hue tower, the intruders were heading towards Dien Chau. At 08:28 hours, the MiG-21s made an 80 degree turn left, and this time they were flying from the direction of the sun. The wingman, Vu Xuan Thieu, climbed 1,000 meters above the clouds to the altitude of 3,000 meters, while the flight leader, Nguyen Dang Kinh, saw two dark spots 15 kilometers away between cloud layers over Nam Dan. The wingman, Vu Xuan Thieu, also saw two F-4s some 8 kilometers away. Nguyen Dang Kinh made a left turn and took up a firing position, but by this time the Americans had also noticed the MiGs and switched on their afterburners to get away quickly, towards the Gulf of Tonkin. Vu Xuan Thieu dropped his fuel tanks and increased his speed in pursuit of the Phantoms. Nguyen Dang Kinh was also chasing a Phantom and from a distance of 1,200 meters launched an R-3S missile. The F-4 started a slow descent at a 15 degree bank before crashing. No F-4 loss was reported by the US Navy.

Vu Xuan Thieu followed another F-4 Phantom turning right, but lost him, so the X3 command post ordered him to break off right, bearing 360 degrees. Tran Manh ordered GCI to watch the Talos SAM on enemy combat ships. Ground control ordered the MiG-21s to fly at an altitude of 1,000 to 1,500 meters. Nguyen Dang Kinh used high speed, changed his direction, and reported an altitude of tact with the command centre and got lost, turning to south of Tho Xuan. He was able to establish radio contact only 5 minutes later. When two MiG pairs came back to Nghia Dan, a second MiG-17 pair, of Hoang Thanh Xuan and Nguyen Phu Ninh, took off to cover Sinh – Doan (MiG-17s) and Kinh – Thieu (MiG-21s). All the pairs of MiGs made a successful landing on that day.

At the end of 1968, the MiG-21pilots of the 921st Fighter Regiment decorate the unit-flag with their air-victory medals. Nguyen Duc Soat (MIDDLE) and Nguyen Van Coc (RIGHT) are two famous Aces of the war. (ISTVÁN TOPERCZER COLLECTION)

In 1968, MiG-21s became more and more effective, even though they were fighting over the unfamiliar territory of the 4th Military District. During the year, 29 enemy aircraft were destroyed by MiG-21 fighters, with the loss of 8 North Vietnamese MiG-21s (only one pilot killed after the air battle).

From the end of 1968, on orders from the Ministry of Defense and of VPAF, only a token force was kept in the 4th Military District. On the 1 November 1968, President Johnson announced a unilateral cessation of bombing. In the 1,305 days from 3 March 1965 to 31 October 1968, the VPAF had launched 1,602 missions and downed 218 US aircrafts of 19 different types. Many of the US pilots became Prisoners of War (POWs). Against the well trained and numerically superior American pilots, the North Vietnamese side with few pilots and aircraft, developed step by step managed to provide a satisfactory response and were able to protect effectively Hanoi and the 4th Military District.

At the beginning, North Vietnam had 36 pilots and 36 MiG fighters, but by 1968 there were two Fighter Regiments with double the number of fighter pilots and five times the number of aircraft. This meant that the VPAF became the strongest service within the People's Army of Vietnam (PAVN).

This Red 3029 MiG-17F participated in many air battles over the Ham Rong Bridge, at Thanh Hoa City. Today it is on display at the Thanh Hoa City museum.
(DANG THAI SON)

After "Rolling Thunder" and before "Linebacker"

Manned MiGs against Unmanned Aerial Vehicles

The first American unit equipped with Ryan Q-2C Firebee unmanned aerial vehicles (UAV), namely the 4025th "Black Knights" Reconnaissance Squadron of the 4080th SW (Strategic Wing), flew its operational missions over North Korea and China, in 1964. In August 1964, this unit moved from Kadena AB, Okinawa in Japan, to Bien Hoa AB, in South Vietnam. They started the first operations, foremost monitoring the work of North Vietnamese air defenses sites (AAA and SA-2 units).

All the drones of the AQM-34 series deployed during the Vietnam War were carried and started from specially modified DC-130 control aircraft, each of them being equipped with systems for carriage, start, control, and guidance of drones. On their return, the drones deployed a parachute and were snared by specially modified CH-3 recovery helicopters. Usually the AQM-34 was used at low levels and at high altitude for different missions. Depending on their tasks, drones could then either continue their mission at the same level or climb to altitudes between 12,000 and 20,000 meters in order to acquire their targets with concrete sensors. The highly upgraded AQM-34L flew no less than 1,600 missions over North Vietnam. In total, between August 1964 and late April 1975, Ryan Firebees flew 3.435 missions over North Vietnam, using 22 different variants of AQM-34s. Over China and North Vietnam 578 drones were lost: 251 were shot down, 80 were declared as missing in action (MIA), 53 were lost during recovery, 30 during winching up, and the rest to different reasons.

The AQM-34L (Ryan Model 147SC) Firebee was used for low altitude photo-reconnaissance missions over North Vietnam. Several hundred examples of the model were built under the "Compass Bin" and "Buffalo Hunter" programs. This "Tom Cat" completed 68 successful missions over North Vietnam. (István Toperczer Collection)

The 921st and 923rd Fighter Regiment of the VPAF started their fights against Firebees in 1966. The first Firebee was shot down by Nguyen Hong Nhi, who launched an R-3S missile from his MiG-21 against the drone, on 4 March 1966. In 1966, the MiGs shot down 7 drones, only one drone in 1967, and they claimed 17 Firebee kills in 1968 over North Vietnam.

Dinh Ton and the ground crew discuss in front of a MiG-21F-13 Fishbed C. On 15 April 1968, Dinh Ton shot down an AQM-34 Firebee, at an altitude of 14,500 meters, west of Lang Chanh, over Thanh Hoa Province.
(István Toperczer Collection)

During 1968, 15 Ryan Firebees drones were shot down by MiG-21 pilots (Nguyen Dang Kinh, Dang Ngoc Ngu, Pham Thanh Ngan, Mai Van Cuong, Dinh Ton, Bui Duc Nhu, Nguyen Van Coc, Nguyen Van Luc, Nguyen Van Ly…) over North Vietnam.

At noon 15 April 1968, the VPAF HQ received information that an AQM-34 Firebee drone would operate, then radar detected a jamming signal at a heading of 160-170 degrees, several enemy groups appeared 100 to 120 kilometers east of Thai Binh, and inforamtion came from observers at Cat Ba Island about other aircraft. North Vietnamese command guessed the enemy might conduct reconnaissance of targets at Route No.18 or Route No.5 and decided to use MiG-17 and MiG-21 fighters as a prepared plan.

At 14:04 hours, a MiG-17 pair of Luu Huy Chao and Le Hai took off from Gia Lam, to orbit at An Thi – Thanh Mien to intercept the drone at low altitude. At 14:10 hours, Nguyen Dang Kinh and Dinh Ton took off with their MiG-21s from Noi Bai. The GCI control "blindly" guided them to Tan Lac to intercept the Firebee, which would come out from the southwest, south or southeast. Radar still did not pick up signals of the target or the MiGs. After ten minutes, the first signal was spotted, the recce-drone took bearing of 200 degrees, at a relatively stable speed 800 km/h and ascended. The MiG-21s took a bearing of 120 degrees and flew over Vu Ban, then turned right, at a bearing of 240, then 230 degrees, at a speed of 950 km/h, and an altitude of 10,000 meters. At 5 kilometers southeast of Quan Hoa, Nguyen Dang Kinh reported a white smoke trail on the right, at an altitude of 11 – 12,000 meters, and GCI control ordered them to an altitude of 13 – 14,000 meters. Nguyen Dang Kinh, bearing of 200 degrees, detected a target ahead at a distance of 5 kilometers, followed and fired an R-3S missile, but missed and had to break off. Dinh Ton also attacked and he shot down an AQM-34 Firebee at an altitude of 14,500 meters west of Lang Chanh. The MiG-21 pair returned back toward Viet Tri and landed at Noi Bai, while the MiG-17 pair landed safely at Gia Lam.

On 8 November 1968, based on an EB-66 Destroyer and C-130 Hercules operation 30 kilometers northwest of Long Vi, radars detected drone coming to Hai Phong, through Hai Duong over the Duong River bridge at an altitude of about 300-500 meters. After, it flew to Viet Tri and then ascended. The weather was complicated, with clouds as low as 1,500

On 8 November 1968, Nguyen Van Coc intercepted and shot down a Firebee unmanned aerial vehicle over Gia Vien, in Ninh Binh Province.
(István Toperczer Collection)

meters. At 09:08 hours, the enemy aircraft was 10 kilometers south of Noi Bai when Nguyen Van Coc took off with his MiG-21. After he reached a safe altitude, the GCI ordered him to turn left, he kept his afterburner on to get altitude and took a bearing of 240 degrees. The enemy arrived over Phuc Yen at an altitude of 2,500 meters and turned left to fly toward Hoa Lac. At 09:11 hours, ground control informed Coc that a target was on the right at 30 degrees and a distance of 5 kilometers. The MiG-pilot was in the clouds, and then a target was ahead at a distance of 6 kilometers, at that moment Coc flew over the clouds. One minute later, the MiG-21 flew over Hoa Lac and the 921st Fighter Regiment command ordered him to turn left, bearing 170 degrees, an altitude of 7,000 meters, and informed him about the position of his target. At 09:13 hours, Nguyen Van Coc detected a drone was flying fast from left to right, below and ahead of him. He fired the first R-3S missile but missed. In the next minute, the drone turned left at Hoa Binh, flew with a bearing of 115 degrees and to an altitude of 9,000 meters. The MiG-21 flew on the left and ahead of the drone.

At the same time a MiG-21 took off from Noi Bai, and command ordered other MiG-21 to start at Tho Xuan, Dong Van Song and Luong The Phuc were guided to Yen Thuy – Cam Thuy.

At 09:15 hours, Nguyen Van Coc was ordered to turn left, ascend, and then follow with a bearing of 115 degrees. One minute later, the enemy was ahead at a distance of 10 kilometers and above an altitude of 1,000 meters, but the pilot could not detect it. At 09:17 hours, the GCI ordered the MiG-21 pair at Cam Thuy to take a bearing of 70 degrees, accelerate from 900 to 1,100 km/h and to an altitude of 12,000 meters. At 09:19 hours, Song – Phuc arrived over Gia Vien and detected both the Firebee and Coc's MiG-21. The command guided the MiG-21 pair to follow them, but only 20-30 seconds after that Nguyen Van Coc detected the target and requested to attack. The GCI ordered Song – Phuc to reduce their speed, turn right and keep a distance of 7 kilometers on the right behind the target. After Nguyen Van Coc fired his second R-3S missile, Dong Van Song reported the Firebee burning. The all MiG-21s landed safely after the air engagement.

In 1969, the two fighter regiments had shot down 14 Firebees, with the 921st Fighter Regiment scoring 12 and the 923rd Fighter Regiment 2 kills. The North Vietnamese fighters – mostly MiG-21s – were scrambled no less than 540 times in order to intercept Ryan Firebee (AQM-34) drones.

On 9 February 1969, based on a UAV operation, two MiG-21s, with Mai Van Cuong and Pham Phu Thai, were put on Class One Alert. At 10:31 hours, they started their engines and took off from Noi Bai. The enemy drone flew from the south of Cat Ba Island to Tra Ly Mouth, then to Hung Yen, at an altitude of 500 meters. Command guided the MiG-21s over Bac Ninh to a holding area and they turned left, 180 degrees twice, to a

DATE OF BIRTH: 5 September 1936
ENLISTED: December 1952
PILOT TRAINING:
1957 – 1958 (Czechoslovakia)
1958 – 1961 (910th Air Training Regiment)
1965 – 1968 (MiG-21 – Soviet Union)
WAR SERVICE AND UNIT:
1961 – 1965 (919th Air Transport Regiment)
1968 – 1975 (921st Fighter Regiment)
AIRCRAFT: Li-2, MiG-21
HERO OF THE VIETNAMESE PEOPLE'S ARMED FORCES: 31 December 1973
RANK: Senior Colonel

AIR VICTORIES: 4 kills
(1 F-4, 1 OV-10, 2 Firebees – VPAF official credit)

DATE	AIRCRAFT	UNIT	KILL – US PILOT (VPAF – US DATABASES)
15 Apr 68	MiG-21	921.	Firebee
26 May 68	MiG-21	921.	Firebee
02 Jun 68	MiG-21	921.	Firebee
16 Jun 68	MiG-21	921.	F-4J – Wilber (POW) Rupinski (KIA)
13 Apr 71	MiG-21	921.	O-2A – US not confirmed
20 Apr 71	MiG-21	921.	OV-10 – US not confirmed

MiG-21F-13 Fishbed C, No. 4527 of the 921st Fighter Regiment, 1968
On 15 April, 26 May and 2 June 1968, Dinh Ton used a MiG-21F-13 type to shoot down unmanned reconnaissance drones over North Vietnam. (ARTWORK: BALÁZS KAKUK)

On the night of April 1969, Nguyen Van Coc prepares to take-off with an unusually camouflaged MiG-21PFM, No. 5017, which wears dark green color on its upper side.
(István Toperczer Collection)

direction of 160 and 340 degrees. At 10:36 hours, the enemy was at Tien Hung, and the MiG-21s took a bearing of 150 degrees and a speed of 900 km/h. Three minutes later, the drone flew 10 kilometers east of Phu Xuyen. As a response, the MiG-21s turned right and approached. Mai Van Cuong spotted the drone on his left, at a distance of 6 kilometers and launched an R-3S missile to shoot it down. Pham Phu Thai had seen the landing parachute deploy from Firebee.

On the same day, a MiG-21 pair of Dang Ngoc Ngu and Nguyen Tien Sam took off from Noi Bai on their way to Vinh, but on the way met with American aircraft, who attacked them. They had to change direction and eventually chose Tho Xuan as the destination, but one of the aircraft ran out of fuel and Nguyen Tien Sam had to eject.

This Ryan Firebee AQM-34 was shot down by a MiG-17 over North Vietnam, in 1969. After being hit, the landing parachute was deployed from drone.
(István Toperczer Collection)

The famous Ace-pilot, Mai Van Cuong shot down no less than 6 Firebees, so he was the best "Drone-killer" during the air war. (ISTVÁN TOPERCZER COLLECTION)

Between February and June, Nguyen Van Khanh, Dang Ngoc Ngu and Nguyen Duc Soat each shot down an AQM-34 drone over North Vietnam.

Mai Van Cuong claimed his next Firebee kill on 24 June 1969. At about 16:00 hours, a C-130 arrived 35 kilometers south of Long Chau Island. Commander Dao Dinh Luyen ordered MiG-17s at Kien An, MiG-21s at Noi Bai and Tho Xuan airfields on Class One Alert to attack drones as adjusted plan. At 16:13 hours, the Firebee was detected 30 kilometers east of Tra Ly Mouth. It then flew to Thai Binh Mouth. Then a command at Kien An ordered the MiG-17 pair to take off and guided them high above the airfield to intercept when enemy came to south of the airfield, but the MiG pilots could not detected a target. When the drone flew to Tu Son at an altitude of 200-300 meters, command ordered the MiG-21 pair of Pham Phu Thai and Mai Van Cuong to take off from Noi Bai and guided them to a holding area over My Hao. However, when a target arrived near Ke Sat, the GCI lost the signal of the enemy. They changed to "blindly" guided, but without result.

Commander Dao Dinh Luyen decided to attack when the enemy turned back and agreed to order the MiG-21s to take off from Tho Xuan. They were at Nam Truc and flew to Thanh Oai, keeping an altitude of 500 meters. The other MiG-21 pair of Thai – Cuong and the MiG- 17s kept their positions. At that time, the Firebee flew over the Noi Bai airbase from east to west, then turned left to Hanoi. At 16:28 hours, GCI reported the target at Gia Lam, bearing 140 degrees, at an altitude of 300 meters. Pham Phu Thai guessed the enemy flight path and turned to intercept. At that moment, Thai – Cuong were ordered to take a bearing of 180 degrees, to speed of 900 km/h. They flew one minute, and then turned left, bearing 90 degrees. The target was on the left at a heading of 30 degrees, at a distance of 8 kilometers and arrived from left to right. Pham Phu Thai detected the drone on the right, at a distance of

On 3 August 1969, Le Hai destroyed an unmanned aerial vehicle with his MiG-17 gunfire. He was credited with 6 US aircraft kills during his service from 1967 to 1972.
(István Toperczer Collection)

5 kilometers. He attacked, but accidentally the missile was guided to and hit a brick-kiln on the ground. His wingman, Mai Van Cuong, also attacked and shot down the drone at an altitude of 250 meters.

In July and August 1969, seven Firebees became victims of North Vietnamese MiGs. On 3 August, two famous "flying aces", Nguyen Van Coc (MiG-21 of the 921st F.R) and Le Hai (MiG-17 of the 923rd F.R.) each shot down a Ryan Firebee drone over North Vietnam.

In 1970, there were 70 missions with six encounters against Firebees, and the MiG-pilots (Nguyen Cat A, Truong Cong Thanh and Ngo Son) opened fire three times. In May 1970, an AQM-34L Firebee was on a mission over the Hanoi area. Finishing its recce mission, the drone turned toward the Gulf of Tonkin and was intercepted by a MiG-21 of the 921st Fighter Regiment. The MiG-pilot tried to shoot it down with two R-3S missiles, but both malfunctioned. He continued the pursuit, trying to down the drone by tackling its wing. After the drone fell into the sea, the MiG-pilot forgot to control his fuel reserves and he found out that his MiG did not have enough fuel to return to Noi Bai airbase. He ejected while flying back toward the coast of the Gulf of Tonkin.

During 1971, MiGs were scrambled six times against Firebees, but only one pilot, Luong Duc Truong, could make a visual contact and hit a drone, but he lost his life in this incident on 9 March. In April 1971, a Firebee flew straight into fierce North Vietnamese AAA fire and was simultaneously intercepted by a MiG-21. While the drone came away the MiG-21 was shot down by friendly AAA fire.

Between 1971 to 1973, MiG-21s shot down only seven drones. In 1972, some MiG-21 pilots (Le Thanh Dao, Do Van Lanh, and Nguyen Van Nghia) of the 927th Fighter Regiment also added Firebee kills to their air victories over North Vietnam. The last AQM-34 Firebee kills were on 4 and 6 January 1973, by MiG-21 pilots – Nguyen Van Nhuong from the 927th and Han Vinh Tuong from the 921st Fighter Regiments.

At the end of the air war, MiG-17 pilots of the 923rd Fighter Regiment claimed three kills over Firebees, although they also lost their drone-killer MiG-pilots – Hoang Cong and Nguyen Van Hung – in January of 1973, and Truong Cong Thanh on 1 May 1974.

The volunteer North Korean pilots who flew the MiG-17 and MiG-21F-13 in their unit of "Doan-Z" returned to their home at the beginning of 1969.

A few MiG-17s and MiG-21s were delivered to the 4th Military District to the Vinh and Anh Son airfields after 21 March 1969, and the training for a future encounter had begun. Some of the MiG-17 and MiG-21 pilots were sent for courses, making training flights primarily in bad weather conditions. Pilots from this group were especially chosen for service in 4th Military District. The unit at Anh Son had reached combat readiness even for night intercepts by the 6 of April 1969.

DATE OF BIRTH: 29 April 1942
ENLISTED: 21 July 1961
PILOT TRAINING:
1961 – 1965 (910th Air Training Regiment, North Vietnam)
1965 (MiG-17 – 923rd Fighter Regiment)
WAR SERVICE AND UNIT:
1965 – 1974 (923rd Fighter Regiment)
AIRCRAFT: MiG-17
HERO OF THE VIETNAMESE PEOPLE'S ARMED FORCES: 25 August 1970
RANK: Senior Colonel

AIR VICTORIES: 6 kills
(4 F-4s, 1 F-105, 1 F-8 – VPAF official credit)

DATE	AIRCRAFT	UNIT	KILL – US PILOT (VPAF – US DATABASES)
28 Apr 67	MiG-17	923.	F-105 – US not confirmed
14 May 67	MiG-17	923.	F-4 – US not confirmed (Shared)
19 Nov 67	MiG-17	923.	F-4B – Teague (KIA) Stier (POW)
14 Jun 68	MiG-17	923.	F-4 – US not confirmed
29 Jul 68	MiG-17	923.	F-8 – US not confirmed
03 Aug 69	MiG-17	923.	Firebee
06 Mar 72	MiG-17	923.	F-4 – US not confirmed

Shenyang J-5 (MiG-17F Fresco C), No. 3020 (7 kills) of the 923rd Fighter Regiment, 1969
During the air war, the silver MiG-17s were painted to overall green color.
Le Hai added also his air victory to these seven "red stars". On 3 August 1969,
he shot down a Firebee drone over North Vietnam. (ARTWORK: BALÁZS KAKUK)

Ho Chi Minh (LEFT) died on the morning of 2 September 1969. After one week, twelve MiG-21 pilots of the 921st Fighter Regiment presented the "honorable fly-past" in memory of Uncle Ho over Ba Dinh Square in Hanoi.
(ISTVÁN TOPERCZER COLLECTION)

Also in April 1969, new training courses were started where the MiG-17 pilots received conversion to the MiG-21 type. The MiG-21 flight based at Vinh was given the order to attack any intruding B-52s. On the 22 April, a pair of MiG-21s was moved to Anh Son, but because of less than adequate camouflage, they were destroyed in an American bombing raid.

Ho Chi Minh died, at 09:47 hours on the morning of 2 September 1969, from heart failure in his home in Hanoi, aged 79. At night the same day, commanders gathered for a meeting with the MiG-21 pilots to order them for a special mission. The next morning, on 3 September, all pilots of the 921st Fighter Regiment focused on Dao Dinh Luyen, Commander of the VPAF. Out of the 50 pilots, 12 had to be chosen for the honorable fly-past, in memory of Uncle Ho, over Ba Dinh Square in Hanoi. All the chosen pilots were fighting in air combat and shot down many US aircraft. The No.1 flight was led by Nguyen Hong Nhi. In his team were Le Toan Thang, Pham Dinh Tuan and Nguyen Duc Soat. Nguyen Van Ly led the No.2 flight with pilots Pham Phu Thai, Le Thanh Dao and Nguyen Hong My. The flight No.3 squad had pilots Mai Van Cuong, Pham Thanh Nam, Nguyen Van Khanh and Nguyen Van Long. The two reserve pilots were Bui Duc Nhu and Dang Ngoc Ngu. Between 3 and 8 September, the pilots were practicing every day, both in the air and on the ground. They took off 3 times per day and flew over Ba Dinh square for the first time on the afternoon of 8 September.

The weather was excellent on 9 September 1969. At 09:00 hours the formation of MiG-21s took off from Noi Bai and turned southeast of Phu Lo. According to preflight plans, the 12 MiG-21s started their engines at the same time and took off in a two-ship formation. After reaching an altitude of 100 meters they built up 3 elements in a trail. The gap between the elements was 600-800 meters, and 20-30 meters vertically. The jets were flying at an altitude of 300 meters at speed of 850 km/h. The "Time on Target" (TOT) was 09:30 hours, when 12 minutes after the funeral speech the 12 aircraft crossed the Ba Dinh Square. After the honorable fly-past, the MiG-formation landed safely at Noi Bai airbase. Shortly after the landing of the MiG-21s, the regimental headquarters called and told the MiG-pilots the task was completed very well!

"Phoenix" is born in 1969

In September 1965, a group of 80 people (pilot cadets and technicians) travelled to China for training on MiG-19s. In 1966, new pilot cadets joined the training. After the initial theoretical part, training flights started. Following the flying time on Yak-18 (Nanchang CJ-6) and MiG-15UTI (Shenyang JJ-2) trainers, the cadets continued training on MiG-19s (Shenyang J-6). The double-seaters version (JJ-6) took off for the first time only in November 1970. Training in China ended in January 1969 and the crews started deployment back to Vietnam. At the end of 1968, the USAF focused on the area south of the 20th Parallel. Sometimes their separated flights made raids in the north. Otherwise

The Chinese instructor shows the maneuver with the aid of an aircraft model to North Vietnamese MiG-19-pilot, Nguyen Ngoc Tiep (Left) in front of a Chinese Shenyang JJ-5 (MiG-17UTI) trainer jet.
(István Toperczer Collection)

The squadron commander demonstrates dogfight – maneuvers to pilots of MiG-19 flights at Yen Bai airbase. The 925th Fighter Regiment was created in February 1969, and used the Chinese-built Shenyang J-6 (MiG-19S). The regiment moved from Kep airbase to Yen Bai airbase during September 1969. (István Toperczer Collection)

only reconnaissance aircraft operated. In February 1969, North Vietnam was enjoying a four-month break from American air raids, and the MiG-19 group moved from China to Kep airbase. The MOD decided on the creation of the 925th Fighter Regiment (Trung Doan Khong Quan Tiem Kich 925) to be equipped with Chinese-built MiG-19 Farmers (Shenyang J-6) fighters. Le Quang Trung was appointed Regiment Commander and Mai Duc Toai as Vice Commander. According to the situation, the North Korean "Doan Z" left Vietnam. Air Force engineers with help from other units and people of Lang Giang (Ha Bac Province) quickly repaired Kep airbase.

After creation, the 925th Fighter Regiment had only the core officers from the 923rd Fighter Regiment, as others still trained in China. It had only staff, political and technical sections. The logistic section was created when it returned to Vietnam. In a short period before the MiG-19s moved to Kep, the ground control section of the regiment quickly organized the training and helped the pilots in terrain research. After the MiG-19s arrived at Kep in February, they had to build up basic combat plans and improve the flight trainings data. For the data, they had to support both the MiG-15UTI and MiG-19, due to their performance differences. At the beginning, there were 37 pilots, using 36 MiG-19s (J-6) and 4 MiG-15UTIs. From March to late August 1969, the ground control section's main task was maintaining navigation for the MiG-19s training flights. The intense tactical and advanced flight training resulted in nine combat-capable MiG-19 pilots by April 1969.

In September 1969, the 925th Fighter Regiment, with MiG-19s and MiG-17s, moved to Yen Bai airbase to protect the northwest airspace of Vietnam. Yen Bai had only one runway and electricity was provided by generators. Preparation for battle was hampered by fuel shortages and a high hardware attrition rate caused by the humid climate, poor maintenance and inadequate logistics. To help with GCI and cooperation between air force and air defense force, the 42nd Radar Company was attached to the 925th Fighter Regiment at Yen Bai. Other pilots of the 925th Fighter Regiment came from Gia Lam to MiG-17s and Soviet flying schools where they had undergone MiG-21 training. From late 1969 to early 1970, with experiences in Kep, the ground control section quickly organized operation in the new base, it supported combat training flights for MiG-19, switched training to MiG-17 for several MiG-19 pilots, supported 10 MiG-19s and 12 MiG-21s that moved from Tuong Van airfield (Kunming, Yunnan) to Yen Bai, and the MiG-21s to Noi Bai airbase. In 1970, mobile MiG-19 flights and a GCI team were sent to Tho Xuan airfield.

During this period, the 925th Fighter Regiment lost three pilots. On 13 September 1969, Duong Trung Tan, who was a MiG-17 pilot in the 923rd Fighter Regiment, between 1965 and 1968, took off for the task flight as a MiG-19 pilot and lost his life for an unknown reason over Kep. The next year, on 6 April, Bui Dinh Doan and Le Quang Trung (both earlier MiG-17 pilots) were on training flights and because of a mid-air collision they did not eject and were killed. Le Quang Trung was a lesser known Ace-pilot on MiG-17 with his 5 victories.

The pilot and technician are seen during a pre-flight check of a Shenyang JJ-5. Besides the MiG-15UTI, North Vietnamese pilots also used this Chinese-built two seat version of a MiG-17.
(István Toperczer Collection)

This Shenyang J-6 (MiG-19S Farmer C), No.6058, flew in the 925th Fighter Regiment, at Yen Bai airbase. Nowadays, it is displayed in the Museum of the 372nd Air Division, Da Nang.
(István Toperczer)

The previously gained MiG-19 experience was taken into account in the expected confrontations. The pilots returned from China after nearly 200 hours of flight time and entered wartime conditions right away. Their combat experience was limited, but they tried to exploit the characteristics of the aircraft. For the Vietnamese People's Air Force, this had been the first two-engined supersonic fighter. Because of the two engines, the MiG-19 needed a lot of fuel, so it was utilized within a limited range. Since these aircraft were unable to attack the American bombers from Combat Air Patrol (CAP) ties, they could only be deployed from ground alert. The horizontal maneuverability of the aircraft was good even at an altitude of 2,000-4,000 meters. It had only three 30 mm cannons, and only had been equipped with air-to-air missiles later, because the Chinese could fit the missile rails onto the aircraft only in 1974. However, if they could get into close range to the Americans, there was an increased risk that the enemy would shoot first and down them. When they approached the enemy at high speed, to prevent the Americans from counter-attack, they usually missed the hit. So the firing power of the MiG-19s firepower could not be fully exploited.

As the Americans often attacked Yen Bai airbase, the aircraft was covered with a camouflage net and had to be hidden from the American aircraft in shelters built from tree leaves and bamboo shelters. Later, dark green spots were painted on the silver fuselage, and then earth revetments were built in the mountains near the airbase. The bunkers under the mountain could house 60 aircraft at a time, which could reach the runway from several taxiways.

In the entrance-hall of the "Operation Linebackers"

At the beginning of next year, the MiG-21s of the 921st Fighter Regiment claimed two kills, an F-4 Phantom and an HH-53B helicopter on a SAR mission.

The weather was rainy during the early morning hours of 28 January 1970. The primary MiG-21 combat alert flight consisted of pilots Vu Ngoc Dinh and Pham Dinh Tuan. In the afternoon, after Capt Mallon and Capt Panek's F-105G was shot down by the by 230th AAA Regiment north of the Mu Gia Pass, several enemy groups operated south of Ngang Pass on both west and east sides of the Vietnamese – Laotian border, from Keo Nua Pass to Mu Gia Pass, to rescue their pilots. The flight of F-105s was accompanied by two RF-4C Phantoms, which were used to search for SAM sites that had fired at American B-52 bombers. Two F-105 pilots ejected and parachuted to the ground, and they had established radio communications with airborne electronic warfare aircraft. The USAF immediately ordered a SAR mission for HH-53 helicopters, A-1H Skyraider and an HC-130P Hercules aircraft. One of the A-1Hs was shot down by a SA-2 missile as it was searching for the downed pilots.

At 14:20 hours, an enemy aircraft operated at an altitude of 3,000 meters 30 kilometers west of the Mu Gia Pass. Four minutes later, Commander Tran Manh ordered the MiG-21 flight of Vu Ngoc Dinh and Pham Dinh Tuan, at Vinh to a Class One Alert. At 14.28 hours, an enemy group appeared at an altitude of 6,000 meters, 45km south-southeast of Mu Gia Pass and flew along the Vietnamese – Laotian border north

The MiG-21 pilot Vu Ngoc Dinh shot down the search and rescue Sikorsky HH-53B Jolly Green Giant helicopter at Vinh on 28 January 1970. It was his sixth and final air victory during the Vietnam War.
(ISTVÁN TOPERCZER COLLECTION)

to Routes No.12 and No.1. Another enemy group of 4 aircraft operated at an altitude of 2,500 meters, 45km west-northwest of Mu Gia Pass and 40 kilometers southwest of Huong Khe.

At 14:31 hours, the X3 command post ordered a MiG-21 pair to take off and then they turned to a heading of 150 degrees to a holding area west of Ben Thuy. Two MiG-21s, which were flying in an extended trail formation maintained radio silence along Route No.12. At 14:35 hours, radars detected an enemy group that turned continuously at the Khe Ve Bridge (Route No.15 and Route No.12 crossroad). Another enemy group appeared, at an altitude of 6,000 meters coming to Khe Ve. A MiG-21 pair flew alongside Route No.15 and changed altitude from 1,000 to 1,500 meters. At 14:40 hours, the GCI ordered the pilots to open their SOD-57 (signal respond generate equipment), and within the next two minutes the MiG-21s turned left, bearing 120 degrees at a speed of 900 km/h, 10 kilometers south of Huong Khe. At 14:43 hours, the command post ordered the pilots to turn right to a bearing of 170 degrees and an altitude of 4,000 meters. The target was 30 degrees to their right front, at a range of 18 kilometers, and an altitude of 3,000 meters. Commander Tran Manh ordered: "Hit fast and finish the target off fast."

In the next minute, the GCI informed the pilot that the target was 60 degrees to the right front, at a distance of 10 kilometers. Pham Dinh Tuan spotted an F-4 Phantom at a heading of 100 degrees to the right at a distance of 8 kilometers. He requested permission to attack and Vu Ngoc Dinh covered him. The X3 command post ordered him to break off bearing 310-320 degrees after the attack. After unsuccessfully trying to get on the tail of the target, Tuan broke off the attack by turning away. At 14:46 hours, he detected on the left ahead two F-4 Phantoms and requested to attack a second time, while Dinh continued to cover him. The two F-4s turned and headed straight out toward the Gulf of Tonkin. One minute later, as Vu Ngoc Dinh was making a turn to the left to resume covering Tuan's MiG, he spotted two helicopters flying in the opposite direction and one helicopter flying in the same direction as his aircraft. This helicopter flew at an altitude of 3,000 meters, very slowly. He decided to attack the helicopter flying in the same direction and requested permission to attack. Dinh maneuvered his aircraft in behind the target. When the helicopter was at a distance of 1,500 meters, he fired an R-3S missile and shot down the HH-53 helicopter. The Jolly Green 71 (66-14434) SAR helicopter burst into flames and crashed. All members of the crew were killed in action (KIA). At 14:48 hours, he shouted in the radio: "It's burning!" and rolled to his left side and pulled into a climb to avoid the ball of flames from the exploding helicopter. He reduced his altitude to 2,500 meters and ordered to his wingman to break off the engagement and turn to a heading of 360 degrees. At 14:50 hours, Pham Dinh Tuan replied: "Roger!", but in the next moment he said: "I am making a counterattack…". When Vu Ngoc Dinh's aircraft was flying past, Huong Son called him, but no answer. Just before Pham Dinh Tuan reached the Hill 2235, the SOD-57 signal was lost from his MiG-21. Due to bad weather, Pham Dinh Tuan crashed into a mountain side and lost his life.

Vu Ngoc Dinh maintained an altitude of 500 meters and a heading of 360 degrees as he flew back to Vinh airfield. After he landed, the technicians found many cracks and holes on his MiG-21caused by missile fragments, because his closing speed had been so great when he launched his missile.

On 27 and 28 March 1970, the Americans had launched several attacks on Muong Xen, but due to bad weather Tho Xuan could not put up a pair of the MiG-21 (Nguyen Duc Soat and Tran Viet), so four MiG-21s took off from Kien An instead. Pham Thanh Nam had no combat experience and lost his life when his MiG was shot down by AAM of a F-4J Phantom from the USS *Constellation* (CVA-64), over Ninh Binh. Bui Van Long and Hoang Quoc Dung gave an extensive support to Pham Phu Thai and the three MiG-21s landed safely at Gia Lam.

After studying the operations of US aircraft, which flew over the Ho Chi Minh Trail, intelligence and command officers assigned to forward command posts and mobile units were able to determine the operational patterns of OV-10 Bronco and O-2 Skymaster observer-reconnaissance aircraft. The VPAF Headquarters ordered the 921st Fighter Regiment to draft a plan and conduct an attack against observer aircraft.

In the afternoon of 13 April 1971, enemy low-speed aircraft appeared, at an altitude of 3,000 meters, 20 kilometers south-southwest of Mu Gia Pass. Four more high-speed enemy groups also appeared, at an altitude from 4,000 to 8,000 meters, 40 to 100 kilometers south-southwest of the Mu Gia Pass. Commander Tran Manh ordered an attack of the low-speed, enemy group.

At 17:27 hours, a MiG-21 pair was ordered to a Class One Alert at Anh Son airfield. After half an hour, Dinh Ton took off and flew low along Route No.7, and at Do Luong turned right to fly along Route No.15. At 18:08 hours, the GCI ordered Dinh Ton to turn to a heading first of 200 degrees, and then to a heading of 210 degrees, and to climb to an altitude of 3,500 meters. As the enemy turned there and back continuously in a small radius in a small area over Route No.12, ground control guided the MiG-21 to turn left, following the target.

The ground control ordered Dinh Ton to keep a heading of 200 degrees, at an altitude of 2,500 meters. The pilot reported his speed at 850 km/h and ascended to an altitude of 3,500, then 4,000 meters, and kept a heading of 210 degrees. The information arrived about the position of the target continuously, which was 40 degrees on the left, at a distance of 30 kilometers. Dinh Ton was guided to turn left, keep a heading of 130 degrees, then 60 degrees. The target was on the left 80 degrees, at a distance of 13 kilometers, then 90 degrees and 7 kilometers, but the MiG pilot had not detected it yet. At 18:14 hours, the sun had

In the afternoon of 13 April 1971, Dinh Ton from the 921st Fighter Regiment took off to attack an O-2A Skymaster. He claimed an O-2 kill, but US records did not confirm it. (István Toperczer Collection)

set behind the mountains and the sky was clothed in a dry mist. He was blinded by the sun making it difficult to spot the target. The command post ordered him to descend to an altitude of 3,000 meters and he continued to turn left to a heading of 270 degrees. At 18:16 hours, Dinh Ton spotted two O-2A aircraft at 30 degrees to the left and a distance of 8 kilometers and an altitude of 2,500 meters. He decided to reduce his altitude and speed and to turn on his radar, but after a short time the radar lost the target. Dinh Ton looked for the target with his naked eyes. He immediately discovered an O-2A Skymaster. He closed in on the target with a speed of 750 km/h and fired an R-3S missile at a distance of 1,200 meters. After launching the missile, he pulled his aircraft into a left-turning climb, then turned to look back. He saw the missile explode right under the belly of the O-2A. After firing his first missile, he requested to turn back and prepared to fire the second missile, but the enemy aircraft went down in a spiral. At 18:23 hours, radars picked up F-4s approaching from the direction of Tha Khet in Laos. He broke off and flew at an altitude of 3,000 meters with a speed of 900 km/h back to Anh Son. At the same time, the enemy groups followed his MiG-21 until Do Luong before turning back. At 18:38 hours, Dinh Ton landed safely at Anh Son airfield. The US records did not confirm his O-2 kill on that day.

On 10 May 1971, enemy prop-driven reconnaissance aircraft operated at the Vietnamese – Laotian border, over Muong Kham – Nong Het – Ky Son. Two MiG-21s, Mai Van Cuong and Le Thanh Dao, took off from Tho Xuan airfield and flew to search and destroy an OV-10 Bronco over the 4th Military District. When Mai Van Cuong discovered the target, Le Thanh Dao was in a holding formation about 300 meters from his flight leader's aircraft. Cuong closed in and fired an R-3S missile, but the OV-10 made two complete circles in a spin, and then it leveled out and flew straight again. Mai Van Cuong ordered his wingman to attack the target. Le Thanh Dao also launched a missile and saw the warhead explode off to one side of the OV-10 Bronco. The enemy aircraft spun a couple of times, but it then straightened out and began flying again. He fired the second missile, but it exploded in front of the target without a result. It was the first air battle for Le Thanh Dao, who later became an "Ace" with his six air victories over North Vietnam.

The North Vietnamese records claimed more than ten OV-10 and O-2A reconnaissance aircraft, which were shot down by Air Defense Forces and MiGs between March and September 1971. Although, the US records did not confirm them, because the files mention seven OV-10 Bronco and three O-2 Skymaster losses over South Vietnam, Laos and Cambodia.

In the second half of 1971, the VPAF MiG-21 pilots continued to try to locate and destroy B-52s in the area of the Vietnamese – Laotian border. When North Vietnamese MiG-21s took off, the B-52s immediately turned and flew away, so the MiG pilots were unable to approach them. The

VPAF Headquarters changed tactics against the B-52 bombers. MiG-21 pilot Dinh Ton was selected from the 921st Fighter Regiment, but he was able to take off and land on short, narrow runways in order to carry out the mission.

In the afternoon of 4 October 1971, at 17.00 hours Dinh Ton took off secretly from Noi Bai. He made two base-changes: Noi Bai – Anh Son and Anh Son – Dong Hoi, both at an altitude of 100 meters, and the aircraft was parked at the end of the runway so that it would be ready to take off immediately. That night, radars detected a group of B-52s more than 200 kilometers from the border. There were indications that the B-52s were planning to bomb Route No.12 and No.15. At 19:10 hours, a MiG-21 took off and pulled up, climbing to an altitude of 11.000 meters. Radars were jammed and could not catch the enemy or their signal, sothe command continued to "blindly" guide and the pilot saw two B-52s' headlights on at an altitude of 9,000 meters. When he turned back to follow them, the enemy turned off the lights. Immediately thereafter F-4 escort fighters swept toward the MiG. The situation was unsuitable for combat and the command ordered to break off and land at Tho Xuan airfield.

This was the first time that a MiG-21 had been able to close in on a group of B-52 bombers.

After North Vietnamese MiG-21 night attacks that threatened the B-52s, the USAF aircraft frequently crossed the Vietnamese – Laotian border into the Hoa Binh area. The VPAF Headquarters command post

Le Thanh Dao (RIGHT) shows his dogfight maneuvers for ground crews, on 18 December 1971. He and his comrade, Vo Si Giap (LEFT), shot down two USAF F-4D Phantoms on that day, over Thanh Hoa Province.
(István Toperczer Collection)

concluded that the Americans might resume air attacks against targets deep inside North Vietnamese territory, including against airfields in the 4th Military District.

On 18 December 1971, the entire VPAF was placed on a high level of combat readiness and increased the number of fighters assigned to combat alert duty at the airfields. The command decided to fight a coordinated battle, including coordination between MiG-21s and MiG-19s; as well as between VPAF fighters and ADF SAM sites.

The 921st Fighter Regiment, placed on combat alert, consisted of four MiG-21 pairs: Mai Van Cuong and Tran Van Sang; Le Thanh Dao and Vo Sy Giap; Nguyen Van Khanh and Le Minh Duong; and Hoang Quoc Dung and Le Khuong. The 925th Fighter Regiment alert force also consisted of four MiG-19 pairs: Bui Van Suu and Pham Cao Ha; Nguyen Tu Dung and Pham Hung Son "C"; Hoang Cao Bong and Nguyen Hong Son "A"; and Nguyen Van Cuong and Vu Viet Tan.

At 13:19 hours, radars detected three groups of F-4 Phantoms operating over Muong Lat, and a section of two aircraft operating over Lang Chanh – Hoi Xuan in Thanh Hoa Province. In order to ensure secrecy and surprise, the VPAF Headquarters command post ordered the MiG-19s to operate over the Northwestern region. At 13:12 hours, a MiG-19 pair, of Bui Van Suu and Pham Cao Ha, took off from Yen Bai and flew over Van Yen.

At 13:20 hours, a MiG-21 pair of Le Thanh Dao and Vo Sy Giap took off from Noi Bai and flew toward Suoi Rut. Two minutes later, the command post discovered a group of F-4 Phantoms flying from Sam Neua toward the Tho Xuan airfield. The MiG-21 pair was guided to intercept the bombers to protect Tho Xuan airfield. The target was at a heading of 15 degrees to Dao – Giap's right front, at a distance of 15 kilometers. Vo Sy Giap spotted a single F-4 flying in front of him and informed his flight-leader. This F-4 was one of the group that was assigned to provide cover for a helicopter landing a Special Forces team in northeastern Laos. Le Thanh Dao increased his speed to get behind his target and fired an R-3S missile at a distance of 1,200 meters. After seeing that the missile was speeding straight at the F-4, he broke away and ordered Giap to make a follow-up attack. Vo Sy Giap turned his aircraft and he saw that Dao's F-4 victim was on fire, so he did not pursue the target. Maj Johnson and 1Lt Vaughan's F-4D Phantom was Le Thanh Dao's first air victory during the Vietnam War.

As Bui Van Suu and Pham Cao Ha, with MiG-19s, and Le Thanh Dao and Vo Sy Giap, with MiG-21s, returned and landed, the command post ordered a MiG-19 pair, of Nguyen Tu Dung and Pham Hung Son "C"; and a MiG-21 pair, of Nguyen Van Khanh and Le Minh Duong, to take off and fly to holding areas over Van Yen and Hoa Binh. To protect against an American attack on Tho Xuan airfield, another MiG-21 pair, flown by Nguyen Tien Sam and Nguyen Cong Huy, was ordered to circle in waiting over the airfield. Based on intelligence information, a large group of enemy aircraft flew from the Gulf of Tonkin to attack Thanh Hoa. The MiG-21 pair was ordered to fly to Vu Ban, up to Vinh Phu, and then to land in order to clear the battle area to allow SAM sites to fire at the enemy aircraft.

In the afternoon, between 14:45 and 15:30 hours, a large number of enemy aircraft were in the Sam Neua area in Laos, and they were preparing to conduct a SAR mission to recover their downed pilots. At same time, two pairs of MiG-19s – Hoang Cao Bong and Nguyen Hong Son "A", the other of Bui Van Suu and Pham Cao Ha – took off and flew to a holding area over Van Yen and Lang Chanh. At 14:55 hours, the command post ordered the MiG-21 pair of Hoang Quoc Dung and Le Khuong to take off and fly to holding area over Hoa Binh to provide support for the MiG-19 pair, which would allow them to attack the American SAR team. At 15:16 hours, a flight of American aircraft flying at an altitude of 6,000-7,000 meters and chased the MiGs. Meanwhile, the command post ordered the MiG-19 pair to descend to a low altitude and return to Yen Bai airbase to land. Dung and Khuong, with their MiG-21s, were ordered to intercept the new targets, which were heading 30 degrees to their left side, at a distance of 19 kilometers. When Le Khuong already spotted the target, his flight-leader, Hoang Quoc Dung, was still unable to discover it, so he ordered the wingman to make the attack. Khuong increased his speed and when the distance was less than eight kilometers, the F-4s turned right and they split into separated two pairs. He decided to attack an enemy aircraft on the left, but the lead F-4 Phantom turned back and sought to launch a missile at Khuong's MiG. The F-4 Phantoms realized that they were being chased by MiG-21s, so they broke hard and took off from the action. The MiGs could not get close enough to attack and they were ordered to return and land. Another MiG-21 pair, of Mai Van Cuong and Tran Van Sang, took off and flew to a holding area at an altitude of 10 kilometers to cover the landings of Hoang Quoc Dung, Le Khuong, Nguyen Tu Dung, and Pham Hung Son "C".

Between 15:40 and 16:00 hours, the Americans sent in three flights of F-4s from Xieng Khuang Province, Laos, to launch a counterattack. At the same time, the US Navy sent three groups of F-4s, A-6s, and RA-5s to attack Anh Son airfield.

The VPAF HQ post ordered the MiG-21 pair, of Mai Van Cuong and Tran Van Sang, to fly out beyond the range of SAM sites at Kep in order to land there. At 16:05 hours, Mai Van Cuong and Tran Van Sang landed safely at Kep.

At 15:46 hours, a MiG-21 pair, of Nguyen Van Khanh and Le Minh Duong, took off and flew to a holding area over Bac Can to intercept the American aircraft during their exit flight from North Vietnamese airspace. Five minutes later, the radar station saw that Khanh and Duong's MiG-21s were flying over Kep and gave them an order to turn to a heading of 330 degrees and fly to Bac Can. The GCI then ordered the flight to change to a direction of 270 degrees. At that time, there was

Czech instructors and North Vietnamese officers stand in front of a camouflaged Aero L-29 Delfin. Twelve ex-Russian Delfins were operated by North Vietnamese pilots from 1971.
(István Toperczer Collection)

a poor coordination among the command elements. The MiG-21 pair should have made a left turn, but they had already made a right turn that took them into the SAM fire zone. At 15:57 hours, the command post made a final effort, by telling Khanh to make a hard turn to a heading of 270 degrees, but he did not respond. At that same moment, Le Minh Duong reported that while they were turning to the right, Nguyen Van Khanh had been hit by an SA-2 missile. At 16:10 hours, Le Minh Duong landed safely at Kep.

Also at the same time, the command post ordered the MiG-21 pair, of Ha Quang Hung and Do Van Lanh, and the MiG-19 pair, of Nguyen Van Cuong and Vu Viet Tan, to take off and fly in a holding area over their airfields. No American aircraft arrived over them, so the MiG pairs returned and landed safely.

In summary, on 18 December 1971, the 925th Fighter Regiment, with four pairs of the MiG-19 and five pairs of the 921st Fighter Regiment, flew three different waves with 24 sorties. Le Thanh Dao and Vo Sy Giap discovered two Phantoms over Quan Hoa, Ba Thuoc, and the leader shot down one F-4D Phantom. The other pair, Nguyen Van Khanh and Le Minh Duong, protected the north area of Hanoi, but Nguyen Van Khanh was shot down by friendly SAM fire over Thai Nguyen, because the MiG-21 flew into a no-fly zone of the SAM unit.

American documents state that two other F-4D Phantoms (65-0799 and 64-0954) were shot down by MiGs more than three hours later, while they were trying to find and rescue their downed pilots.

From November 1968 to the end of 1971, the Vietnamese People's Air Force flew hundreds of combat sorties, fought 31 battles, and shot down a total of 24 American aircraft, 21 of which were unmanned reconnaissance drones, the AQM-34 Firebees. During this period, the air force received 156 MiG aircraft, 72 of these aircraft were assembled and placed on combat alert duty. The fighter force of the VPAF were strengthened by the addition of a MiG-19 fighter regiment in 1969, and the second MiG-21 fighter regiment by the receipt of MiG MiG-21MF (Type 96) aircraft in 1971.

Tran Hanh, the commander of the 921st Fighter Regiment, holds a preflight briefing for his comrades in front of the newly arrived MiG-21MF Fishbed Js, at Noi Bai airbase. (István Toperczer Collection)

Chapter Five

Aces and MiG-Bandits during 1972

The New Regiment of the "Fishbeds"

At the end of 1971, the pilots of the 921st Fighter Regiment moved to use the MiG-21MF (Type F96) Fishbed-J, which has four hardpoints. By the beginning of 1972, all pilots of the 921st Fighter Regiment had now converted to the MiG-21MF, and the number of pilots who were combat ready under adverse weather conditions and for night missions had steadily increased. The command centre was moved to Bach Mai, while a spare unit was based at Chuong My in Ha Tay Province. At the same time, within each regiment, a second spare command group was created that was able to take over the control of the battles at any time.

On 1 December 1971, Major General Tran Quy Hai, Deputy Minister of Defense, signed the order 226/QD-QP regarding the establishment of the 927th "Lam Son" Fighter Regiment (Trung Doan Khong Quan Tiem Kich 927) under the Command of the VPAF, and stationed at Tho Xuan airfield as its base. After a period of preparation work, on 3 February 1972, the 927th Fighter Regiment celebrated the official launch, at the hall of the 921 F.R., at Noi Bai airbase. Colonel Phung The Tai, Deputy Chief of the People's Army of Vietnam, attended the ceremony and awarded the traditional flag for the regiment. The 927th F.R. flying the MiG-21PFM (Type F94) Fishbed-F was also operating north of the 20th Parallel in support of the 921st Fighter Regiment under the command of Nguyen Hong Nhi. The deputy regiment commanders were Maj Nguyen Nhat Chieu, Capt Nguyen Dang Kinh and Capt Nguyen Van Nhien. Senior Captain Mai Ba Quat was the regiment's Chief of Technical Affairs. The

The first MiG-21MF (Type 96) Fishbed Js arrived to the VPAF at the end of 1971. Two war-veteran MiG-21MFs are on display in the Museum of 5th Military District, at Da Nang. (István Toperczer)

On 3 February 1972, the 927th "Lam Son" Fighter Regiment was established under the command of Nguyen Hong Nhi, along with the 921st unit. The MiG-21PFM (Type 94) Fishbed Fs were in service at the 927th Fighter Regiment.
(István Toperczer Collection)

927th Fighter Regiment had two flight companies and was stationed at Noi Bai airbase when it was formed.

The 921st Fighter Regiment continued its operations with MiG-21MF fighters over the 4th Military District, but was available for missions in the north at any time. The western and northwestern parts of the country were allocated to the MiG-19s of the 925th Fighter Regiment, and the eastern and northeastern parts of Vietnam were protected by the MiG-17s of the 923rd Fighter Regiment.

After suffering losses in the air battle of 18 December 1971, the USAF constantly conducted reconnaissance to closely monitor the activities of the VPAF. On 19 January 1972, radar stations detected a group of enemy aircraft flying over the Mai Chau area. The VPAF Headquarters concluded that enemy aircraft would attack the Hoa Binh – Suoi Rut area and targets along Route No.3. The command post ordered the 921st and 925th Fighter Regiments to coordinate their operations to attack USAF aircraft in the area west of Hoa Binh – Suoi Rut.

At the 921st Fighter Regiment, two MiG-21 pairs were placed on combat alert duty: Nguyen Hong My and Tran Van Sang, Nguyen Duc Soat and Ha Vinh Tanh. The 925th Fighter Regiment placed a pair of MiG-19s, consisting of Pham Ngoc Tam and Nguyen Tu Dung, on combat alert.

At 14:18 hours, the command post ordered My and Sang to take off and fly on a heading of 240 degrees at an altitude of 2,000 meters. The MiG-21 pair was later ordered to climb to 8,000 meters. When they flew at an altitude of 9,500 meters, their target was at a heading of 30 degrees to their left, at a range of 20 kilometers. One minute later, Nguyen Hong My spotted the target to the left at a distance of 20 kilometers, bearing 20 degrees over the Muong Luc area. He was flying at an altitude of 11,500 meters and a speed of Mach 1.2, and because he was farther away from the target, he ordered his wingman to attack.

Nguyen Hong My stands in front of his MiG-21MF. He shot down an USAF RF-4C Phantom on 19 January 1972. It was the first air victory of the MiG-21MF type during the air war. (István Toperczer Collection)

Tran Van Sang attacked the target, but his finger slipped on the trigger and he lost his missile. He broke off to the left and My increased his speed to Mach 1.4. When the distance was 1,000 meters, he launched an R-3S missile and broke off to the right, and then rolled his aircraft upside-down to look at the target. The missile warhead exploded about 300 meters in front of the target, but the RF-4 Phantom continued to fly straight ahead. At that moment, the command post at Tho Xuan informed him that the target was right in front of him. Nguyen Hong My closed to the target and, when the distance was down to 1,800-2,000 meters, he fired his second missile at an altitude of over 13,000 meters. He broke off to the right and then rolled his aircraft upside-down to observe the missile explosion. He saw the RF-4C Phantom explode, break in half and fall down toward the ground. Because Nguyen Hong My fired his second missile at too close a range and he flew into the slipstream of the American aircraft, his engine stopped. He descended to below 9,000 meters, but then successfully restarted his engine and landed safely at Tho Xuan airfield. The USAF records mentioned Maj Mock's RF-4C Phantom loss the next day, on 20 January 1972, but VPAF claimed for Nguyen Hong My this air victory on 19 January 1972.

On that afternoon, MiG-19s and MiG-21s took off from Yen Bai and Noi Bai. At 14:26 hours, the MiG-19 pair, of Pham Ngoc Tam and Nguyen Tu Dung, flew to a holding area over Yen Bai airbase. At 14:41 hours, the MiG-21 pair of Nguyen Duc Soat and Ha Vinh Thanh, took off and flew toward Thanh Son – Phu Tho. At 14:48 hours, radar stations detected a target flying down from Nghia Lo. The MiG-21 pair turned back to intercept this target. The command post asked the 925th Fighter Regiment where its MiG-19 pair was located. The GCI of the regiment replied that the MiG-19s were still flying in the holding area over Yen Bai airbase. The central command post directed the MiG-21 pair to engage the target. Nguyen Duc Soat spotted two white painted aircraft, which were not F-4 Phantoms. He asked the central command post: "Are you sure these are not friendly aircraft?" The reply arrived: "They are NOT friendly aircraft!" Soat took aim and fired an R-3S missile at a distance of 1,500 meters; and then an aircraft caught fire. Soat's MiG-21 swept up even with the target and he saw that it was a MiG-19! He immediately ordered Ha Vinh Thanh to break off the attack.

The MiG-19 pilot was a victim of friendly fire, so Nguyen Tu Dung had to eject and he landed safely on the ground. In this incident, the GCI of the 925th Fighter Regiment made a mistake. The VPAF Headquarters had ordered that the MiG-19s were to remain in a holding area over their airbase. The GCI of regiment had decided to have its MiG-19s fly toward Nghia Lo – Van Yen to make a radar check, but it did not inform the VPAF Headquarters command post.

In 1972, when the Americans again attacked North Vietnam, they were using brand new tactics and equipment. On first day of March, Lt Col Kittenger and 1Lt Hodgdon fired three AIM-7 missiles from the famous "MiG-killer" F-4D Phantom (66-7463) and destroyed Dang Van Dinh's MiG-21, but he ejected safely.

On 3 March, an Li-2 transport aircraft (No. 218) brought a group of officers and technicians of the 921st Fighter Regiment to Vinh in order to continue on to the Khe Gat airfield to make preparations for air combat operations to support the 1972 Easter Offensive in Quang Tri – Thua Thien. While preparing to land at the Vinh airfield, the aircraft was

Two MiG-21MFs are seen under pre-flight checks at Noi Bai airbase. Usually, the built-in GSh-23L cannon is mounted under the center fuselage. It has an ammunition supply of 200 rounds and four infrared guided air-to-air missiles are underwing pylons of the MiG-21MF Fishbed J.
(István Toperczer Collection)

hit by friendly fire from an SA-2 missile site and 22 people were killed in this incident. Among those killed was the famous fighter pilot, Le Trong Huyen, and a number of other regimental officers.

On 6 March 1972, based on the operations of the enemy, Army Command had directed the VPAF in Vinh, Anh Son and Tho Xuan. The MiG–17s were on duty at Tho Xuan airfield and MiG-21s were ready to take off at Anh Son airfield, while the crew on duty at the navigation headquarters of Tho Xuan led the MiG-21s to close support missions.

About 12:00 hours, the enemy appeared southwest of Anh Son. After 15 minutes and 30 seconds, a pair of MiG-17s, Le Hai and Hoang Ich, took off from Tho Xuan and flew at an altitude of 400 meters, at a speed of 650 km/h, along Route No.15. At Tan Ky they then ascended to 1,200 meters. At 12:27 hours, the MiGs turned right at a heading of 270 degrees toward Anh Son and discovered the enemy southwest of the airfield. Le Hai saw that the MiG-21s took off from Anh Son and two F-4 Phantoms flew at a distance of 8 kilometers and an altitude of 1,000 meters, two more Phantoms at an altitude of 3,000 meters. Le Hai decided to attack the F-4 Phantom pair at low altitude and shot three bursts, one Phantom caught fire. Le Hai turned right and attacked the second pair, but ran out of ammunition. Hoang Ich also found the enemy, but did not fire and reported about the shotdown F-4 Phantom. Le Hai ordered escapism, Hoang Ich answered, but both had not seen each other. At an altitude of 100 meters flying back, Le Hai called Hoang Ich, but received no answer. In this battle, when the two MiG-17s returned to Tho Xuan, the enemy arrived from the Gulf of Tonkin and shot down Hoang Ich over Nghia Dan. The crew on duty at navigation found the enemy from the aircraft carrier. They did not report to the headquarters of Tho Xuan immediately, so the pairs of MiG-21, Tran Viet and Nguyen Cong Huy could not take off for close air support for the MiG-17s.

The MiG-21 pilots of the 921st and 927th Fighter Regiments are discussing the next mission on a map. Ngo Duy Thu (927) and Tran Viet (921) are walking to squatting Le Khuong (921), Nguyen Ngoc Thien (921), Le Thanh Dao (927) and Dang Ngoc Ngu (921), in April of 1972.
(István Toperczer Collection)

Le Thanh Dao and Hoang Quoc Dung are seen after a demo-flight for the Hungarian delegation in February of 1972.
(István Toperczer Collection)

All VPAF units took part in the action on 16 April by launching 30 aircraft (ten MiG-21s, six MiG-19s and fourteen MiG-17s). From them, the Americans shot down three MiG-21s. Nguyen Hong My, Le Khuong (921) and Duong Dinh Nghi (927) ejected safely. On the 27 April 1972, from the 921st Fighter Regiment, Hoang Quoc Dung and Cao Son Khao took off from Noi Bai for Vu Ban (Nam Ha Province) when they saw a pair of F-4s flying 6 kilometers front of them. From a distance of 3 kilometers, Hoang Quoc Dung fired an R-3S missile at the F-4B Phantom on the left, which burst into flames and crashed. Lt Molinare and Lt Cdr Souder ejected and became Prisoners of War (POW).

The Great Battles of May

Early in May, 1972, under "Operation Pocket Money," the US Navy Task Force 77 aerial mining mission was conducted against the most important ports of North Vietnam. The enemy dropped mines and magnetic bombs to blockade the port of Hai Phong and nearby river mouths and increased the attacks in the northern coastal provinces. VPAF Headquarters decided to move the 921st Fighter Regiment from Tho Xuan to Noi Bai and used forces of MiG-21 and MiG-17 from the 921st, 927th and 923rd Fighter Regiments as mobile alert units at Gia Lam, Kien An, Kep, Hoa Lac, Yen Bai, and Tho Xuan airfields, while the aircraft at Anh Son moved to Mieu Mon. The technical personnel at Vinh and Anh Son were divided between the 921st and 927th Fighter Regiments. The MiG-19s from the 925th Fighter Regiment were concentrated at Yen Bai airbase. From mid-May to early October 1972, besides Yen Bai, the 925th Fighter Regiment also performed mobile combat operations on Noi Bai and Gia Lam airfields. Responding to the US attacks, mobile groups of aircraft (MiG-19s, pilots, technicians) temporarily settled onto other

During "the Great Battles of May," the MiG-21 and MiG-19 were the two main fighters against American combat formations. The famous MiG-21MF, No.5121, and MiG-19S (Shenyang J-6), No.6058, are on display at the VPAF Museum in Hanoi.
(István Toperczer)

airfields. Thus, they were able to join into air battles above different areas alongside of the MiG-17s and MiG-21s.

In the afternoon of 5 May 1972, after launching from Tho Xuan airfield, MiG-17s landed at Gia Lam airfield and MiG-21s landed at Noi Bai airbase. The VPAF Headquarters considered that the enemy would continue to attack Tho Xuan, so they arranged an ambush. The preparations were started with the 923rd and 927th Fighter Regiments.

In the early morning of May 6, 1972, a pair of MiG-17s, Nguyen Van Luc and Nguyen Van Bay "B," flew in secret en route Kep – Gia Lam – Vu Ban – Tho Xuan, at an altitude of 100 meters, over terrain and only used a few cues essential in the air. At 12:50 hours, US Navy aircraft from the USS *Coral Sea* (CVA-43) carrier raided Ham Rong and the Do Len Bridge. Based on the rules of enemy activity in the past few days, the headquarters in Tho Xuan ordered the MiG-17s to take off and MiG-21s were in readiness at Noi Bai as a close air support team. At 13:05 hours, Nguyen Van Bay "B" and Nguyen Van Luc flew over south of the airfield, at an altitude of 300 meters when the radar station commander detected four A-6s from the southeast at an altitude of about 70 meters. Nguyen Van Luc also saw the enemy at nine a o'clock position and a distance of 4 kilometers. He attacked the first two A-6s and Nguyen Van Bay "B" turned to the second pair of A-6 Intruders. Nguyen Van Luc cut the radius, shot two series and saw debris thrown off the enemy aircraft. He fired a third series and the A-6 caught fire. The US Navy records do not mention this A-6 loss. Bay "B" followed the enemies to the east of Trau Mountain. At that moment, two F-4 Phantoms were detected flying from north to south of the airfield. Immediately Bay "B" took an evasive maneuver, but the enemy still clung to his MiG-17. Nguyen Van Luc called his comrade, but got no answer, because he was already sacrificed. On the orders of the base commander, Nguyen Van Luc landed alone on Gia Lam airfield, at 13:28 hours.

On that day, four MiG-21s of the 927th Fighter Regiment were on combat alert duty at Noi Bai airbase and two more MiG-21s were on reserve alert at Kep airbase. Nguyen Tien Sam, Nguyen The Duc, and Nguyen Van Nghia were ordered to take off at 17:31 hours. Following take-off, they were directed to a holding area over south of the Mieu Mon airfield, where they began flying in circles to wait for enemy bombers flying in to attack Nam Dinh. A few minutes later, the MiG-21 flight spotted the target at Dong Giao – Vu Ban. According to the battle plan, the MiG-21s attacked the enemy bombers in order to disrupt the USAF strike formation. After a few minutes, the situation was not too favorable for MiG-21s, so the GCI ordered them to break off the engagement and return to land at Noi Bai airbase. During this maneuver Le Van Lap's MiG was hit by an AIM-9G missile from Lt Hughes' F-4J Phantom of VF-114, USS *Kitty Hawk*. The MiG pilot ejected and landed safely on the ground, while the other three MiGs returned to Noi Bai.

After researching enemy operations, the VPAF HQ focused on the southwest area of Hanoi, to protect important targets, such as Noi Bai, Yen Bai, and Hoa Lac airfields. After general intentions were debriefed, all ground control teams made their own plans for their units. From 21:00 hours of 7 May, ground control teams cooperated with command posts and from 05:00 hours of 8 May, they also cooperated with combat units.

At 08:12 hours on 8 May 1972, enemy flights appeared 50 kilometers southwest from Ky Son to Sam Neua, and at 08:32 hours, from Tuong Duong to Sam Tai. The enemy began approaching from the southwest of Hanoi and the commander on duty, Tran Manh, ordered a MiG-21

MiG-bunkers were built in the hills at Noi Bai, Yen Bai, Kien An, Anh Son and other airfields. The bunkers had camouflaged and armored gates, and about 30-60 MiGs were able to fit inside.
(ISTVÁN TOPERCZER)

In May of 1972, North Vietnamese pilots of the 925th Fighter Regiment run to their MiG-19S Farmer Cs at Yen Bai airbase. (István Toperczer Collection)

pair to take off at Noi Bai. Pham Phu Thai and Vo Si Giap from the 921st Fighter Regiment went through the clouds, and then flew to a holding area over Tuyen Quang, at an altitude of 7,000 meters.

The VPAF Headquarters had ordered the 925th Fighter Regiment to put up a constant CAP over Yen Bai airbase, to protect the Thac Ba hydroelectric power station.

At 08:36 hours, a flight of 8 enemy aircraft flew from the Sam Neua to Van Yen direction. At 08:48 hours, command post reported that the enemy was 15 kilometers north of Van Yen when the two flights of MiG-19s were in air at the opposite end of Yen Bai. Flight Number I in the north was operating four MiG-19 fighters flown by: Nguyen Ngoc Tiep, Nguyen Duc Tiem, Nguyen Hong Son "A," and Nguyen Hung Son "B". Flight Number II was patrolling in the south with: Pham Ngoc Tam, Pham Hung Son "C", Phung Van Quang and Nguyen Manh Tung (instead of Vu Chinh Nghi).

At that time, command post at the 921st Fighter Regiment followed the enemy flight coming from north of Van Yen to Yen Bai and guided Pham Phu Thai – Vo Si Giap from Tuyen Quang to Yen Bai to pull them to altitude of 6,000 meters to give the MiG-19s an opportunity to fight at an altitude of 4,000 meters. The MiG-21s detected F-4 Phantoms head on and made maneuvers to follow them twice, but it was impossible. During the break off, radio contact was jammed, so the MiG-21s had to counterattack many times, when Giap's MiG-21 received a missile hit. The MiG was damaged and lost fuel so he decided to land. He flew the very low altitude and had to avoid a school on the ground. Vo Si Giap made a turn to the other side when his aircraft exploded and killed him over Thuong Trung in Vinh Phu Province.

At 08:56 hours, the command post informed the MiG-19s that they were covered by MiG-21s, at an altitude of 6,000 meters, but the MiG-19 flight already met the enemy because the enemy fired missiles and were following the MiGs. The fight began between MiG-19s and 8 F-4 Phantoms. At 08:58 hours, command post ordered them to fight only over the airbase and without going far away. Nguyen Ngoc Tiep,

Nguyen Hong Son "A," and Nguyen Hung Son "B" had chances to attack. Nguyen Ngoc Tiep and Nguyen Hung Son "B" shot down two F-4 Phantoms. At 09:04 hours, Tiep reported he had less than 1,200 liters of fuel, so command ordered them to land. The MiG-19 pair of Pham Ngoc Tam – Pham Hung Son "C" took off to cover them, while Phung Van Quang and Nguyen Manh Tung stayed on ready. At 09:06 hours, Tiep – Tiem – Son "A" – Son "B" landed safely at Noi Bai.

The second MiG-19 pair apparently did not meet American aircraft. At 09:16 hours all MiG-19s were safely back at the base. The US records did not confirm MiG-19s kills.

While the air battle took place in the sky of Yen Bai, several US flights operated in Kim Boi, Hoa Binh and Viet Tri. A ground control team of the 927th Fighter Regiment guided the MiG-21 flight of Nguyen Duc Soat, Ngo Duy Thu, Nguyen Van Nghia and Ha Vinh Thanh from Noi Bai to Dai Tu, to intercept any Americans from attacking the Noi Bai airbase. The ground control team of the 923rd Fighter Regiment guided the MiG-17 flight of Nguyen Van Tho, Nguyen Xuan Hien, Do Hang and Au Van Hung from Kep to Phuc Yen and the ground control team of VPAF HQ guided the MiG-17 flight of Hoang Cong, Nguyen Van Gia, Nguyen Hung Van and Ngo Son from Gia Lam to west of Hoa Lac, to protect Noi Bai and Hoa Lac airfields.

On 8 May 1972, Nguyen Hung Son "B" shot down an F-4 Phantom, by VPAF records. The North Vietnamese MiG-19s were armed only with three 30 mm NR-30 cannons during the air war.
(István Toperczer Collection)

Operation "Linebacker" was the title of a US Seventh Air Force and US Navy Task Force 77 air interdiction campaign conducted against North Vietnam, from 9 May to 23 October 1972. On 9 May 1972, apart from mining the waters of Hai Phong and other ports, more than 200 strikes were launched against the airfields at Vinh, Tho Xuan, Hoa Lac, Yen Bai and Na San, as well as against transport routes in the region of Hanoi and Hai Phong. This attack was anticipated and the strength of the four fighter regiments was concentrated for the counter attack.

On 10 May, according to plan, all units focused on the southeast of Hanoi, while also protecting Yen Bai airbase and Thac Ba hydroelectric

The three MiG-types of the Vietnam War are on display together at the VPAF Museum in Hanoi. On 10 May 1972, flights of MiG-17s, MiG-19s and MiG-21s took part in air battles over North Vietnam.
(István Toperczer)

plant. At VPAF HQ, ground control officer Le Thanh Chon commanded MiG-21s of the 927th Fighter Regiment at Kep and assisted MiG-19s at Yen Bai, Khong Duc Thi commanded MiG-21s of the 921st Fighter Regiment at Noi Bai, and Do Cat Lam commanded MiG-17s at Gia Lam. At the 923rd Fighter Regiment command post, Tong Ba Nhuong commanded MiG-21s of the 921st Fighter Regiment at Kep and Dang Van Hao commanded MiG-17s of the 923rd Fighter Regiment at Kep. At the 927th Fighter Regiment command post, Vu Duc Binh and Nguyen Van Duoc commanded other MiG-21s of the 927th Fighter Regiment at Noi Bai airbase.

At 08:36 hours, the enemy was detected 100 kilometers east of the Tra Ly River mouth, flying to Long Chau, when commanders Dao Dinh Luyen and Tran Hanh ordered MiG-21s from the 921st Fighter Regiment and MiG-17s from the 923rd Fighter Regiment to take off at Kep.

At 08:43 hours, the MiG-17 flight of Vu Van Dang, Nguyen Cong Ngu, Trinh Van Quy, and Nguyen Van Lam was guided to a holding area at Pha Lai, ready to protect the Lai Vu Bridge. At 08:52 hours, a MiG-21 pair of Dang Ngoc Ngu and Nguyen Van Ngai also took off. When they reached an altitude of 200 meters, the enemy aircraft followed them and fired from behind. Unfortunately, Nguyen Van Ngai's MiG was shot down by an AIM-9 Sidewinder from Lt Dose's F-4J Phantom of VF-92, USS *Constellation*. He was killed in action (KIA). Dang Ngoc Ngu accelerated and continuously changed his direction. After he turned to the north side of Yen Tu range, Ngu detected two F-4 Phantoms flying over him on the left at 15 degrees. He increased his speed and shot down an F-4 Phantom by a missile at 08:57 hours. Command ordered Ngu to break off to the north, then he landed safely at Noi Bai. US records did not confirm his kill on that day.

Pham Hung Son "C" stands in the cockpit of a MiG-19, in May of 1972. Three MiG-19 pilots became the best-known of the air war, because of their similar names. They were known as Son "A", Son "B" and Son "C". (István Toperczer Collection)

From 09:14 to 09:35 hours, the radars detected some enemy flights at Suoi Rut, Hoi Xuan, but could not keep them. The 925th Fighter Regiment commanders Ho Van Quy and Mai Duc Toai judged they would attack Yen Bai, Thac Ba and ordered a MiG-19 flight of Pham Ngoc Tam (1), Pham Hung Son "C" (2), Nguyen Van Phuc (3) and Le Duc Oanh (4) to fight at the south end of the airbase. At VPAF HQ, flight routes of the enemy from Moc Chau to Nghia Lo and southwest of Sam Neua to the Vietnamese – Laotian border were monitored closely. Two MiG-21s of Nguyen Cong Huy and Cao Son Khao, from the 921st Fighter Regiment scrambled from Noi Bai at 09:44 hours heading for Tuyen Quang to distract the Americans' attention. They attacked the enemy fighter flight in the Yen Bai area but Huy – Khao had to fight hard, Cao Son Khao shot down an F-4 Phantom, but he was later killed by enemy AIM-7 missiles, from 1Lt Markle's F-4D Phantom. The USAF records did not confirm Khao's air victory.

Meanwhile, the first flight of MiG-19s flew at the south end of Yen Bai airbase, at 09:44 hours. The second MiG-19 flight was ordered to

Dang Ngoc Ngu

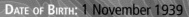

Date of Birth: 1 November 1939
Enlisted: 23 March 1959
Pilot training:
1961 – 1965 (MiG-17 – Soviet Union)
1965 – 1966 (MiG-21 – Soviet Union)
War Service and Unit:
1966 – 1972 (921st Fighter Regiment)
Aircraft: MiG-21
Died: 8 July 1972 – shot down by USAF F-4E Phantom (67-0270 / Hardy – Lewinski)
Hero of the Vietnamese People's Armed Forces: 11 January 1973
Rank: Senior Captain

Air Victories: 7 kills
(3 F-4s, 1 F-105, 3 Firebees – VPAF official credit)

Date	Aircraft	Unit	Kill – US Pilot (VPAF – US databases)
13 Aug 66	MiG-21	921.	Firebee
14 Dec 66	MiG-21	921.	F-105D – US not confirmed
22 May 67	MiG-21	921.	F-4C – Perrine, Backus (KIAs) (AAA)
08 Nov 67	MiG-21	921.	F-4D – Gordon, Brenneman (POW)
24 Apr 68	MiG-21	921.	Firebee
04 Mar 69	MiG-21	921.	Firebee
10 May 72	MiG-21	921.	F-4 – US not confirmed

MiG-21MF Fishbed J, No. 5136 (5 kills) of the 921st Fighter Regiment, 1972
The pilots of the 921st Fighter Regiment credited 5 air victories by this MiG-21MF.
The Ace-pilot Dang Ngoc Ngu added his kill marking to No. 5136 during on 10 May 1972.
(Artwork: Balázs Kakuk)

take off and guided to a holding area over the airbase; bearing 100-280 degrees, at an altitude of 3,000 meters, and a speed of 850 km/h.

After the third turn, and with help from the command post, Pham Ngoc Tam (1) detected F-4 Phantoms at a distance of 6 kilometers, and at an altitude 1,500 meters. The Phantoms saw the MiG-19s too. Both sides fought on the right side over the airbase. Seeing an F-4 was turning from the north end to the south end, Nguyen Van Phuc (3) dove and, in the 16th minute of the dogfight, he fired three short bursts with cannons at an F-4 Phantom from a distance of 2,000 meters. Maj Lodge and Capt Locher's Phantom was hit from its tail to the mid-fuselage, but Nguyen Van Phuc (3) continued with the attack and fired again from a distance of 300 meters, and again, before the American aircraft broke up into two pieces at 09:58 hours. Nguyen Van Phuc (3) attacked another Phantom under the watchful eyes of his wingman Le Duc Oanh (4) when he noticed that they were followed by an F-4 Phantom. Due to too close a distance, Nguyen Van Phuc had to break off with a G more than 10. He opened fire three times but missed his target. In the meantime, Le Duc Oanh was hit by an air-to-air missile over La Hill in Tuyen Quang Province. He was able to eject but later died of his injuries. After the enemy the backed off, the 925th Fighter Regiment command ordered the first MiG-19 flight to return over the airbase and the second MiG-19 flight, Hoang Cao Bong (1), Pham Cao Ha (2), Nguyen Van Cuong (3) and Le Van Tuong (4), was guided to the north end of Yen Bai airbase.

The enemy returned to the Yen Bai area, and the second MiG-19 flight found itself in the heat of the battle immediately. Le Van Tuong (4), spotting the target, fired two bursts, setting Capt Harris and Capt Wilkinson's F-4E Phantom port wing into flames. Nguyen Van Cuong (3) also attacked and fired three times but did not score any hits. The air battle lasted 18 minutes, and even though there were still US fighters over the airbase, the MiGs received an order to land, due to low fuel. Hoang Cao Bong (1) landed safely but Nguyen Van Cuong (3) overran the runway by 50 meters, fortunately with no damage to the MiG-19 or injury to the pilot. Le Van Tuong (4) landed only when he had completely run out of fuel. He started his approach from 1,400 meters and, due to the high speed, ran off the landing strip, which destroyed the aircraft. Le Van Tuong died in the accident. Pham Cao Ha (2) also landed safely.

On that morning, the 923rd Fighter Regiment command guided a MiG-17 pair of Do Hang and Nguyen Xuan Hien from Kep, and the VPAF HQ guided a MiG-17 flight of Luong Quoc Bao, Nguyen Van Hung, Nguyen Hung Van and Ngo Son from Gia Lam. All MiG-17s flew to protect the area of the Kep, Gia Lam and Noi Bai airbases. The VPAF HQ also guided a MiG-17 flight of Nguyen Van Tho, Ta Dong Trung, Do Hang and Tra Van Kiem from Hoa Lac to protect Hoa Lac and Noi Bai. They later moved to Kep airbase.

At 12:25 hours, US Navy F-4s, A-6s and A-7s attacked Hai Duong and the bridges at Lai Vu and Phu Luong. Four MiG-17s, Nguyen Van Tho, Ta

Dong Trung, Do Hang and Tra Van Kiem from the 923rd Fighter Regiment were ordered to take off and protect the northern bridgehead at Lai Vu. They took off from Kep and, when 15 kilometers from Hai Duong, Nguyen Van Tho and Ta Dong Trung spotted the Americans and went into action. Ta Dong Trung chased an American aircraft and opened fire, but missed. When he noticed that he was flying out to the open sea, he turned and flew along the Thai Binh River to land at Kep. Nguyen Van Tho went after an A-7, opened fire once but missed, after which the Corsair was able to escape. He noticed that an F-4 was on his tail and Nguyen Van Tho turned around, but the Phantom flew past him. Seeing that two Phantoms were trailing both Do Hang and his wingman Tra Van Kiem, the leader Nguyen Van Tho warned them of the danger and Tra Van Kiem managed to evade the two Americans. Do Hang was not so lucky as his MiG-17 was hit by two missiles from Lt Cunningham's F-4J Phantom of VF-96 from the USS *Constellation*. Do Hang bailed out but he was killed by 20 mm machine gun fire from the two Phantoms as he was descending with his parachute. Nguyen Van Tho noticed that Tra Van Kiem was chased by an F-4J Phantom and he opened fire but missed. He opened fire two more times but missed again and at the same time ran out of ammunition. Tran Van Kiem did not eject, he died in his fallen MiG-17. By this time Nguyen Van Tho was also under fire from Lt Connelly's F-4J Phantom of VF-96, USS *Constellation*. He was able to eject from his MiG-17 northwest of Tu Ky.

Meanwhile, the 927th Fighter Regiment command guided its two MiG-21s, from Noi Bai to Thanh Son – Phu Yen to attack the enemy when they continued their mission to Yen Bai.

At 12:57 hours, a MiG-21 pair of Le Thanh Dao and Vu Duc Hop took off. The enemy flew straight the Tra Ly River mouth, the MiG-21s turned left, at heading of 360 degrees, at an altitude of 2,000 meters and intended to wait at Kep to fight both in the east and southeast directions. When the enemy flew west of Hai Duong and then turned right to Nam Sach, command ordered Dao – Hop to turn back. At 13:00 hours, the MiG-21s turned to heading of 180 degrees. The enemy was 10 kilometers north of Hai Duong. Command ordered the MiG-21s to fly to heading of 210 degrees and one minute later they turned left to heading of 140 degrees to intercept enemies. North Vietnamese aircraft followed as the enemy continued to turn left. After Le Thanh Dao detected a target on his left 30 degrees, and a distance of 25 kilometers. Vu Duc Hop reported an F-4 on the left, at a distance of 10 kilometers, head on and requested to attack. The enemy discovered the MiG-21s and broke formation to fight back. At 13:04 hours, Hop approached and shot down Lt Cunningham and Lt (jg) Driscoll's F-4J Phantom (155800) by an R-3S missile. One and half minutes later Dao also fired his missile and hit Cdr Blackburn and Lt Rudloff's F-4J Phantom (155797). The command post ordered Dao – Hop to break off and they landed at Kep airbase.

This veteran MiG-21MF Fishbed J, No. 5127, is on display in the Museum of the 5th Military District, Da Nang.
(István Toperczer)

Le Thanh Dao and Vu Duc Hop's air victories were a historical mark for the 927th Fighter Regiment. That was the first air victory for the fighter regiment: two MiG-21 PFMs shot down two F-4J Phantoms in one and half minutes, each pilot fired only one R-3S missile and the air battle lasted 21 minutes between take-off and landing.

On the late morning of 10 May, besides air battles of MiG-17 flight Tho – Trung – Hang – Kiem and MiG-21 pair Dao – Hop, in a southeast direction, the 923rd Fighter Regiment command guided two MiG-17 pairs, Trinh Van Quy and Nguyen Van Lam, Vu Van Dang and Nguyen Xuan Hien at Kep over the airbase to protect it, and VPAF HQ guided the 921st Fighter Regiment's MiG-21 pair of Hoang Quoc Dung and Bui Thanh Liem from Noi Bai to cover Dao – Hop's MiG-21s.

After the hard day of air battles, on 11 May, the VPAF prepared plans for MiG-21s of the 927th Fighter Regiment at Noi Bai, and checked the plan for MiG-19s and MiG-17s at Yen Bai and Kep airbases.

At 14:37 hours, the enemy arrived from the Vietnamese-Laotian border, at an altitude of 8,000 meters. The main MiG-21 pair, of Ngo Van Phu and Ngo Duy Thu was on a Class One Alert when radars detected eight American aircraft from Tuong Duong to Que Phong, at an altitude of 8,000 meters. At 14:42 hours, the decoy MiG-21 pair, of Nguyen Tien Sam and Duong Dinh Nghi, was on a Class One Alert, also. The number of enemy flights from the southwest direction increased at several different altitudes and with jamming to make it difficult for MiGs to find their striking flights.

At 14:45 hours, Phu – Thu took off and they were guided at a heading of 190 degrees, a speed of 800 km/h, and an altitude of 500 meters. After four minutes, the 927th Fighter Regiment commander Nguyen Hong Nhi ordered Sam and Nghi to take off and they flew as decoys, to attract the enemy to Thanh Son. They ascended to an altitude of 7,000-8,000 meters toward Moc Chau, then back to Phu Tho – Noi Bai.

The VPAF HQ with assistance from the GCI, "blindly" guided Phu – Thu. At 14:49 hours, the MiGs followed the enemy flight that crossed the border coming to Mai Chau – Hoa Binh, at a heading of 210 degrees, at an altitude of 800 meters, and accelerated to 900 km/h. Three minutes later, the MiG-21s arrived over Vu Ban, and command ordered them to turn to a heading of 270 degrees, speed to 1,000 km/h and at an altitude of 4,000 meters. At 14:54 hours, they changed their heading to 360 degrees and an altitude of 6,000 meters. The enemy crossed Route No.15, flew to Tan Lac and approached the MiGs. Phu – Thu turned to a heading of 30 degrees and spotted the targets on their left, at a distance of 25 kilometers, 20 kilometers, and then 15km. At 14:57 hours, Ngo Duy Thu shot down an F-105G Thunderchief and broke off to the left and returned to Noi Bai airbase at 10,000 meters. Meanwhile, Ngo Van Phu followed an F-4 Phantom flight and shot down Lt Col Kittinger and 1Lt Reich's F-4D Phantom (66-0230), but he was shot down by Capt Nichols and 1Lt Bell's F-4D Phantom, and ejected safely.

On 18 May 1972, four MiG-17s of the 923rd Fighter Regiment as well as MiG-19 and MiG-21 flights, mixed it up with American aircraft over Kep. The North Vietnamese aircraft were operating in pairs, supporting each other and had managed to avoid American missiles.

The VPAF HQ redeployed combat units at Noi Bai, besides MiG-21s there were four MiG-19s. The 925th Fighter Regiment began to fight as mobile at other airbases while keeping parts ready at Yen Bai. There were four MiG-17s of the 923rd Fighter Regiment and two MiG-21s from the 927th Fighter Regiment at Kep airbase. The command focused on the fighting to the east and west of Hanoi.

At 11:26 hours, several enemy flights were detected at the southwest direction. Commander Tran Manh ordered a MiG-21 pair, of Bui Duc Nhu and Ngo Duy Thu, to take off at 11:42 hours, and they were guided to turn over Tam Dao to Phu Tho. The MiG-21s spotted the enemy head on and could not attack, so they broke off to Noi Bai.

At 11:47 hours, radars detected enemy aircraft from Long Chau Island to Cam Pha and coming in the Yen Tu range direction. The VPAF HQ ordered MiG-19s and MiG-17s to take off. At 11:52 hours, a MiG-17 pair, of Han Vinh Tuong and Nguyen Van Dien, took off, and two minutes later another MiG-17 pair, of Trinh Van Quy – Nguyen Van Lam, were guided to turn over the airbase. They started their afterburners to ascend and discovered the enemy 80 degrees on the left, at an altitude of 3,500 meters and 25 kilometers east of Bao Dai Mountain. At 12:00 hours, Han Vinh Tuong detected four F-4 Phantoms at a distance of 6

On 18 May 1972, Nguyen Hong Son "A", Nguyen Thang Long, Pham Ngoc Tam and Vu Viet Tan discuss their tactics. On this day Pham Ngoc Tam shot down an USAF F-4D Phantom. Unfortunately, Tam and Long were shot down by US Navy F-4B Phantoms, although each MiG-pilot ejected and landed safely.
(István Toperczer Collection)

kilometers and he followed them, firing three bursts to shoot down an F-4 Phantom. The MiG-17 flight broke off and returned to Noi Bai.

At 11.51 hours, the MiG-19 flight, of Pham Ngoc Tam, Nguyen Thang Long, Nguyen Hong Son "A" and Vu Viet Tan, took off from Noi Bai, they flew toward Pha Lai – Luc Nam. During the turn back at 80 degrees; they detected an enemy on the left, at a heading of 20 degrees, at a distance of 4 kilometers and an altitude of 2,000 meters. At 12:03 hours, Pham Ngoc Tam attacked with three bursts and shot down 1Lt Ratzel and 1Lt Bednarek's F-4D Phantom (66-7612), who became KIA status. After the break off, command ordered the MiG-19s to fly over Kep to cover the MiG-17s, and then turn back to Noi Bai.

While the MiG-17s and the MiG-19s were breaking off, the enemy was still in the east, so a MiG-21 pair at Noi Bai took off to cover them. At 12:12 hours, the 927th Fighter Regiment guided Nguyen Ngoc Hung and Mai Van Tue to turn to Thai Nguyen, but there were heavy clouds ahead and regimental command could not catch the MiGs' signals. Commander Tran Manh ordered pilots to make contact with VPAF HQ. At 12:20 hours, an enemy was reported 8 kilometers east of Kep and they flew to Luong Bridge. One minute later, the MiG-21s turned right hard and Hung detected F-4s below on the left, at a distance of 10 kilometers head on. Nguyen Ngoc Hung attacked and shot down an F-4 Phantom, although the US records did not confirm it. Mai Van Tue also fired an R-3S missile but missed. They broke off and landed at Noi Bai.

In the afternoon, US Navy aircraft conducted a strike mission against Haiphong. A MiG-19 pair and a MiG-21 pair were guided from Noi Bai to Kep, where they met enemy fighters.

At 16:30 hours, when two F-4B Phantoms, assigned to MiGCAP mission, were approaching Kep airbase, they spotted the two MiG-19s of Pham Ngoc Tam and Nguyen Thang Long flying toward the airfield. The two F-4Bs from USS *Midway*, immediately fired AIM-9G missiles at

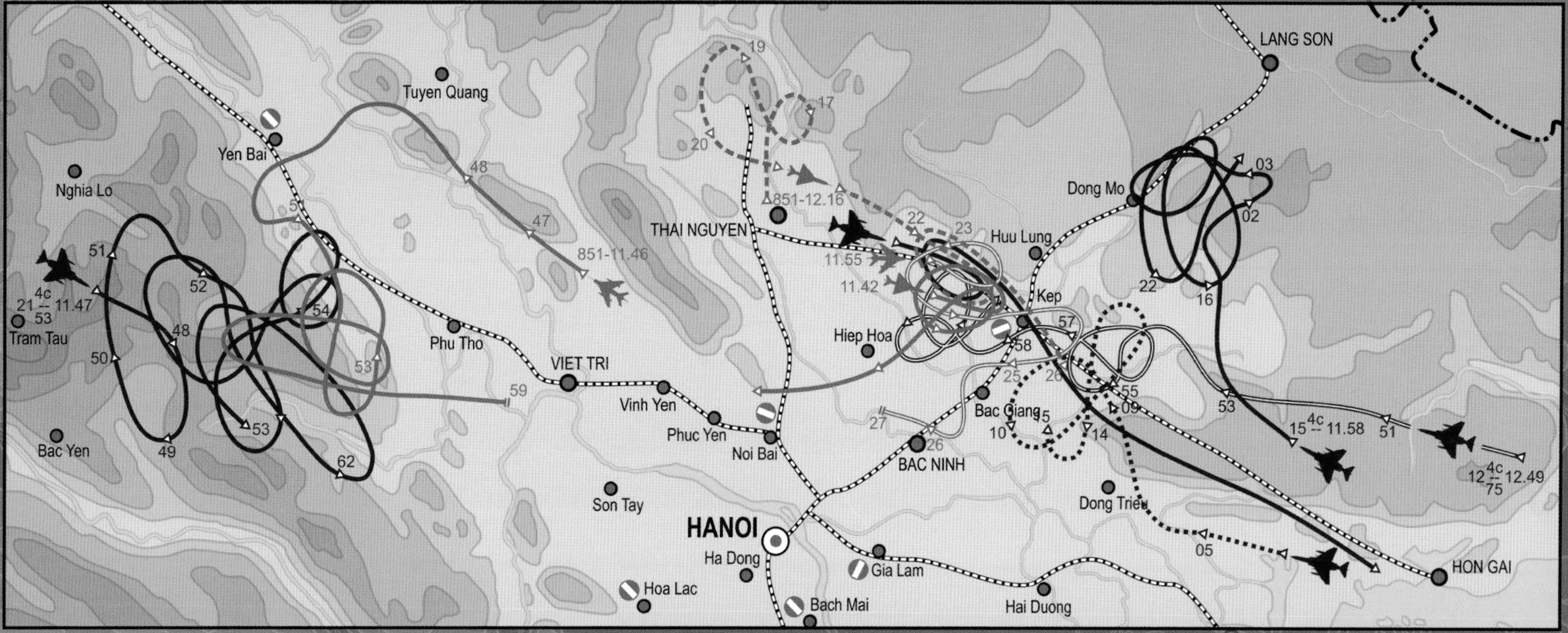

On 18 May 1972, three MiG-21 pairs of the 927th Fighter Regiment and two flights of the 925th Fighter Regiment took part in the air battles over Yen Bai and Kep airbases. (CARTOGRAPH: PÉTER BARNA)

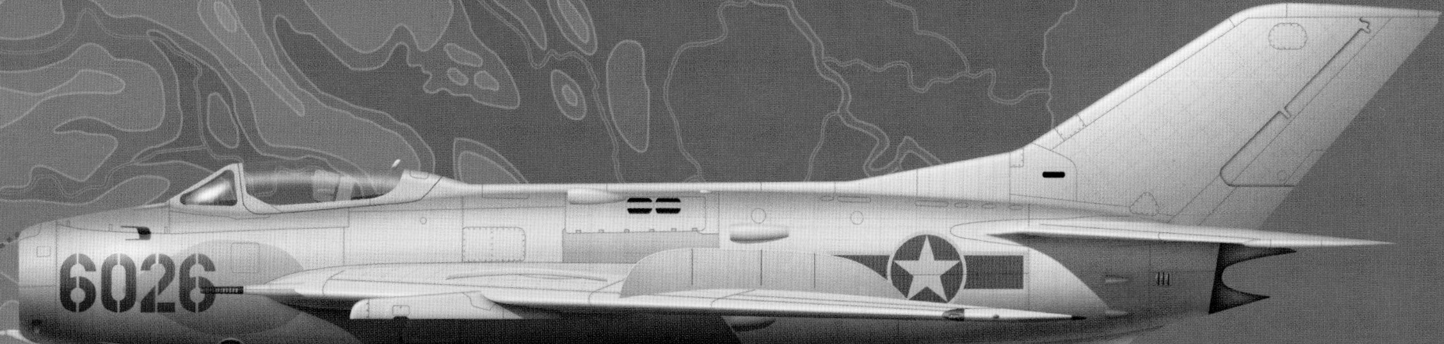

Shenyang J-6 (MiG-19S) Farmer C, No. 6026 of the 925th Fighter Regiment, 1972
Nguyen Hong Son "A" used this Shenyang J-6 during air battle of 18 May 1972, when his flight-leader, Pham Ngoc Tam shot down an USAF F-4D Phantom. (ARTWORK: BALÁZS KAKUK)

the two MiG-19s, which were hit and both Vietnamese pilots ejected and landed safely.

Meanwhile, at 16:29 hours, a pair of MiG-21s from the 927th Fighter Regiment, flown by Nguyen Van Nghia and Nguyen Van Toan, took off from Noi Bai and flew to an eastern area of Kep airfield to cover Tam and Long's MiG-19s. However, as a result of the air battle between the MiG-19s and the F-4s, Nghia and Toan returned and landed safely at Noi Bai.

These air battles confirmed that when the enemy used large strike formations to attack Hai Phong, they used fighters to suppress Kep and Noi Bai, but the North Vietnamese thought they were strike formation which attacked Route No.1.

After moving its operations from Tho Xuan airfield back to Noi Bai airbase, the 921st Fighter Regiment used flights of MiG-21s flying out at low altitudes and, when enemy aircraft crossed the Vietnamese – Laotian border, to unexpectedly appear in the area west of Tho Xuan by climbing to high altitudes and attacking the American aircraft.

On 20 May, a MiG-21 pair, of Luong The Phuc and Do Van Lanh, was on combat alert duty at the 921st Fighter Regiment. At 11:35 hours, radars detected a group of eight enemy aircraft southeast of Sam Neua, and later twelve more aircraft flying at Vu Ban toward Suoi Rut – Viet Tri. After taking off, Luong The Phuc and Do Van Lanh turned left and flew east of Gia Lam airfield, and then followed Route No.1 to go south of Phu Ly. At 11:53 hours, the MiG-21s turned to a heading of 270 degrees and climbed to an altitude of 4,000 meters. Five minutes later, Phuc spotted two F-4 Phantoms on their left at a heading of 60 degrees and at a distance of 15 kilometers. Phuc tried to close in to attack, but

On 20 May 1972, Luong The Phuc and Do Van Lanh intercepted an American fighter group. Do Van Lanh (RIGHT) shot down 1Lt Markle and Capt Williams' F-4D Phantom west of Hanoi. (ISTVÁN TOPERCZER COLLECTION)

was not able to do so because two of the enemy aircraft were making hard turns and maneuvers. Luong The Phuc broke off an returned to land at 12:10 hours.

Meanwhile, Do Van Lanh increased his speed and climbed to 4,000 meters, when he saw two F-4s behind them fire missiles, he gave a warning to his flight-leader. Lanh spotted an F-4 Phantom in front of him, so he started to pursue it and launched a missile from distance of 1,500 meters, at a speed of 1,100 km/h. When Lanh made a hard turn to the left and broke away, he did not see a detonation, but the F-4 Phantom turned right and went down. After breaking off, Lanh saw two F-4s chasing Phuc, who took evasive action and then Lanh fired his second missile at a distance of 1,500 meters. He shot down 1Lt Markle and Capt Williams' F-4D Phantom (65-0600) and broke off to turn to left and landed at 12:15 hours.

On 23 May, the US Navy continued to attack Hai Phong – Kien An, Thai Binh and Route No.1 to the south of Phu Ly – Nam Dinh – Ninh Binh. At Gia Lam airfield, the VPAF HQ deployed another MiG-21 pair from the 927th Fighter Regiment to reinforce the MiG-19s and MiG-17s. In early morning, a MiG-19 flight, of Hoang Cao Bong, Vu Chinh Nghi, Nguyen Hong Son "A" and Pham Hung Son "C," took off as planned to defend Hai Phong – Kien An, but the enemy turned back, so they returned to land at Gia Lam.

At 11:50 hours, several enemy flights were detected at east of Thanh Hoa flying north. All combat units were on Class One Alert at Gia Lam, Noi Bai and Kep. Four minutes later, some enemy flights turned from the Day River mouth to Nho Quan, while other flights came from the Ba Lat River mouth to Hung Yen – Phu Ly. The MiG-21 pair, of Nguyen Duc Soat and Ngo Duy Thu, took off from Gia Lam, while a MiG-19 flight waited for their orders. The MiG-21s accelerated to 950 km/h and flew to Hung Yen. The enemy had bombed Phu Ly and was returning.

At 12:03 hours, Soat – Thu dropped the external fuel tanks, started their afterburners and ascended to an altitude of 3,000 meters, where they were informed continuously about positions of the targets. Two minutes later, Soat detected only an enemy A-7 Corsair, looked around and attacked it. At 12:06 hours, Nguyen Duc Soat shot down Cdr Barnett's A-7B Corsair (154405) from the USS *Midway*, southeast of Nam Dinh. Ngo Duy Thu saw the enemy pilot who ejected from his aircraft. The US Navy loss records state it fell to a North Vietnamese SAM site and Cdr Barnett lost his life in the cockpit. The MiG-21s broke off and landed at Gia Lam.

At 12:10 hours, Commander Ho Van Quy of the 925th Fighter Regiment ordered a MiG-19 flight, of Bong – Nghi – Son "A" – Son "C," to take off, and the GCI guided them to the east and back to Kep. The flight divided into two pairs over the airbase. The enemy fighters came from the east of the airbase and fired missiles at MiG-19s. After some maneuvers with high G, Son "A" – Son "C" fought back and each shot

On 23 May 1972, Nguyen Hong Son "A" shot down the 3,600th enemy aircraft over North Vietnam, by VPAF records, but US records did not confirm his kill.
(István Toperczer Collection)

down an F-4 Phantom. The US records did not confirm these losses. Meanwhile, Vu Chinh Nghi did not change his contact channel in time, so he did not get the order to turn hard and was hit by a missile from Lt Col Beckers and Capt Huwe's F-4E Phantom. His engine and control system were damaged, so Nghi had to eject. Hoang Cao Bong tried to fight back but did not have a chance to fire. Command ordered them to break off and they landed safely at Gia Lam.

In the afternoon, enemies arrived from the Gulf of Tonkin, via Hong Gai, Yen Tu range to Chu and Luc Nam. At 16:35 hours, a MiG-17 flight, of Vu Van Dang, Nguyen Van Dien, Nguyen Van Lam and Nguyen Cong Ngu, took off from Kep airbase and they were in a holding area to the west. At 16:51 hours, over the bridge at Kep, four F-4 Phantoms popped up at an altitude of 1,500 meters and flew towards the Bao Dai Mountains. The two sides fought at low altitudes, chasing each other fiercely. Pilots Vu Van Dang and Nguyen Van Dien shot down one F-4 Phantom, but then they were shot down by Lt Cdr McKeown's F-4B of VF-161 from the USS *Midway* (CVA-41). They jettisoned the canopy just before the aircraft exploded, but the pilots did not eject. Nguyen Cong Ngu's MiG was also hit due to enemy fire, but he was able to eject. Nguyen Van Lam landed on Noi Bai, safely.

A conference was called for the commanders and officers of the VPAF in late May, to analyze the lessons learned from dogfights from 8 May to 2 June. A study was ready by the 12 June, in which enemy tactics and manoeuvres were discussed, together with the current state of VPAF and its combat readiness, as well as recommendations for solving its shortcomings. The study was distributed between pilots of the fighter regiments.

In the second half of 1972, the MiG-21s of the 921st and 927th Fighter Regiments achieved a better record.

Young Aces of the "Linebacker"

The new generation of MiG-21 pilots (such as Do Van Lanh, Nguyen Tien Sam, Nguyen Duc Soat, Le Thanh Dao, Pham Phu Thai, Nguyen Van Nghia) had returned from the Soviet Union in recent years, and they were certified as "combat ready" pilots after the appropriate training hours in Vietnam. They took part in more and more aerial combat and claimed many air victories over American aircraft to become "flying aces" of the VPAF.

Early in the morning of 1 June, the US aircraft continued their attacks against Route No.1, Route No.2, and the Hanoi area, so the VPAF HQ ordered the 921st Fighter Regiment to intercept enemy bomber groups approaching in the Suoi Rut – Thanh Son – Van Yen area.

At 09:30 hours, Pham Phu Thai and Nguyen Cong Huy took off and flew past Son Duong, and then they climbed to an altitude of 8,000 meters. Turning to a heading of 150 degrees, Thai spotted a flight of four F-4s on his right at a distance of 12-15 kilometers. In addition to the F-4s assigned to attack ground targets, some flights were also assigned to help the search and rescue effort to recover Capt Locher, who had been shot down by a MiG-19 on 10 May 1972. When the F-4s discovered the MiGs, the two lead aircraft accelerated and pulled up into a climb while the other two aircraft dove to a lower altitude. Thai pursued the two aircraft that dove. Thai and Huy rolled their aircraft upside down and dove, from their current altitude of 8,000 meters down to an altitude of 2,000 meters. Pham Phu Thai fired a missile from a distance of 1,500-1,800 meters and then turned immediately to break away. He saw the missile explode just left and behind the tail of Capt Hawks's F-4E Phantom. He decided to pursue the F-4 to fire a second missile, but at that moment he felt his aircraft shake hard twice. He saw that his pitot tube had broken in two. It may have broken because his break away maneuver had been too violent in a 9.5 G turn. Thai decided to break off and returned to Noi Bai, where he landed safely. The USAF stated Capt Hawks's F-4E Phantom was a victim of a SAM.

Pham Phu Thai claimed his next kill on 10 June, when he and his wingman, Bui Thanh Liem, attacked a group of twelve aircraft flying southwest of Sam Neua toward Yen Bai. Each MiG-21 pilot shot down an F-4 Phantom, but the US sources did not confirm these losses.

In the next two days, the USAF continued to conduct attacks against a number of road and traffic targets along Route No.1 and Route No.2.

Pham Phu Thai was the most successful MiG-21 pilot during June 1972. He shot down four F-4 Phantoms in a month, by VPAF official sources.
(ISTVÁN TOPERCZER COLLECTION)

B-52s bombed targets in Quang Binh Province and Vinh Linh District. At 08:29 hours, on the morning of 12 June, twenty US Navy aircraft attacked the Do Len Bridge in Thanh Hoa. At 11:55 hours, twenty more US Navy aircraft attacked the Luc Nam area in Bac Giang. Meanwhile the USAF sent forty aircraft to attack the Ngoi Hop Bridge and Yen Bai. To provide cover for the bombers, eight US Navy F-4 Phantoms were assigned to fly in a holding area over Yen Bai, while four other navy fighters flew in a holding pattern over the Thanh Son area in Phu Tho.

At 12:02 hours, from the 927th Fighter Regiment, a MiG-21 pair, of Le Thanh Dao and Truong Ton, took off and they were ordered to fly on a heading of 30 degrees toward Nha Nam – Dong Mo. One minute later, they dropped their external fuel tanks, switched on their afterburners and climb to an altitude of 5,000 meters. Dao spotted four F-4s that were in the process of splitting up into two sections. He had decided to target the two F-4s that were decreasing altitude, when he spotted two more F-4s that were headed straight for their MiG-21s. At this time the Phantoms discovered the two MiGs, so they suddenly turned hard left, but Dao fired an R-3S missile. The missile flew straight as an arrow toward the F-4 Phantom. Because of the short range, Dao made a hard right turn to break away. He looked around but did not see any American aircraft and also could not see his wingman, Truong Ton. He broke off and landed on Noi Bai airfield, at 12:21 hours. Truong Ton, who covered and supported Dao's MiG, saw two F-4s that were trying to move in behind the MiGs. He decided to turn back to make a counterattack, but after two complete circles in a turning dogfight he was not able to get into a good attack position. He also broke off and landed on Noi Bai. The USAF records do not confirm Dao's kill for that day.

On 13 June 1972, Pham Phu Thai was involved in his third air battle on that month and shot down an F-4E Phantom over Vinh Phu. At 08:35 hours, radars picked up one group of four aircraft and another group of twelve aircraft flying from the Vietnamese – Laotian border. Two pairs of MiG-21s, each from the 921st Fighter Regiment, the first consisting of Luong The Phuc and Do Van Lanh and the second consisting of Pham Phu Thai and Nguyen Cong Huy, were placed on combat alert duty and stood ready to take off immediately. After half an hour, the first pair, Phuc and Lanh, took off to attack a group of twelve USAF aircraft flying near Yen Chau and another group of four American aircraft flying from Phu Tho to Tuyen Quang.

After Phuc and Lanh took off east to west from the Noi Bai Airfield, they turned to a heading of 260 degrees, dropped their external fuel tanks and climbed to an altitude of 5,000 meters. At that moment, Phuc spotted four F-4s flying in a trail formation, which were to the left at a heading of 20 degrees, a distance of 20 kilometers and an altitude of 4,500 meters. He immediately climbed to 6,000 meters, and then rolled his aircraft upside down and made a left turning dive toward the F-4 Phantoms. The F-4 pilots saw the MiGs, so both Phantoms made a hard

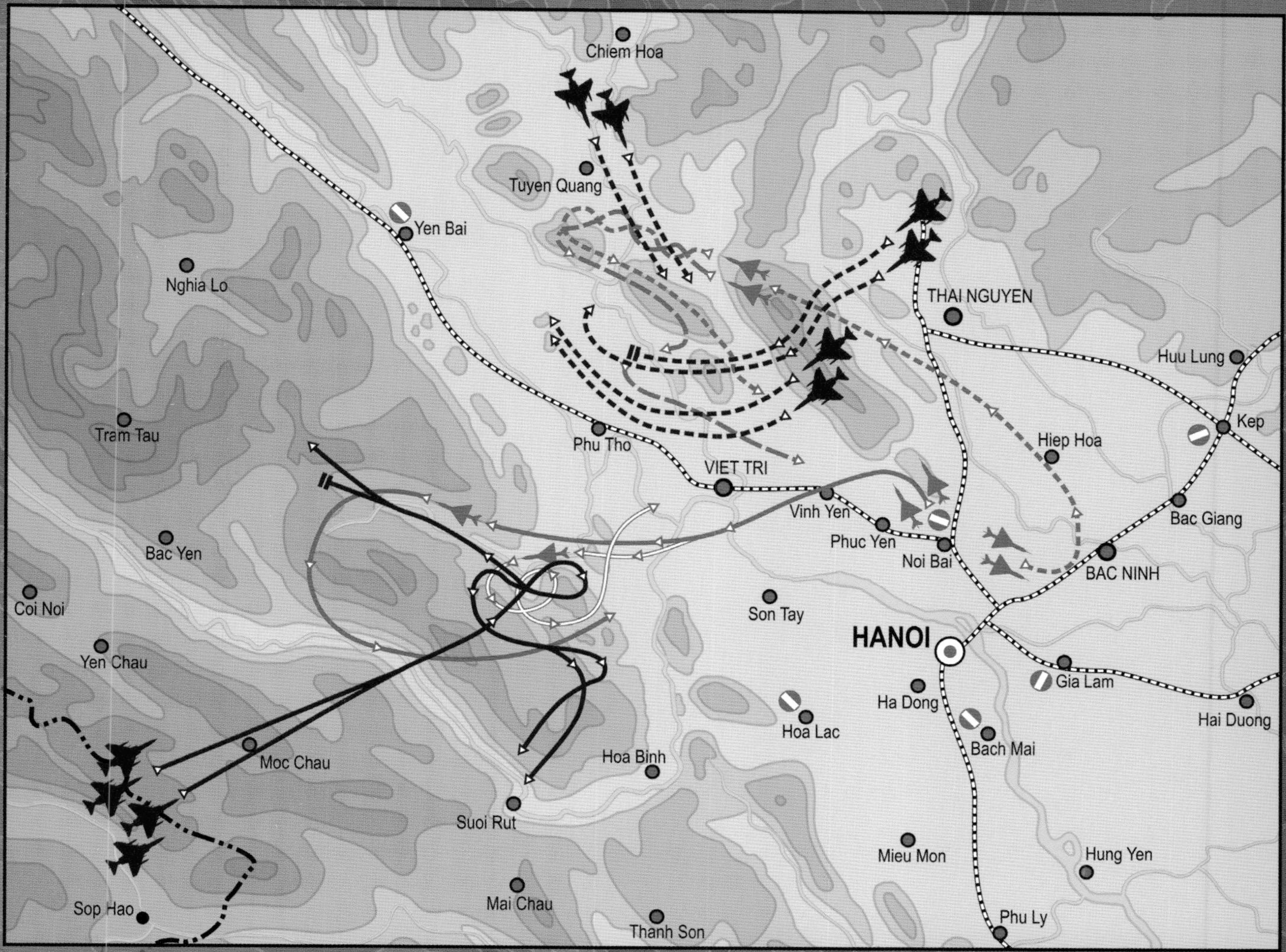

On 13 June 1972, two MiG-21 pairs of the 921st Fighter Regiment intercepted the enemy fighter groups over Vinh Phu Province. Pham Phu Tai and Do Van Lanh shot down two USAF F-4 Phantoms by Vietnamese records.
(CARTOGRAPH: PÉTER BARNA)

turn and passed under the belly of the Phuc's MiG. Luong The Phuc decided to break off the engagement and he returned to land.

While Do Van Lanh covered Phuc's MiG, he spotted four more F-4s at a heading of 30 degrees to the right and at a range of 7 to 8 kilometers. He got on the tail of the closest F-4 on the left, and fired a missile. He saw his R-3S missile explode just above the top of the F-4 Phantom. He quickly broke away by turning to the right when he spotted another F-4 at a heading of 20 to 30 degrees. He attacked this aircraft and launched his second missile from a distance of 1.000 meters. He saw the missile explode to the right of the target and broke off to return to Noi Bai, where he landed safely at 09:24 hours.

Meanwhile, at the west end of the Noi Bai runway, the second MiG-21 pair, with Pham Phu Thai and Nguyen Cong Huy, took off and turned to the battle area of Son Duong – Dai Tu. After the MiGs climbed to an altitude of 4,000 meters and flying past Bac Can, Huy spotted four F-4 Phantoms to the right at a distance of 13 kilometers. When the MiGs turned back, the Thai – Huy spotted four more F-4s to the right at a distance of 12 kilometers. While this flight of F-4s was trying to catch the MiG-19s, they did not realize that the MiG-21 pair had chased them. The separation between Thai and Huy was three kilometers. Thai decided to attack the two Phantoms at a distance of 1,500 meters and he launched a missile against his target. He did not see an explosion, so decided to fire another missile. When he was preparing to press the firing button he saw that the 1Lt Hanson and 1Lt Fulton's F-4E Phantom (67-0365) was on fire. Pham Phu Thai made a hard turn to break away and then landed safely at 09:41 hours. Nguyen Cong Huy stayed a long distance behind Pham Phu Thai and landed safely two minutes later at Noi Bai. On that day only one F-4E Phantom was shot down by MiG-21 over Tuyen Quang by US records.

In the second half of June 1972, the USAF aircraft concentrated their attacks on traffic points and supply stockpiles along Route No.1 (Hoa River Bridge), Route No.3 (supply stockpiles in Thai Nguyen), and Route No.2 (Yen Bai airbase).

During the afternoon of 21 June, two MiG-21s from the 921st Fighter Regiment attacked and scattered an American fighter group which did not reach its intended target. Do Van Lanh added another F-4 Phantom to his score sheet. Over the Red River near Phu Tho, Capt Rose and 1Lt Callaghan's F-4E Phantom (69-0282) was attacked by a MiG-21 pair and the enemy aircraft was hit by Do Van Lanh's R-3S Atoll missile.

On this day, the 927th Fighter Regiment lost an MiG-21PFM in a dogfight. Lt Col Christiansen's F-4E Phantom was an escort mission for chaff force over Route Pack 6. An AIM-9 Sidewinder was launched from his Phantom and guided toward the MiG's tail, which exploded and burned fiercely from the canopy aft. The flight-leader Le Thanh Dao's wingman, Mai Van Tue, was able to eject and landed safely.

Based on intelligence reports, it was considered likely that on 23 June, the USAF and US Navy would continue to conduct heavy attacks on vital traffic points and in the Hanoi area. The USAF would probably continue to send in fighters seven to ten minutes ahead of the bombers to cover the airfields, and the fighters would fly at higher altitudes than the bombers. During their approach flight, the USAF strike groups would fly in large formations, but after they crossed the Vietnamese – Laotian border, the strike groups would spread out to fly in separate smaller groups. The American pilots concluded that in mid-June 1972 the MiG-21s began using a new tactic, which was to use the cloud cover at altitudes of 500-600 meters to hide beneath the clouds. When the auxiliary ground control station informed them that they were close to an enemy target, the MiGs would pull up into a climb and attack the American aircraft.

On 23 Jun 1972, Nguyen Van Nghia and Nguyen Van Toan were on combat alert duty at Gia Lam airfield. They had flown down to Gia Lam

Do Van Lanh

Date of Birth: 21 October 1948
Enlisted: August 1965
Pilot training:
1965 – 1968 (MiG-17 – 910th Air Training Regiment – Vietnam)
1970 (MiG-21 – Vietnam)
War Service and Unit:
1968 – 1970 (923rd Fighter Regiment)
1970 – 1972 (921st Fighter Regiment)
1972 – 1973 (927th Fighter Regiment)
Aircraft: MiG-21
Died: 9 July 1980 – during training flight over Thai Nguyen
Hero of the Vietnamese People's Armed Forces: 11 January 1973
Rank: Lieutenant Colonel

Air Victories: 4 kills
(4 F-4s – VPAF official credit)

Date	Aircraft	Unit	Kill – US Pilot (VPAF – US databases)
20 May 72	MiG-21	921.	F-4D – Markle, Williams (POW)
13 Jun 72	MiG-21	921.	F-4 – US not confirmed
21 Jun 72	MiG-21	921.	F-4E – Rose, Callaghan (POWs)
24 Jun 72	MiG-21	921.	Firebee (Shared)
09 Sep 72	MiG-21	921.	F-4E – Dalecky, Murphy (AAA) (Shared)

MiG-21MF Fishbed J, No. 5128 (4 kills) of the 921st Fighter Regiment, 1972
On 21 June 1972, Do Van Lanh shot down an USAF F-4E Phantom (69-0282), so he added also his air victory to these four kill markings. (Artwork: Balázs Kakuk)

The Ace-pilot Nguyen Van Nghia frequently used this MiG-21MF Fishbed J, No. 5114, during the war. Nowadays, his MiG is stored in the Museum of the 5th Military District, at Da Nang.
(István Toperczer)

on 22 June. At 10:30 hours, a MiG-21 pair of the 927th Fighter Regiment took off and turned, over the south of Hanoi, to Xuan Mai and west of Yen Lap. Command post ordered Nghia – Toan to turn to a heading of 240 degrees, climb to 8,000 meters, and fly toward Hoa Binh. When they caught a large enemy group from the southwest Van Yen, the MiG-21s turned left to a heading of 240 degrees and an altitude of 3,000 meters. After the MiG-21 pair was informed two times about the positions of targets, Nguyen Van Nghia detected two F-4 Phantoms, to the right at a heading of 30 degrees and a distance of 12 kilometers. He used high speed to attack and fired a missile at an F-4 Phantom. Nghia saw both wings of the F-4 catch fire and then dive into the ground. He broke off right away. Toan followed him and they landed on Noi Bai, at 10:51 hours. This was the first American aircraft that Nguyen Van Nghia had shot down, but US records did not confirm his kill.

The Americans attacked the Thai Nguyen industrial center and a few other targets on Route No.1, between Lang Son and Hanoi, on 24 June. The US attack group flew a route over Yen Bai, Phu Tho, Hoa Binh, Cho Ben and Son Duong.

At 15:16 hours, Bui Duc Nhu and Ha Vinh Thanh, from the 927th Fighter Regiment, took off from Noi Bai to intercept the intruders over Thanh Son and Tuyen Quang. At 15:29 hours, radars detected a large enemy group at an altitude from 2,500 meters to 4,000 meters, which were flying from Yen Chau toward Phu Tho. The fighter section of the enemy group broke away and started to chase the MiGs. At this time, another MiG-21 pair of the 927th Fighter Regiment was launched, with Nguyen Duc Soat and Ngo Duy Thu, and they flew at a heading of 270 degrees and an altitude of 2,000 meters.

At 15:34 hours, the enemy was over Van Yen and turned to Son Tay, when command ordered MiG-21 pairs to await them at Son Tay. In the next five minutes, the large enemy group turned back to Doan Hung, so Commander Tran Hanh ordered Soat – Thu to attack them, keeping a heading of 290 degrees, a speed of 950 km/h, and an altitude of 3,000 meters. Two minutes later, they turned right to approach with angle 90 degrees. Ngo Duy Thu reported 8 enemy aircraft on the right at an angle of 45 degrees; meanwhile Soat spotted another 16 enemy aircraft. The MiG-21 pair started to follow the enemy flights. Nguyen Duc Soat launched an R-3S missile on Capt Grant's F-4E Phantom (66-0315), which crashed. At 15:44 hours, Soat reported his kill and continued the attack. He tried to get the American flight-leader, but did not fire due to the close distance. He broke off the engagement only to try another launch, but without success. The Americans turned right and descended to a lower altitude. After 20 seconds, Ngo Duy Thu also managed to score one F-4 kill from another fighter group, but since there were many more targets in front of him, he increased speed and altitude before commencing another attack. The missile he launched on the lead aircraft missed its target due to the high speed and angle of intercept. Command ordered them to break off to the right, and Soat descended to an altitude of 500 meters before landing at Noi Bai. His wingman, Thu also landed safely.

At 15:42 hours, the third MiG-21 pair of the 927th Fighter Regiment took off from Noi Bai, with Nguyen Van Nghia and Nguyen Van Toan, to intercept the enemy group with 24 aircraft, during their turn back. The MiG-21s flew on a heading of 280 degrees, at an altitude of 1,000 meters. At 15:51 hours, the enemy was north of Tam Dao, when Nghia – Toan turned left to a heading of 310 degrees. Two minutes later, Nghia detected enemy aircraft on the left at a distance of 15 kilometers, and an altitude of 4,500 meters. He accelerated to follow them. Six minutes later, Nguyen Van Nghia launched an R-3S missile from a distance of

On 24 June 1972, Nguyen Duc Soat and Ngo Duy Thu attacked an enemy formation over Phu Tho. Soat shot down Capt Grant's F-4E Phantom.
(ISTVÁN TOPERCZER COLLECTION)

The flight-line of the 927th Fighter Regiment at Noi Bai airbase, in June 1972. On 24 June 1972, Nguyen Duc Soat used the MiG-21PFM, No.5020, to shoot down an USAF F-4E Phantom. The No.5015 is overpainted with dark green spots on light green upper surfaces.
(István Toperczer Collection)

1,200 meters before pulling up sharply. 1Lt McCarty's F-4D Phantom (66-7636) crashed in flames under Toan's MiG, 10 kilometers north of Van Yen. Nguyen Van Toan still managed to attack the fighter on the right side but his missile missed its target. Command ordered them to break off to the left and descend to altitude of 200 meters to Noi Bai.

In the early morning of 25 June, the US Navy went on a raid against North Vietnam. At 06:54 hours, the command of the 927th Fighter Regiment ordered a MiG-21 pair to take off from Gia Lam airfield. Le Thanh Dao and Truong Ton flew toward the Hung Yen area and they detected 12 enemy aircraft at a heading of 40 degrees, at a distance of 20 kilometers. The MiG pair followed the final flight which parted two pairs to the left and to the right. Ton – Dao attacked the right pair, but the enemy was able to avoid Le Thanh Dao's two missiles. Meanwhile, Ton also fired an R-3S missile and hit Lt Shumway's A-7E Corsair (157437)

On 27 June 1972, Pham Phu Thai used the MiG-21PFM, No.5023, to shoot down an USAF F-4E Phantom over Da River in Son La Province. This MiG-21MF wears "5023" as its nose number in the city museum of Viet Tri.
(István Toperczer)

The No.5057 was used by Nguyen Duc Soat to shoot down another USAF F-4E Phantom on 27 June 1972. This MiG-21MF wears nose numbers of Soat's MiG-21PFM, because the original No.5057 was shot down by an USAF F-4E Phantom, on 19 August 1972.
(István Toperczer Collection)

from the USS *Coral Sea*. The MiG-21PFMs pair turned to Hanoi and landed safely on Noi Bai at 07:19 hours.

During the two previous days (25 and 26 June 1972), the USAF had attacked targets in the Viet Tri area, transportation targets along Route No.2, and the area of the Bach Mai in Hanoi. The US Navy concentrated its attacks on the area southwest of Hanoi (Dien Bridge and Xuan Mai) and the Hai Phong – Hon Gai area.

In the morning of 27 Jun 1972, from 08:40 to 09:40 hours, the USAF sent 44 bombers and fighters to attack the Bach Mai command post complex, the Kim Lien area and many other civilian targets. The American fighter escorts of 20 aircraft flew in holding patterns over three areas: southeast of the Noi Bai airbase, southeast of the Gia Lam airfield and over the Nghia Lo – Yen Lap – Thanh Ba area. The F-105s were ordered to suppress North Vietnamese air defense and radar units.

From the 927th Fighter Regiment, a MiG-21 pair of Bui Duc Nhu and Ha Vinh Thanh took off from Noi Bai to fight in the direction of west Hanoi. After they detected four F-4 Phantoms below, Bui Duc Nhu followed the last one and fired an R-3S missile, but US records did not confirmed this loss.

At the 921st Fighter Regiment, at 08:50 hours, a MiG-21 pair of Pham Phu Thai and Bui Thanh Liem was ordered to take off and sent to fly a holding area over Van Yen. Because the American aircraft were too far away, the MiG-21s were unable to intercept them, so they returned and landed at Yen Bai. At 09:18 hours, and again at 10:02 hours, a flight of four MiG-19s, flown by Pham Ngoc Tam, Nguyen Manh Tung, Vu Cong Thuyet and Vu Viet Tan, and two MiG-21s, flown by Nguyen Tien Sam and Le Van Kien, took off and flew in holding areas over the Gia Lam airfield and over Nha Nam – Tuyen Quang, but they did not encounter any enemy aircraft and returned to land. While the MiG-19 flight was coming in to land, F-4s were spotted approaching from their rear. Pham Ngoc Tam pulled up to climb, but his aircraft stalled and he was unable to eject safely, so he lost his life.

Two MiG-21 pairs from two fighter regiments were successful in the air engagements on 27 June of 1972. Nguyen Duc Soat – Ngo Duy Thu (FRONT) from the 927th Fighter Regiment and Bui Thanh Liem – Pham Phu Thai (BACK) from the 921st Fighter Regiment shot down four USAF F-4E Phantoms, by VPAF records. (ISTVÁN TOPERCZER COLLECTION)

About three hours later, several USAF enemy groups operated on the axis of Moc Chau – Yen Lap – Van Yen. They tried to rescue the downed pilots, so the VPAF HQ decided to attack. At 11:53 hours, the 927th Fighter Regiment MiG-21 pair, of Nguyen Duc Soat and Ngo Duy Thu, took off from Noi Bai to a heading of 210 degrees, at an altitude of 500 meters and a speed of 900 km/h. Later they climbed to an altitude of 2,000 meters over Hoa Lac toward Moc Chau. The radars detected an enemy group was turning back from Van Yen to Moc Chau and other enemy groups from south of Sam Neua over the Vietnamese – Laotian border. Commander Nguyen Hong Nhi at the 927th Fighter Regiment ordered Soat – Thu to attack the enemy flight that turned back. At 12:02 hours, the MiG-21 pair turned left to a heading of 180 degrees, and climbed to an altitude of 5,000 meters. One minute later, Soat detected two F-4s on the right at a heading of 30 degrees, at a distance of 15 kilometers, and an altitude of 4,000 meters. The F-4s realized that they were being chased by the MiGs, so they switched on their afterburners and fled to try to escape across the border. When it saw that the F-4s had crossed the border, the command post ordered the flight to break off the engagement. Conversely, at 12:06 hours, Nguyen Duc Soat fired two missiles and shot down Capt Cerak and Dengee's F-4E Phantom (67-0243) over Ban Pahang (Laos) 20 kilometers southwest of Moc Chau. Soat broke off and turned to a heading of 90 degrees to land at No Bai. Meanwhile, Ngo Duy Thu followed two other aircraft and after he fired the second missile, an F-4 Phantom crashed at the border. Thu turned to break away and flew to a heading of 90 degrees and descended to low altitude. Because his MiG-21 was low on fuel, he requested permission to land at Hoa Lac, and he landed safely there at 12:18 hours. In the same battle, at 11:59 hours, after the radar unit caught the enemy group that flew over the Vietnamese – Laotian border to Moc Chau

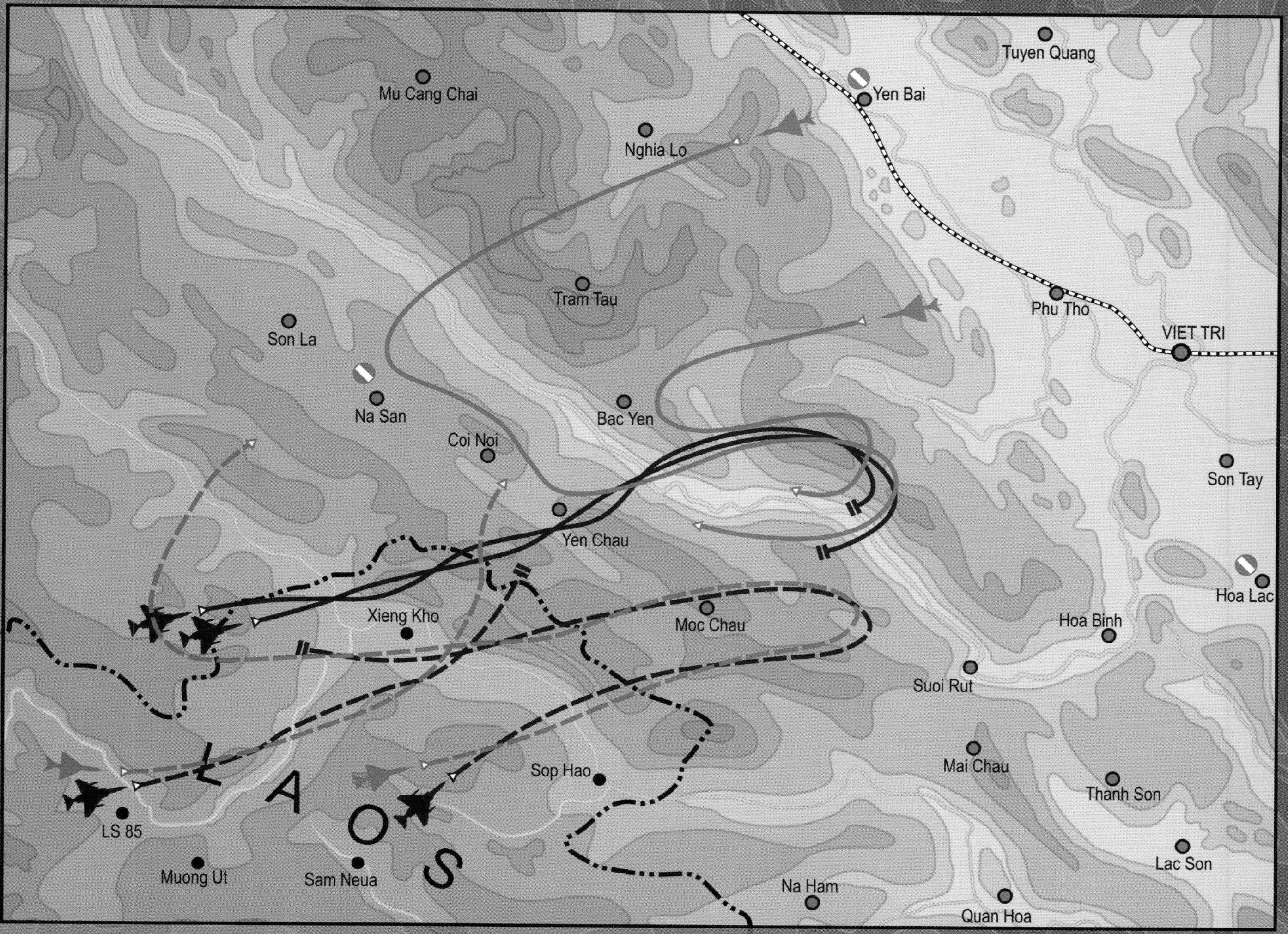

and Van Yen, command ordered a MiG-21 pair, of Pham Phu Thai and Bui Thanh Liem to take off from Yen Bai. They were redeployed from another base the day before. The GCI guided Thai – Liem to Na San at an altitude of 4,000 meters. At 12:06 hours, the MiG-21s flew over the Da River, and turned left to Bac Yen. The MiG pilots detected four F-4s turning right at an altitude of 2,000 meters over Yen Chau, but were unable to follow them. Then enemy aircraft flew under clouds to the north, so the MiGs turned left and waited for them above the clouds. At 12:16 hours, Thai detected four F-4s on the left at a heading of 30 degrees, and a distance of 15 kilometers. He ordered Liem to watch, flew alongside and followed the trailing two aircraft to attack at the same time. From a distance of 1,300 meters Pham Phu Thai launched a missile, with Bui Thanh Liem doing the same from a distance of 1,500 meters. Two minutes later, Thai reported he shot down an F-4E Phantom and a few seconds later Liem also shot down another F-4E Phantom. Both F-4E Phantoms (69-7271 and 69-7296) were hit and crashed while Pham Phu Thai and Bui Thanh Liem landed safely at Yen Bai.

On 27 June 1972, the MiG-21 pair of Nguyen Duc Soat – Ngo Duy Thu from 927th Fighter Regiment and a MiG-21 pair of Bui Thanh Liem – Pham Phu Thai from 921st Fighter Regiment shot down shot down four USAF F-4 Phantom close the Vietnam – Laos border by Vietnamese records. (CARTOGRAPH: PÉTER BARNA)

On this "Black Day," the USAF had lost five aircraft, five of their pilots had been captured after ejecting, and one pilot had been killed. More so, they had not managed to shoot down a single North Vietnamese MiG. Six young MiG-21 pilots, whom the average age was less than 24 (the oldest pilot was only 26 years old) and with an average of less than 250 flight hours in the MiG-21, had fought masterfully, used outstanding air combat techniques, and shot down five enemy aircraft flown by five experienced USAF pilots. By contrast, the USAF records confirmed only three F-4 Phantom losses on that day.

In July 1972, the command of the VPAF approved an order for further training programs, showing that the air force was not only fighting the war but also training new pilots. The new pilots were receiving training primarily for MiG-21MF (F-96) Fishbed-J and conversion training from MiG-17s to MiG-21s also continued.

The fights in the summer of 1972 were still very bloody. A lot of energy was spent on resolving the problems arising at the bases. The Americans constantly changed tactics and caused serious disruption by jamming the radar units and attacking them with anti-radiation missiles, but some of the problems were from within, since some units and certain commanders despised the enemy, which resulted in overconfidence and in serious losses on the North Vietnamese side. Because of the unfolding situation, the Communist Party Committee started a new drive; after each encounter the arising problems were analyzed, and they criticized the ideology, according to which they were not afraid of the enemy. They feared that if the battles were to continue, then the VPAF would sustain serious losses. The idea to go into battle immediately after a defeat was also criticized. Instead, they recommended learning the

On 5 July 1972, Nguyen Tien Sam used this MiG-21PFM, No.5020, to destroy an USAF F-4E Phantom northeast of Kep airbase. (István Toperczer)

DATE OF BIRTH: 15 June 1946
ENLISTED: 2 June 1965
PILOT TRAINING:
1965 – 1968 (MiG-21 – Soviet Union)
WAR SERVICE AND UNIT:
1968 – 1972 (921st Fighter Regiment)
1972 – 1975 (927th Fighter Regiment)
AIRCRAFT: MiG-21
HERO OF THE VIETNAMESE PEOPLE'S ARMED FORCES: 11 January 1973
RANK: Senior Colonel

AIR VICTORIES: 5 kills
(5 F-4s – VPAF official credit)

DATE	AIRCRAFT	UNIT	KILL – US PILOT (VPAF – US DATABASES)
05 Jul 72	MiG-21	927.	F-4E – Spencer, Seek (POWs)
24 Jul 72	MiG-21	927.	F-4E – Hodnett, Fallert (Rescued)
29 Jul 72	MiG-21	927.	F-4E – Kula, Matsui (POWs)
12 Sep 72	MiG-21	927.	F-4E – Zuberbuhler, McMurray (POWs)
05 Oct 72	MiG-21	927.	F-4D – Lewis, Alpers (POWs)

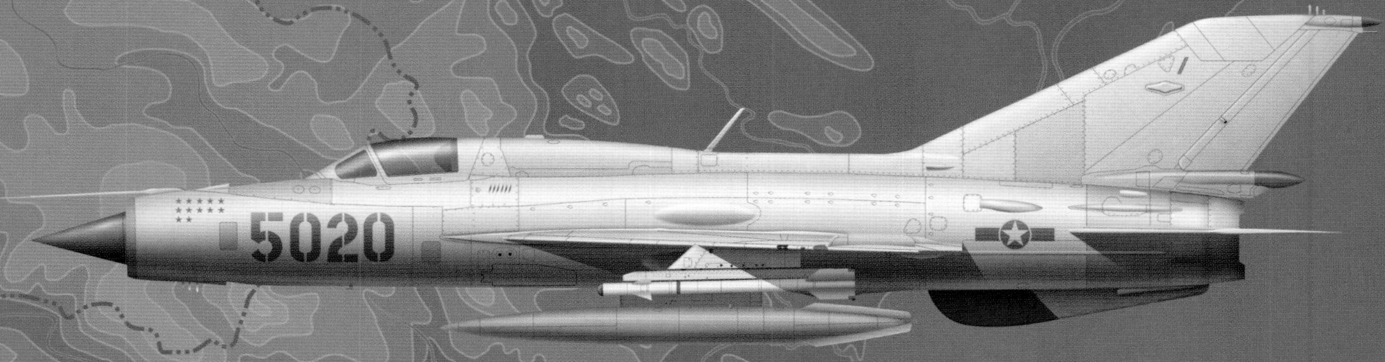

MiG-21PFM Fishbed F, No. 5020 (12 kills) of the 927th Fighter Regiment, 1972
On 5 July 1972, Nguyen Tien Sam used this MiG-21PFM to destroy USAF F-4E Phantom (67-0296), at northeast of Kep airbase. (ARTWORK: BALAZS KAKUK)

lessons of previous battles and to draw up new, more effective tactics before the next encounter.

On 5 July 1972, the MiG-21PFM pair, of Nguyen Tien Sam and Ha Vinh Thanh from the 927th Fighter Regiment, took part in a dogfight over Ha Bac Province.

Between 07:15 hours and 09:20 hours that morning, US Navy aircraft attacked targets in Hai Duong, Hung Yen, Bac Giang and Bac Ninh. From 10:15 to 11:00 hours, 32 USAF aircraft attacked targets in the Thai Nguyen area, and attacked Kep airbase.

At 10:23 hours, Nguyen Tien Sam and Ha Vinh Thanh took off and flew on a heading of 110 degrees. Later the MiG-21 pair was directed to fly on a heading of 80 degrees and informed that the target was 40 degrees to the right at a range of 50 kilometers. They dropped their auxiliary fuel tanks, accelerated their speed, and climbed to an altitude of 6,000 meters. One minute later, Ha Vinh Thanh spotted four F-4s 20 degrees to the left at a range of 25 kilometers. At the last minute, Sam announced that he would attack the leading two aircraft and directed Thanh to attack the two trailing aircraft.

Ha Vinh Thanh launched two R-3S missiles from a distance 1,800 meters. The missile hit Maj Elander and 1Lt Logan's F-4E Phantom (67-0339). Meanwhile, Sam turned hard to pursue an F-4 in the lead section and fired a missile from a distance of 2,000 meters, but the R-3S missile exploded about 50 meters to the right of the target. The F-4 rolled into a right turn. He continued the attack and launched a second missile this time from a distance of 600-700 meters. Capt Spencer and 1Lt Seek's

The Ace-pilot Dang Ngoc Ngu is credited with 7 kills, from 1966 to 1972, while he served in the 921st Fighter Regiment. On 8 July 1972, his MiG-21MF was shot down by an F-4E Phantom, and he was killed in the downed MiG-21.
(István Toperczer Collection)

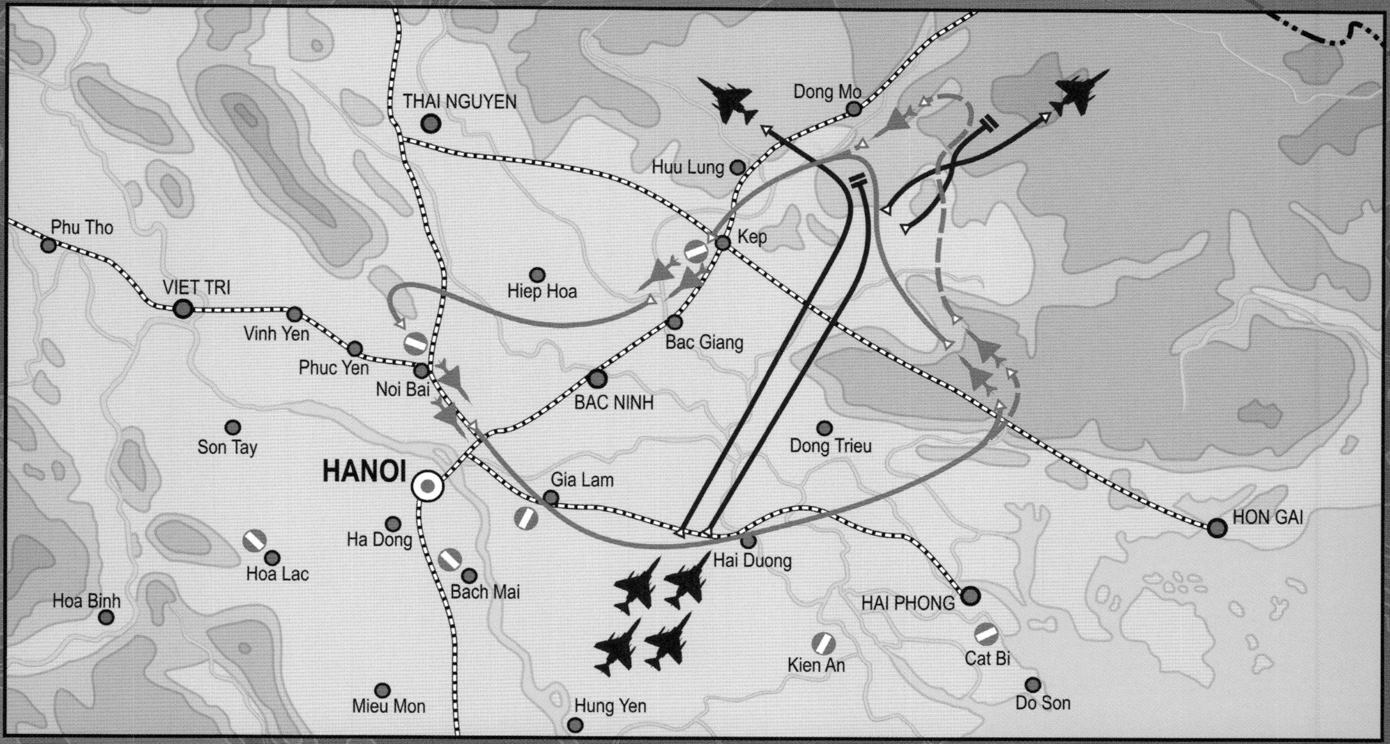

On 5 July 1972, Nguyen Tien Sam shot down an F-4E Phantom and his wingman, Ha Vinh Thanh also claimed another F-4E Phantom kill at east of Kep, over Ha Bac. (CARTOGRAPH: PÉTER BARNA)

F-4E Phantom (67-0296) exploded, its right wing broke off and the aircraft burst into flames. Because Sam was so close, his aircraft flew right through the explosion. When he got out of the ball of smoke, he found that his aircraft was controllable and engine had died. He was able to restart the MiG-engine in the air, and then they returned to the airbase. It was Nguyen Tien Sam's first air victory during Vietnam War.

After three days, on 8 July, MiG-21 flights were being used at Noi Bai, Gia Lam and Yen Bai airbases, to intercept the enemy from far and beyond the AAA units fire perimeter, to protect Hanoi from the northwest, southwest and southeast, by orders of VPAF. In the early morning, at 05:49 hours, radars detected an enemy group coming from Sam Neua to Yen Chau. At the 921st Fighter Regiment Dang Ngoc Ngu and Tran Viet took off from Noi Bai, and then flew to Thanh Son at an altitude of 4,000 meters. At that moment, the enemy flight turned back, so the MiGs were ordered back to land.

At 09:50 hours, radars discovered an enemy group of 12 aircraft which were at 30 kilometers north of Sam Neua, and then they changed their direction to Son La. They attacked Yen Bai and the Thac Ba hydroelectric plant. Luong The Phuc and Do Van Lanh took off from Yen Bai and went through the clouds to turn to a heading of 180 degrees, and an altitude of 3,000 meters. At 10:00 hours, the enemy changed its direction to Yen Chau, so the GCI guided the MiG-21 pair of Phuc – Lanh to attack them south of Yen Chau, and then to turn right back. After four minutes, the enemy aircraft climbed to an altitude of 3,600 meters and MiG-21s climbed to an altitude of 5,000 meters with a speed of 1,000 km/h. After six minutes, Phuc detected the enemy below, and one and a half minutes later they reported that the enemy turned back. The command ordered them to break off to Yen Bai airbase without any counterattack.

Meanwhile, several enemy groups came from the southwest of Hanoi, and radars detected an enemy group of 8 aircraft east of Sam Tai (Laos) coming to Ba Thuoc. At the 921st Fighter Regiment, a MiG-21 pair, of Pham Phu Thai and Bui Thanh Liem, took off from Noi Bai, to keep a heading of 250 degrees, at 10:05 hours. Command ordered Thai – Liem to turn over Hoa Binh, and then to Tan Lac – Vu Ban. The MiG-21s did not meet an enemy, then broke off to Thanh Son and landed at Noi Bai.

At 10:08 hours, an enemy group of 16 aircraft flew to the north area of Hoi Xuan at an altitude of 5,000 meters. After five minutes, Dang Ngoc Ngu and Tran Viet took off from Noi Bai for the second time that day. They flew on a heading of 270 degrees at an altitude of 500 meters and a distance of 25 kilometers from Thanh Son. At that moment, command was not able to determine the enemy group's position and "blindly" ordered the MiGs to turn left to a heading of 180 degrees. At 10:25 hours, the enemy turned back at Hoa Binh, so command ordered Ngu – Viet to change their heading to 120 degrees, climb to an altitude of 5,000 meters, and then turn to 210 degrees, with a speed of 1,000 km/h to intercept the enemy at Suoi Rut. At 10:28 hours, the MiG-21s maneuvered to follow them and Dang Ngoc Ngu detected four F-4s 30 degrees on the left, at an altitude of 4,000 meters and a distance of 15 kilometers, flying across from left to right. Tran Viet informed him that there were two enemy aircraft behind. Dang Ngoc Ngu reduced his MiG-21's tilt and followed the enemy to fire an R-3S missile, and then broke off to the right side. At 10:32 hours, the command post ordered him to fly to a heading of 30 degrees, and from that moment they lost contact with him. According to USAF records, Capts Hardy and Lewinski fired two Sparrows and guided them from their F-4E Phantom toward Ngu's MiG-21. The flight-leader, Dang Ngoc Ngu did not eject after the hit and was killed in the falling aircraft at Hoa Binh. He was a famous North Vietnamese Ace pilot with 7 air victories during the air war.

Tran Viet detected two other F-4s and followed them to fire an R-3S missile from a distance of about 1,600 meters, but could not determine the explosion. He turned right and tried to follow another F-4 Phantom pair. He fired the second missile, and then breaking off to the right saw another aircraft head-on and below. At that time, he had only 450 liters of fuel and discovered the runway of Hoa Lac airfield was far away. He descended and landed at 10:39 hours. The wingman, Tran Viet shot down Lt Col Ross and Capt Imaye's F-4E Phantom (69-7563) 60 kilometers southwest of Hanoi. The Phantom was able to return to Thailand and the crew ejected north of Udorn of the RTAFB.

While the MiG-21 pair of Ngu – Viet was guided, the other MiG-21 pair of Nguyen Ngoc Hung and Vu Duc Hop took off from Gia Lam to Hung Yen and flew at a heading from northeast to southwest, to Suoi Rut, at an low altitude in the holding area. At 10:43 hours, radars detected an enemy group of 8 aircraft at an altitude of 3,000 meters, 15 kilometers northwest of Lang Chanh, coming to Vu Ban. The MiG-21s of the 927th Fighter Regiment were ordered to turn right with a heading of 270 degrees, and to climb to an altitude of 4,000 meters. The radar station lost signal of both enemy aircraft and MiGs. They "blindly" guided Hung – Hop to a heading of 290 degrees with a speed of 1,000 km/h. At 10:48 hours, the MiG-21s should have met the enemy as expected, but they could not spot any American aircraft. They turned left to Hung Yen when the GCI again got good enemy signals and guided the MiG-21s to turn right 310 degrees with a speed of 950 km/h. When the radar station lost the targets' signals again, Vu Duc Hop detected four F-4 Phantoms 30 degrees on the left ahead at a distance of 15 kilometers. At 10:52 hours, Ngu ordered Hop to attack the two enemy aircraft below, while he attacked the others above. One minute later, the GCI lost contact with Hung – Hop's MiG21s. On this day, Capt Ritchie and DeBellevue were flying on a MiGCAP mission west of Phu Tho. They met a MiG-21 pair of the 927th Fighter Regiment. Ritchie attacked the wingman, Nguyen Ngoc Hung's MiG-21, and fired two AIM-7 Sparrows missiles turning the MiG into a huge fireball. They fired another Sparrow to the leader, Vu Duc Hop's MiG-21, who together with his wingman was killed in this air battle.

This pair of veteran MiG-17Fs is on display at the VPAF Museum, in Hanoi. The last air victory of the North Vietnamese MiG-17s was on 11 July 1972, when Han Vinh Tuong shot down a US Navy F-4J Phantom, from the USS Saratoga.
(István Toperczer)

The pilots of the 927th Fighter Regiment used the MiG-21PFM, No.5033, to shoot down three US F-4 Phantoms during 1972. Because the original No.5033 was lost, a MiG-21bis wears the nose number and three kill markings in the Museum of Victory over B-52, Hanoi.
(István Toperczer)

8 July 1972 was a "Black Day" for the VPAF, when two MiG-21 fighter regiments lost three pilots.

On 24 July 1972, after enemy groups were detected 40 kilometers west of Bach Long Vi Island flying to Hong Gai, two MiG-21 pairs of the 927th Fighter Regiment were ordered to take off. Nguyen Tien Sam and Ha Vinh Thanh started from Noi Bai, and three minutes later Le Thanh Dao and Truong Ton were alerted at Gia Lam. The MiG-21 PFM pair of Sam – Thanh flew out at an altitude of 500 meters to Hiep Hoa. At 12:24 hours, the enemy arrived at Hill 1068 of Yen Tu ridge, and then to Hoa River Bridge, while the MiG-21s turned left to a heading of 120 degrees, with a speed of 950 km/h, and climbed to an altitude of 4,000 meters at Nha Nam.

Three minutes later, when the MiGs were at Route No.13B, Ha Vinh Thanh detected 8 F-4s on the left at an angle of 90 degrees, and a distance of 12 kilometers. Nguyen Tien Sam ordered Thanh to accelerate speed, turn left and watch above. When, the MiGs were in a good position behind the enemy, Sam fired two missiles to shoot down Capt Hodnett and Fallert's F-4E Phantom (66-0369). Thanh also launched his two R-3S missiles, but missed. At 12:29 hours, command post ordered them to break off to Vo Nhai northeast of Thai Nguyen. They maneuvered to change direction and descend to low altitude to come back to Noi Bai airbase. On landing, Nguyen Tien Sam used up the last drops of his fuel, to be followed shortly by his wingman landing from the opposite direction. Due to the American presence it was a dangerous situation, and Nguyen Tien Sam landed on the main runway, while Ha Vinh Thanh on the taxiway at 12:42 hours.

After takeoff, the Dao – Ton pair flew on a heading of 150 degrees at a low altitude, but radar could not get any MiG signals. The GCI "blindly" guided the MiG-21s and chose the enemy groups, which flew from Hoa River Bridge – Kep – Luc Ngan to Hong Gai. The MiGs were at the Luoc River when they were ordered to turn left on a heading 60 degrees, a

DATE OF BIRTH: 24 June 1946
ENLISTED: 5 July 1965
PILOT TRAINING:
1965 – 1968 (MiG-21 – Soviet Union)
WAR SERVICE AND UNIT:
1968 – 1972 (921st Fighter Regiment)
1972 – 1973 (927th Fighter Regiment)
AIRCRAFT: MiG-21
HERO OF THE VIETNAMESE PEOPLE'S ARMED FORCES: 11 January 1973
RANK: Lieutenant General

AIR VICTORIES: 6 kills
(4 F-4s, 1 A-7, 1 Firebee – VPAF official credit)

DATE	AIRCRAFT	UNIT	KILL – US PILOT (VPAF – US DATABASES)
13 Mar 69	MiG-21	921.	Firebee
23 May 72	MiG-21	927.	A-7B – Barnett (KIA) (SAM)
24 Jun 72	MiG-21	927.	F-4E – Grant, Beekman (POWs)
27 Jun 72	MiG-21	927.	F-4E – Cerak, Dingee (POWs)
30 Jul 72	MiG-21	927.	F-4D – Brooks, McAdams (Rescued)
26 Aug 72	MiG-21	927.	F-4J – Cordova (KIA) Borders (Rescued)
12 Oct 72	MiG-21	927.	F-4E – Young, Brunson (POWs)

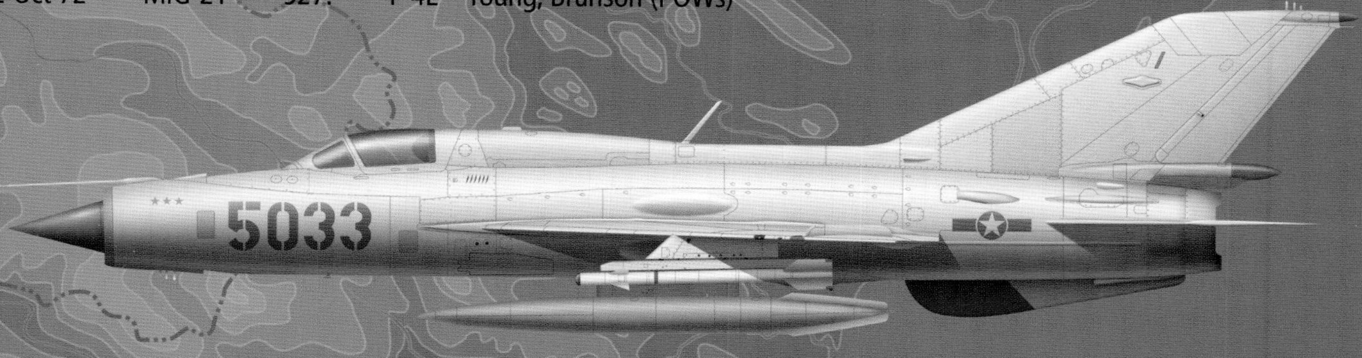

MiG-21PFM Fishbed F, No. 5033 (3 kills) of the 927th Fighter Regiment, 1972
Ace-pilot Nguyen Duc Soat used this MiG-21PFM during air battle of 18 July 1972, when his wingman, Nguyen The Duc lost his life by USAF F-4D Phantom (66-0271). (ARTWORK: BALÁZS KAKUK)

On 29 July 1972, Ace-pilot Nguyen Tien Sam, from the 927th Fighter Regiment, shot down Capt Kula and Matsui's F-4E Phantom east of Kep.
(István Toperczer Collection)

speed of 900 km/h and an altitude of 1,000 meters. At 12:31 hours, Dao and Ton flew east of Hai Duong and accelerated to climb to an altitude of 6,000 meters at a heading of 80 degrees. At that time, the enemy turned back from Luc Ngan and they were over Route No.18. Le Thanh Dao detected an enemy formation of 12 F-4s and informed Truong Ton. The American intruders did not discover that MiGs were behind them. Le Thanh Dao was chasing an F-4 towards the sea and managed to shoot it down, while Truong Ton shot down another F-4 – neither kill can be matched with US losses. At 12:36 hours, Dao broke off to right because he thought the distance to Noi Bai was shorter than Kep, but Ton broke off to left. At that time, they saw a Phantom section approaching to Noi Bai and Kep. Dao's MiG had 900 liters of fuel left and Ton's MiG had 800 liters. Command post ordered them to fly in low consumption mode, and watch all the airspace over Noi Bai and Kep. At 12:51 hours, Truong Ton landed at Kep airbase, and one minute later Le Thanh Dao arrived in Noi Bai airbase under the protection of anti-aircraft artillery.

At the end of July 1972, there was an interesting air incident. On 29 July, Nguyen Tien Sam and Nguyen Thanh Xuan, from the 927th Fighter Regiment took off from Noi Bai and they were guided east of Kep. The leader, Nguyen Tien Sam, shot down Capt Kula and Matsui's F-4E Phantom and his wingman, Nguyen Thanh Xuan was a victim of F-4E Phantom over Huu Lung. According to the US official records, Lt Col Bailey's F-4D (Cadillac 1) on a MiG sweep mission, engaged and shot down a MiG-21. Shortly thereafter, Lt Col Taft's F-4E (Pistol 1) escorting a chaff mission, engaged and shot down a second MiG-21. Almost immediately thereafter, a third MiG-21 shot downed Capt Kula's Phantom (Trigger 04), one of a flight of four that was also escorting the chaff mission. The

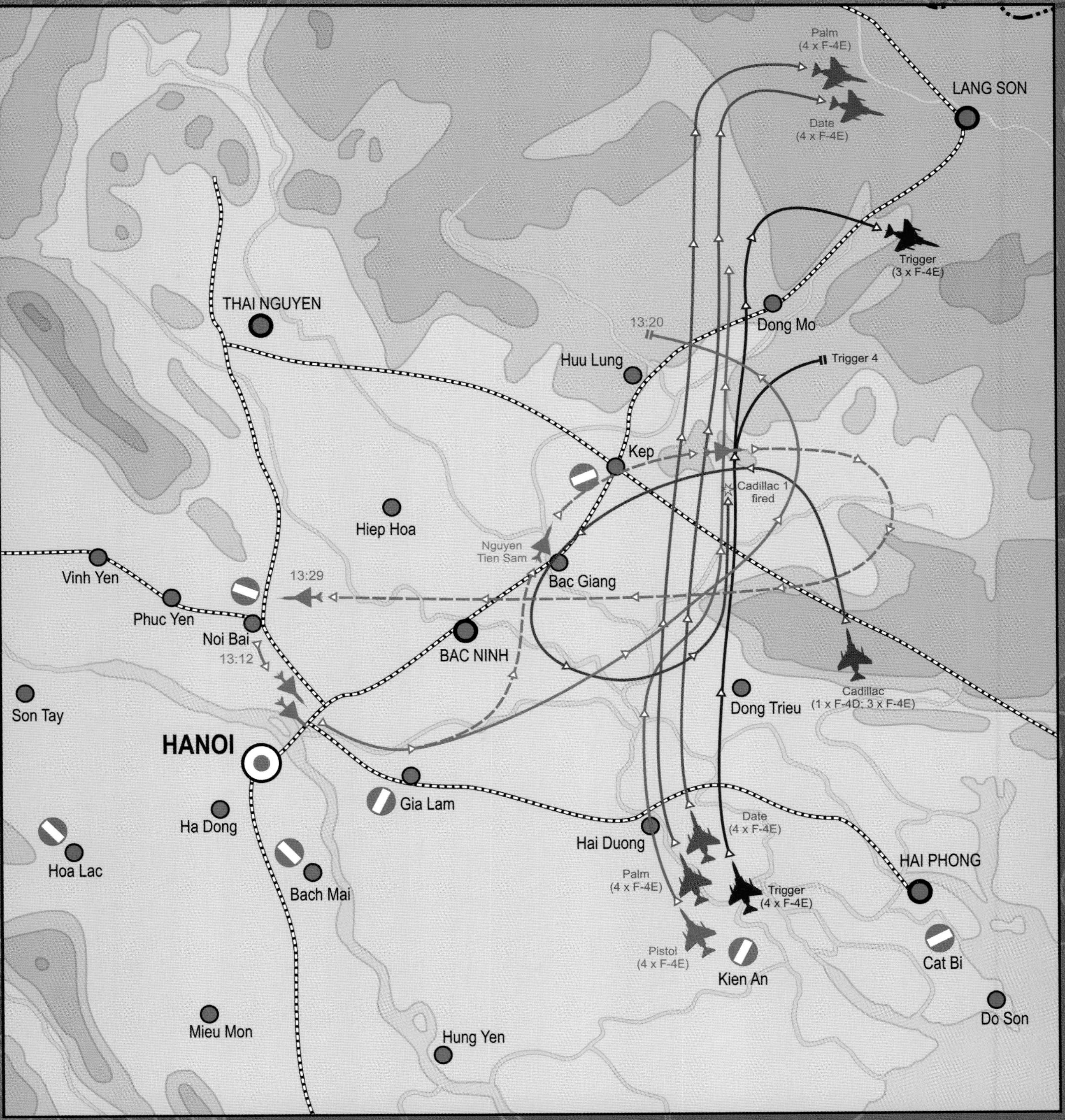

On 29 July 1972, a leader of MiG-21PFM pair, Nguyen Tien Sam shot down an USAF F-4E Phantom at east of Kep during a complicated air battle over Ha Bac Province. (CARTOGRAPH: PÉTER BARNA)

American official record suggested that Trigger 4 was mistakenly shot down by Cadillac 1, who had misidentified the friendly F-4 as an enemy MiG-21. From this aspect, Nguyen Tien Sam saw the fallen Trigger 1, and he thought it was his own kill. Nguyen Thanh Xuan was a victim of the "Pistol 1."

The North Vietnamese official records mention only two MiG-21s on that day – one air victory and one ejection.

Three USAF F-4 Phantoms were lost over North Vietnam on 30 July 1972, according to US sources. Capt Brooks and Capt McAdams's F-4D Phantom (66-7597) was damaged by a MiG-21 during a Combat Air Patrol. Brooks flew out toward the Gulf of Tonkin before he and his weapon system officer, Capt McAdams ejected 60 kilometers east of Thanh Hoa. According to the sources in Vietnam, Nguyen Duc Soat credited this kill to his air victories on that day.

The first half of the August 1972 was to see the VPAF suffer more losses to both USAF and US Navy F-4 Phantoms. At night, on 10 August, a MiG-21 of the 927th Fighter Regiment was involved in air battle over the 4th Military District, and a US Navy F-4J Phantom from the USS *Saratoga* shot down Nguyen Ngoc Thien's MiG. Unfortunately, he was killed in action (KIA).

Two days later, on 12 August, Capt Richard from the US Marines and Lt Cdr Ethell from the US Navy, were exchange pilots with the USAF F-4E Phantom, when they downed the wingman of MiG-21 pair from the 921st Fighter Regiment. Nguyen Cong Huy ejected safely from his destroyed MiG-21 over Phu Ninh District, Vinh Phu Province.

On 15 August, Nguyen Tien Sam and Nguyen Hung Thong, from the 927th Fighter Regiment, took off and were directed to the designated air battle area over Phu Tho to intercept a formation of USAF aircraft that was attacking the Viet Tri electrical power plant. The MiG-21 pair clashed with a group of F-4 Phantoms assigned to escort the attack bombers. The American aircraft made a hard turn to the rear to counterattack and shot down Thong's MiG-21. He ejected successfully. Nguyen Tien Sam returned and landed safely at Noi Bai airbase.

On 19 August, Le Thanh Dao and Nguyen Thang Duoc attacked USAF F-4 Phantoms with their MiG-21PFMs. Dao realized that they were in a bad situation from other F-4s, so he requested permission to break off the engagement and return to airbase. Meanwhile, his wingman had engaged in a dogfight with the F-4s and had been hit by an enemy missile. Nguyen Thang Duoc was able to eject successfully, but while he was descending by parachute two F-4 chased him down and ripped his parachute. He fell into a tree branch, seriously damaging both his arms and spine. Because his injuries were so severe, he died on 21 August 1972 at Son Dong.

On 26th day of the month, two MiG-21 pairs claimed their first kills of August 1972, when each pilot, Nguyen Duc Soat and Nguyen Van Toan, shot down an F-4 Phantom. The US records confirmed only Soat's kill for that day. At 10:00 hours, the radar station picked up enemy electronic jamming signals on a heading of 165 degrees, originating in the Sam Tai (Laos) area. From the 927th Fighter Regiment, a MiG-21 pair, of Nguyen Duc Soat and Le Van Kien, was ordered to take off from Noi Bai at 10:11 hours. When they turned to a heading of 120 degrees and climbed to an altitude of 8,000 meters, Soat spotted two F-4 Phantoms turning to the right front at a distance of 15 kilometers. He increased his speed and fired an R-3S missile from a distance of 1,500 meters. The missile hit 1Lt Cordova and 1Lt Borders' F-4J Phantom (155811) of the VMFA-232 from the US Marines (Nam Phong airbase, Thailand), which burst into flames. Both crewmen ejected in the area of Sop Hao in Laos. The US Marines list this aircraft as the only USMC F-4J Phantom aircraft to have been shot down in an air battle over North Vietnam.

Meanwhile, Le Van Kien pursued another F-4 Phantom making three complete circles in a turning dogfight, but neither aircraft was able to get into position to make an attack. The command post ordered Kien to break off the engagement and to follow the course of the Da River up to Hoa Binh Lake and then turn to reach the Red River. Over Hung Yen, he checked his MiG's fuel status and found that it had only 50 liters of fuel left. One minute later, the MiG-21 engine stopped in mid-air. At 10:43 hours, Le Van Kien ejected safely at a distance of 20 kilometers from Gia Lam airfield.

In September and October 1972, the MiG-21s of the 921st and 927th Fighter Regiments were more successful.

On 7 and 8 September 1972, large numbers of US Air Force aircraft attacked targets along Route 2 and Route 1 North, while US Navy aircraft

Do Van Lanh used this MiG-21MF Fishbed J, No.5108 of the 921st Fighter Regiment, on 9 September 1972, when he and his comrade, Luong The Phuc, shot down an F-4E Phantom north of Thai Nguyen. The MiG-21MF is in the military museum at Nha Trang airbase. (ISTVÁN TOPERCZER)

attacked the Hon Gai, Quang Ninh, and Thanh Hoa areas and also conducted armed reconnaissance missions against many key, important targets.

In according with the general air battle plan, a MiG-21 pair of Luong The Phuc and Do Van Lanh were on combat alert duty at the 921st Fighter Regiment, on 9 September 1972.

After 10:00 hours, the radars picked up a large number of American aircraft. The fighter regiment recommended that the combat alert flight be sent out to Phu Ly – Lang Chanh to attack the enemy aircraft as they approached their targets. At 10:22 hours, the MiG-21s took off and the radar station discovered a group of eight aircraft approaching from Cam Pha – Dinh Lap – Dong Mo. Six minutes later, Phuc – Lanh climbed to an altitude of 6,000 meters and turned to a heading of 100 degrees.

At that moment, the command post informed the pilots that the target was 10 degrees to their left side at a distance of 18 kilometers. The MiG-21 pair pursued the enemy aircraft out toward the ocean, and three minutes later Luong The Phuc spotted four aircraft 30 degrees to the left at a distance of 18 kilometers. He saw four more aircraft flying in a parallel line formation to the right at a range of 8 to 9 kilometers. Phuc attacked the closest enemy aircraft and launched an R-3S missile. After firing, he saw the F-4 nose over and dive toward the ground. Do Van Lanh shouted to him: "They are firing 20mm guns! Turn hard immediately!" Phuc turned to the right and broke off the engagement to land at Kep airbase. His MiG-21 had 450 liters of fuel left while he was flying over Bac Son. When he reached Kep, the airfield control tower ordered him to turn back and make a counterattack. At that moment, he saw two missiles flash over his MiG, which were launched from two F-4 Phantoms behind him. The MiG engine stopped in mid-air and Phuc tried to restart his engine. However, because Luong The Phuc's MiG flew so low, he ejected safely over Lang Giang District, close to Bac Giang.

When Do Van Lanh saw flames under Phuc's MiG-21, he knew that his flight-leader had fired a missile. At that moment he spotted two F-4s closing in to fire M-61A1 20mm guns at Phuc's MiG, so he fired an R-3S missile, but missed. He made a hard turn to follow the two F-4s to his right and fired the second missile to hit the tail of Capt Dalecky and Capt Murphy's F-4E Phantom (69-7565) at a distance of 15 kilometers north of Hanoi. According to USAF records, this F-4E Phantom was damaged by AAA unit. After the hit, Do Van Lanh broke off to turn left and climbed to an altitude of 13,000 meters, and then he descended to return to Gia Lam airfield. After landing, his speed was so great that he deployed his brake chute to slow down, but the MiG-21 overran the runway into a rice paddy filled with water.

On that day, Do Van Lanh received the nickname "Ironbird" in 1972, just like Nguyen Van Coc had in the years between 1965 and 1968.

At 10:41 hours on that day, a pair of MiG-21s flown by Tran Viet and Tran Van Sang took off from Gia Lam and flew to the Nha Nam area to

Le Thanh Dao

Date of Birth: 20 September 1944
Enlisted: 5 July 1963
Pilot training:
1965 – 1968 (MiG-21 – Soviet Union)
War Service and Unit:
1968 – 1972 (921st Fighter Regiment)
1972 (927th Fighter Regiment)
Aircraft: MiG-21
Hero of the Vietnamese People's Armed Forces: 11 January 1973
Rank: Senior Colonel

Air Victories: 6 kills
(6 F-4s – VPAF official credit)

Date	Aircraft	Unit	Kill – US Pilot (VPAF – US databases)
18 Dec 71	MiG-21	921.	F-4D – Johnson, Vaughan (POWs)
10 May 72	MiG-21	927.	F-4J – Blackburn, Rudloff (POWs) (AAA)
12 Jun 72	MiG-21	927.	F-4 – US not confirmed
24 Jun 72	MiG-21	927.	Firebee (Shared)
24 Jul 72	MiG-21	927.	F-4 – US not confirmed
09 Sep 72	MiG-21	927.	F-4 – US not confirmed
11 Sep 72	MiG-21	927.	F-4E – Ratzlaff, Heeren (POWs)
01 Oct 72	MiG-21	927.	F-4 – US not confirmed

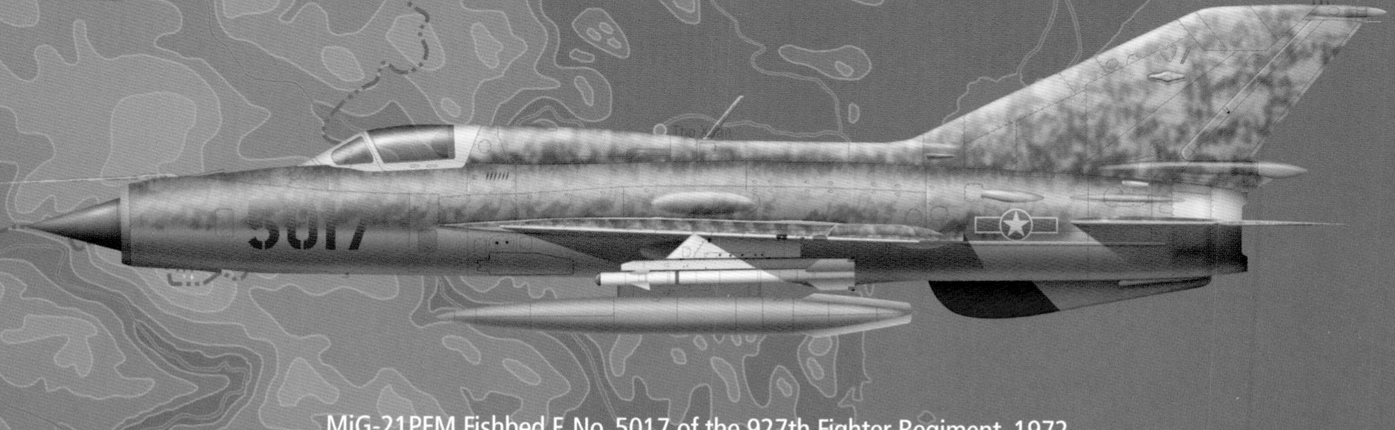

MiG-21PFM Fishbed F, No. 5017 of the 927th Fighter Regiment, 1972
On 11 September 1972, Le Thanh Dao used this unusual camouflaged Fishbed to shoot down USAF F-4E Phantom (69-0288) about 15 miles northeast of Kep airbase. (Artwork: Balázs Kakuk)

support and cover for Phuc – Lanh. Although they discovered the enemy aircraft, the Americans flew too far away to be caught, so the MiG-21 pair returned and landed at Gia Lam.

At the same time as the first MiG-21pair from the 921st Fighter Regiment took off, Le Thanh Dao and Mai Van Tue also started to take off at the 927th Fighter Regiment. After take-off, they turned to a heading of 340 degrees and climbed to an altitude of 7,000 meters. Ten minutes later, Dao spotted two enemy aircraft 90 degrees to the left at a distance of 15 kilometers. He turned to the left and pursued these two aircraft. A moment later, he spotted four more aircraft in a better position to attack, so he launched his missile against this enemy formation. After seeing one American aircraft begin to trail smoke, he broke off to the right and flew back to land at Gia Lam. The US records confirmed only Do Van Lanh's F-4 Phantom on that day.

At the 925th Fighter Regiment, the Air Force Headquarters had ordered two MiG-19s, flown by Nguyen Tu Dung and Pham Cao Ha, to take off and intercept USAF bomber strike groups, and to cover air operations at Noi Bai, Gia Lam, and Kep airfields. During the attack on the four F-4 Phantoms, Pham Cao Ha's MiG-19 had been hit by an AIM-9 missile from Capt Madden and Capt Debellevue's F-4D Phantom. He ejected and parachuted safely to the ground in Phu Lo Village, Kim Anh District, Hanoi.

VPAF HQ ordered the 927th Fighter Regiment to use MiG-21s in both the eastern and southern sectors to fight at Route No.1, on 11 September 1972. Le Thanh Dao and Tran Van Nam were on combat alert duty with their MiG-21 PFMs.

Around 10:00 hours, radars picked up two groups of eight aircraft south of Sam Neua (Laos) and one group of twelve aircraft in the east and flying over Bach Long Vi Island. At 10:14 hours, the MiG-21 pair took off from Noi Bai and climbed to 6,000 meters. The command post informed the pilots that the target was 20 degrees to their right at a distance of 12 kilometers. At this moment, Dao spotted four aircraft to the right and below, and four more aircraft farther away. The MiG-21s attacked them and Dao shot down Capt Ratzlaff and Capt Heeren's F-4E Phantom (69-0288) over Dong Mo, about 45 kilometers northeast of Kep.

Tran Van Nam pursued three other F-4s and launched his two R-3S missiles against enemy aircraft. He claimed one air victory, because an F-4 Phantom began to trail smoke and caught fire.

In the late afternoon of 11 September 1972, two US Marine F-4J Phantoms assigned to MiGCAP attacked an unarmed MiG-21US training aircraft. Major Dinh Ton and a Soviet instructor, Vasilij Motlov, had practiced dogfight maneuvers near Noi Bai airbase. In the MiG fuel tanks only 800 liters were left, when Dinh Ton spotted the F-4s coming in to attack.

They were commanded to escape and the instructor made a defensive maneuver to avoid the missiles that were being fired from two F-4Js. Although Maj Lasseter and Capt Cummings of VMFA-333, from the USS *America*, were credited with shooting down this MiG-21US, in fact, the Vietnamese aircraft ran out of fuel and the engine stopped at an altitude of 500 meters. Dinh Ton and the Soviet instructor decided to eject, and they landed safely. As the two F-4J Phantoms (155526 and 154784) that had attacked Dinh Ton's MiG were passing through Haiphong's air defense zone on their way back out to Gulf of Tonkin, both F-4s were shot down by SAM and AAA units.

The dogfight of 12 September 1972 had witnessed the 3,900th American aircraft to be shot down over North Vietnam by the ADF-VPAF soldiers and civilians. Nguyen Tien Sam claimed this air victory when he was flying with his wingman, and they intercepted an enemy group of eight F-4 Phantom over Luc Ngan District in Bac Giang Province.

Early morning on that day, US Navy bombers attacked the Ha Lam Mine in Quang Ninh. Between 09:00 and 10:30 hours, sixty USAF aircraft attacked Kep airbase, Route No.1 and Phu Tho areas. The 927th Fighter Regiment was ordered to place two MiG-21s on combat alert duty at Kep airbase. At 09:41 hours, Nguyen Tien Sam and Nguyen Van Toan took off and flew on a heading of 180 degrees and climb to an altitude of 5,000 meters. They were informed that the target was 10 degrees to their left at a distance of 20 kilometers. Nguyen Tien Sam spotted the target and informed his wingman, who also discovered the eight F-4 Phantoms. When Sam saw both flights of enemy aircraft make hard right turns, he also made a hard turn, and attacked the enemy aircraft. He launched an R-3S missile from a distance of 1,300 meters, while his MiG speed was close to Mach 1.0 (1,200 km/h). The missile flew straight into Capt Zuberbuhler and Capt McMurray's F-4E Phantom (69-7266), causing it to burst into flames. Nguyen Tien Sam rolled his aircraft upside down and then he turned back to Noi Bai airbase, where he landed safely at 10:00 hours.

Nguyen Van Toan also spotted four aircraft ahead of him and fired a missile, which flew straight into an F-4 Phantom, causing it to begin to burn. He quickly broke away, but two enemy aircraft were chasing him. He switched on his afterburner to climb to 8,000 meters and turned back toward Kep. As he was descending to 4,000 meters, he felt a vibration on his MiG-21. Lt Col Beckers and 1Lt Griffin were behind him; they fired an AIM-9E missile, and then fired 520 20mm rounds, causing the MiG malfunction. Toan was not able to control his aircraft and ejected at the far end of Kep airbase, at 09:50 hours.

At the 921st Fighter Regiment, Pham Phu Thai and Le Khuong were on combat alert duty. At 10:01 hours, the MiG-21 pair took off from Gia Lam airfield and flew toward Phu Ly, where Thai spotted a flight of F-105 Thunderchiefs, as well as other enemy flights. Due to the complicated situation, Thai decided to break off the attack and landed safely at Gia

On 12 September 1972, Nguyen Tien Sam shot down Capt Zuberbuhler's F-4E Phantom northeast of Hai Phong. It was the 3,900th enemy aircraft shot down over North Vietnam, by VPAF records.
(István Toperczer Collection)

Lam at 10:26 hours. Le Khuong was in a holding formation to cover Pham Phu Thai's MiG, when he spotted four more aircraft chasing them. He launched R-3S missiles and its warhead detonated to the right and behind the tail of the F-4 Phantom. At that moment, Capt Mahaffey and 1Lt Shields fired an AIM-9E missile which damaged the tail section of the MiG. Khuong's aircraft began losing speed and descended to an altitude of 250 meters. He ejected, but he hit the ground on a mountainside and seriously injured his spine.

In the first days of October, the 927th Fighter Regiment's mood got a spark with consecutive wins in battles. On the afternoon of 1 October, Le Thanh Dao claimed an F-4 Phantom kill over Chiem Hoa in Tuyen Quang Province, although US records did not mention any loss on that day.

During the late morning hours of 5 October, when a large enemy formation was picked up approaching from the east, the command post ordered Bui Duc Nhu and Nguyen Tien Sam to take off from Noi Bai. They flew over Dong Mo area to attack enemy bomber groups. The MiG pilots detected the enemy at a distance of 20 kilometers, which were under fire from the AAA unit at Dong Mo railway station. The enemy activity was just a deception, so the command post immediately ordered the MiG-21 pair to return and land at Noi Bai airbase. During the preparation for landing at Noi Bai, the command post guided the pilots to Yen Bai and they landed there to stand combat alert duty. They were ordered to create the element of surprise and to attack enemy targets approaching from the west.

At 13:44 hours, radars detected enemy groups from west of Moc Chau coming to Yen Bai. The VPAF HQ concluded that USAF aircraft were approaching to attack Thai Nguyen. At 13:52 hours, a MiG-21 pair of Nhu – Sam took off and was ordered to fly 25kilometers north of Yen Bai, keeping an altitude of 6,500 meters. One minute later, the enemy was at Van Yen and the MiG-21s turned back left, and then accelerated to Mach 1.1 (1,300 km/h). The American aircraft were turning right to Yen Bai, when the MiG pilots spotted 16 aircraft at a distance of 12 kilometers and saw two more aircraft in front of a twelve-aircraft formation flying toward the MiGs head-on. At this time, the American pilots did not know that there were MiGs in the area and continued to fly straight and level. At 13:56 hours, Nhu quickly decided to turn and attack the lead aircraft in the first flight in the enemy formation. He fired an R-3S missile and forty seconds later an F-4 burst into flames. Bui Duc Nhu broke off and landed safely at Noi Bai airbase at 14:03 hours.

Meanwhile, Nguyen Tien Sam spotted two F-4s flying behind Nhu's MiG. He quickly dove to chase them. After making one circle chasing the targets, the command post informed him: "Watch out for enemy aircraft to your right rear." Sam turned right to give up the pursuit of the two F-4 Phantoms. After discovering four enemy aircraft behind

Nguyen Tien Sam received the fifth "Huy Hieu Bac Ho" (Uncle Ho Badge) after his air victory on 5 October 1972. On that day, he shot down Capt Lewis and Alpers' F-4D Phantom over the Yen Bai area.
(István Toperczer Collection)

him, he made a hard inside turn to attack the last F-4 in this flight. Sam had placed his weapons system on the "two missile" firing mode and launched the missiles. The second R-3S missile flew straight into Capt Lewis and Capt Alpers's F-4D Phantom (66-8738), causing it to burst into flames and dive toward the ground. At 13:58 hours, he reported the hit and pulled up into a climb to break off the engagement, while the command post informed him about enemy aircraft on the left at 90 degrees, and at a distance of 12 kilometers. Sam changed his heading to north of Tam Dao, then quickly descended and landed safely at Noi Bai at 14:06 hours. It was Nguyen Tien Sam's fifth and last air victory of the war.

On 6 October 1972, a MiG-21 pair, from the 921st Fighter Regiment at Kep, and a MiG-19 pair, from the 925th Fighter Regiment at Gia Lam, were ordered to protect Route No.1 while the 927th Fighter Regiment stationed a MiG-21 pair, Nguyen Van Nghia and Tran Van Nam, at Noi Bai airbase. At 08:45 hours, a radar station detected several enemy groups west of Sam Neua, over the Vietnamese – Laotian border, coming to Yen Chau – Phu Yen. The GCI requested MiG-21s over Thanh Son to intercept the enemy at Phu Tho – Doan Hung, but then command ordered the MiG-21s over Bac Can to attack enemy groups over Son Duong – Thai Nguyen to bomb north of Route No.1.

At 08:49 hours, Nghia – Nam took off and turned right at a heading of 30 degrees to avoid enemy fighter groups that were turning northwest of Thai Nguyen. The MiGs dropped their external fuel tanks, and switched on their afterburners to get an altitude and speed advantage. Ten minutes later, when the enemy was at Son Duong and the MiGs flew 15 kilometers east of Cho Moi, command ordered them to turn left at a heading of 270 degrees with a speed of 1,200 km/h. One and a half minutes later, the MiGs turned left at a heading of 180, 140, and then 120 degrees. At 09:00 hours, Nghia detected four F-4s on his left side at a heading of 45 degrees, a distance of 18 kilometers, and an altitude of 6,500 meters. When the distance was 10 kilometers, the enemy maneuvered and split up into two sections. Nghia ordered his wingman to watch and attack. Nghia launched his first missile, but because he did not see an explosion, he fired the second missile at Capt White and Capt Egge's F-4E Phantom (69-7573) which burst into flames. When he broke off to the right, he spotted six enemy aircraft head on and above, and descended to an altitude of 200 meters to land at Noi Bai. The damaged Phantom crashed just after crossing the Vietnamese – Laotian border. This was the third F-4 Phantom that Nguyen Van Nghia had shot down over North Vietnam. Meanwhile, Tran Van Nam maintained a separation of about 1,500 meters from his flight-leader and followed the enemy aircraft turning left, fired his first missile without a result. While he broke off to the right, he spotted another target, pursued, and fired the second missile. It exploded under Lt Col Anderson and 1Lt Latella's F-4E Phantom's fuselage. Nam quickly broke off and did not see the missile warhead explosion. He also landed at Noi Bai. The USAF claimed Tran Van Nam's victim, F-4E Phantom (69-7548) was destroyed by SAM near Son Tay, west of Hanoi.

At 08:50 hours, the MiG-19 pair of Nguyen Hong Son "A" and Nguyen Hung Viet, took off from Gia Lam. When the MiGs reached Pha Lai they were ordered to turn to a heading of 270 degrees. At this time a USAF bomber group flew 10 kilometers north of Thai Nguyen. Twelve minutes later, Son "A" discovered the target and ordered to attack. He chased the two enemy aircraft on the left and Viet covered him. At that moment, four F-4s appeared behind them and Viet turned back to counterattack. Son "A" continued to pursue the two aircraft and fired one burst from his guns, but his shells missed. He made a hard turn to the left and break off the engagement. He called his wingman, but got no response from Nguyen Hung Viet. At 09:17 hours, Nguyen Hong Son "A" landed safely at Gia Lam airfield.

When Nguyen Hung Viet turned back to make counterattack, he was on the tail of Capt Barton and 1Lt Watson's F-4E and fired two or three bursts from his guns. Maj Clouser and 1Lt Brunson's F-4E was on the tail of Viet's MiG-19. At approximately 100 meters, Capt Barton pulled his Phantom out of the dive, but Viet could not maneuver and turn at a low altitude, and in the process hit the ground and crashed near Khuon Nang Hamlet, Lien Ninh Village, Vu Nhai District, Thai Nguyen Province.

Nguyen Hung Viet was the last MiG-19 pilot to be killed during the air battle and this incident was the last air battle of MiG-19s during the air war over North Vietnam.

At 08:57 hours, the Kep-based MiG-21 pair of Do Van Lanh and Le Van Hoan had flown up to Lang Son, but they did not encounter any enemy aircraft, so they turned back and landed at Gia Lam airfield.

Nguyen Van Nghia demonstrates the maneuvers of his dogfight for young MiG-21 pilots at Noi Bai airbase. On 6 October 1972, he shot down Capt White and Capt Egge's F-4E Phantom, which was able to return to the Thai – Laotian border, where the crew ejected and were picked up by helicopter. In the background, pilots of the 927th Fighter Regiment also demonstrate their air engagements.
(István Toperczer Collection)

On 8 October, Nguyen Van Nghia and Duong Dinh Nghi from the 927th Fighter Regiment attacked Phantoms at Yen Bai – Tuyen Quang, but Maj Retterbush's F-4E locked up the wingman with a Sidewinder missile, which failed to fire. They switched to 20 mm cannon and fired two series, causing the MiG-21 to burst into flames. Duong Dinh Nghi ejected just before his aircraft hit the ground.

On 9 October 1972, the USAF guided air strikes against targets in the Pho Ni – Trung Gia – Thai Nguyen area, and against the Yen Bai airbase. On the morning of 10 October, there was no USAF and US Navy air activity north of the 20th Parallel, but a large number of B-52s bombed targets from Nghe An to Quang Binh Province and the US Navy aircraft attacked targets south of the 19th Parallel. On 11 October 1972, the USAF concentrated its attack in the area of Yen Bai airbase, while the US Navy aircraft attacked the locomotive-factory area at Gia Lam.

In the second half of October, four MiG-21s were shot down. Only Nguyen Duc Soat was able to shoot an F-4E Phantom about 30 kilometers northeast of Kep airbase on 12 October.

On that day, two MiG-21 pairs were on combat alert duty at Noi Bai. The first pair was Nguyen Duc Soat and Duong Ba Khang, and the other consisting of Nguyen Tien Sam and Nguyen Hung Thong. Because the weather was so bad, the regiment command post decided to change the wingman of the first pair to the experienced pilot Nguyen Tien Sam.

At 10:01 hours, a radar station detected a group of sixteen aircraft north of Son Dong. Nguyen Duc Soat and Nguyen Tien Sam took off and climbed to an altitude of 5,000 meters. They dropped their auxiliary fuel tanks and increased speed to 1,000 km/h. The command post informed the MiG pilots that the target was on their right at a distance of 60 kilometers. As the MiGs were turning to a heading of 240 degrees, Soat spotted four F-4s to the right at a distance of 20 kilometers. Nguyen Duc Soat scanned the air all around and he decided to pursue this flight of F-4 Phantoms. Just as he had begun his turn to attack, the four F-4Cs made a very sharp turn to the left. At that moment, Nguyen Tien Sam spotted four more F-4s on the left.

Six of the F-4s turned to the left and the two other F-4s turned to the right, and then turned back. While the formation of American escort fighters was concentrating on chasing Sam's MiG, Soat got in behind a group of bombers. He once more scanned the situation and pursued the two aircraft below him. Soat fired an R-3S missile, but there were still four F-4s chasing behind him. He broke away immediately without waiting to see his missile explosion. When he turned to the left and rolled his aircraft upside down, he saw that Capt Young and 1Lt Brunson's F-4E Phantom (69-0276) was on fire. Soat dove into the clouds and then he came out of the clouds over Yen Tu Mountain. He descended to an altitude of 300 meters and landed safely at Noi Bai Airfield, at 10:29 hours. Meanwhile, his wingman's MiG crashed because of aggressive maneuvering in a battle with Capt Madden's F-4D Phantom. Nguyen Tien Sam ejected safely at 10:21 hours.

In the afternoon on the next day, Mai Van Tue from the 927th Fighter Regiment lost his life when his MiG-21 was shot down by Sparrow missiles from Lt Col Westphal's F-4D Phantom over Thai Nguyen.

In the afternoon of 15 October, two pilots from each MiG-21 fighter regiment had to eject. Capt Rubus and Capt Hendrickson were flying northwest of Hanoi when they intercepted Le Thanh Dao and Tran Van Nam's MiG-21s from the 927th Fighter Regiment. They used their guns, due to the failure of their AAM to shoot down Dao's MiG. When he descended in his parachute, the other MiG-21s circled around him. From the other F-4E Phantom, Maj Holtz and 1Lt Diehl launched an AIM-9 missile shooting down Pham Phu Thai's MiG-21 from the 921st Fighter Regiment. After ejection, he saw four F-4s firing their guns. The shells shredded his parachute and he used his right hand to control it in order to avoid being shot by the F-4s. He landed safely on the ground and was taken to Tuyen Quang.

Le Thanh Dao remembers this day as follows:

We took off from Noi Bai airbase ascending to an altitude of 3,500 meters toward Ba Vi, where we had already flown at an altitude 6,000 meters. We discovered the enemy Phantoms and intercepted two aircraft in a pair, and I prepared to launch my missile. At this moment, another F-4 hit my MiG-21 and I had to eject immediately. When I descended in parachute a Phantom fired a burst from their cannon to make many holes in my parachute. So I had fallen down and crashed into the big rock at a high speed. I was unconscious for two days; both legs and

The famous Ace-pilot, Le Thanh Dao demonstrates dogfight-maneuvers of 15 October 1972, nowadays in Hoa Lac. (István Toperczer)

Pham Phu Thai

Date of Birth: 30 December 1949
Enlisted: 5 July 1965
Pilot training:
1965 – 1968 (MiG-21 – Soviet Union)
War Service and Unit:
1968 – 1972 (921st Fighter Regiment)
Aircraft: MiG-21
Hero of the Vietnamese People's Armed Forces: 28 May 2010
Rank: Lieutenant General

Air Victories: 4 kills
(4 F-4s – VPAF official credit)

Date	Aircraft	Unit	Kill – US Pilot (VPAF – US databases)
01 Jun 72	MiG-21	921.	F-4E – Hawks, Dingee (SAM)
10 Jun 72	MiG-21	921.	F-4 – US not confirmed (Shared)
13 Jun 72	MiG-21	921.	F-4E – Hanson, Fulton (POWs)
24 Jun 72	MiG-21	921.	F-4 – US not confirmed
27 Jun 72	MiG-21	921.	F-4E – Aikman (Rescued), Hanton (POW)

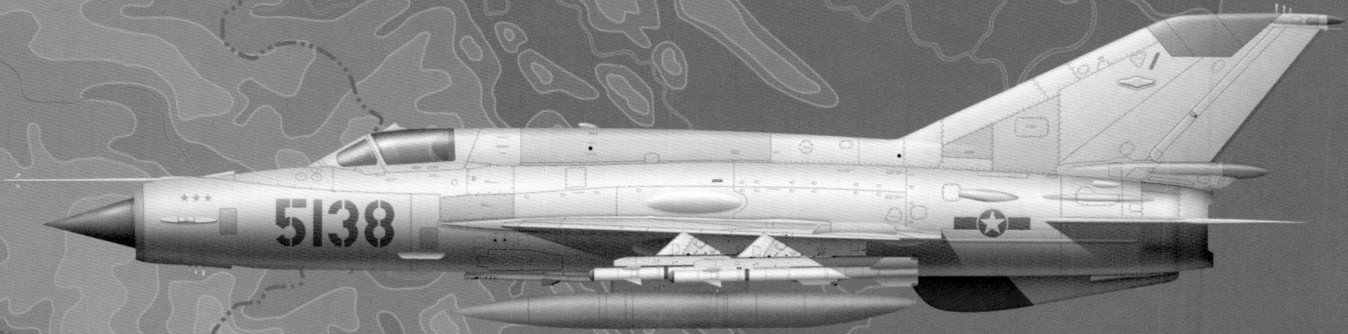

MiG-21MF Fishbed J, No. 5138 (3 kills) of the 921st Fighter Regiment, 1972
Pham Phu Thai used this MiG-21MF, which credited three air victories by pilots at 921st Fighter Regiment. Unfortunately, his MiG-21 was shot down by USAF F-4E Phantom (67-0301), and he ejected safely on 15 October 1972. (Artwork: Balázs Kakuk)

In the second half of October 1972, three famous North Vietnamese pilot's (Nguyen Tien Sam, Le Thanh Dao and Pham Phu Thai) MiG-21s were shot down by USAF F-4 Phantoms. They ejected and landed safely.
(István Toperczer Collection)

vertebra were broken, and my head was also injured. The local people made a stretcher from my parachute and transported me a distance of 9 kilometers, where an Mi-6 helicopter transported me to the hospital. I was in the Hospital No. 108 for 4 months. Then I returned to the unit, and I was able to fly only after one year.

Operation "Linebacker II" started against North Vietnam in the second half of December 1972. This placard demonstrates the "heroic" and hard fighting of the Air Defenses Forces and Vietnamese People's Air Force against large, enemy bomber formations.
(István Toperczer)

The End of the Air War

Operation "Linebacker II" started against North Vietnam in second half of December 1972. The operation received several informal names, such as the American version, "The Christmas Bombings," and the Vietnamese version, "Dien Bien Phu in the Sky."

It was a bombing campaign that combined both the US Seventh Air Force and US Navy Task Force 77, and was conducted against targets such as airfields, army barracks, radio stations, petroleum storages, railroads, and SAM and AAA sites located in the Hanoi and Hai Phong areas. Daylight operations were primarily carried out by F-4 Phantoms and A-7 Corsair bombers, depending upon the weather over the targets. The USAF EB-66s and US Navy EA-6 EW aircraft were used to confuse the radar stations with electronic jamming signals. During the nighttime operations, B-52 and F-111 bombers attacked Hanoi and Hai Phong, while the US Navy ordered its strike formations against airfields and SAM sites. Under "Linebacker II," the US Navy aircraft carriers (USS *America*, *Enterprise*, *Oriskany*, *Ranger* and *Saratoga*) centered their air attack sorties in the coastal areas around Hai Phong. By 29 December 1972, the 650 daytime and 700 nighttime intense bombing sorties flown by USAF and US Navy aircraft convinced the North Vietnamese government to return to the peace table in Paris.

On 17 December, a Class One Alert was ordered for all North Vietnamese units north of the 20th Parallel. At 19:40 hours on 18 December, B-52s and fighter-bombers launched an attack on Noi Bai, Gia Lam, Kep, Hoa Lac and Yen Bai airfields, the Dong Anh, Yen Vien and Duc Giang industrial centers, and the North Vietnamese Radio station at Me Tri. At the same time, the US Navy attacks against Hai Phong also started.

The MiG-21MF (F-96) Fishbed-Js of the 921th Fighter Regiment were on constant 24 hour combat alert duty at Noi Bai, Kep and Hoa Lac airfields, from the 18 December. MiG-21MF pilots had to be ready to takeoff up to 6 minutes during day and to 7 minutes at night.

In according with plans to shoot down B-52s at night, the MiG-21 pilot Tran Cung was ordered to take off from Hoa Lac airfield on 18 December. At 19:28 hours, he was ordered to fly toward the Hoa Binh – Suoi Rut area to attack B-52s flying from south of Moc Chau up to Van Yen. Radars could not detect the target because the electronic jamming was powerful that time. Tran Cung broke off the engagement to return and land at Noi Bai. At 19:47 hours, another MiG-21 pilot, Pham Tuan, was on combat alert duty at Noi Bai. After takeoff, he was guided over the Hoa Binh area where he spotted the B-52 formation and F-4 Phantoms. The F-4s discovered him and they turned to fire four missiles at the MiG-21. Pham Tuan evaded the missiles to pursue the B-52 bombers, but his RP-21 onboard was under electronic jamming signals. He broke off the engagement and decided to return to land at Noi Bai, where the many sections of runway were destroyed by American bombs. After landing, Pham Tuan's MiG-21 ran into a bomb crater in the runway and he was able to get out of the cockpit without any injuries.

In the afternoon of 22 December, a MiG-21 pair from the 927th Fighter Regiment took off from Noi Bai. Because the runway had been so severely damaged by B-52s, the two aircraft had to take off from

The SA-2 missile and Fan Song missile guidance radar are on display in the VPAF Museum in Hanoi. The "fan" refers to radar's fan shaped beams and the "song"' to the bird-like sound of the demodulated radiation. The Fan Song radar operated with ranges of 60-120km depending on the target type, altitude, and operating condition.
(István Toperczer)

At the 927th Fighter Regiment, Nguyen Duc Soat demonstrates the air engagement, on 22 December 1972, to Ngo Duy Thu (left), Tran Viet (middle) and his wingman, Nguyen Thanh Quy (right). Nguyen Thanh Quy's MiG-21PFM was shot down by a USAF F-4D Phantom, but he ejected and landed safely.
(István Toperczer Collection)

The SA-2 Guideline (Soviet designation S-75 Dvina) medium to high altitude surface-to-air missile (SAM) system was used against non-maneuvering targets, such as bombers, during Linebacker II. In the background, the bamboo mock-up of an SA-2 missile is seen, which was used to deceive the American SAM-killer Wild Weasel aircraft formations.
(István Toperczer)

the taxiway, which was just 16 meters wide and was lined with bomb craters along both sides. Nguyen Duc Soat and Nguyen Thanh Quy were ordered to intercept a group of F-4 aircraft flying in from Laos. They climbed to an altitude of 8,000 meters. After they broke through the clouds, Soat began to turn left and instantly found the flight of F-4s to the left at an angle of 90 degrees and at distance of 6 to 8 kilometers. They were flying at an altitude of 6,000-8,000 meters. Nguyen Duc Soat decided to attack the second pair of F-4s and gave the command to his wingman to drop the fuel tanks and switch on the afterburners. Soat made a sharp turn pulling seven to eight Gs, so Nguyen Thanh Quy lost him and tried to bank his MiG-21 into an U-turn. At that moment, four AIM-7 missiles were fired from Lt Col Brunson's F-4D Phantom and hit the MiG-21. Nguyen Thanh Quy ejected and landed safely in the Son Duong area of Tuyen Quang Province.

At noon, on 23 December 1972, radars detected an enemy formation coming from the southwest of Hanoi. Commander Dao Dinh Luyen ordered MiG-21s of the 921st Fighter Regiment to fly as a diversion to the north of Tam Dao, while MiG-21s of the 927th Fighter Regiment were to fight south of Hoa Binh. At 13:34 hours, Tran Van Sang took off from Kep and was guided over Phu Luong, where he climbed to an altitude of 8,000 meters. The enemy group appeared from Phu Tho to Son Duong. The MiG-21s accelerated and turned left, when an enemy F-4 formation also turned left. After spotting them, Sang engaged in an unfavorable dogfight against twelve F-4s. The situation would have not been good to continue, so at 13:53 hours, the command post ordered Tran Van Sang to break off the engagement and return to Kep airbase.

DATE OF BIRTH: 3 May 1946
ENLISTED: July 1965
PILOT TRAINING:
1965 – 1968 (MiG-21 – Soviet Union)
WAR SERVICE AND UNIT:
1968 – 1972 (921st Fighter Regiment)
1972 – 1975 (927th Fighter Regiment)
AIRCRAFT: MiG-21
HERO OF THE VIETNAMESE PEOPLE'S ARMED FORCES: 3 September 1973
RANK: Senior Colonel

AIR VICTORIES: 5 kills
(4 F-4s, 1 Firebee – VPAF official credit)

DATE	AIRCRAFT	UNIT	KILL – US PILOT (VPAF – US DATABASES)
23 Jun 72	MiG-21	927.	F-4 – US not confirmed
24 Jun 72	MiG-21	927.	F-4D – McCarty (KIA) Jackson (POW)
06 Oct 72	MiG-21	927.	F-4E – White, Egge (Rescued)
24 Nov 72	MiG-21	927.	Firebee
23 Dec 72	MiG-21	927.	F-4 – US not confirmed

MiG-21PFM Fishbed F, No. 5073 of the 927th Fighter Regiment, 1972
On 24 November 1972 Nguyen Van Nghia launched R-3S missile from this MiG-21PFM and shot down reconnaissance drone, AQM-34 Firebee over Viet Tri. (ARTWORK: BALÁZS KAKUK)

The MiG pilot Nguyen Van Nghia from the 927th Fighter Regiment became Ace-pilot on 23 December 1972, when he shot down a USAF F-4 Phantom over Hoa Binh Province, by VPAF records.
(István Toperczer Collection)

At 13:40 hours, Nguyen Van Nghia and Le Van Kien took off from Noi Bai and climbed to an altitude of 300 meters. They flew under the clouds and at the direction of 160 degrees. Over Mieu Mon area they changed their direction to 260 degrees and began to climb at maximum thrust. At an altitude of 4,000 meters, Nguyen Van Nghia saw a flight of enemy aircraft on the right at 60 degrees. The Phantoms were flying from west of Sam Tai (Laos) coming to Suoi Rut, at an altitude of 8,000 meters. At 13:51 hours, he decided to attack the trailing pair of F-4s. The MiG-21s turned to the right and closed in on the enemy aircraft from above. At a distance of 10 kilometers, when the pair of MiG-21s had flown into the rear hemisphere of the flight of F-4s, they were discovered. The MiG-21s, having the advantage in speed, quickly shortened the distance. The F-4s kicked on their afterburners and split into pairs. The lead pair began the ascending turn to the right and the trailing pair began the spiral dive to the left. Nguyen Van Nghia decided to attack the trailing pair of F-4s. At the distance of 1,300 meters, he launched an R-3S missile at the trail F-4 and shot it down. Le Van Kien was flying at a distance of 2,500 meters and also launched a missile at the trailing pair of F-4s. Because of the MiG-21's sharp turn at 3.5 G, the R-3S missile flew past the Phantom. The MiGs broke off on the right to fly east and landed at Noi Bai at 14:02 hours. This was the fifth American aircraft that Nguyen Van Nghia had shot down, but USAF records did not confirm this loss.

At 13:36 hours on 27 December, a pair of MiG-21s took off from Noi Bai to intercept an enemy group flying in from Laos. After takeoff and climbing to an altitude of 500 meters, Do Van Lanh from the 921st Fighter Regiment and Duong Ba Khang from the 927th Fighter Regiment flew at a direction of 30 degrees. The flight of F-4s arrived from Thai Nguyen over Kep. The MiG-21s flew under the clouds and

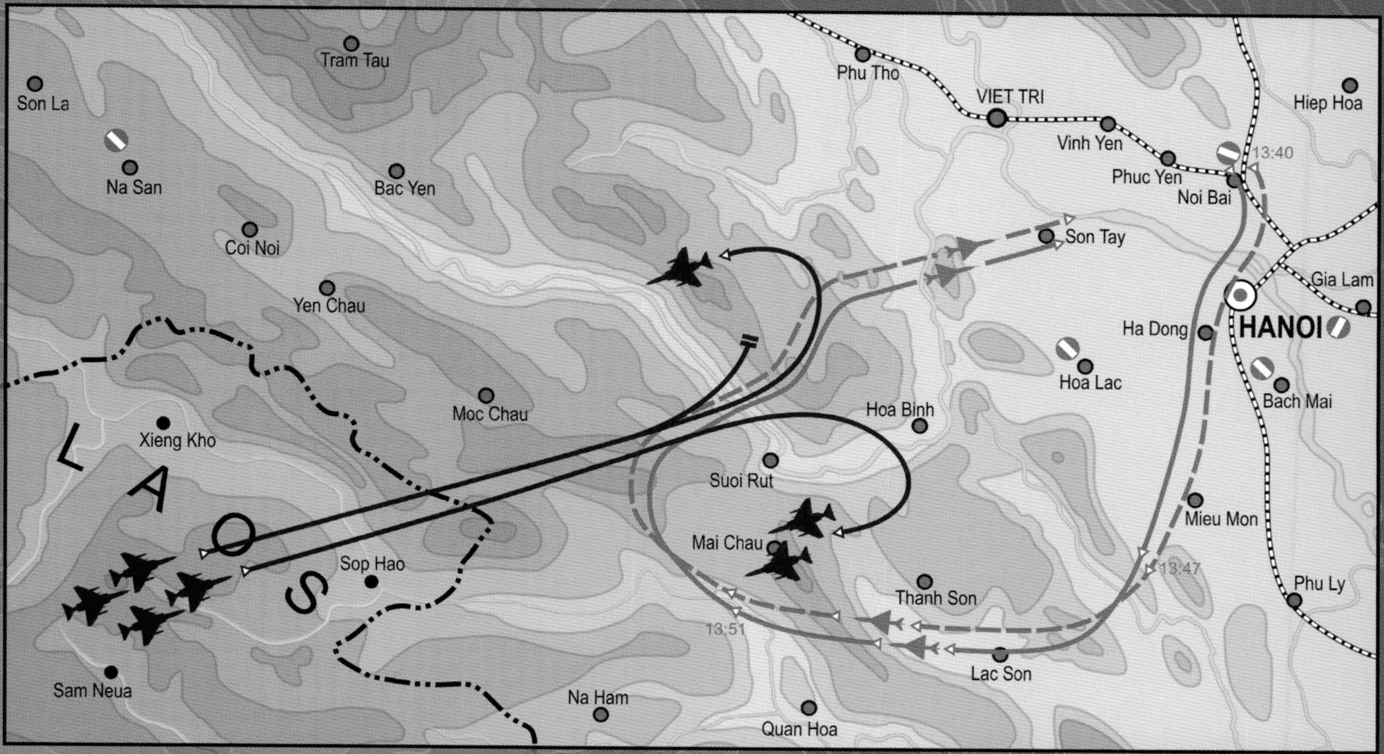

changed their direction to 90 degrees and climbed to an altitude of 1,000 meters, and then it turned to 270 degrees. The Phantoms were 90 degrees on the left and at a distance of 40 kilometers. At 13:44 hours, the enemy flight was over the western area of Kep, so the MiG-21 pair turned to a heading of 180 degrees. The regiment command ordered them to fly under the clouds, and three minutes later Duong Ba Khang fired his first R-3S missile at a distance of 1,800 meters, at a speed of 900 km/h and at an altitude of 200 meters above the ground, but without a result. He increased his speed to 1,200 km/h and he launched a second missile at a distance of 1,300 meters. At 13:55 hours the MiG-21s landed safely at Noi Bai.

After half an hour, at 14:11 hours, a single MiG-21 of the 921st Fighter Regiment, Tran Viet was onboard, took off from Mieu Mon and flew at a heading of 90 degrees under the clouds. Command ordered him to change his heading to 150 degrees and to climb to an altitude of 5,000 meters. At 14:14 hours, the enemy was 15 kilometers east of Hoa Binh, over Kim Bang, at an altitude of 7,000 meters. After two minutes, Tran Viet discovered the Phantoms on the right at 45 degrees, at a distance of 8 kilometers. Taking advantage of his superiority in speed, he closed the distance to the second F-4 pair, and launched an R-3S missile from a distance of 1,500 meters. The missile hit Maj Jeffcoat and 1Lt Trimble's F-4E Phantom (67-0292). The crew ejected 60 kilometers southwest of Hanoi. Tran Viet escaped to the east and turned north, flying across the Red River to land safely at Noi Bai.

In the afternoon of 23 December 1972, Nguyen Van Nghia shot down an F-4 Phantom over Hoa Binh by Vietnamese records. It was Nghia's fifth and last air victory during the Vietnam Air War.
(Cartograph: Péter Barna)

The battle-scarred MiG-21MFs of the 921st Fighter Regiment wait for the next mission at Noi Bai airbase in 1972. A MiG-21UM Mongol B departs on another training mission in the background.
(István Toperczer Collection)

At the end of 27 December 1972, a single MiG-21MF of Pham Tuan took off from Noi Bai and little later landed at Yen Bai with the help of the GCI situated in Moc Chau and Son La. He recalled:

> *At 22:20 hours, I was given the order to take off from Yen Bai at a heading of 200 degrees and broke through the low heavy cloud layer at 200-300 meters only to find F-4s in the vicinity. In the meantime I was informed that the B-52s were approaching Moc Chau and the GCI at Son La and Moc Chau were constantly updating me on the distance of the bombers: 60 kilometers, 50 km and 40 km. As planned, I jettisoned the fuel tank and climbed to 7,000 meters while applying the throttle to increase the speed. The radars were plotting the route of the B-52s and also warned me of the escort F-4s following them. When I saw a yellow light in front of me, I turned left to 40 degrees, increased my speed to 1,200 km/h and climbed to a 10,000 meter altitude where the B-52s were cruising. I radioed to the command: "I have the target in sight, tally target, request order for the attack". The response of the GCI was: "You have permission to fire twice, and then escape quickly". The Americans were holding formation, keeping approximately two to three*

On the night of 27 December 1972, Pham Tuan used this No.5121 MiG-21MF to shoot down a USAF B-52D Stratofortress bomber over Moc Chau. The provincial museum of Thai Binh stores one MiG-21MF Fishbed J with number of 5121 and kill markings, because Pham Tuan came from Quoc Tuan hamlet, Thai Binh Province.
(István Toperczer)

DATE OF BIRTH: 14 February 1947
ENLISTED: 2 September 1965
PILOT TRAINING:
1965 – 1968 (MiG-17 – Soviet Union)
1968 – 1969 (910th Air Training Regiment – Vietnam)
WAR SERVICE AND UNIT:
1969 – 1970 (923rd Fighter Regiment)
1970 – 1973 (921st Fighter Regiment)
AIRCRAFT: MiG-17, MiG-21
HERO OF THE VIETNAMESE PEOPLE'S ARMED FORCES: 3 September 1973
RANK: Lieutenant General

COSMONAUT TRAINING:
From 1 April 1979 (Soviet Union)
IN SPACE: 6th Interkosmos mission
Salyut-6 station, with Soviet cosmonaut Viktor Vassilyevich Gorbatko
7 days 20 hours 42 minutes,
23 July 1980 (Soyuz-37) – 31 July 1980 (Soyuz-36)

MiG-21MF Fishbed J, No. 5121 (8 kills) of the 921st Fighter Regiment, 1972
In the night of 27 December 1972, Pham Tuan used this MiG-21MF, No.5121 to shoot down a B-52D bomber over the border of Hoa Binh – Vinh Phu Provinces. (ARTWORK: BALÁZS KAKUK)

Pham Tuan demonstrates his attack against a USAF B-52 bomber to his comrades, Nguyen Khanh Duy, Tran Viet, Do Van Lanh and Nguyen Van Tho.
(István Toperczer Collection)

kilometers of separation. I made last minute checks on my missiles and when I reached the level of the third B-52 pushed the fire bottom on the control stick. I launched two heat seeking missiles from a distance of 2 kilometers. Big flames were visible around the second B-52 when I broke sharply to the left and descended to 2,000 meters before landing at Yen Bai. The attacked formation of B-52s immediately dropped their load and returned to base.

The loss of Capt Mize's B-52D bomber (56-0599) to MiG activity was never confirmed by the USAF, which, instead, claimed that the bomber was struck by a SAM.

The North Vietnamese first used the SA-3 Goa (Soviet designation S-125 Neva/Pechora) low to medium altitude SAM system at the end of December 1972. The missiles are typically deployed on fixed turrets containing two or four, but can be carried ready-to-fire on ZIL trucks in pairs.
István Toperczer)

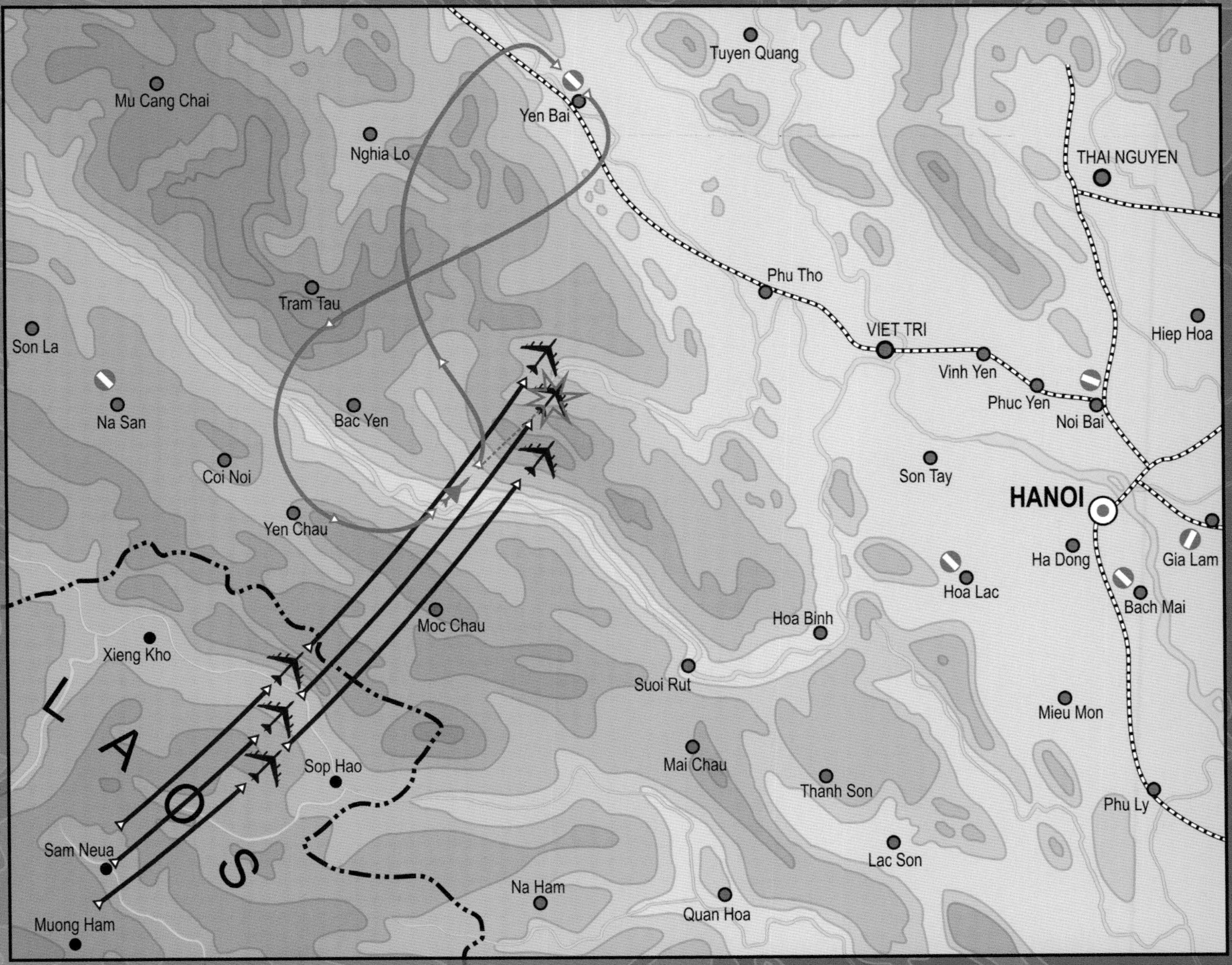

By the time the airfields at Noi Bai, Kep, Yen Bai, and Gia Lam were attacked on the 28 December 1972, the North Vietnamese had already flown, in secrecy, all MiG-21s to the brand new base at Cam Thuy in Thanh Hoa Province.

The last sorties of Operation "Linebacker II" were told by three North Vietnamese pilots. Hoang Tam Hung shot down a US Navy RA-5C aircraft, Vu Xuan Thieu shot down a B-52, and Bui Doan Do killed an F-4 Phantom to increase the number of US losses. Out of the three pilots, two died and only Bui Doan Do survived the war.

On 29 December 1972, three flights of enemy fighters appeared near Thanh Son area; USAF F-111s and F-4s bombed Yen Bai and Kep airbases. Meanwhile, three flights of B-52s appeared from the southwest and another from the southeast. At 23:04 hours, the 921st Fighter Regiment command ordered Nguyen Khanh Duy to take off from Noi Bai, to take the route along Yen Bai – Tuyen Quang – Thai Nguyen – Kep, then return

In the afternoon of 27 December 1972, Pham Tuan attacked a flight of B-52 bombers at Moc Chau and shot down one B-52D Stratofortress over the border of Hoa Binh – Vinh Phu Provinces, by Vietnamese records.
(CARTOGRAPH: PÉTER BARNA)

The Hero Vu Xuan Thieu wears a GSh-4 helmet with VKK-4 green high altitude compensating flight suit before his mission. On the night of 28 December 1972, he attacked an USAF B-52 Stratofortress, and the debris of the exploded bomber hit his aircraft, and he died in his diving MiG-21, by VPAF records.
(István Toperczer Collection)

to Noi Bai. The enemy aircraft entered south of Yen Bai then turned right to go around. At 23:48, the MiG-21 was at Son Duong, when the Tho Xuan command post ordered him to turn left and approach. One minute later, Bui Doan Do reported an F-4 Phantom and requested to attack. He fired two missiles and broke off immediately to land at 21:58 hours at Noi Bai. It was the first F-4 downed by MiG-21 in a night battle. Nevertheless, the USAF records did not confirm any losses on that day. After two weeks, on 8 January 1973, Bui Doan Do's MiG-21 was shot down by an AIM-7 Sparrow from Capt Howman's F-4D Phantom in the Route Pack 3 area. ***It was the last air victory of the USAF over North Vietnam.***

The young pilots of two MiG-21 fighter regiments are seen during a military parade at the beginning of 1973.
(István Toperczer Collection)

Operation Homecoming, from 12 February 1973 to 4 April 1973, returned 591 American "Prisoners of War" from Gia Lam airfield in Hanoi, back to the USA, in 54 missions by C-141A Starlifter transport aircraft. (István Toperczer Collection)

On 6 January 1973, Han Vinh Tuong claimed ***the last air victory of MiG-21 Fishbed during air war***, when he shot down a Firebee over the Suoi Rut – Hoa Binh area.

Luu Kim Ngo from the 923rd Fighter Regiment was on a training flight over Haiphong, on 12 January 1973. Lt. Kovaleski and Lt. Wise launched their F-4B Phantom, from the USS *Midway* (CVA-41), to intercept the MiG-17. The Phantom caught up with the enemy MiG and downed it with AIM-9 missiles. ***This was the last North Vietnamese MiG loss of the air battle during the Vietnam Air War.***

On 15 January 1973, U.S. President Richard Nixon announced a suspension of offensive actions against North Vietnam. U.S. Secretary of State Henry Kissinger and Vietnam's Le Duc Tho met again on 23 January, and the agreement of the Paris Peace Accord was signed by the leaders of the official delegations on 27 January at the Majestic Hotel in Paris. The US government agreed not to intervene in Vietnam and in the internal affairs of the Vietnamese people. Also, they agreed to stop all military action against the Democratic Republic of Vietnam, and call back all forces from South Vietnam.

After a series of diplomatic negotiations, the "Operation Homecoming" started to return 591 American "Prisoners of War" from North Vietnam. Three C-141 Starlifters flew to pick up released prisoners from Gia Lam airfield, on 12 February 1973. The groups of released POWs were selected on the basis of longest length of time in prisons. They had spent 6-8 years as prisoners in North Vietnam. From 12 February to 4 April, the C-141s flew 54 missions from Hanoi, with 40 POWs on board each Starlifter.

Epilogue

According to American databases, the USAF, the US Navy, and the Air America aircraft had managed to shoot down a total of 207 North Vietnamese aircraft and lost 92 of there own aircraft during air battles in the airspace of North Vietnam.

Contrary to the American records, the Vietnamese People's Air Force admits the loss of only 175 aircraft (MiG-17s, MiG-19s, MiG-21s and An-2s) of their own. The North Vietnamese official and non-official sources claimed 316 air victories against American aircraft (F-4s, F-8s, F-105s, RF-101Cs, F-102As, EB-66Cs, A-4s, A-7s, RC-47D, OV-10, HH-53 and Firebees).

During the years of the air war, 6 MiG-17 pilots and 13 MiG-21 pilots became "flying aces" with five or more air victories, however there were no MiG-19 Ace pilots. The MiG-17 Ace-pilots claimed a total of 34 air victories and MiG-21 Ace-pilots shot down 86 American aircraft, so their total score is 120 shotdown US aircraft from 1965 to 1973.

The MiG-17 Ace-pilots shot down 8 F-105 Thunderchiefs, 16 F-4 Phantoms and 7 F-8 Crusaders, while the MiG-21 Ace-pilots claimed 23 F-105s, 40 F-4s and 14 unmanned aerial vehicles, AQM-34 Firebees.

Although an additional eight MiG pilots did not become Ace-pilots, they were also successful during air battles. Each of them had claimed four air victories, so three MiG-17 pilots and five MiG-21 pilots elevated the Aces' results and added a total of 32 shotdown American aircraft.

The North Vietnamese pilots were issued from different "generations" and periods of the air war. During 1966-67, while one group of the MiG-17 pilots (Le Quang Trung, Nguyen Van Bay, Luu Huy Chao, and Vo Van Man) reached the five air victories necessary to become an Ace-pilot in 12-24 months, the other "generation" (Nguyen Phi Hung, and Le Hai) reached this same status in 6-12 months between 1967 and 1968. The early "generation" of MiG-21 pilots (Nguyen Nhat Chieu, Nguyen Hong Nhi and Nguyen Ngoc Do), between 1966 and 1967, became Ace-pilots in 6-12 months, while for the second "generation" (Pham Thanh Ngan, Dang Ngoc Ngu, Mai Van Cuong, Vu Ngoc Dinh, Nguyen Dang Kinh, and Nguyen Van Coc) this took a longer period of 6-24 months, from 1966 to 1968. In 1972, the third "generation" of MiG-21 pilots (Le Thanh Dao, Nguyen Van Nghia, Nguyen Duc Soat, and Nguyen Tien Sam) reckoned downing 5 American aircraft in an extremely short period of 5-6 months.

Below there is a list of very short and also of relatively long success series of MiG-17 and MiG-21 Ace-pilots and sub-Ace pilots.

MiG-17 pilots:
Bui Van Suu – 4 kills during 5 months
Nguyen Phi Hung – 5 kills during 10 months
Nguyen Van Bay – 7 kills during 12 months
and
Phan Van Tuc – 4 kills during 24 months
Luu Huy Chao – 6 kills during 24 months

MiG-21 pilots:
Pham Phu Thai – 4 kills during one month
Nguyen Tien Sam – 5 kills during 4 months
Nguyen Hong Nhi – 6 kills during 5 months
Pham Thanh Ngan – 6 kills during 12 months
Nguyen Van Coc – 7 kills during 12 months
and
Nguyen Dang Kinh – 6 kills during 24 months
Dang Ngoc Ngu – 5 kills during 24 months

Unfortunately, a large number of Ace-pilots and sub-Ace pilots (Vo Van Man, Hoang Van Ky, Phan Van Tuc, Nguyen Phi Hung, Le Quang Trung, Le Trong Huyen, and Dang Ngoc Ngu) had been killed during the war, to which was added the death of Do Van Lanh, who lost his life after the war during a training flight.

After each air victory, the MiG pilot was awarded the "Huy Hieu Bac Ho" (Uncle Ho Badge), on numerous occasions by Ho Chi Minh himself. This badge had been established especially for North Vietnamese pilots and exclusively for shooting down American aircraft.

Aces and sub-Aces of the VPAF

Pilot	Victories	Aircraft	Unit	War period
Nguyen Van Coc	9 US-kills	MiG-21	921st	1967–69
Pham Thanh Ngan	8 US-kills	MiG-21	921st	1966–68
Nguyen Hong Nhi	8 US-kills	MiG-21	921st / 927th	1966–68
Mai Van Cuong	8 US-kills	MiG-21	921st	1966–69
Nguyen Van Bay	7 US-kills	MiG-17	923rd	1966–67
Dang Ngoc Ngu	7 US-kills	MiG-21	921st	1966–72
Luu Huy Chao	6 US-kills	MiG-17	923rd	1966–68
Le Hai	6 US-kills	MiG-17	923rd	1967–72
Vu Ngoc Dinh	6 US-kills	MiG-21	921st	1966–70
Nguyen Ngoc Do	6 US-kills	MiG-21	921st	1967–68
Nguyen Nhat Chieu	6 US-kills	MiG-17/21	921st	1965–67
Le Thanh Dao	6 US-kills	MiG-21	927th	1971–72
Nguyen Dang Kinh	6 US-kills	MiG-21	921st	1966–68
Nguyen Duc Soat	6 US-kills	MiG-21	921st / 927th	1969–72
Vo Van Man	5 US-kills	MiG-17	923rd	1966–67
Le Quang Trung	5 US-kills	MiG-17	923rd	1966–67
Nguyen Phi Hung	5 US-kills	MiG-17	923rd	1967–68
Nguyen Tien Sam	5 US-kills	MiG-21	921st / 927th	1972
Nguyen Van Nghia	5 US-kills	MiG-21	927th	1972
Phan Van Tuc	4 US-kills	MiG-17	921st / 923rd	1965–67
Hoang Van Ky	4 US-kills	MiG-17	923rd	1966–67
Le Trong Huyen	4 US-kills	MiG-17/21	923rd / 921st	1966–67
Dong Van Song	4 US-kills	MiG-21	921st	1966–68
Bui Van Suu	4 US-kills	MiG-17	923rd	1967–68
Dinh Ton	4 US-kills	MiG-21	921st	1968–71
Do Van Lanh	4 US-kills	MiG-21	921st	1972
Pham Phu Thai	4 US-kills	MiG-21	921st	1972

Aces and Heroes Air Battles in the Vietnam War (1965 – 1972)

Date	VN Pilot (Killer)	Aircraft	Unit	Lost	US Pilot (KIA, POW, RESCUED)
03 Apr 65	***Pham Ngoc Lan***	MiG-17	921.	***F-8E***	***Thomas (F-8 damaged)***
	Phan Van Tuc			***F-8E***	***US not confirmed***
	Ho Van Quy				
	Tran Minh Phuong				
	Tran Hanh	MiG-17	921.		
	Pham Giay				
04 Apr 65	Le Trong Long	MiG-17	921.		
	Phan Van Tuc				
	Ho Van Quy				
	Tran Minh Phuong				
	Tran Hanh	MiG-17	921.	***F-105D***	***Bennett (KIA)***
	Pham Giay (KIA)				
	Le Minh Huan (KIA)			***F-105D***	***Magnusson (KIA)***
	Tran Nguyen Nam (KIA)				
17 Jun 65	***Lam Van Lich***	MiG-17	921.	**F-4**	***US not confirmed***
	Cao Thanh Tinh (EJECT)				
	Le Trong Long (KIA)			**F-4**	***US not confirmed***
	Nguyen Nhat Chieu (EJECT)				
20 Sep 65	Pham Ngoc Lan	MiG-17	921.		
	Nguyen Nhat Chieu			**F-4**	***US not confirmed***
	Tran Van Tri				
	Nguyen Ngoc Do				
04 Mar 66	***Nguyen Hong Nhi***	MiG-21	921.	***Firebee***	
	Nguyen Dang Kinh				
	Pham Thanh Chung	MiG-17	923.		
	Ngo Duc Mai			***F-4***	***US not confirmed***
	Tran Minh Phuong				
	Nguyen The Hon				
17 Apr 66	Ho Van Quy	MiG-17	923.		
	Luu Huy Chao			**C-47**	***US not confirmed***
	Nguyen Van Bien				
	Tran Van Triem				
26 Apr 66	Ho Van Quy	MiG-17	923.		
	Luu Huy Chao			***F-4C***	***US not confirmed***
	Nguyen Van Bay			***F-4C***	***US not confirmed (F-4 damaged)***
	Tran Van Triem (EJECT) (FF)				
	Nguyen Hong Nhi (EJECT)	MiG-21	921.		
	Dong Van Song				
29 Apr 66	***Bui Dinh Kinh***	MiG-17	921.	***A-1E***	***Boston (KIA)***
	Bui Van Suu				
	Nguyen Huu Tao				
	Nguyen Xuan Nhuan				

Date	VN Pilot (Killer)	Aircraft	Unit	Lost	US Pilot (KIA, POW, RESCUED)
29 Apr 66	Nguyen Khac Loc (EJECT) Luu Huy Chao ***Nguyen Van Bay***	MiG-17	923.	***F-105D***	***Bruch (KIA) (AAA)***
30 Apr 66	Pham Ngoc Lan (EJECT) Bui Van Suu Tran Tan Duc (KIA) Nguyen Quang Sinh	MiG-17	921.		
12 Jun 66	***Le Quang Trung*** Vo Van Man	MiG-17	923.	***F-8***	***US not confirmed***
21 Jun 66	***Pham Thanh Chung*** Duong Trung Tan (EJECT) Nguyen Van Bay ***Phan Van Tuc***	MiG-17	923.	***RF-8A*** ***F-8E***	***Eastman (POW) (AAA)*** ***Black (POW)***
29 Jun 66	Tran Huyen Vo Van Man ***Nguyen Van Bay*** ***Phan Van Tuc***	MiG-17	923.	***F-105D*** ***F-105D***	***Jones (POW) (AAA) (F-105 damaged)*** ***US not confirmed***
11 Jul 66	***Vu Ngoc Dinh*** Dong Van Song	MiG-21	921.	***F-105D***	***McClelland (Run out fuel)***
19 Jul 66	***Nguyen Van Bien*** ***Vo Van Man***	MiG-17	923.	***F-105D*** ***F-105D***	***Steere (Rescued) (AAA)*** ***Diamond (KIA)***
21 Jul 66	***Nguyen Dang Kinh***	MiG-21	921.	***Firebee***	
29 Jul 66	***Tran Huyen*** ***Vo Van Man***	MiG-17	923.	***RC-47***	***Conklin, Hoskinson + 6 crew (KIA)***
12 Aug 66	Phan Van Tuc ***Luu Huy Chao***	MiG-17	923.	***F-105D***	***Allison (KIA) (AAA)***
13 Aug 66	***Dang Ngoc Ngu***	MiG-21	921.	***Firebee***	
17 Aug 66	***Le Quang Trung*** Ngo Duc Mai	MiG-17	923.	***F-105F***	***Brand, Singer (KIA) (AAA)***
05 Sep 66	***Nguyen Van Bay*** ***Vo Van Man***	MiG-17	923.	***F-8E*** ***F-8E***	***Abbott (POW)*** ***US not confirmed (F-8 damaged)***
16 Sep 66	Ho Van Quy Do Huy Hoang ***Nguyen Van Bay*** Vo Van Man	MiG-17	923.	***F-4C***	***Robertson (KIA), Buchanan (POW)***
20 Sep 66	***Le Quang Trung*** ***Hoang Van Ky*** Tran Minh Phuong Luu Duc Sy	MiG-17	923.	***F-105*** ***F-105***	***US not confirmed*** ***US not confirmed***
21 Sep 66	Nguyen Van Bay Do Huy Hoang (EJECT) Luu Huy Chao ***Vo Van Man*** (MiG damaged) ***Le Trong Huyen*** Tran Thien Luong	MiG-17 MiG-21	923. 921.	***F-4C*** ***F-105D***	***Kellems, Thomas (Rescued)*** ***Ammon (KIA) (AAA)***
08 Oct 66	Tran Ngoc Siu ***Mai Van Cuong***	MiG-21	921.	***F-105***	***US not confirmed***

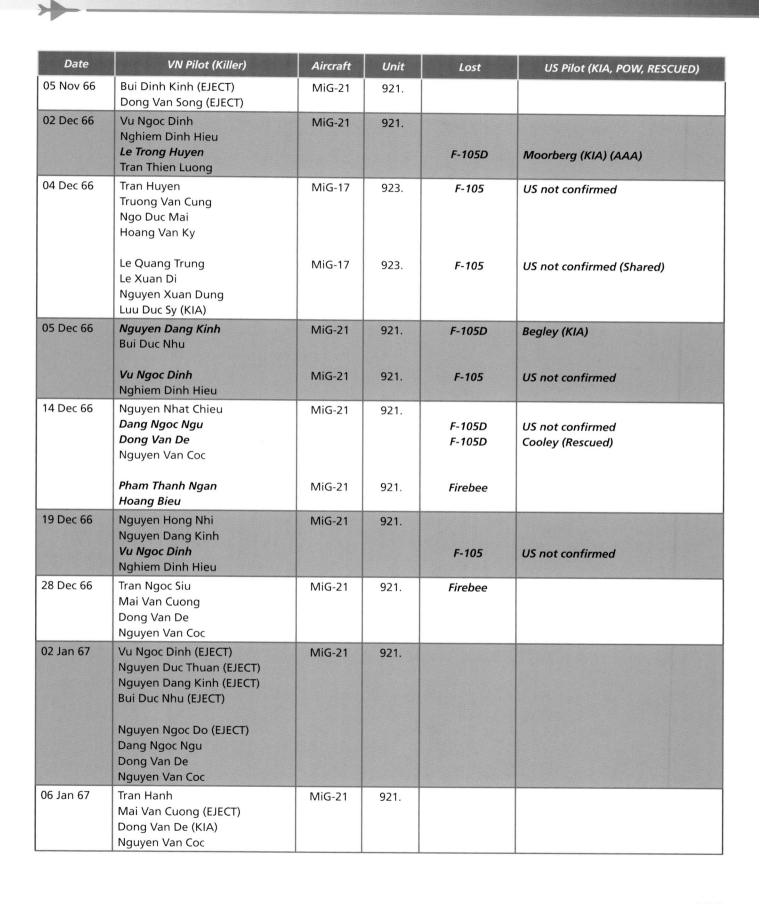

Date	VN Pilot (Killer)	Aircraft	Unit	Lost	US Pilot (KIA, POW, RESCUED)
05 Nov 66	Bui Dinh Kinh (EJECT) Dong Van Song (EJECT)	MiG-21	921.		
02 Dec 66	Vu Ngoc Dinh Nghiem Dinh Hieu ***Le Trong Huyen*** Tran Thien Luong	MiG-21	921.	 ***F-105D***	 ***Moorberg (KIA) (AAA)***
04 Dec 66	Tran Huyen Truong Van Cung Ngo Duc Mai Hoang Van Ky Le Quang Trung Le Xuan Di Nguyen Xuan Dung Luu Duc Sy (KIA)	MiG-17 MiG-17	923. 923.	***F-105*** ***F-105***	***US not confirmed*** ***US not confirmed (Shared)***
05 Dec 66	***Nguyen Dang Kinh*** Bui Duc Nhu ***Vu Ngoc Dinh*** Nghiem Dinh Hieu	MiG-21 MiG-21	921. 921.	***F-105D*** ***F-105***	***Begley (KIA)*** ***US not confirmed***
14 Dec 66	Nguyen Nhat Chieu ***Dang Ngoc Ngu*** ***Dong Van De*** Nguyen Van Coc ***Pham Thanh Ngan*** ***Hoang Bieu***	MiG-21 MiG-21	921. 921.	 ***F-105D*** ***F-105D*** ***Firebee***	 ***US not confirmed*** ***Cooley (Rescued)***
19 Dec 66	Nguyen Hong Nhi Nguyen Dang Kinh ***Vu Ngoc Dinh*** Nghiem Dinh Hieu	MiG-21	921.	 ***F-105***	 ***US not confirmed***
28 Dec 66	Tran Ngoc Siu Mai Van Cuong Dong Van De Nguyen Van Coc	MiG-21	921.	***Firebee***	
02 Jan 67	Vu Ngoc Dinh (EJECT) Nguyen Duc Thuan (EJECT) Nguyen Dang Kinh (EJECT) Bui Duc Nhu (EJECT) Nguyen Ngoc Do (EJECT) Dang Ngoc Ngu Dong Van De Nguyen Van Coc	MiG-21	921.		
06 Jan 67	Tran Hanh Mai Van Cuong (EJECT) Dong Van De (KIA) Nguyen Van Coc	MiG-21	921.		

Date	VN Pilot (Killer)	Aircraft	Unit	Lost	US Pilot (KIA, POW, RESCUED)
21 Jan 67	Ho Van Quy Phan Thanh Hai ***Nguyen Van Bay*** Vo Van Man	MiG-17	924.	***F-105D***	***Wyatt (Rescued) (AAA)***
05 Feb 67	Le Quang Trung ***Hoang Van Ky*** Ngo Duc Mai Truong Van Cung	MiG-17	923.	***F-4***	***US not confirmed***
23 Apr 67	Nguyen Dang Kinh (EJECT) Tran Thien Luong	MiG-21	921.		
24 Apr 67	***Mai Duc Toai*** Le Hai Luu Huy Chao Hoang Van Ky	MiG-17	923.	***F-105***	***US not confirmed***
	Vo Van Man ***Nguyen Ba Dich*** ***Nguyen Van Bay*** Nguyen The Hon	MiG-17	923.	***F-4C*** ***F-4C*** ***F-4B***	***Knapp, Austin (KIA) (AAA)*** ***Knapp, Austin (KIA) (AAA)*** ***Southwick, Laing (AAA)***
	North Koreans	MiG-17	Doan Z	***F-4***	***US not confirmed***
25 Apr 67	Nguyen Van Bay ***Ha Dinh Bon (Nguyen Bon)*** ***Nguyen The Hon*** ***Nguyen Ba Dich***	MiG-17	923.	***A-4C*** ***F-8*** ***A-4E***	***Stackhouse (POW)*** ***US not confirmed*** ***Almberg (Rescued) (SA-2)***
	Le Quang Trung Nguyen Huu Diet (Phan Diet) Phan Thanh Tai Nguyen Van Tho	MiG-17	923.	***F-105***	***US not confirmed***
	Mai Duc Toai Le Hai Luu Huy Chao Hoang Van Ky	MiG-17	923.	***F-105D***	***Weskamp (KIA) (AAA)***
28 Apr 67	Mai Duc Toai ***Le Hai*** Luu Huy Chao Hoang Van Ky	MiG-17	923.	***F-105***	***US not confirmed***
	Duong Trung Tan Nguyen Huu Diet (Phan Diet) ***Phan Thanh Tai*** Nguyen Van Tho	MiG-17	923.	***F-105***	***US not confirmed***
	Dang Ngoc Ngu ***Mai Van Cuong***	MiG-21	921.	***F-105D***	***Caras (KIA)***
29 Apr 67	***Nguyen Van Bay*** Le Si Diep Vo Van Man Truong Van Cung	MiG-17	923.	***F-4C***	***Torkleson (POW) Pollin (KIA) (AAA)***

Date	VN Pilot (Killer)	Aircraft	Unit	Lost	US Pilot (KIA, POW, RESCUED)
30 Apr 67	***Nguyen Ngoc Do***	MiG-21	921.	***F-105F***	***Thorsness, Johnson (POW)***
	Nguyen Van Coc			***F-105D***	***R. Abbott (POW)***
	Le Trong Huyen	MiG-21	921.	***F-105D***	***J. Abbott (POW)***
	Vu Ngoc Dinh			***F-105D***	***Lenski (F-105 damaged)***
04 May 67	Pham Thanh Ngan	MiG-21	921.		
	Nguyen Van Coc (EJECT)				
	Cao Thanh Tinh	MiG-17	923.		
	Hoang Van Ky			***F-4C***	***US not confirmed***
05 May 67	***Nguyen Ngoc Do***	MiG-21	921.	***F-105D***	***Shively (POW) (AAA)***
	Dang Ngoc Ngu				
12 May 67	***Cao Thanh Tinh***	MiG-17	923.	***F-4***	***US not confirmed***
	Le Hai				
	Ngo Duc Mai			***F-4C***	***Gaddis (POW), Jefferson (KIA)***
	Hoang Van Ky			***F-4C***	***US not confirmed***
	Duong Trung Tan	MiG-17	923.	***F-105***	***US not confirmed***
	Phan Trong Van (EJECT)				
	Truong Van Cung				
	Nguyen Van Tho			***F-105***	***US not confirmed***
	Le Trong Huyen	MiG-21	921.		
	Dong Van Song			***F-105D***	***Grenzebach (KIA) (AAA)***
14 May 67	***Vo Van Man (KIA)***	MiG-17	923.	***F-4***	***US not confirmed***
	Ha Dinh Bon (Nguyen Bon)				
	Nguyen The Hon (KIA)			***F-4***	***US not confirmed***
	Le Hai				
16 May 67	***Mai Van Cuong***	MiG-21	921.	***Firebee***	
20 May 67	***Nguyen Nhat Chieu***	MiG-21	921.	***F-4C***	***Van Loan, Milligan (POW)***
	Pham Thanh Ngan				
	Vu Ngoc Dinh (EJECT)	MiG-21	921.		
	Nghiem Dinh Hieu (KIA)				
22 May 67	Tran Ngoc Siu	MiG-21	921.		
	Dang Ngoc Ngu			***F-4C***	***Perrine, Backus (KIA) (AAA)***
05 Jun 67	Ho Van Quy	MiG-17	923.		
	Le Van Phong				
	Hoang Van Ky (KIA)				
	Ha Dinh Bon (Nguyen Bon)				
11 Jul 67	***Le Trong Huyen***	MiG-21	921.	***A-4***	***US not confirmed***
	Dong Van Song				
20 Jul 67	***Nguyen Ngoc Do***	MiG-21	921.	***RF-4C***	***Corbitt, Bare (KIA)***
	Pham Thanh Ngan				***(26-Jul-67 by USAF)***
02 Aug 67	***Nguyen Ngoc Do***	MiG-21	921.	***F-105***	***US not confirmed***
	Pham Thanh Ngan				
10 Aug 67	Bui Dinh Kinh (KIA)	MiG-21	921.		
	Dong Van Song (EJECT)				

Date	VN Pilot (Killer)	Aircraft	Unit	Lost	US Pilot (KIA, POW, RESCUED)
23 Aug 67	***Nguyen Nhat Chieu*** ***Nguyen Van Coc*** ***Cao Thanh Tinh*** Le Van Phong (KIA) ***Nguyen Van Tho*** ***Nguyen Hong Diep*** ***North Koreans***	MiG-21 MiG-17 MiG-17	921. 923. Doan Z	***F-4D*** ***F-4D*** ***F-105D*** ***F-4*** ***F-4*** ***F-4***	***Tyler (POW) Sittner (KIA)*** ***Carrigan (POW) Lane (KIA)*** ***Baker (POW) (Flak)*** ***US not confirmed*** ***US not confirmed*** ***US not confirmed***
31 Aug 67	***Nguyen Hong Nhi*** Nguyen Dang Kinh	MiG-21	921.	***RF-4C***	***US not confirmed***
10 Sep 67	***Nguyen Hong Nhi*** Nguyen Dang Kinh	MiG-21	921.	***RF-101C***	***US not confirmed***
16 Sep 67	***Nguyen Ngoc Do*** ***Pham Thanh Ngan***	MiG-21	921.	***RF-101C*** ***RF-101C***	***Patterson (Rescued) (AAA)*** ***Bagley (POW)***
21 Sep 67	***Ho Van Quy*** Nguyen Dinh Phuc ***Bui Van Suu*** Le Si Diep	MiG-17	923.	***F-4B*** ***F-4B***	***US not confirmed*** ***US not confirmed***
26 Sep 67	***Nguyen Hong Nhi*** Dong Van Song	MiG-21	921.	***F-4D***	***US not confirmed***
27 Sep 67	***Nguyen Ngoc Do*** Nguyen Van Ly	MiG-21	921.	***F-105***	***(F-105 damaged)***
30 Sep 67	Lim Dang An (KIA) Tran Ngoc Siu (KIA) ***Mai Van Cuong***	MiG-17 MiG-21	Doan Z 921.	 ***F-105***	 ***US not confirmed***
03 Oct 67	***Pham Thanh Ngan*** Nguyen Van Ly	MiG-21	921.	***F-4D***	***Moore, Gulbrandson (Rescued)***
07 Oct 67	Nguyen Huu Tao Nguyen Phu Ninh Nguyen Hong Diep ***Nguyen Phi Hung*** ***Pham Thanh Ngan*** ***Mai Van Cuong*** ***Nguyen Nhat Chieu*** ***Nguyen Van Coc***	MiG-17 MiG-21 MiG-21	921. 921. 921.	 ***F-4*** ***F-4D*** ***F-4*** ***F-105F*** ***F-105D***	 ***US not confirmed*** ***Appleby (POW), Austin (KIA) (SA2)*** ***(F-4 damaged)*** ***Howard, Shamblee (Rescued)*** ***Fullam (KIA) (AAA)***
09 Oct 67	***Nguyen Hong Nhi*** Dong Van Song	MiG-21	921.	***F-105D***	***Clements (POW)***
24 Oct 67	Nguyen Dang Kinh Dong Van Song (EJECT)	MiG-21	921.		
26 Oct 67	Duong Trung Tan (EJECT) Nguyen Hong Thai (EJECT) Bui Van Suu Le Si Diep (EJECT) Mai Van Cuong (EJECT) Nguyen Van Coc	MiG-17 MiG-21	923. 921.		

Date	VN Pilot (Killer)	Aircraft	Unit	Lost	US Pilot (KIA, POW, RESCUED)
29 Oct 67	***Nguyen Nhat Chieu***	MiG-21	921.	F-4	US not confirmed
	Dang Ngoc Ngu				
06 Nov 67	Nguyen Huu Tao (KIA)	MiG-17	923.		
	Phan Trong Van (EJECT)				
	Nguyen Van Tho			F-105	US not confirmed
	Nguyen Phi Hung			F-105	US not confirmed
	Bui Van Suu	MiG-17	923.	F-105	US not confirmed
	Nguyen Duy Tuan				
	Le Xuan Di				
	Nguyen Dinh Phuc			F-105D	Hagerman (KIA) (SA-2)
07 Nov 67	***Nguyen Hong Nhi***	MiG-21	921.	F-105D	Diehl (KIA)
	Nguyen Dang Kinh			F-4	US not confirmed
08 Nov 67	***Dang Ngoc Ngu***	MiG-21	921.	F-4D	Gordon, Brenneman (POW)
	Nguyen Van Ly				
18 Nov 67	***Pham Thanh Ngan***	MiG-21	921.	F-105F	Dardeau, Lehnhoff (KIA)
	Nguyen Van Coc			F-105D	Reed (Rescued)
19 Nov 67	Vu Ngoc Dinh	MiG-21	921.		
	Nguyen Dang Kinh			EB-66	US not confirmed
	Ho Van Quy	MiG-17	923.		
	Le Hai			F-4B	Teague (KIA), Stier (POW)
	Nguyen Dinh Phuc			F-4B	US not confirmed
	Nguyen Phi Hung			F-4B	Clower (POW), Estes (KIA)
20 Nov 67	***Pham Thanh Ngan***	MiG-21	921.	F-105D	Butler (POW)
	Nguyen Van Coc			F-105	US not confirmed
12 Dec 67	***Nguyen Van Coc***	MiG-21	921.	F-105	(F-105 damaged)
	Nguyen Van Ly				
14 Dec 67	***Luu Huy Chao***	MiG-17	923.	F-8	US not confirmed
	Le Hai				
	Bui Van Suu				
	Nguyen Dinh Phuc (KIA)				Shared
17 Dec 67	***Vu Ngoc Dinh***	MiG-21	921.	F-105D	Ellis (POW)
				F-105	US not confirmed
	Nguyen Dang Kinh				
	Nguyen Hong Nhi			F-105	US not confirmed
	Luu Huy Chao	MiG-17	923.	F-4D	Fleenor, Boyer (POW)
	Nguyen Hong Thai (KIA)				
	Bui Van Suu			F-4C	US not confirmed
	Le Hai				
19 Dec 67	***Nguyen Dang Kinh***	MiG-21	921.	F-4	(F-4 damaged)
	Bui Duc Nhu				
	Vu The Xuan	MiG-17	923.	F-105	US not confirmed
	Nguyen Quang Sinh				
	Le Hong Diep				
	Nguyen Phi Hung			F-105	US not confirmed

Date	VN Pilot (Killer)	Aircraft	Unit	Lost	US Pilot (KIA, POW, RESCUED)
03 Jan 68	***Nguyen Dang Kinh*** ***Bui Duc Nhu***	MiG-21	921.	***F-105*** ***F-105***	***US not confirmed*** ***US not confirmed***
	Ha Van Chuc	MiG-21	921.	***F-105D***	***Bean (POW)***
	Luu Huy Chao (MiG damaged) Le Hong Diep (EJECT) ***Bui Van Suu*** Le Hai	MiG-17	923.	 ***F-4***	 ***US not confirmed***
14 Jan 68	Ha Van Chuc (WIA) (Died 19 Jan)	MiG-21	921.	***F-105D***	***Horne (KIA)***
	Nguyen Dang Kinh ***Dong Van Song***	MiG-21	921.	 ***EB-66C***	 ***Mercer, Terrell + 5 crew (Rescued – POW)***
03 Feb 68	***Pham Thanh Ngan*** Nguyen Van Coc	MiG-21	921.	***F-102A***	***Wiggins (KIA)***
05 Feb 68	***Nguyen Ngoc Do*** Hoang Bieu	MiG-21	921.	***F-105D***	***Lasiter (POW) (04-Feb-68 by USAF)***
15 Apr 68	***Dinh Ton*** Nguyen Dang Kinh	MiG-21	921.	***Firebee***	
24 Apr 68	***Dang Ngoc Ngu*** Nguyen Van Minh	MiG-21	921.	***Firebee***	
07 May 68	Dang Ngoc Ngu ***Nguyen Van Coc***	MiG-21	921.	 ***F-4B***	 ***Christensen, Kramer (Rescued)***
23 May 68	Nguyen Van Coc Ha Quang Hung (EJECT)	MiG-21	921		
26 May 68	***Dinh Ton*** Nguyen Dang Kinh	MiG-21	921.	***Firebee***	
02 Jun 68	***Dinh Ton*** ***Tran Viet***	MiG-21	921.	***Firebee***	
04 Jun 68	***Nguyen Van Coc*** Tran Van Hoa	MiG-21	921.	***Firebee***	
14 Jun 68	***Luu Huy Chao*** ***Le Hai***	MiG-17	923.	***F-4*** ***F-4***	***US not confirmed*** ***US not confirmed***
16 Jun 68	***Dinh Ton*** Nguyen Tien Sam	MiG-21	921.	***F-4J***	***Wilber (POW), Rupinski (KIA)***
19 Jun 68	***Mai Van Cuong*** Nguyen Van Quang	MiG-21	921.	***Firebee***	
26 Jun 68	Vu Ngoc Dinh (EJECT) Bui Duc Nhu (EJECT)	MiG-21	921.		
09 Jul 68	***Nguyen Phi Hung (KIA)*** Nguyen Phu Ninh	MiG-17	923.	***F-8***	***US not confirmed***
10 Jul 68	Pham Thanh Ngan Pham Phu Thai (EJECT) Dang Ngoc Ngu	MiG-21	921.		

Date	VN Pilot (Killer)	Aircraft	Unit	Lost	US Pilot (KIA, POW, RESCUED)
29 Jul 68	***Le Hai*** ***Luu Huy Chao*** Hoang Ich Le Si Diep (KIA)	MiG-17	923.	***F-8***	***US not confirmed***
01 Aug 68	Nguyen Dang Kinh Pham Van Mao ***Nguyen Hong Nhi (EJECT)***	MiG-21	921.	***F-8***	***US not confirmed***
03 Sep 68	***Mai Van Cuong*** Tran Van Hoa	MiG-21	921.	***Firebee***	
20 Sep 68	***Mai Van Cuong*** Tran Van Hoa	MiG-21	921.	***Firebee***	
21 Sep 68	***Nguyen Dang Kinh*** Nguyen Cat A	MiG-21	921.	***Firebee***	
22 Sep 68	Nguyen Van Ly (EJECT) Vu Dinh Rang (EJECT) Pham Thanh Ngan (MiG damaged)	MiG-21	921.		
26 Oct 68	***Nguyen Dang Kinh*** Vu Xuan Thieu	MiG-21	921.	***F-4***	***US not confirmed***
31 Oct 68	Pham Thanh Ngan ***Pham Thanh Nam***	MiG-21	921.	***Firebee***	
08 Nov 68	***Nguyen Van Coc*** Pham Phu Thai	MiG-21	921.	***Firebee***	
09 Feb 69	***Mai Van Cuong*** Pham Phu Thai Dang Ngoc Ngu Nguyen Tien Sam (EJECT)	MiG-21 MiG-21	921. 921.	***Firebee***	
04 Mar 69	***Dang Ngoc Ngu*** Bui Van Long	MiG-21	921.	***Firebee***	
13 Mar 69	***Nguyen Duc Soat*** Bui Duc Nhu	MiG-21	921.	***Firebee***	
24 Jun 69	***Mai Van Cuong*** Pham Phu Thai	MiG-21	921.	***Firebee***	
03 Aug 69	***Nguyen Van Coc*** ***Pham Thanh Nam*** ***Le Hai*** ***Hoang Cong***	MiG-21 MiG-17	921. 923.	***Firebee*** ***Firebee***	
28 Jan 70	***Vu Ngoc Dinh*** ***Pham Dinh Tuan (KIA)***	MiG-21	921.	***HH-53B*** ***F-4***	***Bell, Leeser + 4 crew (KIA)*** ***US not confirmed***
28 Mar 70	Pham Phu Thai Pham Thanh Nam (KIA)	MiG-21	921.		
13 Apr 71	***Dinh Ton***	MiG-21	921.	***O-2A***	***US not confirmed***
10 May 71	***Mai Van Cuong*** ***Le Thanh Dao***	MiG-21	921.	***OV-10***	***(OV-10 damaged)***

Date	VN Pilot (Killer)	Aircraft	Unit	Lost	US Pilot (KIA, POW, RESCUED)
18 Dec 71	***Le Thanh Dao***	MiG-21	921.	***F-4D***	***Johnson, Vaughan (POW)***
	Vo Si Giap			***F-4D***	***Stanley, O'Brien (Rescued)***
	Nguyen Van Khanh (KIA)(FF)			***F-4D***	***Wells, Hildebrand (POW)***
	Le Minh Duong				
19 Jan 72	***Nguyen Hong My***	MiG-21	921.	***RF-4C***	***Mock, Stiles (20-Jan-72 by USAF)***
	Tran Van Sang				
	Nguyen Duc Soat	MiG-21	921.		
	Ha Vinh Thanh				
	Pham Ngoc Tam	MiG-19	925.		
	Nguyen Tu Dung (EJECT) (FF)				
06 Mar 72	***Le Hai***	MiG-17	923.	***F-4***	***US not confirmed***
	Hoang Ich (KIA)				
06 May 72	Nguyen Van Bay „B" (KIA)	MiG-17	923.		
	Nguyen Van Luc			***A-6***	***US not confirmed***
	Nguyen Tien Sam	MiG-21	927.		
	Nguyen The Duc				
	Nguyen Van Nghia				
	Le Van Lap (EJECT)				
08 May 72	Pham Phu Thai	MiG-21	921.		
	Vo Si Giap (EJECT) (Died 11 May)				
	Nguyen Ngoc Tiep	MiG-19	925.	***F-4***	***US not confirmed***
	Nguyen Duc Tiem				
	Nguyen Hong Son „A"				
	Nguyen Hong Son „B"			***F-4***	***US not confirmed***
10 May 72	***Dang Ngoc Ngu***	MiG-21	921.	***F-4***	***US not confirmed***
	Nguyen Van Ngai (KIA)				
	Nguyen Cong Huy	MiG-21	921.		
	Cao Son Khao (KIA) (FF)			***F-4***	***US not confirmed***
	Le Thanh Dao	MiG-21	927.	***F-4J***	***Blackburn, Rudloff (POW) (AAA)***
	Vu Duc (Van) Hop			***F-4J***	***Cunningham, Driscoll (Rescued)***
	Pham Ngoc Tam	MiG-19	925.		
	Pham Hung Son „C"				
	Nguyen Van Phuc			***F-4D***	***Lodge (KIA), Locher (Rescued)***
	Le Duc Oanh (KIA)				
	Hoang Cao Bong	MiG-19	925.		
	Pham Cao Ha				
	Nguyen Van Cuong				
	Le Van Tuong (KIA)			***F-4E***	***Harris, Wilkinson (KIA)***
	Nguyen Van Tho (EJECT)	MiG-17	923.		
	Ta Dong Trung				
	Do Hang (KIA)				
	Tra Van Kiem (KIA)				

Date	VN Pilot (Killer)	Aircraft	Unit	Lost	US Pilot (KIA, POW, RESCUED)
11 May 72	***Ngo Van Phu (EJECT)*** ***Ngo Duy Thu***	MiG-21	927.	***F-4D*** ***F-105G***	***Kittinger, Reich (POWs)*** ***Talley, Padgett (POWs)***
18 May 72	***Nguyen Ngoc Hung*** Mai Van Tue	MiG-21	927.	***F-4***	***US not confirmed***
	Pham Ngoc Tam (EJECT) Nguyen Thang Long (EJECT) Nguyen Hong Son „A" Vu Viet Tan	MiG-19	925.	***F-4D***	***Ratzel, Bednarek (KIAs)***
	Han Vinh Tuong Nguyen Van Dien Trinh Van Quy Nguyen Van Lam	MiG-17	923.	***F-4***	***US not confirmed***
20 May 72	Luong The Phuc ***Do Van Lanh***	MiG-21	921.	***F-4D***	***Markle, Williams (POW)***
23 May 72	***Nguyen Duc Soat*** Ngo Duy Thu	MiG-21	927.	***A-7B***	***Barnett (KIA) (SAM)***
	Vu Van Dang (KIA) ***Nguyen Van Dien (KIA)*** Nguyen Van Lam Nguyen Cong Ngu (EJECT)	MiG-17	923.	***F-4D*** ***Shared***	***Byrns, Bean (POW) (GF)***
	Hoang Cao Bong Vu Chinh Nghi (EJECT) ***Nguyen Hong Son „A"*** ***Pham Hung Son „C"***	MiG-19	925.	***F-4*** ***Shared***	***US not confirmed***
01 Jun 72	***Pham Phu Thai*** Nguyen Cong Huy	MiG-21	921.	***F-4E***	***Hawks, Dingee (Rescued) (SAM)***
10 Jun 72	***Pham Phu Thai*** ***Bui Thanh Liem***	MiG-21	921.	***F-4***	***US not confirmed***
11 Jun 72	Nguyen Hong Son „A" Pham Hung Son „C" Nguyen Van Phuc (KIA) Nguyen Hung Son „B" (EJECT)	MiG-19	925.		
12 Jun 72	***Le Thanh Dao*** Truong Ton	MiG-21	927.	***F-4***	***US not confirmed***
13 Jun 72	***Pham Phu Thai*** Nguyen Cong Huy	MiG-21	921.	***F-4E***	***Hanson, Fulton (POW)***
	Luong The Phuc ***Do Van Lanh***	MiG-21	921.	***F-4***	***US not confirmed***
21 Jun 72	Le Thanh Dao Mai Van Tue (EJECT)	MiG-21	927.		
	Luong The Phuc ***Do Van Lanh***	MiG-21	927.	***F-4E***	***Rose, Callaghan (POW)***
23 Jun 72	***Nguyen Van Nghia*** Nguyen Van Toan	MiG-21	927.	***F-4***	***US not confirmed***

Date	VN Pilot (Killer)	Aircraft	Unit	Lost	US Pilot (KIA, POW, RESCUED)
24 Jun 72	***Nguyen Duc Soat*** Ngo Duy Thu	MiG-21	927.	***F-4E***	***Grant, Beekman (POW)***
	Nguyen Van Nghia Nguyen Van Toan	MiG-21	927.	***F-4D***	***McCarty(KIA), Jackson(POW)***
	Le Thanh Dao ***Bui Duc Nhu***	MiG-21	927.	***Firebee***	
	Pham Phu Thai	MiG-21	921.	***F-4***	***US not confirmed***
	Do Van Lanh ***Bui Thanh Liem***	MiG-21	921.	***Firebee***	
27 Jun 72	***Bui Duc Nhu*** Ha Vinh Thanh	MiG-21	927.	***F-4***	***US not confirmed***
	Nguyen Duc Soat ***Ngo Duy Thu***	MiG-21	927.	***F-4E*** ***F-4***	***Cerak, Dingee (POW)*** ***US not confirmed***
	Pham Phu Thai ***Bui Thanh Liem***	MiG-21	921.	***F-4E*** ***F-4E***	***Aikman, Hanton (POW)*** ***Miller, McDow (POW)***
	Pham Ngoc Tam (KIA) Nguyen Manh Tung Vu Cong Thuyet Vu Viet Tan	MiG-19	925.		
05 Jul 72	***Nguyen Tien Sam*** ***Ha Vinh Thanh***	MiG-21	927.	***F-4E*** ***F-4E***	***Spencer, Seek (POW)*** ***Elander, Logan (POW)***
08 Jul 72	Dang Ngoc Ngu (KIA) ***Tran Viet***	MiG-21	921.	***F-4E***	***Ross, Imaye (Rescued)***
	Nguyen Ngoc Hung (KIA) Vu Duc (Van) Hop (KIA)	MiG-21	927.		
24 Jul 72	***Nguyen Tien Sam*** Ha Vinh Thanh	MiG-21	927.	***F-4E***	***Hodnett, Fallert (Rescued)***
	Le Thanh Dao ***Truong Ton***	MiG-21	927.	***F-4*** ***F-4***	***US not confirmed*** ***US not confirmed***
29 Jul 72	***Nguyen Tien Sam*** Nguyen Thanh Xuan (EJECT)	MiG-21	927.	***F-4E***	***Kula, Matsui (POW)***
30 Jul 72	***Nguyen Duc Soat***	MiG-21	927.	***F-4D***	***Brooks, McAdams (Rescued)***
26 Aug 72	***Nguyen Duc Soat*** Le Van Kien (EJECT)	MiG-21	927.	***F-4J***	***Cordova (KIA), Borders (Rescued)***
	Bui Duc Nhu ***Nguyen Van Toan***	MiG-21	927.	***F-4***	***US not confirmed***
	Nguyen Van Va Trinh Van Quy	MiG-17	923.	***Firebee***	

Date	VN Pilot (Killer)	Aircraft	Unit	Lost	US Pilot (KIA, POW, RESCUED)
09 Sep 72	***Luong The Phuc (EJECT)*** ***Do Van Lanh***	MiG-21	921.	***F-4E***	***Dalecky, Murphy (Rescued) (AAA)***
	Le Thanh Dao Mai Van Tue	MiG-21	927.	***F-4***	***US not confirmed***
	Pham Cao Ha (EJECT) Nguyen Tu Dung	MiG-19	925.		
11 Sep 72	***Le Thanh Dao*** ***Tran Van Nam***	MiG-21	927.	***F-4E*** ***F-4***	***Ratzlaff, Heeren (POW)*** ***US not confirmed***
	Dinh Ton (EJECT) Vasilij Motlov (EJECT)	MiG-21	921.		
12 Sep 72	***Nguyen Tien Sam*** Nguyen Van Toan (EJECT)	MiG-21	927.	***F-4E***	***Zuberbuhler, McMurray (POW)***
	Pham Phu Thai Le Khuong (EJECT)	MiG-21	921.		
01 Oct 72	***Le Thanh Dao*** Mai Van Tue	MiG-21	927.	***F-4***	***US not confirmed***
05 Oct 72	***Bui Duc Nhu*** ***Nguyen Tien Sam***	MiG-21	927.	***F-4*** ***F-4D***	***US not confirmed*** ***Lewis, Alpers (POW)***
06 Oct 72	***Nguyen Van Nghia*** ***Tran Van Nam***	MiG-21	927.	***F-4E*** ***F-4E***	***White, Egge (Rescued)*** ***Anderson (KIA), Latella (POW) (SAM)***
	Nguyen Hong Son „A" Nguyen Hung Viet (KIA)	MiG-19	925.		
12 Oct 72	***Nguyen Duc Soat*** Nguyen Tien Sam (EJECT)	MiG-21	927.	***F-4E***	***Young, Brunson (POW)***
15 Oct 72	Le Thanh Dao (EJECT) Tran Van Nam	MiG-21	927.		
	Pham Phu Thai (EJECT) Tran Van Sang	MiG-21	921.		
24 Nov 72	***Nguyen Van Nghia*** Le Van Lap	MiG-21	927.	***Firebee***	
23 Dec 72	***Nguyen Van Nghia*** Le Van Kien	MiG-21	927.	***F-4***	***US not confirmed***
27 Dec 72	***Pham Tuan***	MiG-21	921.	***B-52D***	***Mize + 5 crew (SAM)***

Aces and Heroes Air Losses in the Vietnam War (1965 – 1972)

Date	Pilot	Aircraft	Service	Kill	Lost (KIA, POW, WIA)
17-Jun-65	Jack E. D. Batson Jr. Robert B. Doremus	F-4B	USN USN	MiG-17	Nguyen Nhat Chieu (eject) (921)
06-Oct-65	Daniel McIntyre Alan Johnson	F-4B	USN USN	MiG-17	Nguyen Van Bay (MiG damaged) (923)
23-Apr-66	Robert E. Blake S. W. George	F-4C	USAF USAF	MiG-17	Nguyen Dang Kinh (eject) (MiG-21 – 921)
26-Apr-66	Paul J. Gilmore William T. Smith	F-4C	USAF USAF	MiG-21	Nguyen Hong Nhi (eject) (921)
30-Apr-66	Lawrence H. Golberg Gerald D. Hardgrave	F-4C	USAF USAF	MiG-17	Pham Ngoc Lan (eject) (923) Tran Tan Duc (KIA) (923)
21-Sep-66	Fred A. Wilson,Jr.	F-105D	USAF	MiG-17	Vo Van Man MiG damaged) (923)
05-Nov-66	Wilbur J. Latham, Jr. Klaus J. Klause	F-4C	USAF USAF	MiG-21	Dong Van Song (eject) (921)
02-Jan-67	Ralph F. Wetterhahn Jerry K. Sharp	F-4C	USAF USAF	MiG-21	Vu Ngoc Dinh (eject) (921)
	Robin Olds Charles C. Clifton	F-4C	USAF USAF	MiG-21	Nguyen Dang Kinh (eject) (921)
	John B. Stone Clifton P. Dunnegan Jr.	F-4C	USAF USAF	MiG-21	Nguyen Ngoc Do (eject) (921)
06-Jan-67	Thomas M. Hirsch Roger J. Strasswimmer	F-4C	USAF USAF	MiG-21	Mai Van Cuong (eject) (921)
23-Apr-67	Robert D. Anderson Fred D. Kjer	F-4C	USAF USAF	MiG-21	Nguyen Dang Kinh (eject) (921)
04-May-67	Robin Olds William D. Lafever	F-4C	USAF USAF	MiG-21	Nguyen Van Coc (eject) (921)
14-May-67	Samuel O. Bakke Robert W. Lambert	F-4C	USAF USAF	MiG-17	Vo Van Man (KIA) (923)
20-May-67	Robert D. Janca William E. Roberts Jr.	F-4C	USAF USAF	MiG-21	Vu Ngoc Dinh (eject) (921)
05-Jun-67	Durwood K. Priester John E. Pankhurst	F-4C	USAF USAF	MiG-17	Hoang Van Ky (KIA) (923)
10-Aug-67	Guy H. Freeborn Robert J. Elliot	F-4B	USN USN	MiG-21	Dong Van Song (eject) (921)
24-Oct-67	William L. Kirk Theodore R. Bongartz	F-4D	USAF USAF	MiG-21	Dong Van Song (eject) (921)
26-Oct-67	Robert P. Hickey Jeremy G. Morris	F-4B	USN USN	MiG-21	Mai Van Cuong (eject) (921)
03-Jan-68	Clayton K. Squier Michael D. Muldoon	F-4D	USAF USAF	MiG-17	Luu Huy Chao (MiG damaged) (923)
26-Jun-68	Lowell R. Myers	F-8H	USN	MiG-21	Vu Ngoc Dinh (eject) (921) (Talos)
09-Jul-68	John B. Nichols III	F-8E	USN	MiG-17	Nguyen Phi Hung (KIA) (923)

Date	Pilot	Aircraft	Service	Kill	Lost (KIA, POW, WIA)
10-Jul-68	Roy Cash Jr. Joseph E. Kain Jr.	F-4J	USN USN	MiG-21	Pham Phu Thai (eject) (921)
01-Aug-68	Norman K. McCoy	F-8H	USN	MiG-21	Nguyen Hong Nhi (eject) (921)
22-Sep-68		Talos Talos	USN USN	MiG-21 MiG-21	Vu Dinh Rang (eject) (921) Pham Thanh Ngan (MiG damaged) (921)
08-Jul-72	Richard F. Hardy Paul T. Lewinski	F-4E	USAF USAF	MiG-21	Dang Ngoc Ngu (KIA) (921)
11-Sep-72	Lee T. Lasseter John D. Cummings	F-4J	USMC USMC	MiG-21U	Dinh Ton (eject) (921) Vasilij Motlov (eject) (Soviet trainer)
12-Oct-72	John A. Madden Jr. Lawrence H. Pettit	F-4D	USAF USAF	MiG-21	Nguyen Tien Sam (eject) (927)
15-Oct-72	Gary M. Rubus James L. Hendrickson	F-4E	USAF USAF	MiG-21	Le Thanh Dao (eject) (927)
	Robert L. Holtz William C. Diehl	F-4E	USAF USAF	MiG-21	Pham Phu Thai (eject) (921)

Bibliography

Books

Ho Chu Tich Voi Bo Doi Phong Khong - Khong Quan, (Hanoi, Vietnam: Publisher People's Army, 1975).
Quan Doi Nhan Dan Viet Nam (1944-1979), (Hanoi, Vietnam: Publisher People's Army, 1979).
Khong Quan Nhan Dan Viet Nam, (Hanoi, Vietnam: Publisher People's Army, 1980)
Lich Su Khong Quan Nhan Dan Viet Nam (1955-1977), (Hanoi, Vietnam: Publisher People's Army, 1993).
Lich Su Trung Doan Khong Quan 923 (1965 - 2000) (Hanoi, Vietnam: Publisher People's Army, 2000).
Lich Su Trung Doan Khong Quan Tiem Kich 927 (1971 – 2001), (Hanoi, Vietnam: Publisher People's Army, 2002).
Cac Don Vi Va Ca Nhan Anh Hung Luc Luong Vu Trang Nhan Dan Thuoc Quan Chung Phong Khong - Khong Quan. (Hanoi, Vietnam: Publisher People's Army, 2002).
Lich Su Dan Duong Khong Quan (1959-2004), (Hanoi, Vietnam: Publisher People's Army, 2004).
Lich Su Doan Khong Quan 371 (1967 - 2007), (Hanoi, Vietnam: Publisher People's Army, 2007).
Lich Su Trung Doan Khong Quan 921 (1964 - 2009), (Hanoi, Vietnam: Publisher People's Army, 2009).
Nho On Cac Liet Si Khong Quan Nhan Dan Viet Nam, (Hanoi, Vietnam: Publisher People's Army, 2010).
Chan Dung Anh Hung Phi Cong Thoi Ky Chong My Cuu Nuoc, (Hanoi, Vietnam: Publisher People's Army, 2012).
Lich Su Quan Chung Phong Khong - Khong Quan (1963 - 2013), (Hanoi, Vietnam: Publisher People's Army, 2012).
Luu Huy Chao. *Chung Toi & MiG-17,* (Hanoi, Vietnam: Publisher People's Army, 2009).
Nguyen Sy Hung and Nguyen Nam Lien. *Nhung Tran Khong Chien Tren Bau Troi Viet Nam (1965 – 1975) Nhin Tu Hai Phia*, (Hanoi, Vietnam: Publisher People's Army, 2013).

***

Boniface, Roger. *MiG over North Vietnam: The Vietnamese People's Air Force in Combat 1965-1975,* (Manchester, UK: Hikoki Publications, 2008).
Davies, Peter E. *F-4 Phantom vs. MiG-21, USAF & VPAF in the Vietnam War,* (Oxford, UK: Osprey Publishing, 2008).
Davies, Peter E. *USN F-4 Phantom vs. VPAF MiG-17/19, Vietnam 1965-73,* (Oxford, UK: Osprey Publishing, 2009).
Davies, Peter. *USAF F-4 Phantom II MiG Killers 1965–68,* (Oxford, UK: Osprey Publishing, 2004).
Davies, Peter. *USAF F-4 Phantom II MiG Killers 1972–73,* (Oxford, UK: Osprey Publishing, 2005).
Davies, Peter E. *F-105 Thunderchief Units of the Vietnam War,* (Oxford, UK: Osprey Publishing, 2010).
Davies, Peter E. *US Marine Corps F-4 Phantom II Units of the Vietnam War,* (Oxford, UK: Osprey Publishing, 2012).
Drendel, Lou. *...And Kill MiGs,* (Carrollton, Texas: Squadron/Signal Publications, 1997).
Elward, Brad and Peter E Davies. *US Navy F-4 Phantom II MiG Killers 1965–70,* (Oxford, UK: Osprey Publishing, 2001).
Elward, Brad and Peter E Davies. *US Navy F-4 Phantom II MiG Killers 1972–73,* (Oxford, UK: Osprey Publishing, 2002).
Francillon, René J. *Tonkin Gulf Yacht Club – US Carrier Operations off Vietnam,* (London, UK: Conway Maritime Press, 1988).
Futrell, R. Frank. *Aces and Aerial Victories – The United States Air Force in Southeast Asia 1965-1973,* (Washington, D.C.: Office of Air Force History, 1976).
Hobson, Chris. *Vietnam Air Losses,* (Hinckley, UK: Midland Publishing, 2001).
McCarthy, Donald J. *MiG Killers, A Chronology of US Air Victories in Vietnam 1965-1973.* (North Branch, Minnesota: Specialty Press, 2009).
Michel, Marshall L. *Clashes: Air Combat Over North Vietnam, 1965-1972,* (Annapolis, Maryland: Naval Institute Press, 1997).
O'Connor, Michael. *MiG Killers of Yankee Station,* (Friendship, Wisconsin: New Past Press, 2002).

Toperczer, Istvan. *Air war Over North Vietnam: The Vietnamese People's Air Force.* (Carrollton, Texas: Squadron/Signal Publications, 1998).

Toperczer, Istvan. *MiG-17 and MiG-19 Units of the Vietnam War,* (Oxford, UK: Osprey Publishing, 2001).

Toperczer, Istvan. *MiG-21 Units of the Vietnam War,* (Oxford, UK: Osprey Publishing, 2001).

Documentary sources and Periodicals

Red Baron Reports: Air-to-Air Encounters in Southeast Asia Vol. I.: Account of F-4 and F-8 Events Prior to March 1967, (Arlington, Virginia: Institute for Defense Analyses Systems Evaluation Division, October 1967).

Red Baron Reports: Air-to-Air Encounters in Southeast Asia Vol. II.: F-105 Events Prior to March 1967, (Arlington, Virginia: Institute for Defense Analyses Systems Evaluation Division, September 1968).

Red Baron Reports: Air-to-Air Encounters in Southeast Asia Vol. III.: Events from 1 March 1967 to 1 August 1967 and Miscellaneous Events, (Arlington, Virginia: Institute for Defense Analyses Systems Evaluation Division, February 1969).

Project Red Baron II, Vol. II.-III.-IV.: Air-to-Air Encounters in Southeast Asia, (Nellis AFB, Nevada: USAF Tactical Fighter Weapons Center, January 1973).

Project Red Baron III, Vol. I.-II.-III.: Air-to-Air Encounters in Southeast Asia, (Nellis AFB, Nevada: USAF Tactical Fighter Weapons Center, June 1974).